Hollywood Horror
from the Director's Chair

Hollywood Horror from the Director's Chair

Six Filmmakers in the Franchise of Fear

SIMON A. WILKINSON

McFarland & Company, Inc., Publishers
Jefferson, North Carolina, and London

LIBRARY OF CONGRESS CATALOGUING-IN-PUBLICATION DATA

Wilkinson, Simon A., 1976–
    Hollywood horror from the director's chair : six filmmakers in the franchise of fear / by Simon A. Wilkinson.
       p.   cm.
    Includes bibliographical references and index.

    ISBN-13: 978-0-7864-3232-5
    softcover : 50# alkaline paper ∞

    1. Horror films — United States — History and criticism.
I. Title.
PN1995.9.H6W45   2008
791.43'61640973 — dc22   2007030057

British Library cataloguing data are available

©2008 Simon A. Wilkinson. All rights reserved

No part of this book may be reproduced or transmitted in any form or by any means, electronic or mechanical, including photocopying or recording, or by any information storage and retrieval system, without permission in writing from the publisher.

Cover photograph: Jason Miller as Father Damien Karras in *The Exorcist III: Legion*, 1990

Manufactured in the United States of America

McFarland & Company, Inc., Publishers
  Box 611, Jefferson, North Carolina 28640
    www.mcfarlandpub.com

Acknowledgments

I am grateful to many people for their help, both direct and indirect, in writing this book. First and foremost, many thanks and the utmost personal and professional respect must go to my supervisor, Dr. John Osborne, whose unerring support, approachability and faith in both the project and me has been invaluable during the more difficult times. Also playing a part in this process were Professor Mark Jancovich, Professor Neil Sinyard and Dr. David Eldridge, who provided feedback and assistance in shaping the final edit. I would also like to thank Nina Harding from the BFI Stills department for her assistance in the final stages of this process.

On a more personal note, my deepest thanks, sympathy and appreciation goes out to all those friends and family, on both sides, who have been forced to endure my time-consuming forays into numerous cinemas and video shops over the years. Thank you for your patience, tried and tested as it was, and ability to endure — if not necessarily enjoy — the results. Mum, for all the video hunts and times the shopkeepers would offer you a chair out of sympathy, and the subsequent countdowns that followed, I hope you like the result. Dave, Alice, Jenny — each of you has sat through several of these. You've often instigated such evenings and survived, albeit not without regret or recriminations. Dave, I apologize for *Vampires* and only hope my credibility will one day be restored — just as yours will be after *The 25th Hour*. Alice, hope you enjoyed our fashion-unconscious days of bad taste with *Elvira*; and Jenny, your love of *Buffy* knows no bounds.

Finally, the last words of acknowledgement for this book must go to Steve, my partner, husband and best friend, without whom I would have faltered on a number of occasions. From endless cinema visits, both here and abroad, to endless conversations and every extended Blockbuster visit, you have stood by and alongside me day and night until the final edit. Well, here it is — at last! Your support, encouragement and seemingly endless patience and capacity for understanding has been a testament to what we have. Indeed, it is to you that I dedicate this work.

Table of Contents

Acknowledgments v
Preface 1
Introduction 5

1. Don Coscarelli
   In Search of Phantasm's End 27
2. Cursed
   Wes Craven's Franchise Nightmares 51
3. Tom Savini and William Peter Blatty
   They Came from Within 76
4. Joe Berlinger
   Rage Against the Machine 105
5. Jeff Burr
   Divided We Fall 132

Conclusions 157
Hollywood Horror Series Filmography 179
Chapter Notes 219
Bibliography 247
Index 253

Preface

> "It's a perfect night for mystery and horror. The air itself is filled with monsters."
> — Mary Shelley[1]

My love of horror films is a passion that began with a television screening of Carpenter's *Halloween* late one Halloween night. While sufficiently scarred by televised version of *Amityville II* and *Creepshow*, *Clash of the Titans* introduced me to the phenomenon of Home Video. This introduction was closely followed by a memorable viewing of *Superman* that culminated in my running up and down the street pretending to fly. Parentally prohibited from watching such classics as *The Evil Dead* and *A Nightmare on Elm Street* the opportunity to creep downstairs and watch *Freddy's Revenge* or go to a friend's house to see the awful *Spookies* gave me a memorable taste of the forbidden.

Later on, my mother interrupted my first viewing of Joe Dante's *The Howling*. She, following the script of every son's nightmare, entered during the solo sex scene of the movie, in which the two lovers undergo a spectacular transformation into werewolves. Nevertheless, the bars on my brother's and my bedroom window (there when we moved in, I'd like to point out) did not assuage the intrusive fear that the teenage boys from Hooper's adaptation of *Salem's Lot* might one night materialize from the mist. Similarly, a chance encounter with Hooper's *Poltergeist* at a Pontins Holiday Camp screening also reinforced my fondness for watching scary movies on the big screen with an appreciative audience. My interest in Freddy Krueger's notoriety and rising popularity reached new heights after watching

Dream Warriors one Sunday afternoon; while a chance encounter in a comic book shop with publicity for the fourth film led to my first purchase of *Fangoria* (issue 77).

A catalyst for my growing interest in feature film production, *Fangoria*'s luscious and informative coverage of these high profile genre films opened the door, and my eyes, to the many sub-genres, directors and classics that I had previously been unaware of and was now keen to seek out. This obsession led to me bluffing my way into *Child's Play* at the age of 12, and then Craven's 18-rated *Shocker* two years later. Armed with John McCarty's *Splatter Movie Guide* and a growing interest in film journalism, the lure of a twenty-four-hour film festival being held in London at the Scala cinema was impossible to resist!

Consequently, and at the age of 13, I made the journey with my Dad to London for Shock Around the Clock 4, where the hilarious delights of *Meet the Feebles* were surpassed only by the appearance of Clive Barker and Dario Argento to introduce their latest releases. After receiving a response to my thank you letter from co-organizer Alan Jones later that year, it perhaps comes as no surprise that my next birthday celebration attempted to recreate that experience on a smaller yet no less diverse scale. My own mini-festival—an all-nighter in the living room with plenty of snacks, sleeping bags and duvets—was a hit with friends (and cause for concern for parents), with a diverse line-up that ranged from *The Exorcist* to *Day of the Dead*. Further memorable experiences, including trips to the Hyde Park Picture House and the Bradford Playhouse for *Society* and *Henry*, saw to it that my love and appreciation of the genre only grew over time.

When I first conceived of this project in 2000, the idea was to expand upon an assignment I had fulfilled by writing on Wes Craven's postmodernist approach to contemporary Horror cinema, focusing on *Scream* and *New Nightmare*. I had enjoyed and endured a range of films, and began exploring the production histories of these and other such sequels. My research continued with the history of first films and history of the horror genre.

There will be errors, omissions and over-simplifications, for which I take full responsibility, as is customary, while hoping that the rest of the material will offer enough to stimulate new attitudes, approaches and insights into the Hollywood horror franchise. Maybe you'll take a similar trip down memory lane and re-watch a few or seek out new titles to pass the time.

For the first time this century it seems I can face a Halloween without the specter of the Hollywood horror franchise hanging over me. That said, *Texas Chainsaw Massacre: The Beginning*, *The Grudge 2* and *Saw III* are already on our screens, thus proving the theory that some nightmares never end, and there'll always be just one more film...

Introduction

> If you're going to get into the psychology of the filmmaker, you owe it to the filmmaker to understand the psychology of filmmaking and the experiences they had when they were making that movie.[1]
> — David Cronenberg

> It's possible to create a little franchise if you catch a concept at just the right time.[2]
> — Sean S. Cunningham

> Let's face it baby, these days you gotta have a sequel![3]
> —*Scream*

The bastard son of two commonly derided and dismissed forms of filmmaking, the Hollywood horror franchise has dominated feature film production. However, it has rarely attracted serious or substantial critical attention, despite its successful inauguration with Whale's universally renowned *Bride of Frankenstein*[4] in 1935.[5] The critical research in this area is still very much in its infancy, and, as a result, significant gaps desperately need filling before a more thorough understanding can be reached. Consequently, the aim of this book is to present an experiential account of the Hollywood horror franchise from the directors' perspectives.

In casting the director as protagonist, this book will examine the range of factors that have affected directors' involvement with the Hollywood horror franchise. Their range of experience will be placed in an appropriate context in respect to their contemporaries. This will be followed by an examination of the effect studios, stars, audiences, critics and censors have upon their attitudes, approaches and end result.

Indeed, the importance of pleasing or appeasing various factions cannot be overestimated. Therefore, this book will also examine how directors have responded to these pressures and whether any discernible patterns or trends can be found. Finally, to characterize the relationship between the director and the franchise within the horror genre, we must take into account what role the franchise film has played in directors' careers, and the extent to which their involvement has helped or hindered their ambitions.

Limited in its concerns, this book excludes theoretical approaches and issues of reception and consumption, but will take into account the extent to which these elements have influenced directors. In other words, such issues as the fluidity of generic definition and generational shifts in audience taste, expectation and understanding will be considered. Rather than "concentrate on classic moments"[6] or present a stylistic analysis of individual films, shots and set-ups, this book has deliberately taken a step back from theory to focus on five specific patterns of involvement.

To successfully address these issues, and allow for a fuller understanding of these films, evidence has been collated and consolidated from a combination of traditional academic texts and industry-produced journals, including such magazines as *Shivers*, *Cinefantastique* and *Fangoria*. In addition, I have extensively utilized documentaries, interviews and commentaries, and consulted a range of both official and unofficial fan-based Internet sites to cross-reference material and comments. That said, the truth is elusive, and it must be acknowledged that the reliability of such sources, many of which were designed solely as publicity and promotional materials, must be called into question. Indeed, they may not fully depict or even reflect the true extent of a director's attitude or experiences in making a particular film. As has often been the case, inconsistencies in accounts and attitudes often arise, and perspectives shift over time.

Consequently, the majority of pre-release publicity must be treated as commercial promotional discourses deliberately composed for the purpose of persuading readers to see the finished film. Furthermore, those interviews conducted or commentaries recorded in retrospect, while still open to interpretation and biased in their nature, arguably provide a more accurate, yet by no means complete, picture of a film's production history and place in a director's career.

My focus here is based on the interdependence of directors, the franchise, and the horror genre, and this book will take into account the inherently biased and sometimes contradictory attitudes and experiences of filmmakers. However, before the critical context for this investigation is established, these three key terms need defining. Moreover, the parameters and limitations of this study must be acknowledged and set.

The Horror Genre

Writing in 1979, Robin Wood rightly stated, "The horror film has consistently been one of the most popular and at the same time, the most disreputable of genres ... dismissed with contempt by the majority of reviewer critics, or simply ignored."[7] However, a great deal of academic research has since been undertaken, from a variety of ideological and theoretical perspectives, despite critical, commercial and academic derision.

Although Carlos Clarens had published *Horror Movies: An Illustrated Survey* in 1968, with Butler following in 1970, and more substantial works by Derry and Frank emerging in 1977, it was not until the eighties that several more significant texts sought to reevaluate the genre through auteurist accounts and cultural analysis.[8] In their attempts to establish the parameters of the genre, academics have unwittingly served to illustrate the inherent fluidity of the term and our reactionary nature towards it. Moreover, audiences, critics and high caliber marketing departments have often conspired to reconfigure the way in which we define, or in some cases redefine, what constitutes a horror film.[9]

Through reference to Neale,[10] Naremore[11] and Russell,[12] Mark Jancovich has accurately summarized how approaches to genre are problematic, and potentially elusive yet rarely exclusive. Furthermore, narrative histories "tend to repress the diversity within periods"[13] and "simply cannot create a clear narrative line if they are forced to deal with the diversity of horror production from across the world."[14] So the question as to what actually constitutes genre, or even a history rather than "the" history, has been a subjective and fluid one from the outset.

For the purposes of this book I have opted to align myself with Clover by not only concerning myself "chiefly with American cinematic horror,"[15] but also adopting her stance on defining the genre's parameters. In embracing her almost separatist stance, I would like to reiterate how "it has not been my concern to define horror or to adhere to the definitions of others. I have been guided for the most part by video rental store categorizations, which, despite some variation from store to store, seem to capture better than any definition I know what the public senses to be horror."[16] For example, retailers have adopted a less hierarchical approach to stocking films on their shelves by placing such titles as *Aliens*, *The Silence of the Lambs* and *Tremors* within the horror section—despite distributors' attempts to convince us otherwise. In other words, this book deliberately adopts a more inclusive approach to the genre than Hollywood's cautious re-categorization of titles to appeal to a wider anti-horror demographic based on accepted stereotypes of the lowest common denominator.

Rather than representing horror's cinematic history or single-handedly defining its parameters, some scholars sought to isolate and analyze specific scenes, periods, sub-genres, hybrids or trends.[17] Although some focused on horror's cinematic development and Universal's horror films,[18] others settled on Hammer's similar exploits over twenty years later.[19] Two sub-genres addressed have been the supernatural and the appropriately named splatter film.[20] Historically, the rise of eighties slasher films has been a key area of study, and these films formed the basis of Dika's *Games of Terror* in 1990. This was not only followed by McCarty but also Simpson in 2000.[21] However, the period with which this thesis is concerned, despite acknowledging significant influences and inspiration from both Hammer and Universal's classic monster movie series, runs from Hitchcock's *Psycho* in 1960 through to Romero's *Land of the Dead* in 2005.

In 1994, Paul examined the unique relationship between horror and comedy,[22] and this is significant because the links and crossover potential between these two genres has been a real cause for concern for filmmakers. Spielberg, for example, was terrified that "*Jaws* could have turned out to be the laugh riot of 75,"[23] believing it would "be a turkey"[24]; whereas Friedkin had reportedly "gotten so close to [*The Exorcist*] that I thought it was ridiculous and people would laugh at it."[25] Rather than take their subject matter too seriously, other directors infused their films with heavy doses of black humor, self-awareness and comic sensibility. Indeed, this fusion of subtle references and cinematic in-jokes with atmospheric shocks and scares successfully evolved into the cine-literate lunacy of Dante's *The Howling* and satirical social commentary in Harron's *American Psycho*. Elsewhere it has been far less successful. Such a dichotomy between intention and effect highlights the way in which directors' original intentions are subject to audience interpretation, and can potentially leave a film open to commercial failure and critical ridicule.

In addition to the aforementioned generic and historical approaches, academics have applied a variety of theoretical and thematic frameworks. For example, Clover's gender-based research in 1992 was influenced by Williams and impacted upon the work of Berenstein, Grant, Pinedo and Cherry.[26] Similarly, Harry M. Benshoff's work on representations of homosexuality in horror successfully adapted the guiding principles of Russo's 1980 text *The Celluloid Closet*.[27] Indeed, a synthesis of these two seemingly disparate approaches to gender, sexuality and psychoanalysis in horror manifested themselves in Creed's 1993 text *The Monstrous-Feminine*.[28] Paedophobia and the representation of children in the genre has been seen in the work of both Bussing and, later, Westfahl and Slusser,[29] with Tony Williams building on

Wood's assertion that the family is the root of our contemporary American horrors in his *Hearths of Darkness*.[30]

From representation to reception, Weaver and Tamborini also published a collection of investigations in 1995,[31] with several successful compilations and collections of individual essays characterizing genre studies dating back to Britton's *American Nightmares* in 1979.[32] In its wake there have been several such anthologies devoted to the genre, including Grant's *Planks of Reason* and Waller's *American Horrors*,[33] both from the eighties, followed by summative revisions in recent guides edited by Gelder, Silver and Ursini, and Jancovich.[34]

However, what distinguishes this book from these texts is the way in which it is neither theoretical nor historical in its approach. Alternatively, its concerns are rooted in the mechanics of Hollywood horror franchise filmmaking and the director's role and perspective within that challenging process.

The Franchise

A franchise is the authorization to sell a company's product at a particular time and place by exploiting ownership or obtaining the license to it. It is also a popular and profitable approach to starting a new business. In other words, and for the purpose of this book, a franchise is a transferable property that can be legally owned by an individual or institution. Note, therefore, that this definition rules out literary figures, directors and even stars who have the potential to become marketable brand names in their own right. In this respect, all first films have the potential to be a franchise, regardless of their origins.[35]

Commonly associated with a standardized approach to production and promotion, the term implies standardization, a successful formula and an absence of creativity from the outset. Moreover, this term can encompass every consumer product related to the title and licensed by the franchisor, and this includes feature films, TV spin-offs, novels, comics, video games, toys and every other form of official merchandise relating directly to the title.[36] However, this text only recognizes feature films—in the form of prequels, sequels and remakes—as part of the Hollywood horror franchise, irrespective of their fidelity to the first film. Having characterized horror movies as looking "like nothing so much as folktales—a set of fixed tale types that generate a endless stream of what are in effect variants: sequels, remakes and rip-offs,"[37] Clover has also highlighted horror's predominance in sequel production across the budgetary range.

A sequel is commonly understood as being a text that continues the concepts, characters and story begun in a previous text,[38] and is derived from the Latin root sequi, meaning "to follow."[39] In much the same way that the franchise has recently been referred to as "that dreaded F word,"[40] sequels have been described as "cheap carny tricks,"[41] "pure rip-offs,"[42] and "an exploitation of the original film."[43] Their "pulse ... is always this: financial,"[44] and they exist purely as a means of allowing "maximum profit to be derived from success, using a pre-established audience for more systematic exploitation of ancillary markets and merchandising."[45]

In summary, then, "sequels suck,"[46] and these are just some of the common criticisms reiterated by reactionary critics from both inside and outside the industry. Whereas such inflammatory charges are far from fictitious or merely fabrications, this book will highlight the extent to which these negative descriptions fail to present an accurate picture.

Rather than uphold the tradition of calling part one the "original" film, I have chosen to supplant "original" with the less subjective word "first." This is because the former carries with it dual connotations of being both "unprecedented and basic,"[47] neither of which can be applied to many first films, despite their status as entertainment or artistic value. In other words, to avoid bestowing unnecessary simplicity or excessive originality on such films as Romero's *Night of the Living Dead* or Coscarelli's *Phantasm*, the term "first film" is far more appropriate when taking into account issues surrounding intertextuality, adaptation and remakes — all of which highlight the extensive use of referencing and cinematic short-hand so often employed by filmmakers. Certainly, a common misconception regarding the franchise is that it is a relatively new phenomenon plaguing Hollywood feature film production. Contrary to this popular belief, the franchise has, in various forms and guises, been a successful staple of Hollywood's cinematic product and literary history.[48]

Nevertheless, it was not until 1998 that two key theoretical works emerged in order to rectify the dearth of literature regarding two elements of the franchise: the remake and the sequel.[49] Just as McLarty took the male-dominated action genre as her focus, Budra opted to examine the recurrence of the monsters in horror and concluded that it was through a combination of charismatic creatures, incoherence, and a lack of closure that these films have continued to flourish.

Similarly, Horton and McDougal's *Play It Again, Sam: Retakes on Remakes*[50] is another collection of essays. Franchise films are described by contributor Leo Braudy as "close kin"[51] to both the adaptation and the sequel, in that they are "another attempt to get it right"[52] that can be even better than the first — a contentious position to critics who single out the perceived successes as exceptions to the rule. Furthermore, franchise films serve to emphasize the "constant interplay between the desires of artists and the desires of audiences."[53] Naremore also recognizes how these films are in danger of being automatically assigned a low status, or even of "eliciting critical opprobrium, because they are (allegedly) copies of culturally treasured"[54] originals. By way of example, Naremore draws our attention to the *Psycho* franchise and how the "discourse surrounding both its sequels and prequel and its 1998 remake ... encountered nearly universal derision."[55] More recently, Forrest and Koos compiled a number of articles in their 2002 text *Dead Ringers: The Remake in Theory and Practice*[56] which successfully builds on the beginnings of Doris Milberg's introductory guide, *Repeat Performances* (1990).[57]

Whereas the majority of texts devoted to the franchise presented narrative histories,[58] there were initially few genre-specific texts. Foreshadowed by Hanke's *A Critical Guide to Horror Series* in 1991,[59] which spans from Universal's *Dracula* to New Line's *Elm Street* series, later texts by Stell, and Holten and Winchester, adopted this chronological, franchise-specific approach to narrative histories.[60] However, comparisons within or between them were seldom made, with a chronological sequence strictly adhered to throughout.

In contrast, there is widespread availability of texts critiquing successful first films and providing us with a solid foundation upon which to explore franchise development. Just as Newman, Kermode and McCabe all focused on *The Exorcist*,[61] with McCabe also spending some time on follow-ups and spin-offs, Rebello and Leigh and Nickens concentrated on Hitchcock's *Psycho*.[62] Similarly, first film co-screenwriters Russo, (1985) and Gottlieb (1975) wrote extensively on *Night of the Living Dead* and *Jaws* respectively, and critic Nigel Andrews was just one of many critics who selected Spielberg's summer blockbuster as the subject of his 1999 book. On the other hand, informative behind the scenes texts for first sequels to *The Exorcist* and *Jaws* offered detailed and often difficult production histories of these two significant New Hollywood studio sequels, and they proved to be an excellent starting point for such an investigation.[63]

Nevertheless, similar forays into franchise territory have been scarce. They only began to appear in the wake of Stephen King's first wave of adaptations and New Line's phenomenal success with the *Elm Street* franchise. King-based texts were by Jones, Collins and Underwood[64]; while the first *Elm Street* companion appeared the same year, to be followed by Schoell and Spencer's account of the ongoing phenomenon in 1992.[65] Although there are over fifty other contemporary fear franchises, six more have since received similar treatment, with each text taking a chronological look at the origins and evolution of the franchise, both in front of and behind the camera — perhaps a sign that critics and audiences are ready to review and reevaluate these films from a production standpoint.[66]

Consequently, the Hollywood horror franchise has been receiving an increasing amount of critical attention as the film industry continues to invest in its long-term and increasingly expensive development. However, with only the most lucrative movies receiving any kind of critical attention at this stage, many important examples have been rejected and neglected in the process. Therefore, in this book I will strive to incorporate the full extent of the genre's franchises within a case study structure.

The Hollywood Horror Franchise

Despite the prevalence of the franchise across most forms of Hollywood filmmaking, Maitland McDonagh has been right to insist that it has grown "to define the [horror] genre marketplace to a far greater degree than the mainstream marketplace."[67] Due in part to its relative independence from the established star system, and requiring comparatively less financing than other forms of mass entertainment, the horror genre has proven itself time and again to be an attractive option for filmmakers and financiers wishing to break into Hollywood.

Spurred on by cyclic development, and intensified by the unremitting efforts of filmmakers to test and push the boundaries of explicitness and acceptability, horror filmmaking has consistently involved the mass production and aggressive marketing of a tried and tested formula. Although the horror film and the sequel arguably rank as two of the most popular forms of filmmaking, even if only from a producer's point of view, their role within the studio or independent sector has seldom been considered with objectivity. In this respect, this book will provide one more piece of the puzzle — with its focus firmly on the filmmaker.

The Hollywood horror franchise has defined and directed the genre's output since Universal and the 1930s. McDonagh has further pointed out that "horror movies have always gone in cycles ... pivotal movie ... slew of imitations ... diminishing returns."[68] Consequently, it is necessary to offer a brief developmental history of the Hollywood horror franchise, taking into account the technological and industry-based factors behind it. Furthermore, I shall also contextualize the Hollywood horror franchise by re-presenting it as another form of film adaptation sharing similar concerns and critical attacks to those works with direct literary origins.

Despite Bergman's claim that "film has nothing to do with literature,"[69] Vincendeau has argued how most films "originate in some form of writing."[70] Such a statement is also pertinent when looking at the genre and the Hollywood horror franchise. Much like the concept of sequels, the high-profile adaptation of a popular novel, play, short story or even comic book has consistently captured Hollywood's attention. This link has been highlighted in Naremore's negative description of how, "on a theoretical level, the problem of sequels and remakes ... is quite similar to the problem of adaptation."[71] For example, both Browning's *Dracula* and Whale's *Frankenstein* in 1931 not only drew their inspiration from the original source novels but also followed recent Broadway adaptations that had confirmed audience interest.

The release of Universal's *Dracula* and *Frankenstein* saw Hollywood's first horror franchises imported and adapted from the Stage, as well as European film and literature. The influence of the Gothic novel and German Expressionism weighed heavily on these early productions that, for the most part, maintained mythic sensibilities and locations. Plundering the works of Stoker, Shelley and Stevenson, among others, studios were eager to sate the appetites of audiences demanding further installments and the resurrection of their favorite horrors. As Naremore points out, Hollywood "recognized from the beginning that it could gain a sort of legitimacy among middle-class viewers by reproducing facsimiles of more respectable art or by adapting literature to another medium."[72]

Evidence to support this claim can be seen in the wealth of adaptations based on the works of Stoker, Shelley, Stevenson, Poe, and Lovecraft, and such contemporary figures as King, Barker and Rice. However, this has primarily been the case when the resultant film was "an aesthetically and morally conservative form of entertainment."[73] A paradoxical respectability and the genre's status as a profitable contradiction has captivated and confused Hollywood from the beginning. There is an overall consensus that there must be some degree of public awareness of a selected title, topic or theme, be it only in terms of mere recognition or vague association. This presents financiers with a reduced rate of financial and creative risk. The promise of guaranteed profits gleaned from an established and sufficiently prepped audience has been an enormous incentive for Hollywood to embrace and embellish a rich variety of tried and tested concepts.

Specifically designed to exploit the concepts, characters and iconography of its predecessor, the first successful marriage between the horror genre and the sequel was James Whale's *Bride of Frankenstein* (1935). This licentious follow-up, with its literary prologue, was such a resounding critical and commercial success that the series soon gave birth to a third film, a *Son of*

Frankenstein, four years later. Secure in the familiarity of their terror titles from literary sources, and lacking concern as to their legitimacy in literary terms, Universal Studios saw to it that mummies, werewolves, and invisible men (and women) received swift sequelization throughout the thirties and forties. Despite inevitable competition, Laemmle and Universal continued to dominate horror film production before the films inevitably descended into parody and spoof, wherein Abbott and Costello ultimately made their mark. Nevertheless, it was these "Monster Movies," and such later "Creature Features" as Jack Arnold's *Creature from the Black Lagoon*, that became the first fear franchises, spawning numerous sequels and spin-offs.

Forced to compete with external factors beyond its control,[74] the Hollywood of the 1950s had to contend with an influx of independent filmmakers and distributors. Epitomized by Roger Corman and American International Pictures, they competed via an all-too-successful mix of sex, violence and sheer absurdity to capture a growing teen audience. Across the Atlantic, Hammer was also embracing horror, and began emulating Universal's classic series by injecting them with increasingly gratuitous sex and violence, and presenting them in glorious Technicolor. Having proven "themselves the masters of science-fiction,"[75] and the originators of the numerical sequel (with *Quatermass II* in 1956), Hammer's first horror was the appropriately titled *Curse of Frankenstein*.

Following this film's success, the company incorporated Dracula, the Mummy and the Werewolf into their midst before several supernatural films and creature features followed. Indeed, Hammer "revitalized, redefined and revolutionized horror movies around the world."[76] Not only did the company's output influence such Italian masters of the macabre as Riccardo Freda and Mario Bava, it also inspired William Castle,[77] whose penchant for innovative gimmickry, coupled with a pioneering approach to publicity, saw such fifties films as *Macabre*, *House on Haunted Hill* and *The Tingler* promoted with insurance policies, "Emergo" and "Percepto." Corman, on the other hand, eschewed such contemporary interactive horrors in favor of a celebrated cycle of Poe adaptations that belied their meager budgets with sumptuous sets and scenery-chewing performances.

This combination of Corman, Castle and Hammer, coupled with the commercial success of *Les Diaboliques*, inspired Hitchcock to direct an adaptation of Robert Bloch's *Psycho*. A distinctly American nightmare based on the crimes of Ed Gein, *Psycho* was developed against distributor Paramount's wishes, but later championed by critics as "one of the key works of our age."[78] With its shocking star sacrifice, the film also redefined the way in which films were screened and audiences attended them. Cinema exhibition similarly altered as the Drive-in gave automobile-fixated suburbanites — and their offspring — the opportunity to experience the latest releases from the relative comfort of their own front (or, most likely, back) seat as teenagers emerged as the target demographic. This rise in demand for teen-orientated product was swiftly met by A.I.P. and taken to extremes by H.G. Lewis, who, with low-budget gore-fests *Blood Feast* and *2000 Maniacs* (among others), further widened the gap between studio and independent approaches to horror.

This "new age of opportunity"[79] for independent filmmakers stretched so far as Pittsburgh, the drive-in capital of the East, where George R. Romero co-wrote and directed *Night of the Living Dead*. Released in 1968, Romero's black and white drive-in classic coincided with the appearance of the MPAA. Furthermore, it contrasted with Paramount's attempt, in association with producer William Castle, to reclaim the genre through *Rosemary's Baby*. Like Hitchcock, filmmaker Roman Polanski was reportedly convinced that this adaptation "represented [his] chance to conquer Hollywood,"[80] and it is perhaps no coincidence that this studio film became the first contemporary Hollywood horror franchise in 1976.

Three years previous to this date, another Satanically-themed film dominated the box office and propelled horror back into the critically and commercially lucrative spotlight. Friedkin's *The Exorcist* closed the gap between studio-sanctioned highbrow horror and the low-budget exploitation pictures. According to Troma's Lloyd Kaufman, this was yet another example of the majors following "people like Roger Corman ... into the horror field."[81] Generating equal amounts of controversy and success, the film played a significant part in the rise of the big-budget Hollywood Summer Blockbuster that officially began with *Jaws* eighteen months later. Despite Spielberg's need to break from Universal, and the similarities between this project and *Duel*, Spielberg's decision to direct was, according to McBride, born out of his desire to "seek acceptance and approval"[82] with a "big commercial movie."[83] The critical and commercial success of these and other examples firmly established the extent to which new and aspiring Hollywood directors would turn to contemporary literature to legitimize projects and guarantee a high profile release.

However, the existence and involvement of a living author also heralded the potential for an antagonistic relationship to develop between said writer and the director. Sometimes spilling out into the press, examples of such public spats include Peter Benchley and Steven Spielberg on *Jaws*,[84] and Anne Rice and Neil Jordan during the production of *Interview with the Vampire*.[85] Whereas some directors willingly incorporated an author's intentions, others had them imposed upon the production. Spielberg and Jordan, for example, argued that the authors' screenplays lacked the integral cinematic elements;

whereas *The Howling* director Joe Dante simply wrote off Gary Brandner's novel from the outset. Therefore, although directors' attitudes towards source novels and their creators varied, they were seldom reverential. Indeed, Hitchcock's admonition that he "read a story only once, and if I like the basic idea, I just forget about the book and start to create cinema"[86] further supports this claim. Having previously observed how the focus of their text had been shifted, stifled or substituted by a director's own stamp, some authors understandably sought to increase their involvement in, and creative control over, subsequent projects.[87]

This situation has seen writers and literary creators invariably feel the need to publicly defend their work and directly criticize a director's alleged (mis)handling of the material. As we shall see, this is reminiscent of the first film directors' attitude towards subsequent films, and a stance echoed by audiences and critics who characteristically mix direct comparisons with unfair criticisms. Overall, the finished product often fails to live up to any and all subjective preconceptions. Similarly, the Hollywood horror franchise has elicited the same reactions and resentment from fans and creators of first films, in terms of their fidelity to the source material, which underlines its status as another form of film adaptation.

Acknowledging Wood's separatist attitude towards adaptation,[88] Vincendeau has pointed out that this issue of fidelity, and the comparing of literary texts with their cinematic counterparts, has dominated academic discussion. "The critical reception of literary adaptations has been plagued with the urge to assess how 'faithful' the film version is to its original."[89] Ever since the first silent cinematic adaptation of Mary Shelley's *Frankenstein* by the Edison Company in 1910, Hollywood's desire to scare audiences has been tempered by its reluctance to offend the masses. In this, the first of the monster movies, the Edison Company "didn't want to seriously frighten audiences"[90] and so significantly altered Shelley's text to ensure that the monster didn't kill anyone and "eventually vanishes, overcome by Frankenstein's love for his bride."[91] In other words, Hollywood's attitude to the literary text is not as respectful or rigorous as many critics and audiences would like.

Naremore concurs, and has expanded on this statement by pointing out that "even when academic writing on the topic is not directly concerned with a given film's artistic adequacy or fidelity to a beloved source, it tends to be narrow in range, [and] inherently respectful of the precursor text."[92] In applying these issues to the Hollywood horror franchise, we can see how such an approach is unjust, given the nature of studio politics and budgetary constraints as financial support for the franchise dwindles. However, as film criticism continues to evolve, this single-minded over-reliance on fidelity as the primary source of analysis and interpretation has thankfully begun to decline—despite its early domination of academic discussion.

With imitation and creative flattery at the heart of Hollywood filmmaking, rival studios readily cashed-in on successful adaptations of *The Exorcist* and *Jaws* by producing similarly themed and unofficial adaptations of their own—*The Omen* and *Orca: Killer Whale*. Powerless to prevent rival studio productions and low-budget imitations from swamping the marketplace, studios such as Warner Bros. and Universal responded to cinematic plagiarism by producing legitimate numerical follow-ups of their own, thereby creating the first experimental slew of what novelist, critic and screenwriter William Goldman has since referred to as "whore's movies,"[93] and effectively announcing the arrival of the modern Hollywood horror franchise.

Although a rich ancestry stretched back to the earliest forms of Greek tragedy, ones alluded to in Wes Craven's *Scream 2*, shocking climaxes and apocalyptic conclusions actually pre-dated the time when a first film's end was fashioned around a preemptive strike on the part of the studios. Indeed, by prohibiting narrative closure, adaptations of *The Birds* and *Rosemary's Baby* have since been open to (re)interpretation in future films.[94] However, directors have rarely agreed with authors' conclusions, preferring to sacrifice, spare or shift character and meaning to ensure a satisfying cinematic experience. With Michael Mann's *Manhunter* and Dante's *The Howling* being particularly strong examples, Spielberg not only spared his onscreen personas in two monster movies,[95] but also resurrected the T-Rex for the final shots of *Jurassic Park*. That said, the director did not prevail in finishing *Jaws* with a decidedly apocalyptic final shot of "a lot of [shark] fins on the horizon, coming to the island"[96] as survivors Brody and Hooper optimistically kick their way to shore — a shot more in keeping with the director's shrewd sequel-making sensibilities.

Horror's natural tendency towards open-ended and apocalyptic finales finally reached its apotheosis with Brian De Palma's *Carrie*, a film that not only introduced cinema audiences to Stephen King but also to the generic staple known as the shock epilogue. An extension of the aforementioned apocalyptic conclusion in which the "killer always returns for one last scare,"[97] De Palma's shock epilogue was itself "inspired by the end of [John] Boorman's *Deliverance*."[98] This nightmarish scenario, in which the film's antagonist remains alive in some form at the first film's conclusion, dramatically influenced the future of horror filmmaking and facilitated the narrative ease with which franchises were resurrected for one more installment. From the final murderous image of *Pet Sematary* to the resurrection of a female *Candyman*, first films invariably set the stage for future sequels, just as *The*

Howling and *Interview with the Vampire* explicitly indicated the direction follow-ups could take. In other words, filmmakers' narrative choices or compromises allowed production companies to exploit these titles time and again as methods of distribution and exhibition dramatically exploded.

The unprecedented growth in cable, satellite and pay-per-view channels, along with advances in film technology at this time, also opened up the potential for many filmmakers, regardless of budget and backing, to finance, film and distribute their product. Then again, changing methods of distribution and exhibition also contributed to a dwindling interest in venues like the traditional drive-in and grind house, where low-budget horror had cultivated a fertile breeding ground. The introduction of Sony's Betamax videocassette recorder in 1975, along with its rival VHS, ushered in a new era of feature film production, distribution and spectatorship. As had previously occurred in the drive-in, the Home Video market led to an increased demand for new titles and the rediscovery of old ones. Whereas the drive-in merely altered the environment in which films were exhibited, Jancovich has described how:

> The advent of the domestic video machine had been treated with great suspicion by the major Hollywood studios, which feared that it might finally destroy the family altogether. They were therefore originally very cautious about releasing their films on video, and the rental and retail market became dominated by smaller, independent companies, which filled the resulting gap.[99]

Independent and international filmmakers readily exploited this substantial gap in the market and seemingly insatiable demand for product. In order to compete with their big-budget rivals, independents like Roger Corman and Charles Band shrewdly increased the sex and violence quotient in their films, thus distinguishing them from the more mainstream fare on offer. For example, once Spielberg announced his return to the monster movie market with a technologically groundbreaking adaptation of Michael Crichton's *Jurassic Park*, Corman committed to an adaptation of *Carnosaur*. Such was Corman's commitment to the concept that, by the time Spielberg returned for a second installment, Corman had released a third entry in his dino-franchise. Furthermore, as competition increased and many independent production companies went bankrupt, the franchise was embraced by many burgeoning and fledgling companies as a successful method of corporate reinvention and economic survival.

Previously, studios had presented and promoted their actors, auteurs and icons. However, the favorable reception of sequels to George Lucas' *Star Wars* and Sylvester Stallone's *Rocky*, combined with the critical acclaim lavished on sequels to *The Godfather* and *The French Connection*, saw them take over as the industry's most bankable and dependable commodity.[100] In addition to the reduced risk and relative profitability of the franchise, studios were inspired and incensed by the extent to which the independents had cashed in. As previously suggested, Universal's follow-ups to *Jaws* and *Psycho*, for example, could be seen as a direct response to the slew of low-budget imitations and threats to their first film concepts.

Night of the Living Dead director George Romero similarly experienced cinematic plagiarism throughout domestic and international markets with Bob Clark's *Children Shouldn't Play with Dead Things* and Lucio Fulci's *Zombie Flesh Eaters* being marketed as sequels to Romero's own follow-up in various foreign territories. And so, as the seventies drew to a close, no film was safe from becoming a Hollywood horror franchise, highlighting Romero's claim that, although "Hollywood still thinks of horror as schlock, the perpetual poor relative, they're willing to turn to it if it's making money."[101]

This proliferation of sequels, primarily within the horror genre, has led many critics and insiders to diagnose Hollywood with a severe bout of "sequelitis,"[102] the symptoms of which are said to be a lack of creativity and a conservative approach to "playing it safe." Such negative connotations have admittedly been backed up by some undeserving product. Moreover, this growth in the horror, and specifically slasher, genre ironically became the subject of author Robert Bloch's literary follow-up to *Psycho*. Through his work, Bloch criticized Hollywood's cynical approach to filmmaking; and Universal "loathed"[103] this novel's condemnation of their "blood bath tactics."[104] Though the studio was initially reluctant to pursue this franchise, a case of potential copyright infringement (in which the Picture Striking Company had announced *The Return of Norman* as their next feature) sensationally stirred up worldwide media speculation to such an extent that Universal ultimately found the project impossible to resist. By the time *Psycho II* was released in 1982, Fox's *Omen* franchise had reached the end of its current cycle with a fitting yet temporary conclusion after three installments, and Damiano Damiani's *Amityville II: The Possession* had become the first prequel of the Hollywood horror franchise.

As the eighties progressed, New Line's success with the iconic child killer Freddy Krueger[105] inspired courses of action that either involved the accumulation of established titles or the development of more franchise-friendly genre titles in-house.[106] Whereas "The House that Freddy Built"[107] grew in size and stature, companies such as New World, Vestron, Empire and DEG fell into bankruptcy, liquidation or receivership. As the slasher boom dwindled, the collapse of companies like New World encouraged production companies to acquire recognizable product in an overcrowded market.

Elsewhere, Fox fused the remake and the sequel for a follow-up to David Cronenberg's *The Fly*, and Warner Bros. became the first major studio to specifically create horror sequels for the direct-to-video market with Larry Cohen's third *It's Alive* and *A Return to Salem's Lot* in 1987.[108] In this and all respects, Hollywood has demonstrated its ability to meet and then exceed audience demands — to saturation point and at the expense of the independent market.

Technical advances have also helped this situation, with new opportunities for filmmakers allowing the Hollywood horror franchise to take hold. Combined with the growth of cable and pay-per-view channels like HBO, which began its satellite distribution programming in 1975, this avenue has been expanded and explored by competitors such as Showtime. The increase in cable and VCR penetration contributed to the production of franchises specifically designed for the home video market. With such concepts as "product recognition" and "brand identity" built into the franchise mentality, studios and independents capitalized on these benefits, with the added bonus of ancillary markets and additional merchandising. In other words, with the industry no longer restrained by or limited to the theatrical market, an increasing number of films, and particularly their sequels, resurfaced either as direct-to-video, pay-per-view or network/cable television premieres.

Following this expansion, the Hollywood horror franchise has flourished or floundered, depending upon your perspective, by trading on fresh icons in foreign and domestic markets. The resurrection of the *Children of the Corn* franchise is a key success story in this respect. As Trimark, New Horizons, and Full Moon films dominated the direct-to-video horror franchise market with *Leprechauns*, *Puppetmasters*, *Wishmasters* and *Children of the Corn*, spiraling costs saw alternative forms of distribution exploited to secure a return on investments. Indeed, 2005 saw the industry's perception of the home video market dramatically adjust, as companies like Paramount and Universal began investing heavily in direct-to-video fare and opening up specific distribution arms to exploit the DVD premiere market.[109]

Prior to this, the Weinsteins and Miramax specifically established Dimension Films to capitalize on these markets and began accumulating recognizable genre titles like *Hellraiser* and *Halloween* at various stages in their numerical development. Besides their assimilation of these troubled titles into an evolving portfolio, the success of Craven's *Scream* trilogy saw Dimension become the focal point for the financing and distribution of the Hollywood horror franchise in the late nineties. Since 1996, the company has been involved with over twenty different sequels to such first films as *The Prophecy, Mimic, From Dusk Till Dawn, Dracula* and, of course, *Scream*. Through an inconsistent process of farming out sequels and promoting novices and experienced members of its production family into the director's chair, it could be argued that Dimension spearheaded the (sub)standardization and (some level of) experimentation within the Hollywood horror franchise.

Similarly, Michael Bay's Platinum Dunes production company has also built itself around adapting classic genre titles for contemporary audiences, with such titles as *The Texas Chainsaw Massacre* (and a new prequel), *The Amityville Horror*, *The Hitcher* and even plans for a *Friday the 13th* remake. Furthermore, 2007 will see Rob Zombie remake Carpenter's classic *Halloween*, with a shift in focus and a significant prequel element. Promoted as reimaginings, reduxes or simply remakes, these titles, along with a new batch of creature features designed to replicate the success of Universal's first iconic monster movies, have brought the Hollywood horror franchise closer to the literary adaptation.[110] Undeniably, producers have adopted the horror remake revival as a means of resurrecting the profitability of a title and reintroducing the franchise to a younger contemporary audience. Just as these adaptations have dominated horror film production, the Universal trend of combining horror series to ensure their continuation has brought the Hollywood horror franchise full circle.[111]

With the introduction of the DVD in March 1997, horror once again capitalized on its comparatively low costs and high potential for profit in new markets. DVD successfully built on the foundations of the Special Edition and Laserdiscs before eclipsing them completely with the added potential of commentaries, documentaries, deleted scenes and alternative endings. This has generously allowed for the re-release or re-mastering of "old classics," and the digital debut of new ones as a new way of experiencing and analyzing film. Furthermore, DVD sales surpassed those of videos for the first time in 2003,[112] and the Hollywood horror franchise has benefited from its established fan base and a fresh teen audience. In this respect, the Hollywood horror franchise has demonstrated that, like any good cast, it has been one worth repeating through an endless series of sequels, prequels and remakes.

The Horror Film Director

> Auteurism — A theory of filmmaking in which the director is considered the primary creative force behind a film.[113]

The auteurist approach to film theory saw directors ranked and placed in a hierarchy according to their artistic potential and achievements as perceived by critics in *Cahiers du Cinéma*. This influential group of French critics emerged in the 1950s and was responsible for reviving and popularizing the ongoing debate surrounding cinematic authorship. First published in 1951, their manifesto for an auteurist approach to film theory and criticism was eventually epitomized in Françoise Truffaut's 1954 essay "A Certain Tendency of the French Cinema." This advocated that increasing attention be awarded to specific American films and filmmakers.

Dick, in *Anatomy of Film*, stated that "auteurism entered America"[114] through Andrew Sarris, who adopted and adapted this theory first in a 1962 essay and then later in *The American Cinema*. Furthermore, Sarris imposed "a ranking order of his own"[115] and distilled the theory down to three essential principles or criteria.[116] However, many scholars have raised legitimate objections. Citing collaboration and control as dissipating factors, they have countered that the potential for any individual, be it writer, director, producer or special effects artist, to have sole control over the finished film is limited if not impossible. Indeed, this contentious debate brings us back to the key issues of context, content and influences.

Although Twitchell acknowledged the genre's artistry and originality, he considered auteur criticism "quite beside the point when explaining horror."[117] Clover, meanwhile, has concurred: "auteur criticism is at least partly beside the point,"[118] suggesting that directors "operate more on instinct and formula rather than conscious understanding."[119] However, Dickstein, in "The Aesthetics of Fright," has propagated a more extreme view.[120] He argued that "the 'art' of horror film is a ludicrous notion since horror, even at its most commercially exploitative, is generally sub-cultural like the wild child that can never be tamed."[121]

In other words, the genre is not and cannot be crafted, created or controlled, but must be visceral. Insofar as this relates to the Hollywood horror franchise, which seeks to harness the profitability of a proven concept via a series of films, Dickstein would perhaps question its legitimacy and validity on these terms.

Elsewhere, Jancovich has pointed out how writers such as Kitses described the way in which "many directors [have] worked best within specific genres. This observation led them to see genres not simply as formulaic narratives against which directors defined their authorial personality, but rather as a resource on which the director drew — something that was at least as enabling as it was constraining."[122] Indeed, this book will illustrate the extent to which genre and the franchise have been instrumental in establishing a director's auteur status. Moreover, it will examine the extent to which the Hollywood horror franchise provides a "vital structure through which a myriad of themes and concepts"[123] can be explored by directors able to exploit their own fears, neuroses and concerns.

In light of this, scholars such as Kitses have begun to deviate from the established hierarchies of New Hollywood auteurism, as epitomized by the likes of Spielberg, Coppola and Scorsese, to analyze the careers of less prolific figures.[124] Of those directors associated almost exclusively with the genre, only those from the 1970s have, as yet, received similar treatment.[125] More general collections on contemporary Hollywood directors include *The Movie Brats*, *Postmodern Auteurs*, *A Cut Above* and *Directors Close Up*.[126] This profiling and or interviewing of various influential directors has increasingly been applied to the rising number of younger, less experienced directors and those operating on small budgets and outside the traditional Hollywood studio system. However, the majority of this literature has only been produced in the last ten years.

Alternatively, Tom Weaver, and Randy and Lee L'Officier, have compiled interview-based collections entitled *Monster Movie Makers* and *The Dreamweavers: Interviews with the Fantasy Filmmakers of the 1980s*.[127] Furthermore, other writers have profiled directors in a range of self-explanatory titles guaranteed to grab the audience's attention.[128] In addition to these exploitation-focused authors, Dennis Fischer has, in *Horror Film Directors, 1931–1990*,[129] critiqued several sequel directors who, for the most part, have been derided and dismissed by other writers in this field.

As for audiences, S.S. Prawer has pointed out in *Caligari's Children* how audiences, and particularly those attending horror sequels, not only "want to satisfy various latent needs and dispositions ... [but also] want to be surprised by something new or different."[130] In other words, directors must recognize and respond to the external and internal demands imposed upon them. If a sequel rigidly adheres to the established formula, it risks disappointing the audience and jeopardizes the franchise's future; but should it deviate too far from the original concept, audiences will be alienated and consider the film a disappointment. Maitland McDonagh concurs with Prawer in this respect and has commented how this "balance between keeping the elements people loved from the first film while taking the material in a new direction is a tough one."[131] Therefore, this book will also examine the way in which directors of the Hollywood horror franchise have dealt with the dilemmas involved in producing a successful follow-up.

Furthermore, it will provide a considered overview of the production process from the director's perspective by adopting a case study approach. Each of the five chapters will pay particular attention to issues of tone, content, test screenings and censorship by focusing on directors' relationships with the

Hollywood horror franchise. Chapter 1 will chronicle Don Coscarelli's seemingly monogamous involvement with and control of the *Phantasm* franchise. Chapter 2, on the other hand, will address Wes Craven's ambivalent relationship with the Hollywood horror franchise throughout the course of his career. In Chapter 3, the focus will shift to the rise of the special effects artist and the ascension of first film cast and crewmembers into the director's chair by referencing Tom Savini and William Peter Blatty's involvement with the *Night of the Living Dead* and *Exorcist* franchises. Departing from this nepotistic trend, Chapter 4 will then take on the largest category of directors thus far: the franchise outsiders, as represented by *Blair Witch 2*'s Joe Berlinger. Finally,

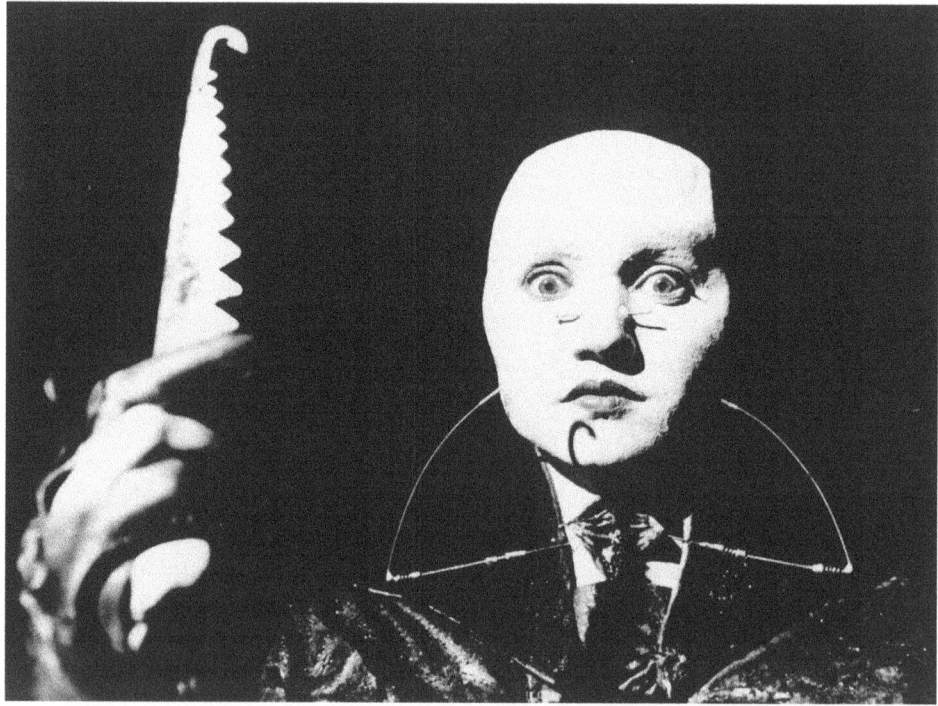

Hellbound: Hellraiser II (Tony Randel, 1988). The Female Cenobite (Barbie Wilde) brandishes just one of the many tools used to torture those who open the box. "We've always been here," she tells a terrified Kirsty (Ashley Lawrence). Her expression blank, her throat exposed, she is in denial as to her origins until the bitter end. Furthermore, her knife is out in anticipation of the kill. And so it is and has been with audiences, censors and critics towards the Hollywood horror franchise. Equally a source of pleasure and pain, these prequels, sequels and remakes have been summoned by audiences on behalf of studios and production companies looking to exploit the past for profit.

Chapter 5 will deal with the inevitable rise of the sequel maker, as epitomized by *Leatherface: The Texas Chainsaw Massacre III*'s Jeff Burr.

Culminating in a series of conclusions, based on the evidence uncovered and provided by directors and key personnel, this text will hopefully begin to redress the critical perception of the Hollywood horror franchise and enlighten audiences as to the myriad issues and inconsistencies that surround so many other cases of film adaptation. And so it began...

1

Don Coscarelli

In Search of Phantasm's End

> Owing to its popularity and marketability, the horror film has traditionally been the proving ground for unknown directors, since it's much easier to find a distributor for horror movies than it might be for a drama or comedy.
> — John McCarty[1]

Having contextualized the development of the Hollywood horror franchise and re-appropriated it as another form of adaptation, Chapter 1 now considers the extent to which directors' continued association has affected and informed their careers. As such, this chapter charts the inspiration and experiences of low-budget filmmakers by addressing the range of push and pull factors that have dictated their repeated return. Whereas mainstream Hollywood filmmakers were drawn to the commercial success of a literary adaptation in the hope of replicating Spielberg or Friedkin's commercial success, from Pittsburgh to Michigan and Texas to New York, independent filmmakers George A. Romero, Sam Raimi, Tobe Hooper and Frank Henenlotter launched their careers by exploiting audiences' fondness for horror. Indeed, they grabbed Hollywood's attention through a series of nihilistic narratives and groundbreaking depictions of violence designed to shock studios and audiences.

Taking a case study approach, this chapter focusses on the career of Don Coscarelli and his twenty-five-year association with the *Phantasm* franchise, spanning four films to date. Other directors in this category include

Ted Nicolaou and Harry Bromley Davenport, in relation to the *Subspecies* and *Xtro* franchises respectively.[2] After assessing directors' attitudes and approaches to the tone and content of a franchise, this chapter addresses these films' methods, modes of production and reception by taking into account the role of studios, audiences and censors. Third, this chapter considers the consequences of Coscarelli's independence from the Hollywood studios and production companies eager to support the Hollywood horror franchise, and the extent to which this has impacted his career.

Don Coscarelli: Phantasm

The promise of greater profits and a higher profile as a result of media exposure and controversy has attracted many directors to the genre. This was reinforced by the perception that the genre was the most cost-effective and therefore attractive to financiers and distributors. Indeed, many first time and relatively unknown filmmakers saw the horror film as an economically shrewd and realistic means of making a successful impact on studios and audiences.

Directors are also drawn to the genre for its enduring popularity, profitability and relative practicality. This choice to work within a traditionally disreputable genre has inspired filmmakers like George Romero, who believed that a low-budget horror film "would serve as a ticket into the film industry."[3] Similarly, Tobe Hooper and Sam Raimi selected the scary movie format as "something we could do for very little money and still have the prospect of getting it into theaters,"[4] and "the most easily marketable film to make."[5] Indeed, Raimi knew that "if I made a horror picture I could get the money and make the movie."[6] And so, from *Dead* directors Romero and Raimi to serial killer creators Carpenter and Hooper, horror has guaranteed the necessary financing, distribution deal, and access to the widest possible audience.

In contrast to Romero, Raimi and, to a lesser extent, Hooper, Coscarelli had already infiltrated Hollywood with his first two pictures. Raised in Southern California, Coscarelli practiced the art of filmmaking throughout his formative years. He became the youngest director to have a feature film distributed by a major studio when he sold his independently produced and critically acclaimed drama *Jim, the World's Greatest* to Universal at nineteen. In his follow up, released by Twentieth Century–Fox in 1976, Coscarelli continued to target the pre-teen market with *Kenny & Company*.

Having eschewed film school in favor of practical experimentation (with some degree of critical and commercial success), Coscarelli gathered together his key cast members before starting work on his third feature. Ultimately entitled *Phantasm*, this film pre-dated the rubber reality aesthetic of Craven's *Elm Street* and Cunningham's *House* franchises with its nightmarish narrative and open-ended approach. Released in 1979, *Phantasm* was one of the more innovative first films of the period and soon acquired cult status. Furthermore, it has spawned three sequels to date — all written and directed by Coscarelli.

Clover has concluded that "horror filmmakers turn remarkably often on fantasies, dreams and childhood memories, or mention myths or folk tales or legends by way of establishing archetype, or directly or indirectly reveal a dependence on Freud."[7] However, these first films were also hugely indebted to horror's cinematic heritage in that sections, scenes or entire scenarios were often grafted, "*homaged*" or simply plagiarized from previous films or documentaries.[8] A fine example of first film intertextuality can be seen in Myrick and Sanchez's *The Blair Witch Project*. This film drew inspiration from Benjamin Christensen's witchcraft documentary *Haxan* and elements of Deodato's *Cannibal Holocaust* and Craven's *Last House on the Left*.[9] Similarly, Raimi fused *Night of the Living Dead* with *Dawn of the Dead* for his first feature.[10] More in keeping with Clover's Freudian assertion, Coscarelli's inspiration stemmed from a recurring nightmare in which the director was "fleeing down endlessly long marble corridors, pursued by a chrome sphere intent on penetrating my skull with a wicked needle."[11] The effects of this personal investment and attachment to first film concepts, characters and themes saw directors like Coscarelli reluctant to relinquish their creative control of the franchise and allow others to (re)direct their Hollywood horror franchise.

Due to their inexperience, unconventional approach or geographical location, directors found that the majority of these first films tended to avoid or be ineligible for studio financing. Consequently, the use of promo reels, trailers and pressbooks, along with sample footage or shorts, proved instrumental in securing investors and facilitating the original and any additional funding needed. Following Romero's formation of Image Ten,[12] the creative trinity behind *The Evil Dead*[13] joined "together and formed the grandly named Renaissance Pictures,"[14] with the sole aim of finally making a feature length film. *Sleepaway Camp*'s Robert Hiltzig, however, apparently "got [his] film financed by raising $50,000 in shares,"[15] whereas Hooper took a more complex approach to financing *The Texas Chainsaw Massacre* by combining private investors with the corporate approach.[16] Coscarelli, on the other hand, was in a comparatively more secure position, and financing for *Phantasm* came from previous successes and parental support. Free from industry trappings, investors and co-producers, Coscarelli was spared from several complications as the franchise expanded — a marked contrast to those whose financing and overall control became the root of conflict.

Moreover, the grueling schedules, perpetual lack of money and unorthodox financing impacted the way in which they were shot. Schedules for *The Evil Dead* and *Basket Case*, for example, were erratic and extended over the course of several months, with shooting only taking place when money was available. Of all these first films, *The Blair Witch Project* was unique in its execution. Improvisation and manipulation were combined with "reality" television to produce a contemporary, Internet-based incarnation of the elaborate horror hoax film. Rather than reflect reality, Coscarelli's film challenged our notions of it and was the direct result of a "very long, very difficult and very challenging"[17] year-and-a-half production process. During this time *Phantasm*'s overlong script and themes were repeatedly refined and restructured well into shooting, perhaps inadvertently contributing to the film's disjointed, dream-like quality.

With no official studio backing, many first films were forced into the process of trying to secure a distribution deal during or after post-production. In some cases, however, this stage of the (post) production process also saw films fall foul of corporate carelessness, creativity and control. For example, Romero's refusal to reshoot *Night of the Living Dead*'s ending and "have Ben survive"[18] cost him a distribution deal with Columbia Pictures and American International Pictures.[19] Nevertheless, what amazes about embryonic and experimental low-budget independent first films like *Phantasm* (as opposed to their studio-endorsed counterparts) is the fact that they were ever finished at all. Despite its origins, Coscarelli's film was fortunate enough to secure a traditional platform release through distributor Avco-Embassy,[20] and, similar to *Halloween* and Compass International Pictures, it followed the traditional low-budget distribution method of "bicycling prints"[21] to build up its core audience.

Building awareness of a first film that has no direct literary or cinematic precedent involves infiltrating the market through innovative publicity campaigns — a technique explored and exploited by William Castle in the fifties and sixties. Fictional ratings, curses and creative gimmicks have often accompanied the release of horror pictures that have also benefited from an embittered or antagonistic relationship with the media. Even prior to *Variety*'s condemnation of *Night of the Living Dead* as "'an unrelieved orgy of sadism' which worked for this film rather than against it,"[22] horror traded on its notoriety as critics inadvertently helped raise the profile of a first film.

Alternatively, critics have intentionally contributed to the cult success of a first film, with Stuart Gordon's *Re-Animator* finding an appreciative

Phantasm II (Don Coscarelli, 1988). In response to Father Meyers' (Kenneth Tigar) betrayal, the Tall Man (Angus Scrimm) has despatched one of his loyal spheres to terminate their temporary alliance. After first severing his ear with a mini rotor-blade, the silver sphere of Coscarelli's nightmares doubles back to perform a graphic power drill lobotomy. With studio backing, Coscarelli also had to make sacrifices, but could live up to the sequel mantra of bigger, bloodier, better in this exceptionally gory sequel. Indeed, a similar sequence from the first film had to be cut to avoid the dreaded X rating, while this far bloodier reprise slid by virtually unscathed. Whether just a case of inconsistency or evidence of a double standard, many filmmakers have nevertheless felt betrayed and punished by the MPAA on account of their past interactions and transgressions.

audience at a midnight Cannes screening where it was awarded a special Jury prize. In addition to this unsolicited accolade, the film also received a begrudging level of respect from *Chicago-Sun Times* critic Roger Ebert, who quoted Kael's sane observation that "the movies are so rarely great art, that if we can't appreciate great trash, there is little reason for us to go"[23] in his review. Indeed, Kael had previously rebuked negative reviews of Carpenter's *Halloween* and helped improve that film's mainstream "credibility,"[24] spearheading its reassessment. Furthermore, this vocal *Village Voice* reviewer also encouraged her readers to seek out Henenlotter's *Basket Case* as the perfect antithesis to the "sweetness and light"[25] of Spielberg's *E.T* in the summer of 1982.

In a similar vein, literary sensation Stephen King single-handedly championed Raimi's *The Evil Dead* around the same time by describing it as "the most ferociously original horror film of the year."[26] The success afforded Raimi's *The Evil Dead,* following its introduction at the AFM (American Film Market), was repeated by *The Blair Witch Project* at the Sundance Festival, where Artisan picked it up for distribution. Furthermore, Roger Ebert of the *Chicago-Sun Times* heralded it as an "extraordinarily effective ... celebration of rock-bottom production values."[27] Whereas some directors, like *Re-Animator*'s Gordon, adopted a preemptive strike by writing off critics from the outset, Coscarelli's attitude and approach has been far more condemnatory in describing their role as largely "irrelevant,"[28] and declaring that reviews are governed by a "herd mentality"[29] that highlights their "disdain"[30] for the genre.[31]

The success of these low-budget exploitation pictures either made or confirmed these relatively new directors' status. It also suggested the potential for respectability and employment within the Hollywood film industry. With directors like Coscarelli starting their careers outside Hollywood, in both financial and geographical terms, the next step involved balancing bigger-budget, studio-based projects with creative freedom. For some, like *Re-Animator*'s Stuart Gordon, this meant familiar themes and comparatively similar scripts firmly rooted in the horror genre (and, more specifically, another H.P. Lovecraft adaptation, based on the short story "From Beyond"). Nevertheless, other directors resisted the temptation to remain within the genre and/or trade in their autonomy, and pursued more personal projects. Very few, however, were allowed to gravitate towards mainstream filmmaking during this time.

Having selected horror as a route to commercial and creative development, many directors experienced an increase in the opportunities available to them. Ever since *Psycho*'s success entrenched Hitchcock within the Universal Studio system,[32] directors have similarly dealt with shrewd corporations keen to secure their services, and, perhaps more importantly, their titles and back catalogues. Since *Psycho*, many studios and production companies have purchased the rights to a filmmaker's picture, and any sequels, leaving directors with little or no (financial) stake, interest or incentive in a franchise. For many other first film directors, their initial cult success resulted in a brand name identification whereby author and director were to be forever associated.

Although Raimi eschewed repetition in his collaboration with roommates Joel and Ethan Coen on *Crimewave*, Hooper eventually caught Spielberg's eye for *Poltergeist* after suffering a legion of interference on his *Chainsaw* retread, *Eaten Alive*. Coscarelli was also "seduced"[33] into shooting an adaptation of Andre Norton's teen-orientated fantasy novel *The Beastmaster* for MGM. However, these experiences were characterized by interference, disappointment and a sense of frustration at an industry overrun with bureaucracy and proverbial red tape. Coscarelli came from an autonomous scenario on *Phantasm* to one where he was essentially a hired hand, with little or no input into the scripting or editing process.

In light of this, the director has since argued that his vision of *The Beastmaster* was castrated from the outset, with casting choices vetoed and final cut denied.[34] In the wake of studio–based disappointment, Coscarelli became embroiled in Dino De Laurentiis' desire to successfully adapt King by signing on for *Silver Bullet*—a werewolf project from which the director eventually resigned—before shooting the fantasy film *Survival Quest* for ill-fated independent New World pictures. Despite the cult status of *Phantasm* and the success of his previous pictures, Coscarelli found it increasingly untenable to relocate and produce anything resembling a satisfying or satisfactory film; as such, his reputation faltered.

During this difficult period, the director was given the opportunity to direct what he later described as being "pretty low end horror sequels"[35] to *A Nightmare on Elm Street* and *Conan the Barbarian*, declining such offers on the grounds that he had "an aversion to doing sequels to other people's films."[36] Indeed, as the industry rabidly pursued the franchise, established genre directors were approached to take on all manner of franchise films, with even David Cronenberg tempted to direct *Basic Instinct 2* on account of its "very perverse, dark, complex script."[37] Just as *Re-Animator*'s Stuart Gordon was "informally propositioned"[38] by Anthony Perkins to helm *Psycho IV: The Beginning*,[39] *Piranha*'s Joe Dante was not only attached to a planned *Orca II* for De Laurentiis, but was also instrumental in the development of *Halloween III* and *Jaws 3* for Universal.[40]

With Hollywood coveting the success of horror sequels, and the director reluctant to work on any of the many sequel projects offered, Coscarelli was reportedly put "under pressure"[41] to return to the film which established his cult reputation. Typical of Hollywood's determination to exploit a filmmaker's perceived market value, he was later offered sequels to *Warlock* and *The Texas Chainsaw Massacre*.[42] Indeed, as the eighties progressed and the opportunities to direct non-franchise films dwindled, a disenfranchised Coscarelli faced two options as an established genre filmmaker — to sequelize himself or somebody else.

A Universal Phantasm 2

With many first films funded and filmed outside Hollywood, first film directors were not contractually obliged to return. Indeed, a director's partial or outright ownership of these potentially lucrative properties even served to prohibit others from making a follow-up without them. This placed filmmakers like Coscarelli in an enviable position, both creatively and financially. Even when studios controlled sequel rights, they were anxious that first film directors remain involved, and adopted increasingly aggressive strategies to secure their return. Through a combination of creative and financial incentives, they tried to ensure that the creative forces behind first films participated fully in the development of the Hollywood horror franchise.[43]

As with Whale's triumphant return with *Bride of Frankenstein*,[44] Fischer has argued, "Romero's big break came when he decided to do a sequel to *Night of the Living Dead*, something long anticipated after the success of the first film."[45] Soon after Romero's return, Larry Cohen worked with Warner Bros. on *It Lives Again* as a negative pick-up following their successful re-release of the first film. Although both directors had continued to make low-budget exploitation fare in the meantime,[46] a return to the franchise was a return to form for some filmmakers. Similarly, it was the complications and comparative failure of *The Beastmaster* and *Survival Quest* that confirmed Coscarelli's return to his own first film — and the Hollywood horror franchise — rather than participation in the development of someone else's sequel.

Like Coscarelli, Sam Raimi found financing for a second *Evil Dead* installment comparatively easier to secure than for a new project or his previous efforts. After soliciting interest from Embassy Home Entertainment, Raimi eventually defected to De Laurentiis after five months of deliberation and delays. Wary of films whose marketability was unproven, studios and production companies were less resistant to financing any number of follow-ups, particularly with first film directors attached. The financing for Coscarelli's

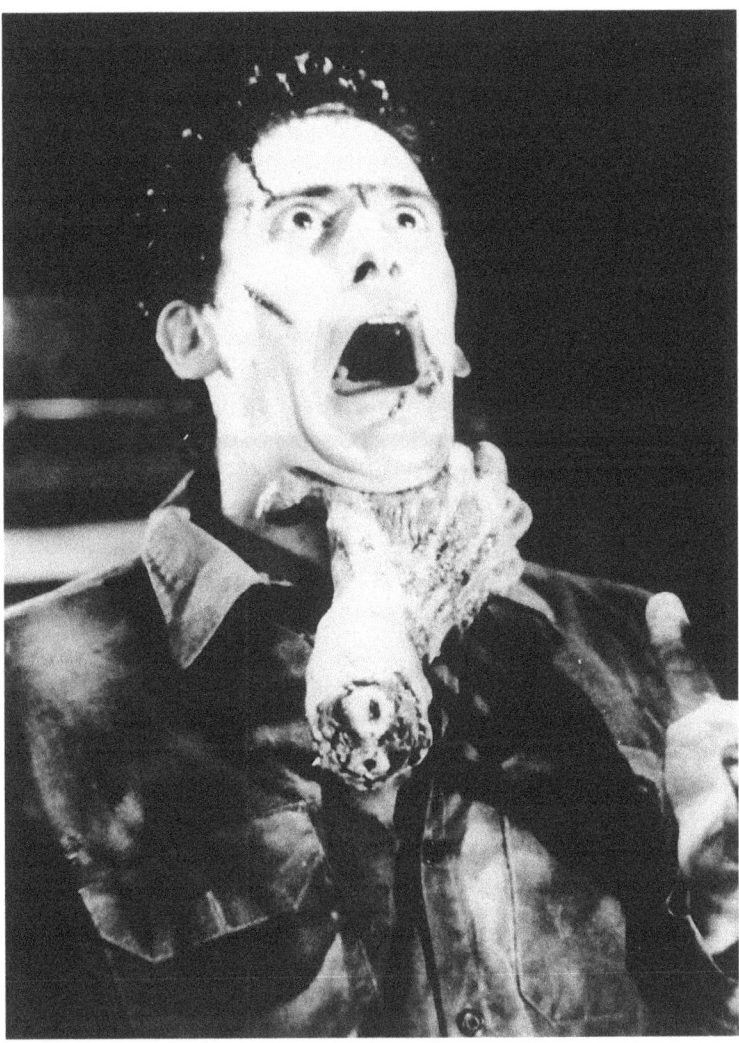

Evil Dead II: Dead by Dawn (Sam Raimi, 1987). After being possessed by the same Kandarian demons the book set free, Ash (Bruce Campbell) takes a chainsaw to his own murderous hand, screaming, "Who's laughing now?!" as his face is splattered with blood. However, this painful severing of ties is by no means the end, as the hand continues to take on a life of its own, tormenting Ash and attacking him once more by grabbing him by the throat. Although Raimi released the first film unrated, financier Dino De Laurentiis insisted on an R-rated sequel; and so, this time around, slime replaced blood, and scenes such as this were apparently re-shot with this mandate in mind. Even with cuts, concessions and compromises, the sequel still received an X-rating, and so De Laurentiis set up Rosebud Releasing for the express purpose of distributing the film.

Phantasm sequel "came from Tom Pollack, who was at Universal, and was really interested in getting a horror franchise"[47] following New Line's success with *Elm Street*. Such an endeavor proved particularly attractive as a low-risk, high-return investment when placed alongside flagship features and potential Summer Blockbusters. Indeed, the demand for previously established concepts and themes that could be transformed into a lucrative franchise was a strategic priority for Universal, who actively campaigned to control the future of Hollywood horror franchise production, with or without first film directors at the helm.[48]

One incentive, or consolation, for those directors returning to the franchise was an increase in both the schedule and budget afforded the production. According to Coscarelli, the budget for *Phantasm II* was set at $3 million, a sum the director has since described as "the lowest amount of money that Universal has ever spent on a movie in that decade but the largest amount of money that *we've* ever received."[49] Similarly, *Maniac Cop*'s Bill Lustig was another returning director who publicized the sequel as an opportunity to "deliver on the action and thrills"[50] with "four times the production value of the first."[51]

These incentives were apparently also a deciding factor in H.G. Lewis' decision to commit to *Blood Feast 2* almost forty years after the first film, and thirty years since his last film.[52] However, it was not until working with Universal on *Army of Darkness* that *Evil Dead* director Raimi issued a frank statement to directors in describing how "when you work with a studio ... you're saying, 'I will trade creative autonomy for studio money, studio marketing and a studio release.'"[53] Nevertheless, this opportunity to work with a bigger budget allowed directors like Coscarelli to indulge their imaginations further and improve upon their first effort. With the benefit of better production values and more technical experience, this lure successfully enticed directors back to the franchise.

Raimi's experience notwithstanding, another incentive employed by increasingly desperate studios keen to recreate a first film's success, besides an increase in budget, fees and or profit points, was the offer of more or complete creative autonomy. Although horror film directors like Raimi were excluded from this, others such as Romero and Lambert, who had previously only co-authored or supervised the final scripting of *Night of the Living Dead* and *Pet Sematary*, respectively, were free to develop concepts, characters and ideas in keeping with their own creative concerns. Lambert, for example, pointedly saw *Pet Sematary II* as "a big raw lump to which I could bring some of my own taste, feeling and story ideas."[54]

Similarly, and more in keeping with the Blockbuster mentality, both

Tim Burton and Joe Dante were seduced by Warner Bros. into directing *Batman Returns* and *Gremlins 2* on the condition that there would be "no compromises this time 'round,"[55] and they "could do whatever they like."[56] Having endured substantial restrictions and studio reservations on first films, returning directors increased their creative autonomy for second installments. Burton's *Batman Returns*, for example, adopted a much darker tone — to the extent that the director's final cut temporarily flirted "with losing its essential PG-13 rating"[57] before coming under fire from within for being "a supposed children's picture that wasn't for children."[58] Despite their apparent fondness for expensive follow-ups and willingness to negotiate with first film directors, Warner Bros. were unimpressed and disappointed by Burton's and Dante's

Batman Returns (Tim Burton, 1992). A feisty Catwoman (Michelle Pfeiffer) fights off the sexual advances of a lecherous Penguin (Danny DeVito). Found sprawled on his bed stroking the black cat, he tells her how she is "just the pussy I've been looking for." Such blatant double entendres and images shocked studios and audiences alike as Burton exploited Warners' offer of creative freedom in exchange for his services. The end result? A darker, perverse, more sexual film than anyone had counted on, and one that pushed the boundaries of the PG-13 rating. Previously submissive on the first film, Burton too was also transformed into a formidable yet subversive ally of the studio keen to get its flippers on an equally successful sequel. The relationship was a strained détente which resulted in a film that lacked the commercial impact of the first.

sequels, with Dante later recalling how "they really disliked the picture almost as much as they disliked the original — after all, they hated the first one."[59]

Hoping to follow in the footsteps of Francis Ford Coppola and *Godfather Part II* (with the retention of the first film director), studios attempted but failed to retain William Friedkin and Richard Donner for sequels to *The Exorcist* and *The Omen*, respectively. Similarly, Universal approached Steven Spielberg twice to helm the sequel to his phenomenally successful Summer Blockbuster *Jaws*. However, he was, for the time being at least, refusing to indulge in "corporate business"[60] after failing to convince the studio that a prequel of sorts, surrounding Quint's experience on the USS Indianapolis, was a viable option. Wary of unfavorable comparisons to first films, and/or eager to embark on new projects on account of their success within the genre, these and many other directors were unable to overcome their reluctance to return.

Back in the low-budget independent arena, however, and in the wake of complex legal wranglings, box office receipts and video rentals, directors apparently felt an obligation to their original investors. Sequels were a means of acquiring further financial remuneration on their behalf. Although not entirely altruistic in their endeavors, Hooper and Raimi cited this concern as the partial inspiration behind their return to *The Texas Chainsaw Massacre* and *The Evil Dead*. Initially attached as producer, Hooper has since commented how he reluctantly saw his *Chainsaw* sequel as a "vacation"[61] that "looked like fun at the outset,"[62] and one that "Cannon wouldn't have time to fuck up like they had done with *Lifeforce* and *Invaders from Mars*."[63] As a major shareholder in the franchise, Hooper had urged the designated trustee to license the sequel rights to Cannon, with whom he had just signed a three-picture deal that included these ill-funded-and-received forays into science fiction.

Despite a fierce resistance to a *Basket Case* follow up, Henenlotter finally succumbed because it was perhaps the only means by which he could get another project off the ground. After getting "the money for *Frankenhooker* by agreeing to do *Basket Case 2*,"[64] the director traded on the brand name and role of franchisor to see his "terrifying tale of sluts and bolts"[65] reach fruition. Consequently, returning directors saw to it that their somewhat reluctant return contained some form of creative and financial compensation through which they could secure the necessary financing and support to make other pictures.

Having cited autonomy, altruism and the ability to direct another film as reasons behind their return, first film directors like Coscarelli publicly chose to frame their follow-up as a means of "going back to my roots."[66] However, it is apparent from directors' testimonies and limited post-mortems that the alternatives to such an approach ranged from the unappealing to the harsh reality of unemployment. With financing the key to any filmmaker's career, the Hollywood horror franchise functions as an invaluable safety net and bargaining tool which many directors saw fit to utilize on an increasingly regular basis as the eighties progressed and the financing and distribution options for low-budget independent first films dried up.

In contrast to his filmmaking experiences within the Hollywood studio system, Coscarelli later described his experience on the first film as "wonderful,"⁶⁷ and intended to recreate a similar situation in which he was surrounded by friends and students (as opposed to employees and executives). In the wake of studio interference on subsequent films, such nostalgic and rose-tinted reflections were common among directors. This was after corporations keen

Army of Darkness (Sam Raimi, 1992). After Ash (Bruce Campbell) is impregnated by one of the many mini–Ash assailants, "Evil Ash" is spectacularly born, and the two, for a time, share the same body, squabbling in the manner of the Three Stooges until their separation. Surrounded by studio executives, Raimi traded his autonomy for studio support, and the price was a prolonged postproduction period involving reshoots, re-edits and an alternative upbeat ending. Caught between mainstream teen fantasy and marginal adult horror, the film was further hampered by the MPAA's refusal to grant Raimi's request to apply a PG-13 rating to what was really *Evil Dead III*.

to capitalize on an existing trend transformed their first films into potential franchises.

As Raimi has indicated, however, this studio backing, a bigger budget and over-dependence on previous successes usually came at a price, one that would encroach upon the tone, content and running timing. Accordingly, Universal's decision to fund Coscarelli's *Phantasm II* hinged upon his adhering to specific creative and casting criteria. Forced to re-cast the role of his central character and protagonist, Mike, using a relatively well-known actor,[68] Coscarelli was also told to ensure that "the film made sense."[69] These demands for narrative clarity and cohesion contradicted the first film, yet Coscarelli attempted to frame this interference in a positive light. His representation of events in pre-release interviews explained how there was now "some narration flowing through the picture ... so that even the least intelligent members of the audience would know where they were and who the bad guys were."[70] Such concessions to a perceived audience, either unfamiliar with the first film or with narrative surrealism, immediately set an unfair distinction between the first two pictures, which the director sought to offset with a bigger budget and an experimental shift in tone and content.

Like the majority of first films created prior to the early eighties slasher boom, *Phantasm* was designed as an "effective low budget ... stand alone film."[71] Consequently, the director "had no master plan"[72] or fleshed out story arc to fall back on after ten years. With other sequels released in swift succession,[73] directors were anxious to ensure that audiences "who liked the original picture were going to like the sequel."[74] To fulfill those demands and extend the life of the franchise (in keeping with Universal's plans), Coscarelli portrayed his sequel as being "bigger and better,"[75] and including those "things that genuinely worked in the first picture."[76]

From the outset then, repetition and familiarity were essential ingredients in returning directors' safety nets. Just as Lambert's *Pet Sematary 2* deliberately courted contemporary audiences with a predominantly teenage cast, *Phantasm 2* liberally borrowed from "buddy movie" clichés and adopted a road movie sensibility to secure a wider audience. Added to this recipe was an obligatory damsel in distress, complete with romantic subplot. Furthermore, Coscarelli's approach was in keeping with the pressure to reveal more of and about a story's monsters, and he made extensive use of advances in special make-up effects. At its weakest point, this first sequel seemed constructed around a series of startling special effects set pieces that partially detracted from the horror of the first film.

Returning directors repeatedly dealt with studios more interested in repetition, running times and recouping their original investment than in releasing the films as intended. They also faced pressure from audiences, critics and censors to conform to their preconceived expectations about a film.

Romero's *Dawn of the Dead*, for example, underwent significant re-editing at the hands of Italian director and distributor Dario Argento, who allegedly "didn't get it"[77] and so "deleted all the funny scenes, and made the film more action-oriented."[78] Prior to these edits, the film was given an X-rating, apparently forcing Romero, Rubinstein and independent distributor United Film Distribution "to ignore the existence of the MPAA and the ratings board altogether."[79] Consequently, this early sequel was released unrated, with a "disclaimer notifying patrons of the film's spectacularly violent content"[80] to distinguish it from hardcore pornography.

However, Romero's *Dawn of the Dead* is a rarity in the genre, since the majority of filmmakers are contractually and economically bound to work within the confines of the MPAA's R-rating. Such subjective and intangible notions as tone and intensity have become keywords in the MPAA's attitude and approach towards genre pictures, and a source of intense frustration for filmmakers trapped within a subjective and studio-owned system. Moreover, to present the MPAA's CARA (Classification and Ratings Administration) as an optional, self-regulatory, non-censorial entity is to deny the reality of economic censorship that most filmmakers contractually face.[81]

Furthermore, directors' experiences at the hands of the MPAA are diverse and inconsistent, with big-budget studio-backed productions allegedly receiving a more favorable reception than lower-budgeted films. For example, Spielberg's family-orientated and PG-rated *Jaws* successfully pushed the envelope with an intensity that was matched only by its box office success. Indeed, from *Jaws* and *Jurassic Park*, through to productions of *Poltergeist* and *Gremlins*, the director's ability to assault a family audience with monsters, murder and mayhem is perhaps best illustrated by the furor surrounding his first sequel, *Indiana Jones and the Temple of Doom*. Furthermore, both the festive violence of *Gremlins* and Spielberg's partially disowned sequel, which featured sadistic torture and a sequence in which a man has his heart ripped out, have been cited as the impetus behind the introduction of an intermediate PG-13 rating.

Whereas Spielberg's appeals for re-ratings were successful, some directors reportedly employed Hitchcock's well-documented tactics of purposefully layering shooting scripts (or films) with additional controversial elements that they could use as negotiating tools,[82] or simply returning films to the censor untouched. Pre-production consultation with the censor was another way in which directors endeavored to preempt problems, cuts and deletions. Harking back to the days of the Hayes Office and the necessity of script approval, the majority of daunted directors shied away from excess, with most adaptations diluted and distilled for mass audiences. Graphic sequences in particular have been dropped or delicately shot and re-shot by directors in light of studio concerns and a contractually obliged R-rating.

Having challenged or sidestepped censorship issues on a first film, the demands of second installments saw directors like Romero, Hooper and Raimi adopt a similar stance on sequels. Indeed, Raimi's attempts at appeasement on *Evil Dead II*, involving the substitution of slime for blood (or altering its color), highlighted these concerns when the film was also released unrated by a specifically-created subsidiary of DEG.[83] However, the majority of returning directors were caught between contractual obligation and the aforementioned preconceptions that sequels should raise the bar, with the MPAA accused of double standards and grudge-bearing. That said, Coscarelli's *Phantasm* sequel for Universal was particularly graphic for its time and appeared to slip by the censor relatively unscathed, perhaps elevated by its status as a studio-endorsed product.

In the low-budget arena, however, directors Jean-Paul Oullette and Frank Henenlotter were not so fortunate or well funded, and had to pull back from their original intentions for their *Unnamable* and *Basket Case* sequels to receive the R-rating. Although regrets, recriminations and battles with the ratings board often dogged directors' experiences on first sequels, the new opportunities and experiences afforded to them have undoubtedly aided, or in some cases revived, their directorial careers. Furthermore, it provided the opportunity to learn from previous experiences and produce a more accomplished feature than before, if only in terms of the overall production process.

The extent to which studios, stars and audiences had the propensity to influence the tone and content of future installments is perhaps best illustrated by the case of Clive Barker's *Hellraiser* franchise. According to *Hellbound* screenwriter Peter Atkins, it was Barker and producer Christopher Figg's "theory when the series started ... that Julia would be the continuing character."[84] Consequently, the sequel's original ending depicted Julia "rising from the mattress as Queen of Hell."[85] However, test screening reports demonstrated that "you can't knowingly create a villain,"[86] since "the public had taken Pinhead to its heart"[87] instead. New World responded to this feedback by placing him at the forefront of their marketing campaign for the film. Coupled with actress Clare Higgins' reluctance to return for a third film and become their "Boris Karloff,"[88] the script was modified to accommodate Pinhead's resurrection and cement his position as franchise icon.

Similarly, Coscarelli found it "hard to hang on to [his] original concept because every person who sees either of the pictures has very definite opinions about who and what each person is — after all, it was the audience who elevated our little tale into myth."[89] With this acknowledgment, Coscarelli has highlighted the role and importance of audiences in adapting any first film concept. In other words, once a first film becomes a franchise, returning directors must take into account, and be accountable to, the interpretations and expectations of audiences.

To propel the narrative forward, directors indulged audience curiosity and studio imposed simplicity with the inclusion of contextual back-story and first film footage to summarize previous events. Through a combination of dream sequences, introductory voice-overs and flashbacks, Coscarelli was one such director who endeavored to help the uninitiated and also introduce Mike's love interest. Similarly, Raimi virtually re-shot scenes, after being denied access to first film footage, to "bring people up to speed,"[90] and examined the Book's origins though a specifically-designed prologue. As expected and sometimes demanded, several first sequels explicitly left the door open for further installments, with shock epilogues that either left their protagonists in jeopardy or their antagonists resurrected. Just as Henenlotter's cliff-hanger not only brought his *Basket Case* narrative full circle by reuniting twins Dwayne and Belial, and setting the scene for the Freaks' revenge, Raimi's open-ended *Evil Dead II* epilogue transported Ash through time to face the Deadites in his originally intended Medieval setting.

A notable exception to this type of Hollywood ending is Hooper's much-maligned revisionist sequel *Texas Chainsaw Massacre 2*. Here the first film's conclusion is subverted in favor of allowing triumphant Final Girl Stretch to survive what Hanke has called "a massacre of her own making,"[91] and succumb to the way of the (Chain)saw in the final shot. In contrast, Coscarelli's follow-up to *Phantasm*, in keeping with the first film, supposedly kills off characters and ends on an apocalyptic conclusion. Coscarelli's episodic approach to the narrative not only remains true to the essence of the first film but also satisfies studio requirements in propagating the potential continuation of the saga.

In much the same way, Hooper's *Chainsaw* sequel focused on its dysfunctional family "to the detriment of the film itself."[92] Larry Cohen's rationale that "if people came back and paid another five dollars, they had the right to see a little bit more"[93] of *It Lives (Again)* saw him equally "trapped."[94] The decision of whether to follow this edict or preserve "some of the magic"[95] undoubtedly compromised the effectiveness of many a Hollywood horror franchise. The majority of directors adhered to audiences' tastes and expectations, with Coscarelli's sequel proving no exception by taking audiences on an extended tour of the Tall Man's dimension and revealing the unsightly visages of his Jawa-esque henchmen. Following Mike's release from the sanatorium and reunion with Reggie, the pair take an extended road trip, tracking the Tall Man. The duo pass through numerous ghost towns until Mike is united with his "dream" girl, and they face an adversary whose henchmen and otherworldly weaponry are seemingly endless. Although Coscarelli's first sequel avoided, for the most part, the camp splattery excess of Hooper's and Raimi's films, it embraced Romero's action-orientated apocalyptic stance. However, by the time the director had signed on for a second sequel, black comedy was very much on his agenda, and the director seized the opportunity to incorporate a variety of generic strands into the story within the relative security of his franchise.

Surviving the Franchise

Historically, first film directors (such as James Whale and Jack Arnold) refused to return to the franchise for a third time, forcing Universal to find replacements for Whale and Arnold on *Son of Frankenstein* and *The Creature Walks Among Us*, respectively. Although Hammer was unsuccessful in securing Val Guest and Hammer stalwart Terence Fisher for the third installment *Quatermass and the Pit* and *The Evil of Frankenstein*,[96] a third official Dracula outing, *Dracula: Prince of Darkness*, saw Fisher become the first filmmaker to complete his own horror trilogy (in 1966). For those contemporary horror franchises deemed worthy of a third film, a director's continuing involvement was guaranteed, with a few notable exceptions.[97] Having succumbed to studio pressure or the need for financial security once before, many returned to the franchise and prevented another director from capitalizing on or altering their creations.

Having failed to raise the necessary financing for other films, both Cohen and Raimi fell back on their relationships with franchise financiers Warner Bros. and De Laurentiis, respectively, and exploited the franchise as a means of continuing their careers. Raimi recalls that when he "made the deal with Dino to make *Army of Darkness* ... things were very bleak,"[98] insofar as "it was my only job opportunity at the time."[99]

Similarly, Larry Cohen approached Warner Bros. "with the idea of sequelizing or remaking Andre De Toth's *House of Wax* ... or making *The Exorcist Part III*."[100] Denied the opportunity to do either, Cohen suggested sequels to *Salem's Lot* and *It Lives Again*. This proposal met with more success — so long as they were made for the direct-to-video market — with reduced financial backing from Warner Bros.

With many directors falling back on the franchise to continue or further their careers, Coscarelli has since commented how "the reality of the business is that you get a little bit of success in one area and that's where your opportunities end up staying,"[101] despite having "a lot of non-horror projects in mind."[102] After being approached by an independent production company to "make *Phantasm III* and *IV* back to back,"[103] Coscarelli's career has highlighted the franchise's function as a dependable commodity in an unpredictable market. In this respect, the franchise can be described as a director's most faithful ally and a guaranteed property to fall back on in times of financial insecurity.

Regardless of whether parts two and three appeared in quick succession or several years apart, a major factor for these directors was the amount of money made available, with many concepts reworked in light of budget decreases. For example, Romero's refusal to be bound to an R-rating cost him the necessary financial backing to go ahead with *Day of the Dead* as written (described as his "most elaborate zombie film yet").[104] A similar back to basics approach characterized the production of many third films, *Phantasm III* included. Despite a significant reduction in budget, Coscarelli's marketing for the third film, six years after part two, assured audiences that this new film had allowed him to "tie some things up and deal with some character elements we never really explored."[105] According to the director, this was after consulting with fans to find "out what they wanted to see."[106]

In this respect, the interactive evolution of the franchise through directors' consultation with Internet fan sites and forums has been illustrated. This form of feedback allowed Coscarelli to incorporate the fans' wishes into the evolution of his Hollywood horror franchise. After claiming he always "had a third *Phantasm* in mind,"[107] the director attempted to justify his return in creative terms.[108] Re-presenting the narrative as an intended trilogy, Coscarelli's misrepresentation was apparent when it was revealed that an open-ended finale was written into his contract for the third film[109]—although that footage was left on the cutting room floor. While Universal had first refusal on the film in terms of distribution, this third movie saw no enforced casting or narrative coherence; as such, Coscarelli returned to a rubber-reality aesthetic and reverted back to his original casting of Mike.

Third films not only saw a sharp drop in budget but also heralded a shift in tone and content. Many directors emphasized or turned to slapstick, fantasy and political satire to keep the material fresh. Described by Raimi as "not so much a horror film as it is an adventure film,"[110] *Army of Darkness* was an extended homage to Ray Harryhausen, fantasy and science fiction in which flawed hero Ash must successfully complete an Arthurian quest in order to travel back to the future. Referencing *Superman III* and *Back to the Future*

Part III in equal measure, Bruce Campbell is literally divided and forced to defeat his alter ego and save a small community before entering into a Rip Van Winkle–style finale.[111]

Similarly, Coscarelli's declaration that it had "never been a slasher series"[112] can be interpreted as a means of distancing the franchise from the negative connotations of other films. Featuring a trio of *Evil Dead II*–inspired ghouls as the Tall Man's stooges, the film also sports several eye-catching special effects gags and devilish black humor. Despite continuing the road movie narrative of the second film, this third installment also featured a post–Apocalyptic dysfunctional family, with the thrust of Coscarelli's narrative lying in the formation of this nuclear family, complete with a homicidal Macaulay Culkin clone. Seeping into *Return of the Jedi* territory, this third film also explored the relationship between its adversaries, with the help of returning character Jody as a sometime–Spherical Spirit Guide, and the revelation that Mike was another vessel for the Tall Man's spheres and instrumental to his plan.

Returning third film directors also experienced further difficulties obtaining the desired rating. Just as Raimi appealed in person against his R-rating for *Army of Darkness*, Lustig, Henenlotter and Coscarelli all received X/NC-17 ratings for *Maniac Cop 3*, *Basket Case 3* and *Phantasm III* respectively, despite their satirical or comic tone. As a low-budget independent filmmaker, Henenlotter has repeatedly argued that the difficulties his pictures experienced have resided in the board's attitude toward blood, a substance that has often proven vital in obscuring "a multitude of sins."[113] Having described the process as one in which "the first thing they consider is where the film is coming from and what studio is behind it,"[114] Henenlotter harked back to Hitchcock's approach and allegedly resubmitted his film two weeks later "without anything cut … and it was given an R rating."[115] As previously mentioned, this complaint, that the board favors the big-budget studio enterprises over their independent endeavors, is made repeatedly throughout interviews with directors—even though all such charges have been fervently denied by the board through its then–President Jack Valenti.

Having failed to negotiate another two-picture deal at SGE using *Basket Case 3* as an incentive after SGE allegedly "hated with a vengeance"[116] every other idea he pitched, Henenlotter begrudgingly applied himself to a third *Basket Case* film based on the $1.2 million budget available. Reportedly sick of his central characters, and confident that so "long as you don't disappoint the audience you can do whatever you want,"[117] the director shifted the film's focus onto Granny Ruth and her school bus of unique individuals, complete with cartoonish gore effects and an absurd sing-along sequence.

Despite reports to the contrary, it was ultimately the dwindling schedule and limited budget that forced the director to "turn it into a comedy,"[118] albeit "more of a comedy than I would have liked."[119]

Unlike Coscarelli, who was contractually obliged to end *Phantasm III* with another cliff-hanger, *Basket Case 3*'s Henenlotter deliberately left his third film "on an up note"[120] to avoid any possibility of "doing *Basket Case 4*,"[121] since "neither of the two sequels should have happened in the first place."[122] With such third installments ultimately disowned by their creators, and even referred to with regret in certain circumstances, filmmakers such as Henenlotter have since resisted the temptation and belief that he "could get money for *Basket Case 4* tomorrow."[123]

Although Coscarelli has made similar remarks about raising the financing for another *Phantasm* sequel "whenever I want to,"[124] he has yet to raise the necessary funds to shoot his most ambitious entry to date. In a marked departure from his previous attitude and approach, Coscarelli has actively embraced Oscar-winning scriptwriter Roger Avery's[125] *Phantasm* sequel script entitled *Phantasm 2012 A.D.* Furthermore, he has tried to secure the $10 million it would take to put Avery's script up on the screen, despite the fact that the first three entries were nomadic enterprises. Described as "*Phantasm* meets *The Stand*, with a dash of *Escape from New York*,"[126] this epic "final" entry in the series sees the Tall Man take over the majority of North America. However, Coscarelli has found it "very difficult to gain respect from the people who finance movies,"[127] and feels frustrated by these "suits and big-shots [who] just don't get it."[128]

In his attempts to elevate the size and scope of his Hollywood horror franchise in financial terms, Coscarelli has discovered a definite budgetary ceiling, insofar as the future of the *Phantasm* franchise was concerned. Ultimately, the project was hampered by his genre-based cult status, even with an Academy Award winner attached as screenwriter. Faced with what seemed to be insurmountable limitations with regard to his status and potential to raise the necessary financing, the director chose to embark upon a comparatively less ambitious self-penned follow-up. Limited, at least in terms of its overall scope and scale, this new installment was designed as a suitable "stop-gap"[129] that could be "produced for peanuts"[130] until his collaboration with Avery could be made.

Released in 1999, and admittedly "concocted for strictly commercial reasons,"[131] Coscarelli's fourth entry was a time-traveling prequel and follow-up to his unplanned trilogy. In combining prequel elements, flashbacks and unused footage to create a further franchise installment, the film's narrative picked up from the climactic scenes of *Phantasm III*.[132] As an epic yet low-key tale, Coscarelli's fourth effort catapulted his characters through time to not only explore the paradoxical origins of the Tall Man but also flesh out their connections in preparation for Avery's take on the franchise.

Best described as a "Dickensian tour of the Tall Man's past, present and future"[133] that belies its budget and status as a solely economic enterprise, *Phantasm OblIVion* eschews the traditional cliff-hanger ending in favor of a decidedly subtle and understated final fade-out. Working with his lowest budget since the first film, financial necessity once again proved to be the mother of invention as Coscarelli justified his decision to "loop back to part one"[134] and "pretty much finish off this story arc of *Phantasm* ... the basic core story of Mike, Reggie, and the Tall Man."[135] The director cited the demands for clarification on numerous fan sites and their feedback as the motivation behind this economically sound attempt at closure.

After publicizing an altruistic agenda, and with his role as creative filter defined, Coscarelli attempted to sidestep the economic reality of the situation and the financial security the franchise has provided. Such an approach effectively echoes the rationale adopted by New Line's Robert Shaye in Wes Craven's satirical *New Nightmare*. Cast as himself for the first time, Shaye's stated impetus for further sequels was: "The fans, God bless 'em, they're clamoring for more."[136] With filmmaking distilled to a process of supply and demand, this franchise, like any other, could continue indefinitely in various forms and permutations. Coscarelli has highlighted its function as a means by which audiences can immerse themselves "in the nightmarish world of horror, and experience these strange characters and bizarre situations over a substantial time period."[137] Furthermore, Coscarelli has understandably praised the role of the Hollywood horror franchise by stressing its longevity and importance as a fundamental part of the genre.

Although Coscarelli has reflected on his career without recriminations, he has expressed some regret regarding his attitude towards studio-based offers and other sequels. Unsure as to whether he should have concentrated on breaking into the system in a more conventional way, Coscarelli has confessed that "making movies with balls, dwarves, hearses and four-barrel shotguns"[138] has nevertheless been "a hoot."[139] Keenly aware of the audience anticipation and financial success that surrounded the franchise face-offs *Freddy vs. Jason* and *Alien vs. Predator*, Coscarelli has attempted to combine the *Phantasm* and *Evil Dead* franchises,[140] and revive interest in Avery's script by casting Bruce Campbell "to fight the Tall Man."[141] Similarly, New Line hoped to include Raimi's flawed hero in a *Freddy vs. Jason* follow-up. However, as co-owner of the *Evil Dead* franchise, Raimi has rejected both ideas and opted to remake the first film with his Renaissance partners as a Ghost House Pictures Production.

Having lost the opportunity to develop this franchise, New Line has refocused its energies on resurrecting Freddy, *Friday the 13th*, *Final Destination* and Leatherface as part of its genre line-up. Furthermore, the studio has also announced its intention to resurrect and remake the *Phantasm* franchise, with Coscarelli attached as producer. With this development, the director has benefited from Hollywood's frenzy to remake seventies classics. Such a move also signals the director's assimilation and highlights the power of the franchise to open doors so long as the director is willing to sign away his autonomy and creative control.

With plans for further installments in the *Phantasm* franchise caught up in various stages of development, the director shifted his focus and shot his most groundbreaking feature since the first *Phantasm* in 1979. Based on the short story by Joe R. Lansdale, *Bubba Ho-Tep* featured Bruce Campbell as an aged Elvis Presley under threat from the undead in an unassuming retirement home. This offbeat adaptation has been embraced by audiences and critics alike, and also featured Ossie Davis as JFK. The winner of national and international awards after successful screenings at such film festivals as Scotland's Dead by Dawn, and defying traditional genre classification, *Bubba Ho-Tep* has reinvigorated Coscarelli's career, raised his Hollywood profile and caused him to reflect on his thirty-year tenure as a director. Indeed, this film represents a key point in his career in which literary adaptation has overtaken and then fused with his approach to the Hollywood horror franchise.

Following *Bubba Ho-Tep*, the director has also adapted Lansdale's slasher-esque short story "Incidents On and Off a Mountain Road" for Showtime's *Masters of Horror* anthology series. Reminiscent of Hooper's and Craven's films, Coscarelli's populist addition was one of the first season's highlights, featuring a cameo from Tall Man Angus Scrimm. In keeping with his franchise history, the director intends to adapt the prequel to *Bubba Ho-Tep*, entitled *Bubba Nosferatu*, with Campbell's Elvis fighting off a coven of Southern she-vampires. Indeed, with Lansdale's work functioning as another reliable franchise, Coscarelli's attitude and approach has begun to echo Stuart Gordon's successful career-long affiliation with H.P. Lovecraft.

Whether acknowledged thematically, conceptually or numerically, a continuation of style, tone and content is vital in raising a director's profile in the collective minds of critics and audiences. A franchise or literary equivalent can increase directors' potential to raise the necessary financing and support for future projects. However, as can be seen in the case of Don Coscarelli, this approach cannot be successful in isolation, and directors must be prepared to participate in studio-based productions and politics if they are to prosper. Throughout Hollywood's history many directors have found that their greatest success has come from being associated with one particular genre, just as many actors are celebrated and remembered for one role.[142]

Insofar as studios and audiences are concerned, certain directors indicate a particular type of film, and together they have come to expect, and increasingly demand, a degree of predictability and certainty within a director's body of work that some filmmakers have found constricting. Despite the dangers of career stereotyping and the challenge of directing sequels to your own film, many directors have exploited the franchise as a vital element in their creative and commercial development.

In spite of industry trappings, an increasing number of first film directors chose to direct sequels because of commercial and creative incentives. The rising trend for first film directors to commit to subsequent installments has guaranteed some freedom and success. Increasingly, studios are contractually binding first film directors to subsequent installments before a single frame of the first film has been shot, in order to negate the potential for negotiation. Studios and production companies have been keen to replicate the success of previous films and emulate the success of the *Elm Street* franchise. In this respect, first film directors like Coscarelli have placed themselves in the controversial position of propagating the continuation of the franchise and those single-minded policies that have relegated their output since the seventies.

Coscarelli's attempts to control the tone and content of his franchise over a twenty-five-year period have demonstrated the extent to which the franchise can allow for a greater degree of experimentation and evolution than previously credited, and without the benefit of a big budget. Moreover, the role of audiences as critics has been elevated and incorporated into the franchise's evolution, with the added benefit of new technology. Therefore, the Hollywood horror franchise has demonstrated its ability to assume different forms, and provide a definite function for directors unable to escape or compromise and yet keen to reassert some control over their careers.

2

Cursed

Wes Craven's Franchise Nightmares

> "The necessity of making a profit will inevitably lead to questionable public relations exercises, to the taking of easy options and the exploitation and over-exploitation of what has been proved attractive in the past."[1]
> — S.S. Prawer

With Chapter 1 having addressed Coscarelli's experiences as sole director of the *Phantasm* franchise, this second chapter focusses on Wes Craven's relationship with the Hollywood horror franchise. Taking into account the experiences of fellow first film directors John Carpenter and Sean S. Cunningham, it also considers the cumulative effect it has had on Craven's career and the extent to which the filmmaker has been successful in avoiding and accepting the limited options afforded him within and outside of the horror genre. By charting the director's creative development and professional relationships with several Hollywood studios over a thirty-year period, this chapter also demonstrates the extent to which the Hollywood horror franchise has been the critical and commercial backbone of his career as one of the genre's leading directors.

Ever since cannibalizing Bergman's *The Virgin Spring* in his directorial debut *The Last House on the Left*, and referencing the Sawney Bean case to create "two mirror families"[2] for *The Hills Have Eyes*, Craven has consistently turned to the tabloids when crafting screenplays—fusing his knowledge of psychology and literature with autobiographical elements.[3] Relishing the opportunity to address socio-political issues and the glamorization of violence, Craven's first film at the age of thirty-two allowed him to take unprecedented risks and provide audiences with a vicious assault on the senses. Indeed, the film was constructed to challenge notions of entertainment via scenes of physical and emotional cruelty. The infamy and fervor afforded to *Last House*,[4] and its status as a cult classic thereafter, successfully saw to it that Craven, along with producer Cunningham, became associated with a specific type of film. This was despite his best efforts to develop a range of scripts and potential projects far removed from the gritty exploitation feel of this first film.

However, a few years after this first taste of commercial success and several failed attempts to raise the financing for other films, the director was contacted by producer Peter Locke, who wanted to finance Craven's second film — so long as he stayed within the confines of the genre and allowed the producer to capitalize on his *Last House* notoriety to promote the film.

Similarly, Cunningham "kept getting phone calls from people wanting to do a really disgusting ugly film,"[5] while he attempted to develop endless non-genre projects. Professing not to like or enjoy "brutal ugly horror movies,"[6] Cunningham's return to the genre as producer and director was inspired by the phenomenal success of Carpenter's *Halloween*. Apparently using the "tail end of his savings,"[7] the producer placed full-page ads in *Variety* and *The Hollywood Reporter* to promote his next project: *Friday the 13th*—a film only intended "to be a pot-boiler, to keep me afloat until the TV series or kid's movies took off."[8] The money raised by this effective publicity stunt led to commissioning a writer, Victor Miller, to collaborate on the script before receiving the backing from his theater-based *Last House* financiers.

The enduring legacy of *Friday the 13th*, a film Kermode credits with having "brought Bava and H.G. Lewis into the American mainstream,"[9] stems from the groundbreaking way it was unleashed. Cunningham has since recalled how he had Paramount, United Artists and Warner Bros. "bidding against one another."[10] Ultimately, Paramount clinched the deal by vowing to break exploitation film tradition and "treat it like an A title,"[11] an appealing alternative to the low-budget technique of "bicycling" prints.[12] However, when Cunningham's film was rated R in 1980, with Paramount's logo and support, it set an industry standard for liberal violence that the MPAA regretted in retrospect. Courting controversy and condemnation from censorship groups across the country, the high profile release sparked a heated debate surrounding violence in cinema and set in motion an escalating depiction of graphic murder in mainstream cinema. However, the profile and impact of this release led to increasing censorship problems as the franchise progressed, with the title scrutinized and reviled as the epitome of exploitation by critics and campaigners across the board.

For Craven, *The Hills Have Eyes* not only continued his familial theme but also continued *Last House*'s dramatic reversal of fortune, with apparently "civilized" characters harboring more monstrous tendencies than their antagonists. A relatively simplistic and clichéd story by modern standards, in which two families collide against the backdrop of a desolate landscape, *The Hills Have Eyes* featured attractive teen protagonists and charismatic villains. Encompassing elements of Hooper's *Texas Chainsaw Massacre*, with its cannibalism subtext and exposé of alternative American family values, Craven's second feature found a receptive audience. It also cemented his reputation and abilities as an effective genre director capable of garnering solid critical reviews.

Similar in both tone and content to *Last House*, yet with significantly higher production values, *Hills* firmly established the fledgling director's trademark characters and narrative techniques. The combined effect of these two features raised Craven's profile and allowed him to build on his success within a relatively narrow framework. Having accepted Locke's genre-specific support, and adding a more shocking conclusion at his request, Craven demonstrated an individual style by conforming to the type of genre stereotyping that limited the assignments offered to him.

In switching sub-genres via such TV terrors as *Stranger in Our House* (aka *Summer of Fear*) and *A Deadly Blessing*, Craven injected a more subtle and supernatural element into his resume. Furthermore, he encountered resistance and producer politics with regard to a film's climax. Attempting to broaden his experience outside of the horror genre, Craven, like many of his contemporaries (Coscarelli included), relied upon a tried and tested concept from another medium. An adaptation of the comic book cult classic *Swamp Thing* was a shrewd choice in terms of crossover potential, despite the finished film being marred by poor production values, a less-than-engaging script and a far-from-trouble-free production.

A second return to television resulted in an *Invitation to Hell*— a desperately average production in which the dark secrets of an idealistic suburbia (read: Stepford) are exposed through the justified paranoia of its protagonists. In this respect, Craven has attempted to combat issues of generic stereotyping and firmly established his ambivalent yet long-standing relationship with television that has reoccurred throughout his career (to varying degrees of success).

Craven's First Franchise

Despite the soft-core content and decidedly luke-warm reception of these early small screen films, Craven remained relatively free to flex his directorial muscles outside of the exploitation arena. As such, he attempted to move away from his early reputation for rape revenge exploitation films (and moniker as the Sultan of Slash). However, Craven's next project was a follow-up to his second film — a *Hills Have Eyes* sequel that reunited surviving cast members and resurrected others. For his first sequel, the director indulged the worst excesses of the Hollywood horror franchise to produce an unworthy follow-up that was similar to *Silent Night Deadly Night Part II* and *Boogeyman 2*. With an unhealthy overuse of first film footage to pad out the running time (via flashbacks and nightmares from key survivors — including Beast, the family dog!), the film embraced the standard trappings of a substandard slasher film devoid of subtlety, scares or narrative cohesion.

The director has since confessed that his prime motivation in directing a *Hills* sequel was a severe lack of alternatives, in that he "hadn't worked for three years"[13] (to the extent that he would even have directed "*Godzilla Goes to Paris*"[14] by that point in his career). Nevertheless, the film damaged his reputation and continues to be heralded as one of the worst examples of self-sequelization to date. In his own defense, Craven has maintained that the film "was not completed"[15] nor "intended to be released as it was,"[16] and is therefore a misrepresentation.[17] However, as writer and director, Craven must accept responsibility for the finished product, irrespective of the form in which it was released, particularly since he waived his right to apply to the DGA for an "Alan Smithee" credit.

In spite of the haphazard nature of production and disappointing end result, the *Hills* sequel served its purpose — it provided the director with money in the bank and apparently helped him regain his confidence. Born of desperation, as opposed to directorial inspiration, *The Hills Have Eyes Part II* proved to Craven, and confirmed the industry's belief, that the franchise could provide financial and job security in an unstable and competitive market.

Even though Craven had not yet achieved independent brand name status, his name, coupled with a recognizable title, was enough to secure financing and shop pet projects to studios, independent production companies and potential investors. One such project was *A Nightmare on Elm Street*— one he was pitching as "a fantasy, an impressionistic thriller,"[18] rather than a horror film, as a potential way of distancing himself from his reputation. In light of this, Craven has repeatedly reinforced Hollywood's hypocrisy towards the genre with his adherence to a narrow and negligent definition of its parameters and potential.

Craven's script was developed through a fruitful combination of news reports and personal fears, and with the uncredited assistance of Cunningham protégé Steve Miner. It was inspired by a series of unrelated articles in the *L.A. Times* in which several Cambodian immigrants, all young men, died in the middle of severe nightmares after desperately trying to stay awake.[19] Similar to Coscarelli's experience with *Phantasm*, Craven's personal experiences, real and imaginary, played a part in the film's evolution. For example, the *Elm Street* antagonist's name was "inspired by Craven's least favorite person in junior high school, a boy who always wanted to fight with Wes during their daily paper routes."[20]

A tale of vigilantes and revenge, whereby their "innocent" children pay for the sins of the parents, Craven's film featured four teen protagonists united in their experience of familial dysfunction and nightmarish encounters with a sinister scarred dream demon. A classic coming of age story and fable for its target audience, *A Nightmare on Elm Street* celebrated the self-sufficiency and independence of final girl Nancy, and introduced the genre's most prolific contemporary icon.

However, the script had been passed over by all the major studios,[21] and the director was forced to borrow money from close friend Cunningham just to pay his taxes. Similarly, Bob Shaye's independent distribution company, New Line Cinema, was struggling to survive in an evolving and fiercely competitive market. Having made a genre-specific name for itself by boldly (re)distributing such classics as John Waters' *Pink Flamingos*, Hooper's *Texas Chainsaw Massacre* and, later, Raimi's *Evil Dead*, Shaye was searching for a new project to take to Cannes and set up for a lucrative Halloween release. In backing Craven's script and agreeing to arrange the financing, both parties entered into a mutually beneficial relationship of financial and creative interdependence, and what Shaye later referred to as their "last big shot."[22]

Whereas Carpenter shrewdly negotiated 10 percent of the film's profits, in addition to his $10,000 fee to write, direct and compose music for *Halloween*, Craven faced a series of creative and economic compromises that included script approval and property rights in perpetuity. With Craven cut out of the potential to financially benefit from the film's success, profit participation became a key issue as the franchise developed. This played a part in the deterioration of the director's professional relationship with the company, and later became a focal point in future negotiations to secure his return. Nevertheless, Craven has since conceded how "when you're starting out in this business, you've almost got to expect to give up most or all of your rights to get something done. It's business reality."[23]

After being shot on the tightest of budgets[24] and under threat of bankruptcy and closure, Craven and the New Line production team finally made it into the editing room; and it was there, according to Craven, that the film "was made as much ... as anywhere else."[25] Operating under Shaye's supervision, Craven, who had already added a *Carrie*-esque jolt to *The Hills Have Eyes*, was once again forced to compromise on his apocalyptic conclusion in favor of one more in keeping with dominant sequel ideology. Shaye's suggested ending was designed to fit in with audience expectations and lent itself to a potential sequel. For Craven, this third experience with an imposed ending caused a great deal of post-production contention. The dispute was to some extent mediated and resolved by bringing in the jury — that is, the audience — and shooting "three endings and testing them all."[26] With no single ending working for test audiences, the decision was made to include aspects of all three — but not, to Shaye's dissatisfaction and Craven's insistence, have Freddy driving the car at the final fade out.

Such experience of appeasement later caused Craven to comment how "the ghost of *Carrie* haunts us all, unfortunately. There's hardly a producer alive that will allow a film to end classically — you must have that final shock."[27] The final shock for Craven, however, was the extent to which New Line would deviate from his original premise, and openly contradict the first film's conceit within the first five minutes of *Freddy's Revenge*. Indeed, the importance of these final moments cannot be overestimated, with *Friday the 13th*'s Cunningham maintaining that the "real success of the film had to do with those last few minutes ... [they] made the film work."[28] Despite being an extension of the shock epilogue, writer Miller has since argued that the ending was "never intended to be the precursor for what came afterwards."[29] This discrepancy between directorial intention and cinematic reality in the collective minds of studios and audiences has become a veritable constant in the development of the Hollywood horror franchise.

According to Shaye at least, the production process detracted from any form of singular authorship or auteurist sentiment, with even the film's title an issue for discussion. Just as *Last House* was tested under three separate titles, several other first films have undergone significant title changes to attract the widest possible audience.[30] According to Schoell and Spenser, Shaye was even considering changing the title to *Bad Dreams* to "class it up"[31] a little and avoid any association with exploitation films. As for Shaye's support of Craven's vision and development as an auteur (and, indeed, auteur filmmaking in general), the producer has since contradicted any such notion and

Carrie (Brian De Palma, 1976). Prom night survivor Sue Snell (Amy Irving) slowly walks down an overly bright suburban street towards the recently demolished White house. Both Carrie and her murderous mother are buried under the stones, and the makeshift cross is made from the white picket fence. As Sue bends down to lay the flowers she has brought, Carrie's bloodied arm reaches out and grabs her. We then cut to Sue suffering from a nightmare and being comforted by her mother before the final credits role. This scene represents the first of the shock epilogues — that one last scare and a genre staple enforced upon countless filmmakers since *Carrie*'s release. Echoed in Wes Craven's *A Nightmare on Elm Street*, the staple has since descended into cliché but lives on through more recent additions to the genre.

explicitly described New Line's feature films as "the creative children of a real complicated, complex gene pool."[32]

This power play between producers and directors within this gene pool is contentious, and filmmakers have often charged that their concepts have been compromised in favor of a more commercial vision or aesthetic. As a producer, *Re-Animator*'s Brian Yuzna similarly adopted Cunningham's encompassing definition and belief that the producer is "responsible for everything, from the time the idea is hatched to the time the film reaches theaters."[33] In transforming an overtly artistic black and white series into a commercially viable film script, Yuzna also took control during postproduction on the film. However, the tendency for producers to relegate directors during production is also a serious issue, and one that saw director-turned-producer Steven Spielberg reprimanded by the DGA (Director's Guild of America) following his over-involvement with Hooper's direction of *Poltergeist*.[34]

In light of such concerns and conflicts, Shaye has also stated how "any belief in auteur filmmaking, I think, does a disservice to the process because it's too hermetic and way too inbred."[35] With such a remark stressing the collaborative process of filmmaking, it also calls into question Craven's legitimacy as creator of the franchise. As the author of his movies, John Carpenter, coming to Craven's defense, has rejected such a statement, despite his personal feeling that *A Nightmare on Elm Street* was "the beginning of the end"[36] for 1980's horror.

After an association with independent Avco-Embassy following *Halloween*,[37] Carpenter returned to the franchise as a writer and producer for Dino De Laurentiis and Universal Pictures (a decision which granted him the support and financing for his ill-received remake of *The Thing*). Having relinquished the directorial reins of the *Halloween* sequel to film school graduate Rick Rosenthal,[38] Carpenter assumed an active role in shaping the sequel, convinced that audiences only wanted to see "the same movie again."[39] However, in the wake of *Friday the 13th*'s success and splattery excess, the director was concerned that Rosenthal's rough cut would prove unpopular with contemporary audiences looking for a faster pace and more gore. Consequently, he shot additional footage and violent scenes in time for its release.[40]

With Carpenter willing to use the franchise to further his career, despite his contempt for the process and end product,[41] Cunningham was similarly content to walk away from Paramount's plans for a *Friday the 13th* sequel. He dismissed their offers to let him direct it, and he readily signed off in favor of a percentage of the profits. Although Cunningham made "a ton of money,"[42] he disagreed with Paramount's decision to establish Jason as the antagonist, and saw the title as "just a generic name for a kind of movie"[43] and a vehicle for the same anthology-themed format Carpenter later applied to *Halloween III*. Moreover, the director considered Jason's resurrection "stupid"[44] and "laughable"[45] since it undercut the first film in favor of replicating Carpenter's franchise. Despite his contempt for this classic example of cross-franchise cannibalism, Cunningham regrets the way in which he failed to understand or take advantage of the ability his success gave him to "generate [his] own projects"[46] and fully exploit his association with the Hollywood horror franchise.

Following *A Nightmare on Elm Street*'s success on Home Video, Wes Craven's status as an established and celebrated director of horror (and franchise founder) was secure, as was his ability to pursue other projects and infiltrate the major Hollywood studios. Consequently, Craven turned down the chance to direct *Nightmare 2* once New Line had balked at the suggestion of making significant changes to former publicist David Chaskin's script. From this point, New Line prioritized style and special effects over content and coherency by commissioning a sequel that so openly contradicted a first film's premise. As producer, Shaye brought in *Alone in the Dark*'s Jack Sholder on the basis of his star-studded first feature and prior association with the producer, who, according to Craven, wanted "to make Freddy like ... a good hamburger and sell it all over the world."[47] Despite harboring a dislike of horror movies, from Chaskin's point of view,[48] Sholder reportedly found it "very necessary"[49] that he conform to Shaye's vision, particularly when it came to shooting his ending for the first film as an opening sequence. This sequence then, in which Freddy became the driver of the stereotypical High School Bus, is emblematic of Shaye's attitude and approach to the Hollywood horror franchise following Craven's departure.

In direct contrast to Richard Franklin's reverential approach on *Psycho II*—a dissertation on Hitchcock's first film—Sholder's *Nightmare 2* clearly "lost the dream side of the story."[50] With an androgynous yet romantic tale of possession and exploding parrots in the "style of Beauty and the Beast,"[51] horror's function as a modern fairy tale came to the fore in *Nightmare 2*, and the film was daring only in its contentious portrayal of "a teenage bisexual male virgin."[52] In reference to *Nightmare 2* and the *Friday the 13th* franchise, it is understandable why McDonagh has argued that this process "almost invariably debases the initial idea,"[53] often against the intentions of its creators.

Having marketed Kruger "as if he was a rock and roll band"[54] after an intense test screening process that led to numerous re-shoots and re-editing, Sholder's sequel was a commercial success for New Line. Specifically, it made a huge impact on the Home Video market as the fan base grew to encompass mainstream viewers, highlighting the concept and character's crossover potential. Nevertheless, criticisms from audiences and critics have since seen producer Shaye fall in line with popular opinion and recently refer to Sholder's sequel as a "misstep"[55] and "wrong-minded foray."[56] For Craven, the sequel as a source of disappointment inadvertently elevated his first film, and its status as a contemporary classic was highlighted by the overall failure of this ineffective companion piece.

Craven's conspicuous absence from the second installment, coupled with his well-publicized criticisms and condemnation of it, saw New Line actively campaign for the director's involvement on the third film. Despite their overtures, the director turned them down in the hope that Warner Bros., with whom he had just completed *Deadly Friend*,[57] would allow him to direct *Superman IV*. This high profile mainstream picture would allow him to break out of previous genre stereotyping and, despite the film's sequel status, into a different league. However, according to Craven, star Christopher Reeve "felt I couldn't handle a big picture"[58] and, with director approval a part of his contract, vetoed any chance Craven had. Retreating back into the franchise, the director agreed to co-write a third *Elm Street* film, with partner Bruce Wagner, as a means of renegotiating percentage points in this and future sequels. This exploitation of the Hollywood horror franchise as a means of strengthening financial security also demonstrated Craven's intention of regaining some of the creative control he had signed away on the first film.

Returning to Elm Street

After choosing to "discount"[59] the disappointing first sequel, the director originally hoped to reject the current trend for sequel narratives[60] by making a prequel that went "back to Freddy's birthplace."[61] Unfortunately, New Line, who preferred his subsequent idea of bringing Nancy back to lead a squad of surviving "dream warriors," rejected the notion. Successfully combining elements of Krueger's back-story with returning characters and an innovative direction, Craven's populist script exposed the franchise's potential for development and special effects sequences. By accepting an executive producer credit, Craven thought he could "patch up old differences"[62] and take "a real creative part in the picture."[63]

According to the disgruntled director, New Line had a different take on his role, and "all they wanted was to have my name on the script."[64] Ignored and cut out of the production process, Craven has stated that *Dream Warriors* "was ultimately not made to my satisfaction."[65] To make matters worse, Shaye employed *Dreamscape* scripter Chuck Russell[66] to take Craven's place. With the script rewritten by Russell and Frank Darabont, the pair took a screenplay credit, and this situation spiraled into a Writer's Guild dispute — one which supported the sequel director's significant changes.[67] Having exploited Craven's name as a means of legitimizing their third film, New Line expanded their audience, appeased the critics of *Freddy's Revenge*, and captured the attention of the first film's core audience.

During his overwhelmingly negative experience with Warner Bros. on

A Nightmare on Elm Street 3: Dream Warriors (Chuck Russell, 1987). Kristen Parker's (Patricia Arquette) opening dream: She enters the familiar Elm Street house and encounters a young girl. "This is where he takes us," the child explains as we hear the sound of Freddy's glove. Kristen runs down endless corridors, is chased by Freddy and stumbles into a large warehouse full of bagged teenagers, nooses around their necks. Kristen looks down and realizes she has been tricked — the girl is now a corpse. For this second sequel, Craven also went back to Elm Street as co-scriptwriter and executive producer; but with his script dramatically altered and his views sidelined, the director felt manipulated and shocked when he saw the finished film.

Deadly Friend,[68] a film chosen because of the networking studio-based opportunities it would provide, Craven lost out on *Beetlejuice* and becoming a mainstream sequel-maker with Warners' flagship franchise, *Superman IV*.[69] Just as his professional relationship with Warners was failing to work out as hoped, the director also had to contend with a civil lawsuit stemming from an *Elm Street* copycat crime. Furthermore, tabloid headlines connected the third film with a rise in teen suicide, citing the film's alleged glamorization of it. These professional trials were confounded by Craven being "raked over the financial coals"[70] in a divorce. The cumulative effect of these events intensified the director's need to escape the industry, its trappings and geographical locale, and take on another project.

In this respect, Craven has recalled how *The Serpent and the Rainbow* "was good because it got me out of the country awhile and onto a big picture."[71] Relocating to Haiti for this adaptation of Wade Davis' autobiographical tale of politics, voodoo and modern medicine, Craven's cast and crew confronted real-life horrors. In many ways this politically unstable environment added to the authenticity of the piece. Made for Paramount Pictures, who had previously offered Craven the chance to direct their *Friday the 13th* clone *April Fool's Day*, this film was a further attempt to broaden his resume[72] and provide him with an opportunity to integrate other genres into his work. For Craven, *Serpent* had real crossover potential in that "it had all the things I'm known to be strong at ... but also things I wanted to demonstrate I could do — a love story, political content."[73]

Indeed, the finished film was an impressive addition to the voodoo/zombie sub-genre that received solid reviews upon its release. It was also dependable in its inclusion of all the hallmarks associated with a Wes Craven film — nightmares and hallucinations, followed by a climactic confrontation between a protagonist and horribly scarred villain whose power comes from previous victims. Although parallels with *Elm Street* are undeniable, this decision to adapt a literary text as an alternative to the Hollywood horror franchise or imitations echoes Coscarelli.[74]

As if to consolidate the fact that there was no escaping Freddy or the franchise, Craven was contacted by New Line regarding a fourth *Elm Street* film. So far the franchise had "defied the law of diminishing returns,"[75] but, according to Shaye, Craven's proposed time-traveling narrative within dreams "was not workable,"[76] with the company preferring William Kotzwinkle's *Dream Master* proposal. Without a finished script throughout production, New Line drafted in at least four other writers to impose some form of coherency upon the special effects–laden proceedings. Despite the chaotic schedule and seemingly disparate approach to the formulaic narrative structure, *Nightmare 4* met its mid–August release date. Furthermore, it supplanted Carpenter's *Halloween* as the most successful independent film up to that time. (Whereas New Line allegedly contacted Craven as a matter of creative courtesy, *Halloween* financier Moustapha Akkad was unable to exploit his stake in the franchise without Carpenter's active support. Consequently, he began applying legal pressure for Carpenter to "put up or shut up,"[77] in his bid to finance Michael Myers' resurrection.)

Regarding *Elm Street*'s success in New Line's growth and expansion, Shaye has publicly drawn a line in the sand at his company being called "The House that Freddy Built." Nevertheless, the producer has conceded that the franchise certainly "catalyzed"[78] the company and allowed it "to gain some sales momentum"[79] in the marketplace. In keeping with its over-exploitation of the franchise—with the syndication of *Freddy's Nightmares*[80]—New Line prematurely threw itself into a fifth film to accompany a multitude of official merchandising agreements.

Having replicated part four's recruitment strategy and over-complicated script development period, New Line's *The Dream Child* was astutely likened to an old MGM musical "built around huge production numbers, slick high-tech dream sequences featuring Freddy dancing around and cutting into slower moving partners."[81] With Krueger's iconic success inspiring independent production companies and studio sources alike to compete and create their own franchise-friendly serial killers,[82] Shaye was attempting to preempt the competition within a dwindling window of commercial opportunity. And so, with the 1980s drawing to a close, the genre was overpopulated by a myriad of slavishly designed and poorly executed Krueger-clones.

Following his foray into voodoo territory, Craven returned to Hollywood with a vengeance. Like Carpenter, the director signed a genre-specific deal with Universal/Alive films that guaranteed "complete autonomy"[83] and the opportunity to create a rival franchise to Freddy on his own terms.[84] Perceived as bankable commodities and franchise creators, Craven and Carpenter were attractive to Alive on account of their profile and association with the Hollywood horror franchise. Craven's first picture was a self-conscious attempt at creating the next great anti-hero for American audiences. *Shocker: No More Mr. Nice Guy*, however, was an ambitiously flawed variation on a common theme that bore more than a passing resemblance to Cunningham's *The Horror Show*,[85] which featured its own wisecracking serial killer, Max Jenke. The resurrection of serial killers sent to the electric chair functioned as a springboard for both these special effects–laden narratives. Whereas Cunningham's film placed the family at the heart of its police procedural narrative, Craven's was the more successful of the two, with its channel-hopping premise and high school protagonist. Irrespective of directors' intentions, the franchise predominantly depends upon a first film's success, and in these cases, box office and video rental receipts have failed to justify a return to the material—at least for the time being.[86]

Craven's failure to consciously create the next Freddy Krueger led to a retreat of sorts into his news-related research files. Also inspired by his previous attachment to an adaptation of Virginia Andrews's bestseller *Flowers in the Attic*, itself the first in a long-running literary franchise and family saga, *The People Under the Stairs* conspicuously dropped Craven's signature dream sequences and producer-imposed shock epilogues. Nevertheless, it sharpened his focus on dysfunctional family values, and added a socio-economic subtext.

Even though this second project fared better with audiences and critics on account of its claustrophobic setting and fable-like qualities, Craven returned to the relative confines of television horror with the short-lived *Nightmare Café* in 1992. This fondness for diversification to facilitate career development has been a staple of Craven's career in conjunction with the franchise. In much the same way that Carpenter sought to emulate Hitchcock anthology series with Showtime's *Body Bags*, Craven's concept co-starred a post–*Freddy's Dead* Robert Englund as Blackie, the enigmatic proprietor of a *Twilight Zone*–esque last stop for lost and disconcerted souls.

Shocker (Wes Craven, 1989). As Freddy Krueger emerged as a cultural phenomenon and New Line's iconic cash cow, industry rivals attempted to cash in on the current vogue for wise-cracking serial killers with a number of similarly themed features. From *Trick or Treat* to *Brainscan*, *Dr. Giggles* and beyond, none lived up to the hype. In 1989 both Sean Cunningham and Wes Craven also attempted to market their newest films, *The Horror Show* (*House III*) and *Shocker*, in a similar vein. Both featured serial killers returning from the grave after being sent to the electric chair; but, despite a few sparks of wit and originality, Max Jenke and Horace Pinker (pictured) made little impact at the box office. However, market saturation ensured that both films found an underwhelmed audience on their release.

As mediator and franchise star, Englund suggested that Shaye should contact Craven if they were indeed intent on cheating audiences with a seventh Nightmare after the 3-D disappointment of *Freddy' Dead*. Although first film directors Ridley Scott, Paul Verhoeven and John Carpenter have all been tempted to return to the franchise in the wake of numerous sequels,[87] only Wes Craven has returned to the franchise that cemented his reputation.[88] Prior to Craven's return, New Line had similarly approached *Friday the 13th* creator Sean Cunningham about reacquiring the rights to his franchise, with the ultimate goal being *Freddy vs. Jason*. Previously unable to compromise with Paramount on this project, New Line was keen to secure Cunningham's support and participation as part of a lucrative negative pick-up.[89] Having failed to create or participate in franchises for Universal, Warner Bros. or even Paramount, Craven's decision to reinvent the *Elm Street* franchise was a solid business choice. His participation provided New Line with the necessary hook to sell the sequel to audiences and gave the director the opportunity to show Shaye and studio executives how the sequels should have been done.

When asked to reflect on their treatment and evolution of the franchise, Craven has since remarked:

> I would have hoped that the *Elm Street* films would have been treated with absolute respect all along the way. That's not a snipe against New Line, but I would have liked to have seen somebody sit down each time they set out to make one of the sequels and really get into the philosophy and the heart behind it. My first film was about some very serious and important subjects. I felt that with *2* they immediately threw all the important issues out the window and made it a series of strange, freaky events and the same old raunchy teenagers. I tried to wrestle it back with *3*, and then the series tended to wander, depending on the talent of the directors and the commitment of the writers. Sometimes I had the feeling that they just went with somebody who could knock out a script rather than somebody who had a true vision.... I'd be a very wealthy man right now if I'd done them all, but I really don't know if I could have done it.[90]

Despite questioning his creative ability to sustain the franchise throughout five sequels, Craven is nevertheless aware of the financial incentives involved and the need to be (publicly, at least) more diplomatic towards New Line. Under their supervision, however, continued association with the franchise meant supporting the company's mainstream aspirations and Shaye's formulaic framework. According to Craven, the conditions of his return revolved around "being satisfied with the deal and my demands being met"[91] "in both an artistic and business sense."[92] Indeed, it was in the wake of a diplomatically termed "very frank discussion"[93] with Shaye that "significant payments and a very uniform and predictable accounting of profits"[94] took place, and New Line "made good on many things."[95] Armed with an excellent lawyer, Craven found it "attractive to come back from a position of strength,"[96] whereby he could not only insist on a bigger budget than previously allocated, but could also redirect the Hollywood horror franchise on his own terms.

With the financial side addressed and redressed to the director's satisfaction, Craven had the task of creating "a way to bring Freddy back without violating the nature of the story or offending the audience,"[97] despite the filmmaker having no "idea of what kind of film to make."[98] In reassembling key cast members and fusing key elements of the franchise with real-life events and a film-within-a-film framework, Craven shot the picture as a "documentary in both look and concept."[99] Attributing an added depth to his movie during publicity interviews, Craven stated that his *New Nightmare* owed "more to films about Hollywood than traditional horror films."[100] Pitched as a multi-layered look at the violence in cinema and our culture, and how it affects audiences and filmmakers, Craven's *New Nightmare* was the "first almost unintentional deconstruction of the horror film."[101]

With a premise similar to King's *The Dark Half*,[102] this self-conscious examination of the Hollywood horror franchise was carved from an insider's perspective and expanded on the first film's conceit. A reactionary return to the character's "darker origins"[103] was accompanied by several satirical swipes at New Line's approach that "watered [it] down ... to make it an easier sell."[104] Furthermore, the casting of Shaye and co-producer Sara Risher as themselves allowed Craven to comment on their exploitation and mismanagement of the franchise. And so, in returning to the Hollywood horror franchise, Craven was able to reestablish himself as its on- and off-screen creator, address some of his own concerns, and respond to critics of both the franchise and the genre within his effective fairy tale premise.

With the film completed under budget and on schedule, test-screening results saw New Line allocate extra funds to "punch up"[105] its final act. Nevertheless, Craven was ultimately reminded of past experiences in the form of suggestions from Shaye's executives as to the film's tone, title and marketing campaign.[106] This situation brought Craven's involvement with the franchise full circle and confirmed his need to "say goodbye to it."[107] In terms of reception, this seventh installment created a dramatic discrepancy between audiences and critics. Whereas the box office gross failed to live up to expectations and marked the lowest for the series, mainstream reviewers responded favorably to the self-referential plot and fairy tale analogy, with the director receiving "some of the best reviews"[108] he'd ever had. Though *New Nightmare* was regarded as a commercial misstep, Craven nevertheless subverted and experimented with the formula to reevaluate his first film concept and concerns.

New Nightmare (Wes Craven, 1994). Freddy Krueger (Robert Englund, left) uses Dylan (Miko Hughes) as bait to bring Nancy (Heather Langenkamp, not pictured) back one last time. Painting Krueger as part ogre and part witch, Craven's revisionist take on the character and the material explicitly linked the franchise and the genre to its Grimm fairytale roots (Krueger even calls out, "Come here, my piggy. I've got some gingerbread for ya!"). Praised by critics for its postmodern take on the material and documentary style, Craven's film is further proof that the franchise can be fresh and creative. Perhaps it also places such narratives in context.

Furthermore, this film demonstrates the distance that exists between a first film director's diverse intentions and audience's formulaic demands that constrict the versatility and potential of the Hollywood horror franchise.

After leaving New Line and his *New Nightmare* behind, Craven was approached by writer-producer-star Eddie Murphy to direct his latest horror-comedy, *Vampire in Brooklyn*, a project the star had been developing with his brother at Paramount. This was an opportunity for Craven to work with a high profile cast on a bigger budget. Moreover, it would allow him to demonstrate his flair for comedy by collaborating with Murphy, a star who was in need of a hit at this point in his career. This situation was similar to the way in which John Carpenter had courted mainstream credibility with the comic assistance of Chevy Chase in 1992's *Memoirs of an Invisible Man*.

Conceived as an homage to such early blaxploitation horrors as *Blacula* and its sequel, *Scream, Blacula, Scream*, *Vampire in Brooklyn* emerged as a desperately inconsistent horror-comedy hybrid in which vampirism and culture clash comedy were unevenly combined. Unfortunately for Craven, the chances of success were untenable from the outset. Creatively compromised, Craven was caught between meeting the needs of the star or the studio, as Murphy's determination to escape his own stereotyping saw him push for a more terrifying film than Paramount, and perhaps even Craven, wanted. None too surprisingly, and in light of such production infighting, the film suffered a similar fate to Carpenter's special effects extravaganza (*Memoirs of an Invisible Man*) and fell flat between the two genres, achieving little in the way of laughs or screams.

Completing the Trilogy

First written as a 25-page script by Kevin Williamson, and based on an idea he had watching a Barbara Walters TV special on the Gainesville murders,[109] this *Scary Movie* was intended to be "sold to Roger Corman for $5000."[110] However, a bidding war involving Universal, Paramount and Morgan Creek saw Williamson accept a $500,000 offer from Miramax, whose Dimension label was in need of a flagship property. More importantly, the writer also submitted a five-page treatment for *Scream 2* and *3*, shrewdly suggesting that "if they bought this script they would have a possible franchise on their hands."[111] Aware of the project's franchise potential, Bob and Harvey Weinstein aggressively courted Craven to direct, despite the director's deliberate attempts to escape such projects and the trappings of genre filmmaking. Currently involved with the Weinsteins at Miramax in developing a remake of Shirley Jackson's *The Haunting*, a remake with a more mainstream feel, Craven passed on *Scream* at this stage.

After the search went from Robert Rodriguez and Danny Boyle to Anthony Waller, Dimension put Craven's project into turnaround and immediately offered him *Scream* for the second time. By this point, the film was in production, with star Drew Barrymore attached. With no other projects on the immediate horizon, Craven warmed to the film's tricky mix of horror and humor, aware that he, and many others, had done it badly in the past. Nevertheless, the director was understandably reluctant to re-embrace the genre, having struggled for so long to diversify his interests and enhance his mainstream reputation. Due to the combination of a strong script, rising star and a stalled project, Craven committed to making the film and, in some respects, a return to his *Last House* roots.

Scream's basic prerequisite is the knowledge and familiarity of its audience with the rules, formulas and conventions of the genre. Its success lies in the playful subversion of these rules, explicitly stated by the virgin Randy,[112] to manipulate the audience. "Never meant to be anything but a wicked film,"[113] *Scream* was a self-referential homage to *Terror Train* (1980), *Prom Night* (1980) and, of course, *Halloween* (1979). United through "Scream Queen" Jamie Lee Curtis, these three earlier films provided the blueprint for *Scream*'s fresh take on a previously exhausted formula. From the expertly executed opening that borrows heavily from *When a Stranger Calls* (a movie conspicuously not acknowledged yet recently remade) to its blood-soaked climax, *Scream* is littered with references for the cine-literate. Furthermore, *Scream* juggled shocks and scares more effectively than any other "slasher" film that preceded it.

Craven's return to the intensity of his earlier films also paved the way for further controversy. Despite early conflicts with the Weinsteins over their need for consultation, further pressures emerged when the Santa Rosa City School District Governing Board withdrew permission to shoot at the local High School at the eleventh hour. The situation escalated when the local media incited the community to protest and jumped on the bandwagon with complaints, petitions and letters to the editor singling Craven out and attacking the director personally. Despite receiving no such complaints or negative comments from test-screening reports regarding intensity and gore, Craven recalls how the MPAA classified the movie as being "a wonderful example of an NC-17,"[114] adding that it would "probably never be able to get an R rating."[115] Submitted to the board several times, a protracted battle over intensity, imitation and the movement of innards resulted in the removal of twenty seconds of footage. In addition, the film's soundtrack was similarly targeted for complaints, leaving the director frustrated that his best work was not allowed to find his audience as intended.

Following impressive test screenings, after which the film "scored in the 80's and 90's for everything,"[116] the studio offered Craven a two-picture deal stipulating one other horror picture (*Scream 2*) and the opportunity to select one of the non-genre projects they had in production. Confronted with the opportunity to finally experiment outside the confines of his career-long genre stereotyping, Craven agreed.

His eventual selection was 1999's *Music of the Heart*, with Madonna originally set to feature in the starring role. Previously known as *Fifty Violins* and *Fiddlefest*, the $7 million movie was based on an award-winning short film. Craven had connected with its focus on classical music, and depiction of schoolteachers, divorce and a broken home. Eventually starring Meryl Streep, the film was based on the inspiring true story of a teacher battling for the right to teach music in a tough Harlem school. For Craven, then, it took a deliberate return to the genre and the Hollywood horror franchise for him to finally break out of it — demonstrating its role and potential to provide filmmakers with new opportunities.

Further exploiting his association with a critically and commercially successful franchise, Craven, as the genre's answer to Steven Spielberg,[117] has supported the next generation of fear filmmakers by using his name to endorse specific projects. Propagated by the likes of Spielberg, and taken up by directors like Cunningham, Carpenter and Craven, the role of industry-based mentor has allowed those directors with marquee names to use their brand name value as a means of publicizing and promoting films involving fresh talent. This trend has increased in recent years, and, as we will see in Chapter 3, the Hollywood horror franchise has played a vital role in its development.

It began by experienced genre directors like Craven and Carpenter having their names incorporated into film titles as part of the marketing campaign[118]; and producer Cunningham has used both the *House* franchise and more recent installments in New Line's *Friday the 13th* franchise to "try out directors and writers I'm interested in."[119] Indeed, from *Friday the 13th* directors Steve Miner and Adam Marcus, through to *House* screenwriters Ethan Wiley and Lewis Abernathy, Cunningham has actively supported directors' debuts through his franchise ownership.[120] Initiated by Craven under the guise of nepotism on 1995's *Mindripper*,[121] this new stage in his career has since extended to several titles.[122] Although a second experience as presenter/executive producer involved supporting Special Effects artist Robert Kurtzman's directorial debut with *Wishmaster* in 1997,[123] it was not until Adam

Grossman's misguided and much-maligned *Carnival of Souls* remake in 1998 that Craven described his newfound function as a "mixed experience."[124]

Also in 1998, Craven's production company, Craven/Maddalena films, followed *Scream 2* by branching out into television and co-producing Larry Shaw's *Don't Look Down*.[125] Additionally, Craven signed an agreement with Dimension which saw his name used to promote in-house projects and acquisitions alike. Dimension exploited the director's name in promoting Robert Harmon's *They* in 2002,[126] and falsely advertised it as "A Wes Craven film" in the UK. Such dishonest and misleading tactics are in danger of displacing, if only for publicity purposes, the role and responsibility of the director.

More recently, Craven has been a producer on Ben Affleck and Matt Damon's moviemaking talent contest, *Project Greenlight*. The reality series' third season deliberately focused on the horror genre, emphasizing its commercial potential as a means of guaranteeing a return on its investment, with *Feast*. Similarly, the director has supported and executive produced first features by long-serving crew members Patrick Lussier and Nicholas Mastandrea,[127] and mentored Vince Marcello's second feature — an adaptation of the musical *Zombie Prom*. Having supported Alexandre Aja's selection as the director of a *Hills Have Eyes* remake after viewing *Haute Tension*, Craven has also committed to producing several other projects. However, in this role of mentor, Craven is admittedly "at the mercy of [directors] and how well they can do it,"[128] with varying levels of participation in these projects potentially dragging his marketable brand name into disrepute.

Passing the $100 million mark, *Scream* evolved into a modern Hollywood phenomenon that saw the major studios green light a slew of imitations and similarly themed films.[129] Consequently, the Weinsteins were equally keen to cash in on its success and rushed into its loosely outlined sequel. Forced to put his werewolf opus, *Bad Moon Rising*, on hold, Craven once again returned from a position of strength without a fleshed out script from Williamson. According to the writer, *Scream 2* "should have sucked for the way we made it [but] Wes did a phenomenal job — a better job than he did on the first ... it was a nightmare."[130] A "nightmare" that Craven recalls involved "a lot of collaboration."[131] Nevertheless, this situation allowed him to develop the material in keeping with his own interests and concerns. Shrouded in secrecy and dogged by eager fans desperate to discover the latest plot twists, the shoot consisted of many embellishments, amendments and additions throughout the rushed schedule. Publicized by Craven and the studio as the second part of a trilogy, despite the absence of a "cliff-hanger,"[132] Craven once again used the Hollywood horror franchise to address his critics and redress the balance in the film/media/violence debate.

Departing from standard slasher sequel conventions by focusing on a trio of core protagonists (as opposed to the literal resurrection of the first film's killers), *Scream 2* brought horror back to its theatrical roots. The film's structure focused on spectatorship within society, with each of the three acts and slasher set pieces played out on one kind of stage or another. Swiftly reestablishing old characters and introducing new ones, the film referenced college-based splatter films[133] before settling on *Friday the 13th* for its true inspiration. In terms of thematic approach and "message," Craven satirically responded to the genre's critics but lacked conviction on the merits of the Hollywood horror franchise.

For its final act, the director has since recalled how Mickey's motivation and dialogue was "done in conference"[134] to encapsulate the filmmakers' collective response. Indeed, Mickey's seemingly absurd and calculated plan to blame the movies is smothered with irony as he highlights his trial's potential for celebrity, notoriety and media frenzy. Unlike its predecessor, however, Craven's final cut of *Scream 2* was left untouched by the censors. Whether this was the result of Craven learning to work within the system, a studio playing it safe or a censor reluctant to "take on" a high profile release is debatable.

Debuting with a box office weekend of $32.9 million just one year after the first film, *Scream 2* soon outstripped the financial success of its predecessor. It also earned what John Muir deemed a "grudging respect"[135] from critics, despite Clive Barker's warning that "if you make a picture that has some real originality in the market place you're gonna get kicked hard on the second picture whatever happens critically."[136] However, the price for this success was the standard tabloid controversy, moral panic and industry-wide repercussions. In this respect, Craven's *Scream* franchise was no exception. A worldwide media backlash associated the franchise with a series of alleged copycat crimes and killings in various countries. The Columbine Massacre emerged as a catalyst for potential political intervention and a nationwide discussion of violence in the media, and this placed the franchise in the spotlight. Nevertheless, as Craven's third attempt at directing a Hollywood horror franchise, *Scream 2* revealed the extent to which a concept could evolve, and encompass cultural and thematic concerns, in conjunction with the expectations of audiences and critics.

Craven's chance to complete the trilogy was secured once scriptwriter Williamson declined the assignment in favor of pet project *Killing Mrs. Tingle*.[137] In direct contrast to his relationship with New Line's *Nightmare* franchise, Craven maintained his commitment, and even compared the trilogy to Coppola's *Godfather* films. Williamson's departure provided Craven with an ideal opportunity to create *Scream 3* in accordance with his own vision, and this meant a "complete page-one rethinking of everything"[138] rather than the proposed *Return to Woodsboro*. Despite his willingness to complete the trilogy, intense media speculation and scapegoating of the franchise caused Craven to reconsider his role in an "increasingly chancy business."[139] With the combined threat of a Congressional witch-hunt and potential legal action looming on the horizon, Craven later confessed to a "moment of introspection"[140] prior to shooting.

As a key member of the DGA's Task Force on Violence and Social Responsibility, the director nevertheless drew the line at the studio's suggestion he shoot the sequel "bloodless, with no violence at all."[141] With both its script and schedule in a perpetual state of flux, and multiple versions, subplots and scenarios entertained, shot and ultimately discarded,[142] Craven was once again placed under the intense pressure of conflicting schedules, media speculation and a high profile Christmas release date.[143]

Similar to the way in which *Scream* referenced *Halloween*, and its sequel homaged *Friday the 13th* the third film evoked Franklin's *Psycho II* (itself a variation of the 1964 film *Strait-Jacket*, scripted by Robert Bloch). Presenting Sidney as a potential latter-day Norman Bates, the movie dared the audience to question her sanity, with Mother's voice and image pushing her closer to the edge. A double mystery drives the narrative, with Sidney as the fundamental link between them. In contrast to the first two films, *Scream 3* turns duplicity into duality as characters confront and interact with their cinematic counterparts. In presenting a concise and coherent defense from within, Craven sought to preempt criticism with comedy and satire. He also offered audiences alternative theories and explanations by holding society to account and stressing the notion of personal/parental responsibility.

However, in blatantly ignoring its "super trilogy rules," *Scream 3* shied away from dispatching its core trio and built towards a relatively satisfying yet predictable climax. Here, Sidney functions as the Final Girl and returns to the role of Laurie Strode by coming face to face with her own half-brother. Furthermore, by stabbing him in the back with an ice pick, in true Hollywood fashion she becomes a better Sharon Stone than her mother ever was.

With a budget increase to $40 million and yet another large publicity campaign, *Scream 3* exploded across 3,467 U.S. cinema screens on February 4, 2000. Thanks to Miramax's market saturation strategy the film took almost $35 million in its first three days. Whether a reflection of the current climate, numerous imitations or less than enthusiastic reviews from audiences and critics, *Scream 3*'s takings dropped in subsequent weeks, and the film failed to top the $100 million mark. That *Scream 3* plays so well, despite its fraught production and revisionist scripting, is a testament to both cast and crew, with some exceptionally sharp dialogue and strong set pieces offering audiences something fresh in among the familiar codes and conventions. Shying away from the explicit "knowingness" of the previous entries, but retaining the use of cameo roles (with Carrie Fisher a standout), the franchise's tonal shift from cutting edge post-modern slasher to romantic murder mystery clearly betrayed a more mainstream sensibility at work, one the director had been cultivating long before *Scream*. In this respect, Craven's success with the *Scream* trilogy has demonstrated the extent to which a director can fuse personal concerns with mainstream profitability through directing the Hollywood horror franchise.

Having sufficiently distanced himself from New Line's *Freddy vs. Jason* after a decade in development hell, Craven's initial post–*Scream* output was hampered by a series of unfortunate setbacks, stalled projects and closed doors, despite the creatively shrewd choices he made. From a video game adaptation of *Alice* to a remake of the Japanese success story *Pulse*,[144] the director sought to capitalize on the latest crazes and follow up his franchise success with a suitable crossover project. Similarly, attempts to raise support for an adaptation of his first novel, *Fountain Society*, have yet to reach fruition, despite the project finding a more supportive home at Dreamworks after Dimension failed to meet the script's budgetary requirements.

Having considered *Scary Movie* a lesson in "how quickly Hollywood can render you obsolete,"[145] and openly rejecting any possibility of directing *Scream 4*, Craven experienced a profound sense of déjà vu when the Weinsteins once again pulled out of the director's proposed remake of *Pulse* to push for a reunion with screenwriter Williamson on *Cursed*. A werewolf project following the UK's *Dog Soldiers* and Canada's *Ginger Snaps*,[146] *Cursed* initially saw the Weinsteins predict *Scream*-like success, mistakenly setting their sights and expectations, along with those of the industry and audiences, exceptionally high from the outset.

However, what began as a relatively high concept film featuring Hollywood werewolves, in the same vein as Joe Dante's *The Howling*, altered over the course of two years. According to Craven, the film underwent "four major shoots"[147] as it transformed into a soft-core adaptation of Mike Nichols' analogous *Wolf* for a teen audience. Arguably reminiscent of the director's experiences on *Deadly Friend*, the final straw was the Weinsteins' decision to edit the film for a PG-13 rating,[148] by which point Craven had fulfilled his contractual obligations to the project and chose to walk away.[149]

Having experienced extreme levels of interference from New Line, Warner Bros. and now the Weinsteins,[150] Craven sought to immerse himself in a new project, and has pointedly commented how he was "treated with more respect"[151] by Dreamworks on *Red Eye*. A claustrophobic conspiracy thriller with mainstream potential, this late summer release addressed Craven's specific structural and thematic concerns. With survival, self-sufficiency and the home invasion integral aspects of the production, *Red Eye* was a calculated return to form that was safe, formulaic fun yet featured a third act that was classic Craven — complete with false scares and knife-wielding Final Girl. Despite the film's mainstream potential and PG-13 rating, Dreamworks deliberately emphasized the director's reputation and role as the creator of *Scream* and *A Nightmare on Elm Street* throughout its promotional material, thereby highlighting the continued importance and exploitation of the Hollywood horror franchise.

In Hollywood Craven has found an industry where "everything is so short-term, dependent on the whim of the public and business things you have no control over, like how the economy is going, and how well your film is distributed, or what ad campaign they come up with, or even what the title is."[152] Nevertheless, the director has emerged as one of the most influential filmmakers working in the genre, despite several attempts to distance himself from it. In scripting a second *Hills Have Eyes* sequel with his son Jonathan, the director has continued to combine his franchise exploitation with a fondness for nepotism. By taking on the mantle of mentor through numerous film and television projects, Craven has undoubtedly exploited and capitalized on his success — and that of the Hollywood horror franchise — within his own back catalogue. Such titles have undeniably opened the studio door on several occasions. Furthermore, he has weathered the limitations and controversy that invariably accompany such accolades and has repeatedly stressed how horror has been "a lonely watch"[153] at times.

Working with and against such stereotyping at various junctures in his career, Craven has exploited his critical and commercial status. Moreover, he has temporarily broken out from under the horror banner, supported the next generation of genre filmmakers and consistently attempted generic diversification, despite an ambivalent attitude towards it. Although the demands of studios, audiences and censors are paradoxical, Craven has survived, and indeed thrived, by negotiating a difficult path through these potential pitfalls in the Hollywood film industry. In this respect, and during the course of thirty-five years, Wes Craven has not only made the most classic mistakes associated with the genre, but also participated in some of its most recognizable advances and achievements, particularly within the Hollywood horror franchise.

3

Tom Savini and William Peter Blatty

They Came from Within

"Basically, sequels mean the same film. That's what people want to see. They want to see the same movie again."[1]
— John Carpenter

Like John Carpenter, many first film directors were reluctant to indulge in what was often dismissed as cinematic regurgitation. Instead, they seized the opportunity to promote and recommend trusted crewmembers and production assistants, maintaining various degrees of involvement.[2]

Having survived the rigors of low-budget filmmaking, production assistant Steve Miner, for example, was Cunningham's "logical choice"[3] for *Friday the 13th Part 2*, in much the same way that Carpenter turned to close friend and production assistant Tommy Lee Wallace for *Halloween II*. However, Wallace rejected the offer on the grounds that such a project amounted to little more than "hack work."[4] Nevertheless, Wallace's decision to decline Carpenter's offer, on the basis that it would provide little room for individuality or invention, was later rewarded when Joe Dante's departure from *Halloween III* allowed him to create a separate film for his directorial debut.

Rather than recruit from outside the pool of talent that had produced the first film, studios actively supported first film directors' selections, and similarly promoted various members of the production into the director's chair prior to Carpenter's and Cunningham's generous overtures.[5] Since these early examples of studio-imposed sequel nepotism, various members of a first film's cast and crew have sought to put their own indelible stamp on the material, irrespective of their practical filmmaking experience.[6] This third chapter, then, addresses the success with which the Hollywood horror franchise has been used as a career-shifting incentive to retain and reward the creative loyalty of cast and crewmembers.

Keen to recreate the spirit and financial success of the first film, the promotion of literary creators and other key production personnel was often considered to be a logical progression on both sides. As producer, financier and key collaborator on *Re-Animator*, Brian Yuzna exploited his relationship with the franchise to ensure the longevity of his career and secured a three-picture deal with fledgling production company Wild Street Pictures, who stipulated a sequel to Gordon's first film but allowed Yuzna to direct his first feature prior to it.[7] Similarly, 2003's *Beyond Re-Animator* allowed Yuzna to set-up the Hammer-inspired, Barcelona-based Fantastic Factory label using the franchise as a recognizable commodity to give the label a marketable "credibility"[8] factor from the outset.

More recently, Yuzna has returned to America and formed Halcyon International Pictures, with plans for a whole new series of films, starting with *House of Re-Animator* (although this project appears to have stalled). In this respect, the Hollywood horror franchise has not only launched the career of its first film director but also spearheaded and supported the career of an independent franchise owner.

With many installments subjected to dwindling budgets and increased expectations in terms of impressive and expensive special effects, the continuation of the Hollywood horror franchise has often dictated that special effects artists[9] have been similarly approached to take on the role of director. According to McDonagh, the success of the Hollywood horror franchise has "made the careers of a generation of effects artists."[10] As their fortunes flourished, their interdependence reached a seemingly natural conclusion in which the roles of special makeup effects artist and director have been fused together to create horror's first official "goreteurs." The aim of this first section is to chronicle the rise of the modern goreteur and their function as economically viable brand names before addressing their selection and experience at the hands of producers, studios and audiences.[11] In order to illustrate this trend, and highlight the problems experienced by these fledgling directors, this chapter first deals with the career of Tom Savini and his association with George R. Romero's *Dead* franchise.

With a focus on the way in which the Hollywood horror franchise has highlighted and facilitated alternative approaches, the second section of this chapter addresses William Peter Blatty's relationship with the *Exorcist* franchise. It also considers the extent to which he, as author, screenwriter and producer of the first film, has propagated a revisionist approach to the franchise and exploited his association with it.[12]

To place Blatty's experiences within an appropriate context, I also refer to Universal's *Psycho III*, *Halloween III* and *Jaws 3-D*, and the experiences of such screenwriters as David S. Goyer, Don Mancini and Ethan Wiley, who directed sequels to *Blade*, *Child's Play* and *House*. By taking into account franchises' relationships with their literary creators, this second section also begins to consider the extent to which franchisors, financiers and fans of the previous films have been allowed to impact upon the creative process and dictate the direction of future films.

The Rise of the Goreteur

In 1915, a twenty-nine-year-old Willis H. O'Brien impressed Hollywood with two innovative shorts — *Morpheus Mike* and *The Dinosaur and the Missing Link: A Prehistoric Tragedy* — and arguably introduced the industry to this pioneering and profitable concept. Serving as an effective precursor to his work on RKO's *King Kong* (1933), O'Brien secured his legacy as mentor to Ray Harryhausen. Similarly, Cecil Holland is considered to be "the Father of the Make-Up Profession,"[13] just as Lon Chaney would be remembered as "the Man of 1,000 Faces." Cast in the dual role of creature and creator, Chaney contorted his features and appearance to fit a range of tragically disfigured characters.

However, such a marriage of performance, and what would later become prosthetics, was frowned upon by makeup artist Jack P. Pierce, whose "crowning achievement"[14] was the conception and construction of classic creatures like Frankenstein's Monster, the Wolf Man and the Mummy. As Universal's chief monster maker in the thirties and forties who sketched, sculpted and supervised their application, Pierce strictly advocated that make-up's sole purpose was "not to proclaim the skill of the artist, but to help tell the story."[15]

By the mid–1950s, science fiction was one of the decade's most dominant cinematic trends.[16] The combined success of *The Thing from Another World*, Universal's *Creature from the Black Lagoon* and *Invasion of the Body Snatchers* paved the way for further monsters and mutations in *The Blob* and *The Fly*. However, the fondness with which audiences looked back on Universal's films was due to Forrest J Ackerman, the man responsible for coining the term "sci-fi" in 1954. As an avid fan and literary agent hooked on the

Amazing Stories magazines since childhood, Ackerman single-handedly established the magazine that would come to attract and inspire a new generation of special effects artists.

Beginning in 1958, *Famous Monsters of Filmland* contained a mixture of lightweight features, interviews, reviews and retrospectives that also introduced fans to William Castle's latest gimmick-laden shockers. Refusing to wallow in mere publicity and promotion, *Famous Monsters* also revealed how stop-motion and the new split-screen[17] technique allowed filmmakers to depict what were incredibly realistic effects sequences at the time. As one of the pioneers of this technique, stop-motion specialist Ray Harryhausen built on O'Brien's success with *The Beast from 20,000 Fathoms*, *The 7th Voyage of Sinbad* and his most popular special effects showcase, *Jason and the Argonauts* (1963), before ending his career on the classic *Clash of the Titans* in 1981.

However, in 1963 the concept of special effects had splintered into two distinct segments. On the one hand it was Oscar's first year to present an Academy Award for Best Visual Effects,[18] while on the other Pittsburgh-born director and special make-up effects artist H.G. Lewis was busy cementing his cult status and reputation as "the Godfather of Gore."[19] By reveling in its amateurish origins and outrageously over-the-top sequences, Lewis' *Blood Feast* has, with the help of John Waters, famously been dubbed "the *Citizen Kane* of Gore Movies."[20] However, according to Bissette, *Famous Monsters* and the more adult *Castle of Frankenstein* "usually vilified or simply ignored"[21] Lewis' films and actively "went out of their way to warn readers away from [them and] ... the gutsier European horrors"[22] of the day.

Five years after Lewis' landmark film, another Pittsburgh native, George A. Romero, directed *Night of the Living Dead*—specifically designed to appeal to the drive-in audience and released without the recently established MPAA's seal of approval. In eschewing mainstream standards and practices, Romero's debut film, with its explicit violence and shocking finale, garnered "scathing reviews,"[23] which secured the interests of exhibitors and audiences alike.

Having confessed to being "a person who's not fond of blood and gore,"[24] Dick Smith nevertheless delivered a series of controversial effects sequences in *The Exorcist* almost five years later.[25] Released under a storm of controversy, with tales of curses, faintings, walk-outs and scandal, the film became the biggest box office draw to date and "gave birth to"[26] the Blockbuster era. The phenomenal success and media frenzy surrounding *The Exorcist*, which saw the MPAA come under attack for awarding the film an R-rating, inevitably spawned such imitations as Richard Donner's *The Omen* in 1976, which, according to McCarty, was one of the first studio-based "splatter"[27] films. As another entry in the Satanic cycle,[28] *The Omen* was elevated above mere exploitation by studio support and an all-star cast.

However, what really set Donner's derivative film apart was its introduction of what McCarty has called "the device of the creative death,"[29] an instrumental feature at the heart of every splatter movie.[30] Indeed, this Grand Guignol approach to filmmaking was adopted by independent and studio productions, transforming films into virtual showcases for special effects artists to create breathtaking and stomach-churning illusions to shock the viewer.

In this decade dedicated to the trampling of taboos, Romero returned to his zombie roots with a satirical "comic book"[31] sensibility. Described by Fischer as "the first American horror film with a substantial budget to really paint the walls red,"[32] Romero's sequel *Dawn of the Dead*, also issued "a clear illustration of the dawning trend in which the makeup effects would replace the story as the show."[33] The work of such rising stars as Tom Savini[34] saw the amateurish effects that dogged many first films replaced by an array of fantastic yet anatomically correct depictions that proved problematic for the MPAA. When the MPAA threatened *Dawn* with an x-rating, lumping it in with hardcore porn, Romero, Rubinstein and distributor United Film Distribution ignored the MPAA and released the film unrated, with a disclaimer notifying patrons of the film's spectacularly violent content. With Savini's groundbreaking special effects singled out by audiences and critics, *Dawn of the Dead* introduced Savini's work to audiences and producers alike. This first point of fusion between the horror franchise and the special makeup effects artist was an important step towards goreteurism.

Although Romero satirized mass consumerism via *Dawn*'s mall setting, and painted an "epic view of a civilization in decline,"[35] it was Savini who shocked and educated audiences on the mechanics of special effects filmmaking and the experimentation behind numerous "gags." Prevented from participating in Romero's first film because of his involvement in the Vietnam War as an army photographer, Savini later confessed that his exposure to extreme images of murder and mayhem during this period influenced and informed his approach to creating increasingly realistic effects. Indeed, with the battlefield and mass media a desensitizing training ground, special effects artists like Savini created an array of fantastic yet anatomically correct depictions of death and dismemberment that eschewed the amateurish look of Lewis' films. This led to their elevated status as role models and made them the subject of interviews, profiles and reverence in the pages of *Fangoria* magazine.

Accurately described by Kermode as the "new bible of hard-core horror fandom,"[36] *Fangoria* (founded in 1979) has also been described by Dick Smith

Dawn of the Dead (George A. Romero, 1978). This was just one of Savini's many zombie creations as head of make-up effects. However, the film not only highlighted his ingenuity and flair for creating shocking set pieces, but also his fondness for acting and stunt work. After his work on *Martin* (1977) and this relatively high profile sequel, the Hollywood horror franchise opened doors for Savini from the start.

as "one of the leading factors in spreading the gospel of special make-up effects."[37] Indeed, the favorable reception given to an article on *Alien* and a shot of an exploding head from *Dawn of the Dead* in its first issue strongly indicated the direction the magazine would increasingly adopt, particularly in the pages of its spin-off magazine *Gorezone*. Nurtured through its infancy by a range of interviews with, and profiles of, established and emerging special effects artists, *Fangoria* found its audience and capitalized on the success of films like *Friday the 13th*, which introduced mainstream cinema-goers to Savini's cutting edge techniques.

Having impressed the director through *Dawn of the Dead*, Savini recalls how Sean Cunningham "didn't believe we could achieve some of the stuff,"[38] with murders going off like "fireworks, one effect after another."[39] Returning to the impact of *Fangoria*[40] on his career, Savini argued that it was "clearly the magazine [which] made me famous. It got my name out — even though it was as the King of Splatter."[41] With industry stereotyping and a restrictive appellation the standard price to pay for rising popularity and success, Savini's career has been entwined with the development of the Hollywood horror franchise from the outset.

With splatter lavishly spread across magazines and cinema screens, the combined big-budget efforts of Spielberg and Lucas (with the exception of *King Kong* and *Alien* in 1976 and 1979) continued to dominate the category for Best Visual Effects. This has been the Academy's way of simultaneously appeasing and acknowledging the success of box office giants, with advances in make-up effects notoriously overlooked, save for two honorary awards.[42]

However, in 1981 a category for Best Makeup Effects was permanently adopted by the Academy, with the first winner being Dick Smith protégé Rick Baker for *An American Werewolf in London*. As an artist who went on to a productive career in designing increasingly realistic primates and lycanthropes,[43] Baker credited *Fangoria* as being "the *Famous Monsters* of the '90s,"[44] which has "really helped popularize the art of special make-up effects."[45] Rob Bottin was behind the early eighties' second werewolf extravaganza, *The Howling*, and moved on to the Universal lot in his tireless bid to realize *The Thing* the following year. Even though John Carpenter's FX-laden update was forgotten at the box office, Bottin's special effects threw down the gauntlet to his contemporaries — a challenge picked up by Chris Walas in David Cronenberg's reworking of *The Fly*, a film for which Walas received the coveted Academy Award.

Savini's Living Nightmare

Just as Chris Walas' Oscar win convinced Mel Brooks to back Walas as director of Fox's *Fly* sequel, a combination of Academy recognition[46] and second unit experience previously enabled Cameron protégé Stan Winston to direct *Pumpkinhead*, aka *Vengeance: The Demon*. With Winston the only FX artist to start a franchise until Kurtzman's special effects–laden *Wishmaster* in 1997, special effects artists were shrewdly promoted into the director's chair on a series of films whose origins were single-mindedly economic. Walas, for example, confessed that Fox's motivation for commissioning *The Fly II* was purely a way of filling "an available release slot."[47]

In the case of Savini's 1990 remake of *Night of the Living Dead*, George Romero similarly revealed that the new *Night* was designed "to just lockdown the title and the copyright"[48] and compensate those "twenty six original investors who had gotten ripped off by the original."[49] Even though the first film was a huge financial success, very little money made its way back to the financiers, and the company went bankrupt. Moreover, a reorganization at Continental Pictures saw an all-important copyright notice line left off the picture, with many video companies taking advantage of the fact that the film had fallen into the public domain. Indeed, the long-term effects of this lesson have been costly and led to many different permutations of this unregulated Hollywood horror franchise.[50]

After turning down the chance to direct the *Night of the Living Dead* remake in favor of adapting Stephen King's *The Dark Half*, Romero agreed to rewrite the *Night* script and executive produce the film on the condition that Savini directed. As an established director within the genre, Romero had already exploited his role as mentor through his association with the Hollywood horror franchise by recommending cinematographer and sound editor Michael Gornick to a "very nervous"[51] Stephen King as the director of *Creepshow 2* in 1987. Although this was his first feature-length film, Gornick had, like many first time directors, acquired invaluable experience on genre-based television work. Due to the episodic nature of *Creepshow 2*'s anthology format, he was regarded as a "safe bet."[52]

Similarly selected on the basis of his status and relationship with Romero and the franchise, Savini's experience also included second unit work and the "Inside the Closet" episode of TV's *Tales from the Darkside*.[53] However, in using his limited participation in the project as a bargaining tool to ensure Savini's appointment, Romero inadvertently sowed seeds of resentment in the eyes of his fellow investors keen to reassert their control and ownership over the title in the wake of Romero's singular success.

As another goreteur who cut his directing teeth on TV horror,[54] *Hellraiser IV*'s Kevin Yagher credited the *Elm Street* franchise and "the pages of *Fangoria*"[55] with having a significant impact on his career. Just as Yagher negotiated second unit directing duties on the *Child's Play* sequel as a means of ensuring his participation as the doll's designer and puppet master, Full Moon stop-motion animator David Allen also traded on his pivotal role as puppet creator and operator to direct *Puppet Master II*. However, Charles Band's support of this was, according to executive producer David DeCoteau, his shrewd way of securing "a dozen or two more movies worth of special effects"[56] out of the experienced stop-motion supervisor. As the only goreteur with previous feature film experience,[57] Empire Pictures alumnus John Carl Buechler was similarly targeted by Paramount Pictures for *Friday the 13th Part VII* (1988). With such reciprocal and exploitative strategies (supported by Buechler's account),[58] it is clear that many studios and production companies sought to save money by combining two roles and focusing on the more sensational aspects of the sequel.

According to Kevin Yagher, who accepted the *Hellraiser: Bloodline* assignment at the eleventh hour, part of his motivation lay in a profound sense of frustration, similar to that experienced by writers like Blatty, at having "so many of my ideas ... stifled or changed ... as I began working with as many bad directors as good ones."[59] Advocating the idea that special effects artists were more efficient directors within the horror genre, in that they could "get the angles that translate into the audience getting more out of the effects," [60] Yagher's extensive second unit work fuelled his aspirations.

Walas, on the other hand, traces his aspirations back even further in stating how "most effects people today started out making little Super-8 movies just so they could stick their bloody heads in front of a camera. It's the next logical step to direct."[61] Whether born of frustration or a sense of natural progression, the majority relied upon a combination of support, coercion and mutual exploitation to ensure their directing ambitions were fully realized through the Hollywood horror franchise.

Having seized the directorial reins of relatively high profile releases, many of these filmmakers had strong ideas as to how they wanted their installment to develop. Although Romero had sidestepped directorial involvement in the *Night of the Living Dead* remake, his role as scriptwriter gave him the opportunity to update his and Russo's screenplay for contemporary audiences. According to Savini, however, it was *his* idea to revamp the characterization of Barbara, perhaps in keeping with Clover's Final Girl theory, and keep "the zombie explanation nebulous."[62] Despite proclaiming that Romero gave him "a lot of freedom"[63] on his "remake plus a sequel,"[64] Savini was not allowed to deviate too far from the first film (losing his proposed black and white subjective camera shots and many of the director's impressively storyboarded sequences). Indeed, Savini deferred to Romero as the leading authority on the sub-genre and franchise, and this included "cutting stuff before we started shooting"[65] for reasons of practicality, thereby curtailing his plans for the film.

Whereas Savini experienced some collaboration, in that Romero's revised script subverted the first film in line with cultural changes, many other sequel directors were far less fortunate with regard to scripting. Based on Barker's idea, and guided through an endless series of rewrites by scriptwriter Pete Atkins, the *Bloodline* script[66] that initially attracted Yagher to the *Hellraiser* franchise was, according to Atkins, "a classic case of too many chiefs and not enough Indians."[67] In this case, conflicting ideas and budgetary concerns left little room for a first time director's input.

Similarly, and in spite of their alleged protestations, Walas and Buechler were equally disappointed by studio decisions to take the least adventurous options and settle for either a "nearly verbatim remake"[68] or "moments of standard stalk and slash." [69] Subjected to round table rewrites and production infighting from the outset, scripts were the main source of conflict for many special effects artists, with Walas recalling how he tried to "quit the picture"[70] before a single frame had been shot. Issued scripts that were either deemed crowded and formulaic, unrealistic and over ambitious, or simply clichéd and condescending,[71] directors nevertheless abided by contractual obligations, since the alternative would end their directing careers before they had even begun.

For Savini, filming was the catalyst for a range of professional and personal issues. This period saw the director caught up in a custody battle for his daughter and distracted by sabotage on the part of envious on-set

Night of the Living Dead (Tom Savini, 1990). Apparently suggested by Savini, Barbara's (Patricia Tallman) character undergoes the most significant change in the remake. No longer passive or catatonic, she follows the trend set down by Weaver's Ripley and emerges as an action-orientated survivalist who is no longer afraid to fight back. She gladly picks up the shotgun and starts shooting. Savini was placed under enormous pressure by the producers, who did not share Romero's confidence in him as a director; they refused to let him shoot the film his way, and such an attitude extended into the editing room.

detractors. Moreover, the director's version of events traces the trouble back to Columbia's purchasing of the film halfway through the shoot and a deal[72] which saw the editing time reduced. After a series of meetings in which Romero was allegedly "told many lies"[73] about what was happening, the first film director eventually appeared on set to help consolidate shot lists and keep the picture under control. Since plagued by rumors that the film was taken away from him, Savini has refuted such claims and maintained his position that "no one ever came in and took over the reins."[74] With internal and external conflict characterizing the production process, from Savini's perspective at least, directing failed to live up to his expectations as protective producers and mixed agendas characterized these filmmakers' experiences with the Hollywood horror franchise.

Despite being hired on the unspoken understanding that special effects were increasingly the star, many first time directors attempted to rebel and dared to try and defy studio and audience expectations. After stating how "effects guys like me spoiled people, the more we showed them the more they wanted to see,"[75] Savini adopted a more holistic approach to filmmaking. In creating his deconstructive commentary on the first film by playing with and upon the audience's entrenched expectations, Savini hoped to challenge the stigma and criticism directed at his debut by dispensing with the first film's storyline "in sixteen minutes"[76] and filling the remainder of the running time "with action ... twists and turns and a lot of different effects."[77] Consequently, Savini's conclusion dramatically deviated from what we might expect, with Ben actually becoming one of the Living Dead and Barbara emerging as Harry's executioner — a move that destroys any sense of moral superiority yet sustains some element of shock for jaded audiences.

Keenly aware of audience expectations surrounding a Romero/Savini collaboration, the director was nonetheless adamant that his first feature was not a splatter film. During the obligatory promotional tour he insisted that "as a director I have aspirations that go beyond gore and splatter,"[78] even though it was "that background that gave me [the] chance to direct"[79] in the first place. Similarly, Yagher attempted to publicly take a step back from the "makeup FX extravaganzas"[80] that were *Hellraiser II* and *III* and abide by Jack Pierce's edict.

Despite pledging to show less and focus on the actual techniques involved in crafting "a truly suspenseful film,"[81] Savini's movie suffered a similar fate to the Russo-produced *Children of the Living Dead* and was taken away prior to the ratings process, where it was subjected to further scrutiny and restrictions under the MPAA. In keeping with previous entries, the *Night* redux was initially branded with a solid X-rating, a move indicative of the franchise's controversial ratings history. Contractually bound to deliver an R-rated picture, however, the producers slavishly removed all offensive shots without appeal. According to Savini, this final lack of support resulted in a "sterile film,"[82] despite his intended emphasis on action and suspense that was out of synch with previous entries.

Indeed, the onset of post-production often heralded greater demands for compromise, particularly in relation to *Bloodline*'s Yagher, whose first cut failed to impress the same Miramax executives who had approved the script.[83] For Yagher, the studio-dictated changes were understandable but difficult to carry out, and rather than see it change into something unrecognizable, the director opted to leave the project.[84] This decision paved the way for Miramax to demand even more drastic changes under the direction of *Halloween 6*'s Joe Chappelle.

Although Isaac's serial killer thriller *House III* experienced a similar fate to Savini's film, with many of its most graphic scenes relegated to the cutting room floor, Buechler's *Friday the 13th Part VII* suffered more as a result of its reputation than actual content. Effectively castrated to such an extent that almost all of the visceral impact was diluted, if not removed, the promised *New Blood* was reduced to no blood.[85] Having captured a more realistic representation of their work on screen, special effects artists as first time directors were removed from or frustrated by the post-production process. And so, like the very footage for which they had become famous, these goreteurs found themselves excised from the Hollywood horror franchise.

Ratings battles aside, Buechler considers his entry in the *Friday the 13th* franchise to be "flawed in those predictable aspects which are standard in this genre"; and rather than criticize the MPAA, the director has accused Paramount of being "ashamed of their horror labels."[86] Nonetheless, the director is proud of his Jason design, the range of effects audiences were not permitted to see, and his sequel's opening and closing sequences that, for Buechler, made the film "worth making."[87] Whereas Buechler is one of the few goreteurs able to reflect favorably on the experience, Walas has candidly pointed out that *The Fly II* "got made the wrong way for all the wrong reasons,"[88] and "never quite recovered from the reason it was being made."[89]

Alternatively, *Hellraiser IV*'s Kevin Yagher disengaged from the process and successfully petitioned the Director's Guild of America to have his name removed from the troubled sequel's credits. As a direct result of such restructuring and reshoots, the director left the film with the infamous Alan Smithee credit rather than his own. In light of such experiences and troubled relationships, the goreteurs have consistently singled out their respective studios

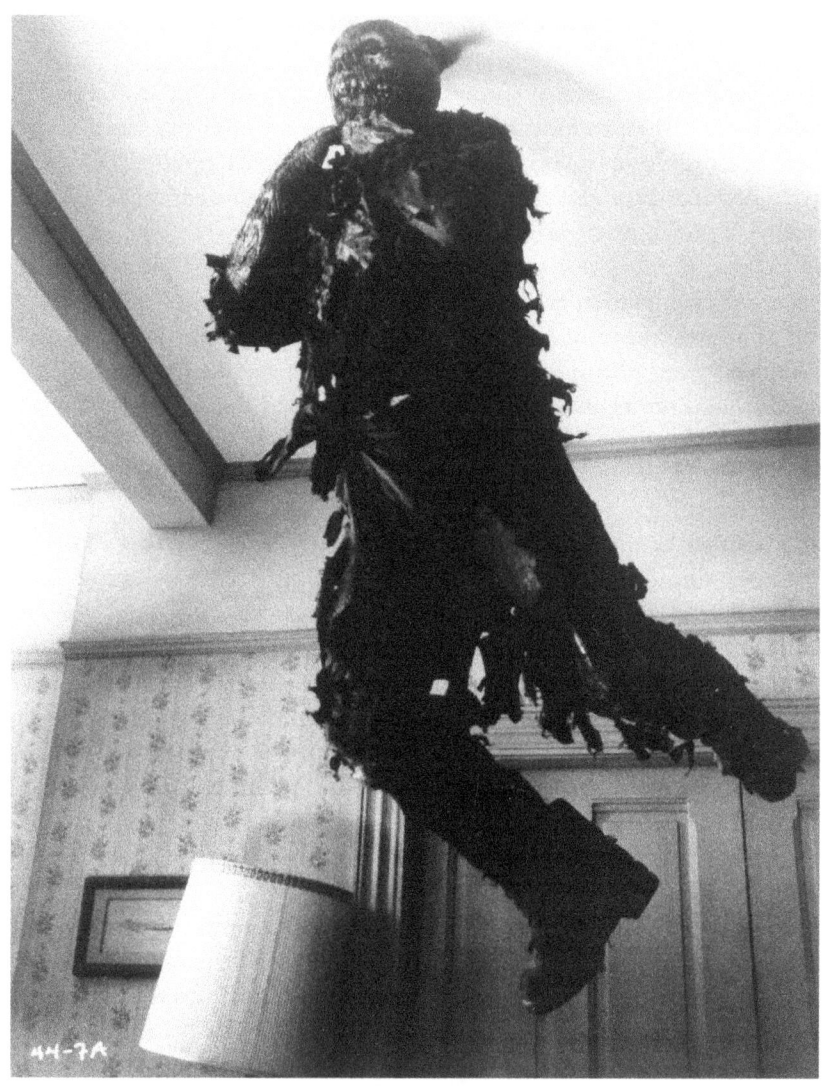

Friday the 13th Part VII: The New Blood (John Carl Buechler, 1988). During their climactic showdown, Carrie-clone Tina (Lar Park Lincoln) first causes Jason's (Kane Hodder) iconic hockey mask to crack open before manipulating the wiring to wrap around his neck and hoist him up off the floor, at which point he struggles to get free and falls into the basement. This extended final sequence featured a range of practical effects that made it into the final edit. However, several of the film's special effects, and kill scenes in particular, did not get past the producers, Paramount or the MPAA, who imposed enough cuts to render the film bloodless and the director bitter about that aspect of the production. Hampered by these constraints and a weak script, director Buechler was equally incapacitated when it came to satisfying the established fan base familiar with the clichés and conventions of the franchise.

and producers as the main source of frustration and their film's comparative critical and commercial failure.

Indeed, with his presence resented and his picture subject to sabotage, and denied any semblance of the support he had enjoyed on *Tales from the Darkside*, Savini has since described his debut as "one of the worst experiences of his life."[90] With the finished film representing only "forty percent of what I originally envisaged on over 700 storyboards,"[91] the director claims to be baffled as to why directing his first film under Romero's guidance was not "the most wonderful situation."[92] Instead, the experience severely affected the pair's personal and professional relationship for many years afterward.

However, now that responsibility has been taken on both sides, the director has lamented that all he ever "wanted was to keep [Romero's] respect."[93] Having survived the franchise, Savini has continued to cement his status as a genre icon through a combination of acting,[94] stunt work and special effects jobs, with the most recent being Steve Miner's *Day of the Dead* remake. In addition to his personal development in the industry, Savini has also secured his reputation in much the same way as O'Brien, Pierce and, more recently, Smith. In the role of teacher and mentor, by establishing an accredited special make-up effects course for aspiring effects artists, Savini continues to influence the potential goreteurs of tomorrow.

The Writer's Cut

In an interview with Dennis Fischer in 1990's *Faces of Fear*, William Peter Blatty cited *Psycho* scribe Robert Bloch as being the one who inspired him to begin writing. However, having already found fame working alongside Blake Edwards in the 1960s, Blatty was much better prepared than Bloch to take on the Hollywood studios when it came to negotiating a deal for the rights to his novel *The Exorcist*— one which was similarly inspired by newspaper reports and an actual case.[95] After being contacted by producer Paul Monash in New York as he completed his manuscript, Blatty gave the producer an exclusive six-month option in exchange for $400,000. Although Monash was successful in securing a deal with Warner Bros., his plans to significantly alter aspects of Blatty's text did not sit well with the author. Consequently, Blatty arranged for Warner Bros. to buy Monash out, leaving the writer on board as sole producer.[96] And so, even from the outset, it is clear that Blatty refused to be overruled or relegated as author, and would be involved in all aspects of production, from completed script to casting choices.[97]

To preempt issues of fidelity and interference, Blatty entered into further negotiations with the studio to ensure he was attached to the project as sole scriptwriter and producer. He also negotiated a 10 percent cut of the film's profits and mutual directorial approval before agreeing to take the project any further. After compiling an agreed list of seven Hollywood directors, ranging from Stanley Kubrick to Mark Rydell, Blatty was reportedly dissatisfied with Warners' preference, and has since stated that "had I the technical expertise to be a director at that time, I would have asked to direct it"[98]—a request the studio would have rejected outright as a result of his inexperience.

Consequently, the writer held out and even threatened legal action on account of Warners' negotiations with Rydell, championing the less established William Friedkin on account of his honesty and documentary realism. The studio finally supported Blatty after the critical and commercial success of Friedkin's *The French Connection*, for which Friedkin became the youngest filmmaker to win the Academy Award for Best Director. With Friedkin proclaiming that "Blatty was always my first audience for this movie; it was him I had to please first and foremost,"[99] the writer had seemingly secured a faithful adaptation of his novel and found a creative and collaborative ally in the guise of Friedkin.

However, fresh from his Academy Award–winning triumph, Friedkin was not afraid to challenge Blatty on his scriptwriting capabilities, and any initial reverence did not prevent the director from rejecting Blatty's first draft outright.[100] As such, the writer revised his script in accordance with the source novel and Friedkin's concerns. With cinematic success and studio indulgence on his side, Friedkin embarked upon an exhaustive casting call and physically demanding shoot, with Blatty acting as an efficient buffer between him and an anxious studio.

Retiring to the editing room behind schedule and over budget, the director edited the picture up until the last minute (in time to qualify for Oscar consideration), while trying to select a suitable score.[101] During postproduction, Friedkin shifted loyalties and sided with the studio in describing Blatty's ending as "a lame way to end this movie ... a pastiche of *Casablanca* ... and anticlimactic."[102] Furthermore, his ruthless approach to editing saw the director delete several sequences to reduce the running time, in keeping with concerns regarding audiences' attention spans.

Reportedly omnipresent throughout the production process, Blatty has consistently argued that he witnessed a masterpiece reduced to a "mere" classic as Friedkin trimmed key exchanges and the conclusion. The writer has since accused the director of removing the "moral core"[103] of the story and

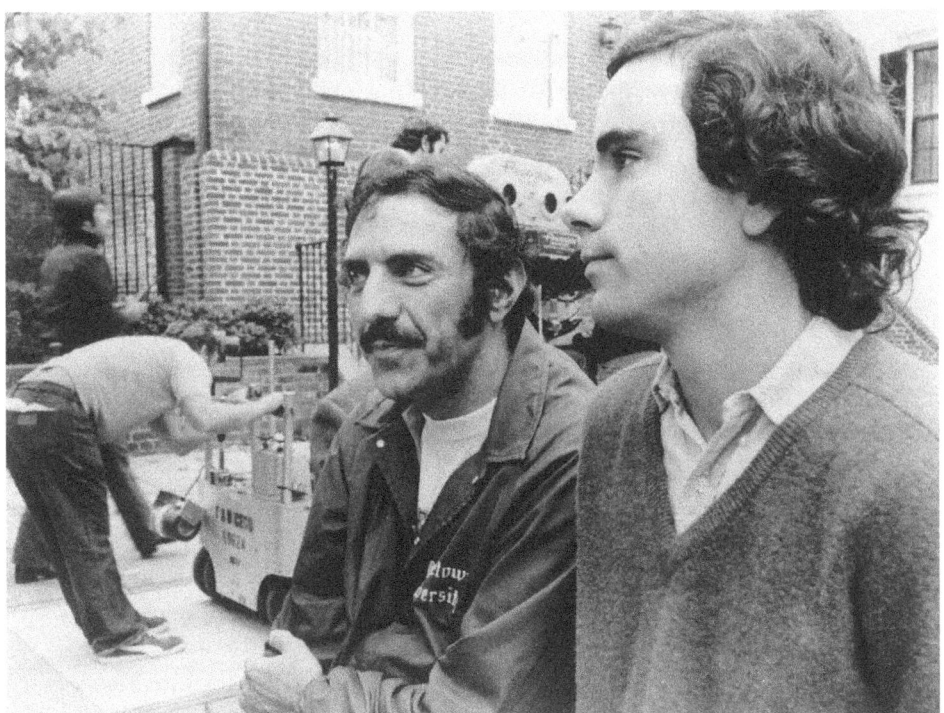

The Exorcist (William Friedkin, 1973). After collaboration, compromise and clear direction, Friedkin (right) and William Peter Blatty (left) eventually agreed on a shooting script and relocated away from Hollywood and Warners to Georgetown for the actual shoot. During this time Blatty was a key ally and clear presence on set while acting as a buffer between director and studio. Indeed, producer/writer Blatty continued to support and protect his director when it came to both the schedule and budget. However, decisions during postproduction over the editing process, and the removal of key scenes, divided the two of them until 1998 when Blatty's preferred cut of the film was released in theaters.

"leaving gaping holes in the carpentry."[104] Speaking years later about their tumultuous relationship around this time, Friedkin recalls how their collective and combative arrogance led to both men being "given over to a lot of pettiness in those days ... [and being] completely full of ourselves."[105]

Despite engineering the film's evolution and shepherding the project throughout its production history, Blatty's agenda and thematic aspirations were thwarted in these final stages by Friedkin, who, as director, was permitted to submit his final cut to the board for rating, and for some time after maintained that he "ultimately prevailed ... for the good of the film."[106] Indeed, it was this incident in the history and making of the film that the writer has consistently returned to in his writings, and a matter he intended to pursue throughout his career and association with the Hollywood horror franchise.

Released in December 1973, and breaking box office records on the back of censorship controversy, *The Exorcist* exploited reports of a manufactured curse, overzealous audience members and ten Oscar nominations. Blatty also benefited from a higher media profile in time for him to publicize his autobiography *I'll Tell Them I Remember You*. After winning the Academy Award, Golden Globe and Writer's Guild Award for his *Exorcist* screenplay, Blatty continued to cash in on his newfound notoriety by publishing *William Peter Blatty on The Exorcist: From Novel to Film* in 1974. This text not only contained his original screenplay but also a brief introduction in which the writer put forward his criticisms and concerns.

Eager to embark on more "original" projects (like first film director Friedkin, who spent the next seventeen years exploring film adaptation across various genres[107]), Blatty was quick to turn down Warners' sequel requests. Distancing himself from Warners' follow-up, Blatty attended a public screening of John Boorman's film in Georgetown and later likened the experience to watching Mel Brooks' *The Producers*, becoming the first to reinterpret the film as a comedy.

Such an unfavorable critical reception paradoxically dragged *The Exorcist* franchise, and thereby Blatty's name and association with it, into disrepute while elevating the iconic status and stature of its predecessor. In response to the overwhelming backlash directed at Boorman's sequel and elevation of the first film, Blatty exploited this second opportunity to expand and elaborate upon his 1974 text and publish *If There Were Demons Then Perhaps There Were Angels: William Peter Blatty's Own Story of the Exorcist* in 1978.

As writer and producer of *The Exorcist*, Blatty's extensive account of his experiences researching and writing the novel further contributed to the author's attempts at repositioning himself in the minds of audiences. He capitalized on Warners' publicity for the follow-up yet abhorred Boorman's revisionist approach. Because of the box office failure of *The Exorcist II: The Heretic*, Blatty experienced difficulty raising the financing for his pet project, *The Ninth Configuration*. Like many authors and scriptwriters,[108] Blatty felt both spurned and spurred on by such frustration, and sought to exert control over future adaptations as director.

However, Hollywood has only reluctantly allowed inexperienced directors behind the camera, particularly when the budget exceeds a certain level. Having proven himself as a screenwriter and established his name in the minds of audiences, Blatty was able to exploit the success of *The Exorcist* and audiences' obsession with it. He persuaded Pepsi to finance a loose reworking of his 1966 novel *Twinkle Twinkle Killer Kane* under the title *The Ninth Configuration* after previous attempts to set up a deal with the recently burned Warner Bros. fell through.

Reportedly "terrified at first,"[109] Blatty effectively paved the way for such literary figures as King and Barker to adapt their own novellas and short stories for the screen with *Maximum Overdrive* and *Hellraiser*, respectively. King's first and only directorial experience to date involved working under Dino De Laurentiis while battling drug and alcohol addiction, a series of events which not only marred the director's recollection of events but the overall quality of the finished film.[110] Barker, on the other hand, successfully adapted his *Hellbound Heart* novella as "a show-reel ... made for a small amount of money to show people I could write and direct movies and turn their investment into a profit."[111]

For Blatty, however, *The Ninth Configuration* was designed to be the second in his self-appointed faith trilogy, thus eclipsing Boorman's numerical follow-up in favor of a thematic and theological connection. Indeed, Blatty's presentation and framing of the film suitably preempts *Psycho* scriptwriter Joseph Stefano's declaration that Russell's *Crimes of Passion*, featuring Perkins as an outsider infused with sexual hang-ups and a penchant for voyeurism, was "the real sequel"[112] to Hitchcock's *Psycho*.[113] Although thematic continuations are not exclusive to the Hollywood horror franchise but hallmarks of directors like Wes Craven, Blatty's theological reappropriation of the first film was part of the writer's sustained attempt to rewrite cinematic history.

Released in 1980 and featuring a tenuous character link to *The Exorcist*, *The Ninth Configuration* focused on military service–induced madness. Through increasingly experimental forms of therapy and a solitary act of redemption, Blatty's theological concerns were given ambiguous expression. For other writers turned directors, the possibility of helming a relatively high profile franchise film meant proving yourself on a low risk property. Though writer-turned-directors' knowledge of and affinity for the material was indisputable, Hollywood sought proof and basic assurances that they were technically competent.

Whereas David S. Goyer and John Lafia directed such comparatively low-budget pictures as *ZigZag* and *The Blue Iguana* before taking the directorial reins of the *Blade* and *Child's Play* franchises respectively, Blatty's high profile association with *The Exorcist* franchise left him bereft of interference as writer, producer and director. Location shooting in Budapest provided Blatty with a suitable shelter from interference in much the same way as Friedkin's Georgetown shoot. Blatty's editing room experience saw him assemble a three-hour rough cut from which he had to fashion a coherent film. With two different cuts assembled from Blatty's three hours of footage, and the film ultimately released under two different titles with little financial backing, what remained was a clearly exploited connection to the first film. Moreover, and quite ironically, the film's controversial yet comparatively low-key release paralleled that of Boorman's official *Exorcist* sequel in this respect.

Blatty's Franchise Film

During this time, Blatty had begun working on an *Exorcist* follow-up inspired by a Priest's experiences on a Disturbed Ward. Set in the aftermath of the first film, without contradicting, rewriting or even referring to the events of Boorman's sequel, this script was firmly in keeping with his previous work. By concentrating on the concept of multiple possession in a psychiatric hospital setting, Blatty resurrected his beloved Lieutenant Kinderman for an investigation into a series of murders entwined with the fate of Damian Karras and the non-fictional Gemini Killer.

Featuring a clear generic shift, Blatty's script was strong enough to temporarily secure the interest of producer Jerry Weintraub and first film director Friedkin. However, despite significant studio interest, Friedkin ultimately backed out of the proposed sequel, citing a myriad of concerns. In the wake of this disappointment, Blatty temporarily gave up on his plan for a theatrical follow-up, rejected the low-budget independent route,[114] and transformed his screenplay into the novel *Legion*, which became a bestseller in 1983. Indeed, with little control over the cinematic future of their creations, writers have often attempted to regain creative control and some degree of proprietorship over the Hollywood horror franchise by returning to these characters and stories to rewrite and sometimes even contradict cinematic history.

Prior to Blatty's retreat into literary horror, Bloch exercised his literary rights to *Psycho* in two savagely satirical sequels—*Psycho 2* and *Psycho House* in 1982 and 1990. These texts were specifically designed to express "his feelings about splatter films,"[115] sadistic film directors and Hollywood studios, with their sensationalist theme parks and keen eye for marketing and merchandising opportunities.[116] Not surprisingly, Bloch's novels were rejected by Universal, yet they remain fascinating pieces of pointed pulp fiction.

Similarly, *Night of the Living Dead* co-scripter John Russo published *Return of the Living Dead* in the wake of Romero's superior sequel. This novel was then rewritten, re-released and adapted by Dan O'Bannon to create the first alternative zombie franchise. Much like Blatty, Russo also returned to the first film and wrote *The Complete Night of the Living Dead Filmbook* in

1985, which celebrated and highlighted his role in the film's production and success. Ira Levin has also written a literary sequel to *Rosemary's Baby*, entitled *Son of Rosemary*, in 2000 that substantially deviated from Sam O'Steen's TV sequel, *Look What's Happened to Rosemary's Baby*.

Moreover, Peter Benchley has spent the latter half of his career redressing the environmental repercussions of *Jaws* with a series of ecologically sound yet similarly themed underwater monster stories entitled *The Beast*, *Great White* and *The Creature*, along with several non-fiction accounts of shark behavior. More recently, Clive Barker has written his final *Hellraiser* story, which kills off franchise icon Pinhead, as a means of drawing a creative line underneath his association with the character and ongoing film franchise.

The literary success of Blatty's mutated script led to the potential resurrection of the film franchise at Lorimar in the mid-eighties. Blatty characteristically returned to *The Ninth Configuration* in time for its 1985 re-release through New World Pictures. Although the film had achieved some nominations and awards, and some level of cult status, the first time director seized this opportunity to clarify ambiguities in the film's conclusion, and subtly reframe the final act as an act of self-sacrifice rather than suicide, in a 117 minute, 37 second approved Director's Cut.[117]

Although post-release editing, restructuring and re-shoots were not uncommon in Hollywood,[118] Blatty's revisionist approach five years after release preempted the more sensational Special Editions and Director's Cuts that became a Hollywood staple after *Aliens*, *The Abyss* and *Terminator 2*.[119] As a creative opportunity to rewrite history, and a commercial ploy to sell more units, this re-releasing of films in and on different formats has provided directors like Blatty with the opportunity to revise their films in the wake of media criticism, acclaim or, more recently, a change in classification policy.

As literary creators of a Hollywood horror franchise, directors like Blatty (the *Exorcist* series), David S. Goyer (the *Blade* franchise) and Don Mancini (the *Child's Play* films) were seemingly in a position to reassert their intentions and reshape the nature and content of the franchise in line with their own concerns. However, such assumed authority and affinity for the material did not go unchallenged by studios and production companies eager to preserve longevity and satisfy perceived audience expectations. Although Goyer's aim was to redress an alleged lack of action in previous films, his concept for an apocalyptic conclusion to the franchise was rejected outright by New Line early in pre-production. Similarly, Mancini's gender-bending plans for a follow up to *Bride of Chucky* were met with strong resistance from Stacey Snider at Universal.[120]

Previously pursued by Larry Cohen and allegedly turned down by John

Carpenter, Blatty's *Exorcist III* finally elicited financial support from Carolco and Morgan Creek. However, this was after the author had sufficiently rewritten the climax in favor of a more visually satisfying conclusion in which Kinderman saves Karras with a single gunshot to the head. When Carolco suggested a new plot twist — that "Kinderman's daughter should become possessed"[121] — Blatty walked and the project found a permanent home at Morgan Creek. With the courage of his convictions and willingness to walk away with the project as literary creator, Blatty's enviable position is the exception within the Hollywood horror franchise.

Whereas some directors opted for a change of location, others adhered or returned to the iconic settings of previous films. Just as Brent Maddock's *Tremors 3*'s subtitle explicitly informed renters that this third entry would go *Back to Perfection* in terms of location and cast, the second of Blatty's stipulations, besides being attached as director, was that he shoot the film in Georgetown rather than some studio back lot. Indeed, Blatty's initial shoot was a marked contrast to Anthony Perkins', who had little choice but to shoot *Psycho III* on the Universal back lot,[122] thus placing him and the production under the watchful eyes of the Black Tower. Despite McCarty's assertion that Perkins had assumed a logical and inevitable process in directing *Psycho III*,[123] the actor-turned-director had little leverage when it came to convincing Universal of "his idea to film *Psycho III* entirely in black and white."[124]

Negotiating from a position of relative strength as the author, Blatty, on the other hand, was seemingly able to direct the tone, content and location of his film to escape the prying eyes of Fox and Morgan Creek. Like Perkins, he too adopted a thorough and comprehensive approach by extensively storyboarding the film and focusing on (re)casting the key roles in keeping with his own attitude and approach to the franchise.

Having acknowledged Hitchcock and Russell's influence, Perkins proclaimed to the press that his follow-up would "be a little more unreasonable and a little more off the wall,"[125] in much the same way that Blatty brought his sequel closer in line with his "idea of terror."[126] Subtle manipulation, dialogue and disorientation were the tools with which Blatty sought to terrify audiences, as "opposed to turning heads and all the rest."[127] This switch from splatter and shock effects to suggestion and surrealism is most evident in the suspenseful build up and subsequent dream sequence surrounding Father Dyer's murder.

Blatty's confident style during this section alone, whereby the camera is kept perfectly still (in homage to Hitchcock's *Psycho*) when Kinderman encounters the recently deceased Dyer in a "fantasy depiction of heaven in terms of a bad 1940s Hollywood musical,"[128] elevates the film above standard

Psycho III (Anthony Perkins, 1986). For *Psycho III*, Universal finally agreed to let star Anthony Perkins into the director's chair. However, his ability to break from the formula, or even leave the studio lot, was severely hampered by the production team and studio regime. Ideas went unsupported, and disagreements put him in a vulnerable position — one which left him disappointed with the end result. Further proof that publicity departments could place a positive spin on the proceedings, this photo portrays Perkins as confident, comfortable and relaxed when he was, in fact, feeling anxious, unsupported and under pressure. Also note how, as ever, the shadow of the Bates House is just over his shoulder and remained there throughout the rest of his career.

genre fare. However, Blatty still faced gentle pressure from the producers to move the camera during this highly effective sequence, heralding the first signs of interference that plagued the remainder of production.

After apparently canvassing the opinions of potential audiences, Morgan Creek persuaded Blatty to recast and reshoot the Patient X scenes with Jason Miller, who was now available, reprising his role from the first film to ensure continuity. This was in spite of the fact that Brad Dourif had already been cast and filmed these scenes back in Wilmington.[129] With Dourif about to be excised from the film, Blatty solved his casting conundrum by presenting audiences with a visual representation of "the schizophrenic nature of Patient X, cutting randomly between the two and evoking a psychological battle between Damien Karras and the Gemini Killer."[130] This left room for both actors to take on the role, although Dourif had to reshoot his scenes over an intense two-day period.

In another instance, Blatty resisted external pressure and internal temptation when it came to not zooming in on a scheduled subliminal "shot of the decapitated priest holding his head in his lap,"[131] since he, like Perkins, was "meticulous about not making it a bloodbath."[132] However, according to Winecoff, Perkins put up little resistance when the studio demanded that he "gore-enhance the murder scenes to appeal to a jaded teenage audience,"[133] and tone down the "wild and sexual"[134] aspects of his film. Successfully thwarted in respect to any form of final cut, Perkins succumbed to Universal pressure and curtailed his original concept to fall in line with their preconceptions of what audiences wanted from this third installment.

For Blatty, who was contractually entitled to one preview before Morgan Creek could "go and do what they want with the picture,"[135] the invited audience played an integral part in the film's fate. With studios embarking on both qualitative and quantitative studies throughout the test-screening process, Blatty's creative input as an authority on the *Exorcist* franchise was silenced in favor of what the director has since described as "the lowest end preview audience I have ever seen in my life. They dragged in zombies from Haiti to watch this film. It was unbelievable."[136]

According to producer Carter De Haven, studio head James G. Robinson's demand for an exorcism, "no matter how small,"[137] was based on the assumption that it would "keep the audience from being disappointed."[138] Not content with recasting the picture in postproduction, Robinson graciously gave Blatty the option of restructuring and re-shooting the climax to incorporate a "graphically gory final exorcism"[139]—or be replaced. With the project essentially complete, and Blatty's name contractually attached for publicity and promotional purposes, the studio sought to legitimize their sequel as part of the franchise in terms of specific set pieces and shocking scenes.

Faced with such a decision, Blatty attempted to turn this metaphorical "pig's ear into a silk purse."[140] This necessitated the shooting of additional scenes to introduce Nicol Williamson's character, Father Morning, to justify this new conclusion. At a cost of over $4 million, and four months after principal photography, director, producer and production company attempted to present a united front to promote the film's new and improved FX-laden finale. This featured Williamson's character being skinned alive, and George C. Scott's character flung around the cell as lightning bolts, flames, an army

The Exorcist III: Legion (William Peter Blatty, 1990). Lt. Kinderman (George C. Scott) returns to Patient X's (Brad Dourif) cell for the final time. He is subjected to the demons' taunts and is confronted by his old friend Father Damien Karras (Jason Miller). As part of this last temptation, the floor is first engulfed by fire and then a sea of snakes before lightning shatters the ground beneath them both. From this pit emerges Karras in mock crucifixion, surrounded by the damned and fighting for his soul. However, this entire sequence was a studio-imposed afterthought reluctantly directed by Blatty who, like Karras, was losing the battle on account of audience feedback from a test screening and studio head James G. Robinson's demands. Blatty reluctantly cooperated and attempted to make the sequence his own — with some degree of success.

of previous victims and a sea of snakes emerged from a Hell mouth beneath. Blatty publicly declared that his new ending "repeated everything that was in *The Exorcist*,"[141] but his real distaste for the entire spectacle has since been documented, along with the saving grace that he persuaded the producers to drop the classic obscenities imposed on the film's soundtrack throughout these "ultimately unnecessary"[142] scenes.

The cumulative effect of this interference saw to it, for the second time in the franchise's three-film history, that Blatty's approved version was systematically gutted and the emphasis unduly shifted — except this time the writer-director was co-opted into performing the postproduction operation himself. And so, although Blatty could apparently stall, if not overcome, studio misgivings, he eventually found it impossible to dismiss the preconceived notions of studio heads and audiences who demanded convention and conformity during the test-screening process.

Just as the studio/producer's perception of audience expectations shaped the casting and conclusion of *Exorcist III*, Joe Alves' aspirations for *Jaws 3-D*, having rescued the concept from self-parody, came under threat from a dramatically reduced budget and the sequel's relegation to an Alan Landsburg production.[143] According to screenwriter Carl Gottleib, Alves' difficulties were compounded by Landsburg's meddling, which included producer Rupert Hitzig shooting "a montage of effects that break the screen."[144] Included to ease Universal's anxiety, this two-minute sequence apparently had "all the 3-D delights everyone [was] crying out for without stopping the dramatic action."[145]

Despite his franchise experience, Alves' technical experience was exploited without any concession to his creative concerns. Similarly, even Blatty's experience mirrored many others whose sequels were either overshadowed by the unwelcome specter of previous films or a targeted teen demographic. Nevertheless, Blatty has consistently defended his sequel in interviews with such heavy-handed bias that he considers his installment to be a "superior film ... [and] more frightening film than *The Exorcist*."[146]

A final cause of contention for these directors was studio mis-marketing. Just as *Halloween III* antagonist Conal Cochran's scheme was "a joke on the children,"[147] Universal's marketing of the film was similarly perceived by audiences. The studio's refusal to address the film's alternative approach as "a pod movie ... instead of a knife movie"[148] in their advertising was a sin of omission that left those fans in search of the Shape, a sharp knife or even Jamie Lee Curtis severely dissatisfied. When it became obvious that *Halloween III* was regarded by fans as more trick than treat, director Tommy Lee Wallace blamed the studio's decision to "play it safe ... [and] get their money back in the first week-end"[149] for the overwhelmingly negative response.

With Fox similarly motivated to "cash-in on the title,"[150] Blatty has since recalled how he "begged them ... not to name it *Exorcist* anything because *Exorcist II* was a disaster beyond imagination."[151] Preferring the source novel's title of *Legion*, complete with its Biblical connotations, Blatty's expectation that the studio would not exploit the film's franchise history was unrealistic. Indeed, its association with the internationally renowned first film, and status as the next installment in the Hollywood horror franchise, was the cornerstone of their marketing campaign.

Having predicted a poor box office response on account of Fox's titling, Blatty presented this situation as a preemptive defense for critical and commercial failure. Furthermore, the sequel also had to contend with Bob Logan's PG-13–rated *Exorcist* parody *Repossessed*, starring franchise veteran Linda Blair. In keeping with Hollywood's reactionary approach to popular concepts, whereby rival studios and production companies green-light similarly themed projects and rush them through the production process to meet a release date, Logan's timing was fortuitous at best. However, first film star Linda Blair has since claimed that Morgan Creek and Fox were capitalizing on her profile and accused the companies of attempting to confuse potential audiences at the multiplex.[152]

As the third installment in a horror franchise with a tumultuous past up against a film specifically designed to ridicule its overall concept, *Exorcist III* ran the risk of market saturation and audiences' inability to take it seriously. When Blatty's follow-up indeed failed to inspire audiences and many critics, the director was ironically informed that the lack of success could be attributed to enduring memories of Boorman's sequel and an association with that film. In light of this, the Hollywood horror franchise demonstrated the potential to orchestrate its own downfall due to the success and failings of previous installments or misleading marketing campaigns. In this respect, both Blatty and Wallace's experience is similar to Walas', since many films were unable to recover from the reasons they were made.

Surviving the Franchise

With his interest in furthering the *Exorcist* film franchise stunted, Blatty returned to his literary roots and channeled his frustration with Hollywood, the horror franchise and studio politics into a new work of fiction entitled *Demons 5, Exorcists 0: A Fable*, published in 1995. An analogous satire sprinkled with thinly veiled elements of autobiography, Blatty's text echoed Altman's *The Player* in its keenly observed expose of Hollywood's insider trading.

Having further mined his association with the Hollywood horror franchise and the industry in literary terms, Blatty was nevertheless recruited by Fox TV with the promise of adapting his original *Exorcist* text into a four-hour mini-series. Once again, Blatty seized the opportunity to try and rewrite franchise history and resurrect his theological concerns in an alternative format that advocated further exposition at the expense of the novel's more sensationalist or shocking elements. Although Blatty's hopes of challenging Friedkin's first film adaptation failed to reach fruition, Stephen King was able to adapt *The Shining* in 1997 using this four-hour format for Warner Bros.

However, such an artistic endeavor ultimately proved unnecessary for Blatty once Friedkin agreed to re-edit and restore the all-important footage to the first film after a sustained 25-year campaign. According to Blatty, Friedkin had cited the audience's limited attention span as the reason why he had trimmed his first cut. In keeping with Hollywood's fondness for exploitation and returns, the director has since conceded retrospectively in several interviews that he did, in fact, make a mistake and "would redo all of my films if I had the chance, because to some extent I've changed my attitude about a lot of the way I used to make"[153] them.

Promoted as *The Exorcist: The Version You've Never Seen*, Warners' high profile 25th Anniversary re-release offered audiences an updated and enhanced version which, although certainly not a "director's cut" in the strictest sense, fulfilled Blatty's need for a "writer's cut." Similarly, *Night of the Living Dead* co-writer Russo had released a revisionist version of that first film two years previous.[154] For Blatty, however, such a dramatic and unabashed turnaround signaled a significant creative and commercial triumph. As co-owner of the rights to the first film, Blatty has recently fought to keep the franchise under his control. By joining together with Friedkin in 2003 and filing a lawsuit stipulating that Warners had tried to cheat them out of profits they had been promised, their relationship has come full circle.

Nevertheless, Blatty remains a singular authority on the franchise and was privy to an early screening of Paul Schrader's *Dominion: Prequel to the Exorcist*. Despite being vocal as to the superfluous nature of another prequel, especially after the significant flashbacks of Boorman's film, Blatty described Schrader's spiritual entry as both "well directed"[155] and containing some "exceptional performances."[156] With the prequel possessing an aesthetic more in keeping with his own sensibilities, Blatty was perhaps relieved that Schrader's entry subverted the first film's narrative and "stayed away from everything identifiable with the Friedkin blockbuster."[157] However, this vision also differed from Morgan Creek's, who had failed to communicate their mainstream intentions from the outset.

After effectively scrapping Schrader's version and hiring established sequel maker Renny Harlin for a re-do, Morgan Creek specified that this version should sufficiently incorporate key images and scenes reminiscent of Freidkin's film, along with a more action-orientated approach. Endowed with what Kermode has called the "dubious distinction of being one of the very few movies to be remade before it even opened,"[158] the fourth film in the franchise continued the reactionary tradition. Indeed, Harlin's take on the prequel was followed by Schrader's version almost a year later, finally giving audiences the chance to compare the two.

With such issues of (mis)interpretation and adaptation surrounding the development of the *Exorcist* franchise over a thirty-year period, Blatty has remained steadfast in his attitude and approach. Furthermore, franchise family members have demonstrated the franchise's ability to regenerate or degenerate, depending upon the intentions and interference of those involved. Having exploited the title's money-making potential in film and literature, and been exploited by Morgan Creek in their continuation of it, Blatty is more optimistic since the production company has finally agreed to search their vaults for *Legion*'s alternate footage. Just as Savini told several interviewers that he wished they "could have seen the movie I wanted to make,"[159] Blatty has potentially been given an opportunity to reconstruct a genuine "director's cut"[160] and allow audiences to once more decide for themselves. Furthermore, Blatty could then join the ranks of his fellow franchise directors in being a part of the most revised horror franchise in Hollywood history.

Although Blatty has all but retired from the industry, Savini's directorial career has been characterized by a series of stalled projects and short-lived forays into television, despite ongoing success with acting roles, stunt co-coordinator work and special make-up effects courses. Blatty and Savini are alike in their experiences with the Hollywood horror franchise in that both filmmakers were forced to follow in the footsteps of an industry phenomenon. Having to contend with a first film's place in popular culture, they were forced to compete with, and against, previous entries. Moreover, they faced the challenge of contradicting various representations of possession or zombies in sequels and spin-offs. In other words, both Blatty and Savini were charged with having to make the concept scary again after the outright parodies of *Repossessed*, Jackson's *Thriller* and Russo's *Return of the Living Dead* franchise. As a goreteur and member of the franchise family, Savini has rightly described how he and his contemporaries were captives of their own success.

In much the same way that Savini's reputation conjured up outrageous special effects and a proliferation of blood and gore, Blatty's name brought up the most iconic scenes from the first film in *The Exorcist* franchise. Both professionals have been stereotyped and exploited as a result. Studios and production companies that narrowly saw the special effects artist as a means of guaranteeing graphic or fantastic content, and the writer as a dependable commodity upon which to continue the franchise, targeted them.

As aspiring filmmakers they were frustrated by their experiences, despite their status and standing within the industry. Indeed, despite being celebrated by directors, the industry and fans in the pages of magazines like *Fangoria*, authors and goreteurs were similarly seduced by these projects and willingly exploited their status to advance their careers. In this respect alone, the Hollywood horror franchise has played an important role within the industry as a vehicle whereby cast and crewmembers can realistically aspire to the director's chair.

Nevertheless, studios continued to assert their ownership of the Hollywood horror franchise after a first film director's absence. Moreover, the attitudes of modern audiences were prioritized and seen as paramount, and their role in the success, failure or formulaic nature of any franchise installment cannot be ignored. Characterized by intense conflict and infighting, these and other such franchise families were arguably condemned from the outset, with many members caught in a crossfire involving audiences, critics and the industry. Consequently, many franchises have only served to disenfranchise their new directors at various stages throughout the production process. As showcases for their talents, the Hollywood horror franchise frequently disappoints; yet it also demonstrates some potential—if only financiers could prevent themselves from transforming these literary creators and monster makers into mere puppets.

4

Joe Berlinger

Rage Against the Machine

"Often the writer and director are cogs in a much larger and sometimes very cruel machine."[1]

— Clive Barker

Promoting from within the franchise family ensured some degree of marketable fidelity, and the rise of the special effects artist represented a form of logical progression. However, the reluctance and/or unsuitability of former directors or crewmembers to take over the sequel saw to it that replacements from outside the franchise had to be found. Consequently, this fourth chapter is devoted to franchise outsiders' relationships with the Hollywood horror franchise, with a focus on Joe Berlinger's *Blair Witch 2: Book of Shadows*.

In doing so, this chapter considers the extent to which outsiders are directed by executives, marketing departments and the preconceived notions of the audiences, critics and censors. Moreover, the chapter addresses the lasting effects the franchise has had on directors' careers and how their films can be reconciled with their body of work. In order to examine these issues fully, I also refer to David Fincher's *Alien 3*, John Boorman's *Exorcist 2* and Stephen Hopkins' *A Nightmare on Elm Street 5: The Dream Child*, among other key examples.

Reportedly made for $30,000 and acquired by Artisan for one million dollars at the Sundance Independent Film Festival, *The Blair Witch Project* grossed over $250 million worldwide, becoming the most profitable film of all time. As a fledgling company keen to make its mark, Artisan latched onto the film's potential and shepherded it through the final stages of post-production to create a film that would raise their profile and profit margins. Funded through the generous assistance of John Pierson, host of the Independent Film Channel's *Split Screen* series, first time filmmakers Daniel Myrick and Eduardo Sanchez merely wanted something they could sell "to cable, [or] maybe get HBO or Showtime to pick it up."[2]

Having drawn their inspiration and company name from Benjamin Christensen's witchcraft documentary *Haxan*, the pair combined the style and structure of *Cannibal Holocaust* and *Last House on the Left*[3] to create an internet-reliant incarnation of the elaborate horror hoax film. Although far from original in its endeavors, *The Blair Witch Project* effectively updated and fused the "snuff" film format with the supernatural elements of American folklore. However, Artisan took this increasingly complex and compelling mythology and exploited its potential through one of the most successful and innovative marketing campaigns in recent film history.

After six months of pre-release publicity and post-purchase tinkering, Artisan released the film on July 30, 1999, fully embracing the range of merchandising opportunities available. Although the film's box office total soon surpassed the all-important $100 million mark, audience reaction to the movie was fiercely divided. Indeed, this profound difference of opinion set in motion a series of events that would see Berlinger's sequel consumed by an unprecedented backlash. With the film teetering on the edge of cultural phenomenon, Artisan were eager to exploit the title and ensure that the numerous imitations and parodies fast-tracked through development did not diminish the power of any possible follow-up. However, such a reactionary policy towards feature film production has an adverse effect on a sequel's potential success and increases the cumulative pressure placed upon the production.[4] Motivated by a combination of fear and greed, Artisan followed in the footsteps of its competitors by rushing into pre-production on a legitimate sequel.

As proven in previous chapters, the seeds of a franchise film's problems were often sown early in the production process, and this is the case here, with a tight twelve-month release schedule firmly in place to ensure it could be in theaters by Halloween. Coupled with an outsider's unfamiliarity with the material and a studio's way of working, the need to acclimatize and focus on finishing the project often left little room for experimentation or negotiation when shooting a franchise entry. Nevertheless, many directors were equipped with enough optimism, enthusiasm and determination to deliver a piece of filmmaking that was both creative and commercial.

The Outsiders

Just as William Friedkin refused to return for *The Exorcist II*,[5] Steven Spielberg twice rejected[6] Universal's advances when it came to creating a sequel to his summer blockbuster *Jaws*.[7] Following his second refusal to indulge in what he publicly considered "corporate business,"[8] and the DGA's decision to veto a waiver which would have given the job to *Jaws* editor Verna Fields as an esteemed member of the franchise family,[9] Universal entrusted one of its most treasured commodities to a veritable outsider. Thirty-eight-year-old Frenchman Jeannot Szwarc, a TV veteran who had sufficiently impressed the studio with his first feature, *Bug*, was not "afraid to go back in the water."[10] Despite only three weeks' preparation time, Szwarc, attracted by the opportunity of a high profile franchise film, believed he "would have been an idiot to turn it down."[11] Easily seduced by studios keen to minimize budgetary expenditure and ensure the longevity of the franchise, filmmakers often found the tone and content explicitly dictated as a result.

As the director of *Alien 3*, following the departure of Renny Harlin and Vincent Ward, David Fincher represents Hollywood's willingness to support the directorial debuts of advertising executives and MTV directors.[12] However, such appointments have been accompanied by expressions of concern and hypocritical accusations that these directors would favor style and special effects over script content and performance. Prior to these attacks, film school graduates Rick Rosenthal, Adam Grossman and, more recently, J.T. Petty had been given the opportunity to direct sequels to *Halloween, Sometimes They Come Back* and *Mimic* on the basis of their thesis films *The Toyer, Trap Door* and *Soft for Digging*. In this respect the film school route has established itself as a valid gateway into the profession by way of the Hollywood horror franchise.

Elsewhere, graduates from the small screen included *Child's Play 3*'s Jack Bender and *Omen: The Final Conflict*'s Graham Baker. That said, *Omen* producer Harvey Bernhard had "a very strong idea of how the film should look"[13] and intended to be "always on set to see what he is doing."[14] Indeed, this decision to focus on novice directors who had demonstrated both passion and promise through their scripts, short films and show reels saw studios, production companies and producers tap into raw talent at an affordable and potentially lucrative rate, and maintain a firm control over their properties.

An alternative approach was to recruit from a pool of directors who had already tasted success with their first genre film. These directors were eager to work on a project with a significantly higher profile as a means to an end (ingratiating themselves with the Hollywood studios). Therefore, the franchise proved irresistible to those interested in furthering their careers,[15] and it was within the slasher sub-genre that such a trend often dominated director selection.[16] Operating in a similar vein, studios and production companies often expanded their search outside of the domestic arena and increasingly looked to the international film market. Hoping to exploit unfamiliar filmmakers as a means of rejuvenating their franchise titles, directors Renny Harlin and Guillermo Del Toro (who infiltrated Hollywood through Empire's *Prison* and Dimension's *Mimic*, respectively) were approached by New Line for *A Nightmare on Elm Street 4* and *Blade II*.

Prior to these sequels, Australian-based filmmakers Richard Franklin and Philippe Mora were also recruited in the early eighties.[17] Brian Trenchard-Smith was yet one more director who initially approached Hollywood with his own project, *The Paperboy*, only to be offered a franchise film. Similarly, Fox and Universal approached directors such as Jean-Pierre Jeunet and Ronny Yu to direct fourth entries in the *Alien* and *Child's Play* franchise on account of their stylistic success and international reputations.[18] Seduced by the idea of accessing a wider international audience with a big-budget, high-profile release, established international filmmakers were persuaded to put aside self-penned projects in favor of assimilation and the opportunity to establish a credible reputation through the Hollywood horror franchise.[19]

Based on this evidence, the franchise has focused on fresh talent and first-time filmmakers. Nevertheless, studios also approached established and experienced independent filmmakers with some proven genre experience who were renowned for operating outside of the studio system. Just as Morgan Creek and Paramount recruited Paul Schrader and Peter Medak for *Exorcist: The Beginning* and *Species II*, their first genre films in almost twenty years,[20] the late eighties saw John Hough and Joseph Sargent direct fourth entries in *The Howling* and *Jaws* franchises.[21] Furthermore, *Alien* director Ridley Scott was approached by producer Dino De Laurentiis to direct *Hannibal*,[22] and Gus Van Sant used his Oscar "get of jail free card"[23] to get support for his controversial *Psycho* remake.

Having exhausted Hollywood's indulgence on his philosophical fairy tale *Zardoz*, John Boorman, who had turned down *The Exorcist* on the grounds that "it would be rather repulsive,"[24] was an unlikely choice to helm the sequel.[25] Simultaneously spurred on by the frustration of developing two scripts without either of them reaching fruition, and seduced by Warners' offer of "an almost unlimited budget, a cool million dollar director's fee, and, best of all, total artistic control,"[26] this combination of push and pull factors secured his involvement. As such, the Hollywood horror franchise has not only been approached by directors as a calculated yet challenging career move, but also accepted as a chance to redress the past.

Since Myrick and Sanchez were unwilling to direct a *Blair Witch* sequel, Artisan was consoled by their intention to return for the third film, one they envisioned as a prequel. With a background in advertising, Joe Berlinger was inspired by Wiseman's controversial 1967 documentary *Titticut Follies* and worked with Bruce Sinofsky on the comic short *Outrageous Taxi Stories*. This led to the formation of Gray Matter Productions,[27] the company through which they released the award-winning *Brother's Keeper* in 1992. A showcase for concerns that would dominate the director's career, *Brother's Keeper* highlighted Berlinger's interest in the U.S. criminal justice system and the media's role in shaping small town America.

After directing episodes of *Homicide*, Berlinger and Sinofsky returned to documentary filmmaking with the multi-award-winning *Paradise Lost* in 1996. Venturing back into America's heartland, the pair investigated the murder of three eight-year-old boys and the subsequent manhunt that found three local teenagers responsible. In examining society's reaction, the pair exposed the flaws in the prosecution's case and the way in which the accused were branded as "Satanic" by the local media. After years of research and reels of footage, Berlinger concluded the teens were innocent, and followed up this investigation with a sequel, entitled *Paradise Lost 2: Revelations*, four years later.

Having lived with and through the trials of the West Memphis Three for over five years, Berlinger felt in need of a break from both the subject matter and frequent collaborator Sinofsky. Despite his status as an acclaimed documentarian,[28] Berlinger experienced frustration as he began pitching ideas to raise the financing for his first feature. However, after soliciting sufficient support from celebrated independent producer Christine Vachon and Killer Films, Berlinger brought his project about a bizarre 1930s murder case[29] to Artisan.

Under the impression that they were genuinely interested, Berlinger was shocked to be offered the *Blair Witch* sequel, given its profile and reputation. According to Berlinger, Artisan was in search of a director who could lend "a certain level of credibility"[30] to the follow-up and considered him a "calculated choice"[31] in light of previous critical acclaim and an apparent affinity for the material's documentary style and backwoods "true-crime" content. From this we can see how the participation of outsiders like Berlinger, Boorman and Cohen was often at the expense of self-penned personal projects turned down by these studios and production companies.

However, Berlinger was cautious about accepting the assignment on account of his ambivalent attitude towards the first film. Although the director in him appreciated its conceit and fictional examination of occultist folklore, as a documentarian he was "deeply disturbed and almost offended by"[32] the clichéd way it was put together and then "marketed through misinformation."[33] Like Boorman before him, Berlinger accepted the sequel out of sheer frustration, tired of "banging my head against the Hollywood wall."[34] He seized this ironic opportunity to explore key thematic concerns and comment on the first film's success. Much later Berlinger also cited an altruistic reason as partial motivation, in that it would help raise the profile of the Memphis Three and an alleged miscarriage of justice. Meanwhile, Artisan sought to harness the director's reputation as a means of maintaining the quality and content of the franchise.

Overwhelmingly in favor of this financial risk reduction strategy, studios and production companies enticed experienced and fledgling directors alike into the franchise. Such offers forced a temporary adjustment in aspirations and outlook for directors in exchange for raising or resurrecting their profile within a potentially safe and structured environment. Irrespective of their relative innocence, age or experience, outsiders recruited to take the franchise forward often discovered that such an arena was fraught with punishing schedules and oppressive budgetary constraints, within which they had to satisfy the demands and expectations of producers and audiences alike. Furthermore, the work of inexperienced sequel writer/directors Ken Wiederhorn and Bruce Starr, of *Return of the Living Dead Part II* and *Silent Night, Deadly Night Part 2*, who had no specific filmmaking background to speak of, adversely affected the reputation of the Hollywood horror franchise for all concerned.

As outsiders, many filmmakers inherited or courted key members of the first film's cast or crew to elicit their cooperation and support. Although comparatively rare in the horror genre, where big-name actors and performers were not only unwilling to return but also unaffordable, the participation of some key players was still considered pivotal, particularly in the first sequel. Boorman's *Exorcist II*, for example, not only featured the return of Blair's character but also required Max Von Sydow to return as Father Merrin. Similarly, Fox was unwilling to make *Alien 3* without Weaver and allowed the star to directly influence the tone and content of the picture.[35] Weaver's lucrative return in Jeunet's follow-up, *Alien Resurrection*, not only meant a rewrite of Joss Whedon's script, but also, as Kermode has rightly summarized, saw the actress "ascend to the throne of Alien Queen."[36]

Indeed, franchise stars like Anthony Perkins, Robert Englund and, later, Jamie Lee Curtis were able to raise their fees and increase their level of creative control.[37] Present since the first film, and perceived as an integral part of the previous films' success, returning franchise actors inevitably affected a director's ability to offer their own interpretation of a character and increased the potential for conflict.[38] With inherited cast and even crewmembers tending to act as self-appointed guardians, the potential for outsiders to experiment within the confines of the franchise dwindled. Consequently, directors of literary sequels or later entries recast starring and supporting roles to accommodate either their own interpretation, a reduction in budget, and/or an actor's reluctance to return.[39]

Although such a practice contributed to the notion that all cast members were expendable or replaceable, stars' participation was certainly preferred by producers keen to forge marketable links and legitimize the project. Whereas some directors welcomed cast members with creative input, and others had it imposed upon them,[40] overseas outsiders Jeunet and Yu shrewdly surrounded themselves with previous collaborators on *Alien Resurrection* and *Bride of Chucky* as a means of ensuring stylistic continuity, cooperation and support. With no surviving characters to consider, Berlinger's *Blair Witch* sequel sidestepped these issues by featuring a cast of unknowns in the style of the first film. Alternatively, other outsiders killed off returning cast members as a means of shocking audiences, cutting costs and keeping the material fresh after using them to reconnect with the audience.[41]

With their outsiders selected, release dates set, and the cast and crew in place, a key area of contention for franchise productions became script development. In some cases, studios commissioned scripts from various writers as a means of exploring numerous options through subsequent drafts. Just as the final incarnation of Fincher's *Alien 3* script was rewritten throughout pre-production, director Stephen Hopkins experienced a similar set of circumstances on *A Nightmare on Elm Street 5: The Dream Child*, despite New Line's attempts to avoid the scriptwriting chaos that threatened to engulf part four.[42] Whereas Hopkins and Fincher shepherded these unsatisfactory scripts, outsiders such as Danny Steinmann, Eric Freiser, Adam Grossman and Dominique Othenin-Girard adopted a more hands-on approach to *Friday the 13th: A New Beginning*, *Warlock III*, *Sometimes They Come Back Again* and *Halloween 5* by redrafting their scripts to such an extent they became eligible for credit.[43]

Depending on studio attitudes, others were subjected to varying levels of involvement in the scripting process. At the other end of the scale, intense producer involvement from Harvey Bernhard (*The Omen*), Robert Shaye (*A Nightmare on Elm Street*), Hilton Green (*Psycho*) and David Giler and Walter Hill (*Alien*) overrode a great deal of directorial control. Linked to the level of financial risk involved and the status of previous entries, the majority of comparatively low-budget sequels were subjected to far less studio input at this stage. For their *Blair Witch* sequel, Artisan followed MGM's approach to *Species II* and commissioned scripts from three relatively unknown, and therefore inexpensive, writers.[44] However, Berlinger convinced Artisan to drop these cliché-ridden concepts, featuring Heather's relatives or news crews going in search of the missing trio, in favor of his own suggestion of a satirical and post-modern follow-up. After submitting a two-page treatment to Artisan seven weeks prior to shooting, Berlinger wrote his script with experienced screenwriter Dick Beebe, whose previous credits included the 1999 *House on Haunted Hill* remake.

Following in the outsider footsteps of Scott Spiegel, Greg Spence and Scott Derrickson (on *From Dusk Till Dawn 2*, *Prophecy 2* and *Hellraiser: Inferno*, respectively), Berlinger's franchise experience began under an approved banner of relative free reign. Similarly, Morgan J. Freeman and Larry Cohen, on *American Psycho 2* and *Return to Salem's Lot*, demonstrated how only the most tenuous of connections were required under the guise of creative carte blanche. At least during this stage of production then, the Hollywood horror franchise offered some outsiders a remarkable amount of creative freedom, even if only within the confines of its central conceit.

Berlinger's Blair Witch

Outsiders often entered the Hollywood horror franchise with fresh ideas, keen to create a film that would paradoxically bear their own stamp and stand alone, as well as satisfy the rudimentary franchise requirements. By employing a range of strategies, these outsiders simultaneously sought to fulfill their contractual obligation to the Hollywood horror franchise and create a film that would enhance their careers.

Berlinger, for example, adopted a reactionary and revisionist attitude in his refusal to continue the documentary style of the first film — in the same vein that Boorman and Schrader approached their *Exorcist* sequels. Just as Schrader intended to "stay away from all the things that people identify with the Friedkin film"[45] in favor of a more "introspective"[46] approach, Boorman departed from Warners' derivative ideology to atone for the alleged damage done by Friedkin's movie. Accordingly, the director described *The Heretic* as a "healing movie,"[47] painting Father Lamont's metaphysical questions of faith with striking imagery on sumptuous sets.

As a documentarian who was equally critical of the first film and its subsequent reception, Berlinger was against making *Blair Witch 2* "derivative or dishonest to the documentary tradition,"[48] or perpetuating "a hoax and wallow[ing] in the clichés of bad documentary."[49] Moreover, Berlinger believed himself damned, irrespective of which avenue he pursued, and decided "to

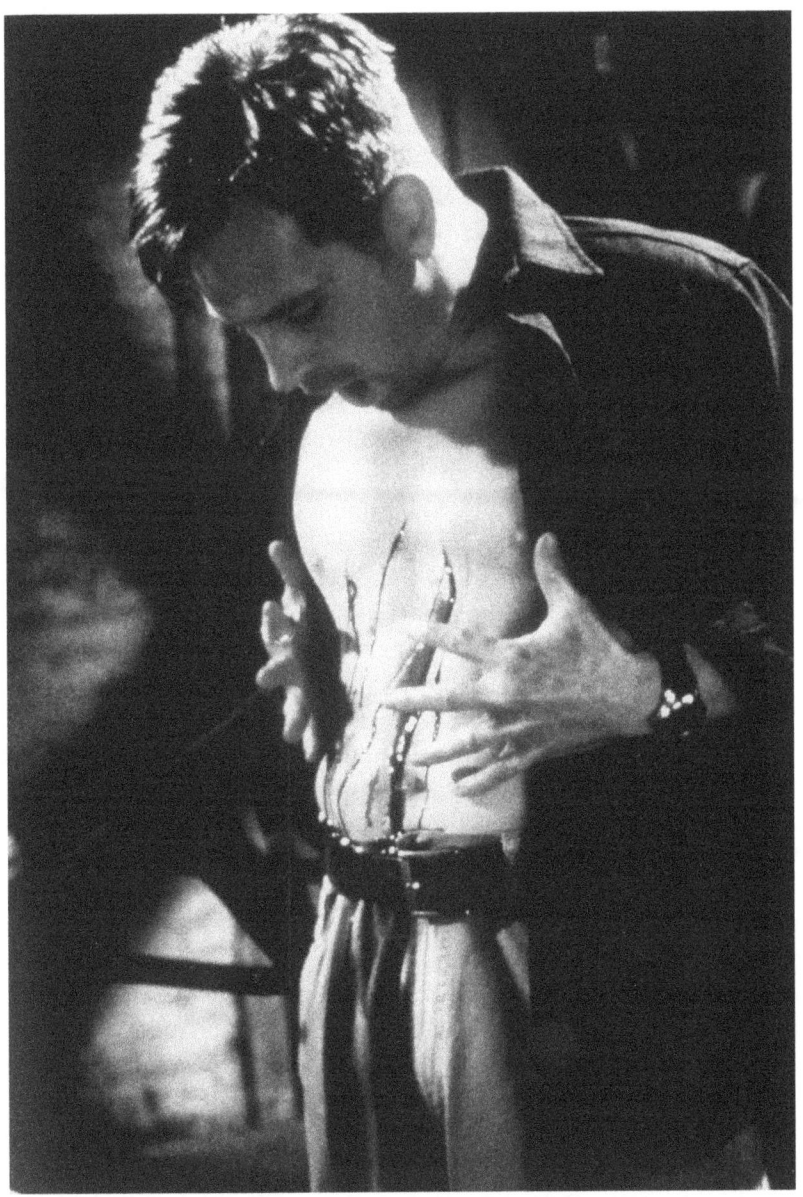

Book of Shadows: Blair Witch 2 (Joe Berlinger, 2000). Despite having an approved script prior to shooting, Artisan were shocked to discover that Berlinger's film was not a slasher film or gore-fest. Consequently, re-shoots were demanded during postproduction to ensure that the final cut contained the requisite blood and guts guaranteed to appease the targeted wider audience. In this image, Jeffrey Patterson (Jeffrey Donovan) is equally shocked to discover that he had been gutted in favor of a more satirical take on the first film's phenomenal status and reception.

make a movie that was relevant to my work."[50] Consequently, he described his film as an "anti-sequel,"[51] intending to "do everything possible and go against expectations."[52] This statement suitably echoed one critic's description of Boorman's film as "an anti–*Exorcist*,"[53] with its prequel and sequel elements in the mold of Coppola's *Godfather Part II*. Openly opposed to the tone and content of first films, directors like Berlinger, Boorman and Schrader were explicit and up front with the studios about making a sequel that would not compromise their personal agendas.

Other outsiders also took steps to rebel against previous entries and returned to the darker tones of first films. Fincher and Hopkins, for example, actively sought to counteract the populist, action-orientated feel of *Aliens* and *Nightmare 4*, with Fincher convincing Fox to "do something that was dark, mean and adult,"[54] and Hopkins hoping to take Freddy "back into the shadows"[55] to be "less jokey and more brutal."[56] Similarly, Scott Derrickson's *Hellraiser* sequel (*Hellraiser: Inferno*) addressed an over-exposure of franchise icon Pinhead by focusing on the nightmarish journey of a male protagonist, and offering a narrative more in keeping with Barker's first film.

In direct contrast to such an approach, yet in keeping with the reactionary mentality, *Alien Resurrection* outsider Jeunet was under strict studio instructions to follow Cameron's successful formula by adopting the action-orientated feel of *Aliens*.[57] Aided and abetted by advances in technology, Gus Van Sant, on the other hand, remade *Psycho* as part of an elaborate experiment that emphasized the theatrical essence of the franchise by redressing the representation of women and fulfilling Hitchcock's original intentions.[58] However, even though these outsiders endeavored to appeal to fans with these comments and declarations, their redirection of the Hollywood horror franchise often failed to find an appreciative audience or maintain much commercial viability.

As previously demonstrated, the remake often played and preyed upon the representation of gender roles as an assured method of updating the story. Whether assigned the role of "the final good guy"[59] in *Red Dragon* or merely allowed to kick out at a sister's killer in *Psycho*, the shackles and screams of the Final Girls of yesteryear have been shrugged off in favor of a newfound assertiveness and capacity for aggression denied to them in previous incarnations. Indeed, Marcus Nispel's *Texas Chainsaw Massacre* not only featured a more aggressive and resourceful Final Girl but also recast its infamous Chainsaw clan to incorporate female antagonists. Outsiders combined the monstrous-feminine[60] with the self-sufficiency of the "modern woman" to appeal to their core demographic with more challenging representations and role models.

With their target audience defined, Artisan "constantly reminded"[61] Berlinger that he was supposed to be making a "teen psychological thriller."[62] Consequently, the director populated his follow-up with a cast of appealing twenty-something archetypes. Such attempts have been popular ever since Universal cynically geared *Jaws 2* towards this growing market by featuring a slew of teen protagonists.[63] And so, from Jack Bender's *Child's Play 3* to Gary Sherman's *Poltergeist III*, outsiders have focused on depicting the trials and tribulations of this target group to provide teen audiences with a specific point of reference within the Hollywood horror franchise.

Since first film directors Myrick and Sanchez had laid claim to a *Blair Witch* prequel, Berlinger was forced to steer clear of any such designs. Furthermore, the director chose not to incorporate any flashbacks or first film footage in his follow-up.[64] However, this approach has been liberally adopted, particularly by other outsiders who made concessions to an audience's perceived need for familiarity. Second sequels to *Poltergeist, Child's Play* and *Hellraiser* featured flashback therapy sessions and slideshow summaries to place the current film in context. *Hannibal's* more innovative Ridley Scott, however, attempted to appease the audience's need to see Starling and Lecter "on screen together as much as possible"[65] through a liberal use of audiotapes, pictures, letters and telephone calls. Alternatively, directors Richard Franklin and Brian Gibson boldly began sequels to *Psycho* and *Poltergeist* with a reminder of the first film's most memorable or climactic moments, and then spent the rest of the running time trying to surpass them.

Back in the mid–1970s however, it was Warner Bros. who initially adopted the most detrimental approach to franchise filmmaking in their early plans for an *Exorcist* sequel. Pointedly referred to as a "rather cynical approach,"[66] this follow-up would heavily feature "unused footage, [and] unused angles from the first movie"[67] to create a "low budget rehash"[68] of the first film. Although Warners ultimately dispensed with this idea, it was a technique slavishly adopted by Lee Harry's dismal *Silent Night, Deadly Night Part 2*, which featured "an astonishing twenty-five minutes of flashback footage."[69] Such tactics illustrated the way in which some filmmakers and franchisers used flashbacks and first film footage as an easy way to save money and increase a sequel's running time.

Although Berlinger decided against using first film footage, he deliberately referenced and incorporated recognizable clichés from several classic genre films.[70] As a means of emphasizing the way in which certain characters are subject to the hypodermic model of media consumption, this iconography has been used to underline the sequel's central conceit as to the dangerous nature of the media. Indeed, outside directors often felt the need to demonstrate their knowledge of the genre by grafting scenes onto existing frameworks, with *Nightmare 5*[71] and *Amityville II* borrowing liberally from *Rosemary's Baby* and *The Exorcist*.

Just as Richard Franklin's *Psycho II* uncannily resembled *Strait-Jacket*,[72] and Adam Marcus' *Jason Goes to Hell* mirrored elements of *The Hidden*, some directors also attempted to graft storylines from non-genre films onto their sequels. Larry Cohen, for example, used Thornton Wilder's play *Our Town* as "a model,"[73] with vampires as "the ultimate Americans"[74] in *A Return to Salem's Lot*, and Del Toro similarly referred to *Blade II* as a vampiric "variation on the *Dirty Dozen*."[75] Therefore, directors' inclination to inject, update or transplant material from a range of sources demonstrates the cannibalistic nature of the medium, the genre and the Hollywood horror franchise.

Rather than continue, replicate or compete with the first film's narrative, Berlinger used the franchise as an opportunity to comment on the *Blair Witch* phenomenon. As an alternative, he created a self-proclaimed "meditation on violence in the media"[76] within the confines of a "post-modern sequel."[77] Arguably inspired by Wes Craven's *New Nightmare*, Berlinger's *Blair Witch* embraced a similarly subversive approach that eschewed any pretence at "mockumentary." Moreover, it also opened the door to the type of social commentary and content he was renowned for. A self-confessed fan of *Rosemary's Baby* and *The Shining*, Berlinger sought to embrace a similar level of ambiguity and leave the film open to interpretation. However, without an established literary text or international reputation to back him up, Berlinger's chances of being allowed to follow through on such aspirations were slim.

Reportedly pitched as an "edgy adult satire,"[78] most aptly demonstrated in the sequel's opening montage, *Blair Witch 2* focused on the subject of evil "as something quite human, quite banal."[79] This was in direct contrast to its predecessor, which approached the subject matter in deadly earnest. Believing a particular concept or creature's ability to scare audiences had diminished or disappeared, many outsiders took the relatively easy option of presenting parody and humor as a substitute. (Scott and Jeunet, in *Hannibal* and *Alien Resurrection*, later adopted such an approach.[80]) However, their choices did not always fall in line with what audiences anticipated or necessarily wanted, and Berlinger's bold sense of experimentation critiqued the mythology, madness and hype that surrounded the franchise.

Rather than descend into parody at the expense of previous entries, other outsiders either ignored the tone and content of previous films or re-wrote franchise history. Although the director publicly claimed to have the freedom to do what he wanted,[81] Berlinger's "sequel to the phenomenon"[82] was studio-approved at the earliest stage. In forfeiting any chance of stand-alone status, the director shrewdly took Franklin's academic approach on *Psycho II* to the next level, albeit without the reverence or twenty year hiatus.

Despite protestations to the contrary, few franchise directors have been able to dispense with a first film's tone, content and characters to such an extent that the only connection is the title. By acknowledging the first film's events as fact, the absolute opposite of Berlinger's approach, and offering only the most tenuous of links to a first film, *American Psycho II* director Morgan J. Freeman admitted that his contravention would be "a let down."[83] With the title its greatest commercial asset—*and* creative liability—the director was nevertheless hopeful that people would warm to its jigsaw-like structure and campus setting before consigning it to the rejection pile.

Similarly, Dimension Films repackaged existing scripts and strategically inserted the iconic Pinhead into the narratives for the *Hellraiser* sequels *Deader* and *Hellworld*. However, with the notable exception of Brett Ratner's *Red Dragon*, which attempted to erase Michael Mann's first film (*Manhunter*) from the franchise to create a more cohesive trilogy, this option to create a stand-alone film has been relegated to direct-to-DVD premieres—an avenue of distribution unavailable to Berlinger, whose $12 million sequel was scheduled to open across America on over 3,000 screens.

Some Kind of Monster

Whereas production was fraught with the pressure of deadlines, potential conflict with established cast members and the specter of studio executives, post-production often posed insurmountable difficulties for outsiders. Having co-written the script and shot without any franchise family members on board, Berlinger had been able to bring his own sense of perspective to the Hollywood horror franchise prior to this point.

Indeed, many outsiders entered into a complex tripartite process of post-production scrutiny and consultation wherein feedback from test-screenings, studios and censors could re-determine the film's content. The effects of this stage ranged from minor alterations to extreme cases of buyer's remorse. The term buyer's remorse was diplomatically employed by Schrader to describe the way in which Moran Creek took the unprecedented and expensive option of rejecting his *Dominion* prequel outright in favor of a fresh start with established sequel director Renny Harlin at the helm. The term is an appropriate way of describing the most extreme reactions on behalf of some studios with regard to the very sequels they had not only developed but also previously approved. Required to submit a rough cut, this stage of production saw many filmmakers forced to endure a series of creative compromises, irrespective of a film's budget, franchiser or financial backer, in favor of alleged mainstream sensibilities.

Just as Artisan rejected Berlinger's first cut in favor of what Berliner has called a traditional "teen slasher movie,"[84] *Alien 3* suffered the indignity of a surgical strike[85] by a studio desperate to avoid the recent excess of *The Abyss* and *Die Hard 2*. With a $50 million budget, Fincher's film warranted a great deal more scrutiny and interest from Fox in comparison to those sequels produced for considerably less. Indeed, *Alien 3*'s financial success was a high priority within the higher echelons of the studio. After screening an assembled rough cut of 2 hours and 17 minutes, a "sobering experience"[86] for all, as far as Fincher was concerned, Fox chairman Joe Roth issued his verdict. With the key comment that this follow-up "needs to be more like a traditional

Alien 3 (David Fincher, 1992). As co-producer and star of this third installment, Sigourney Weaver sought to protect her director protégé from both Fox and Brandywine. Isolated, alone and shooting without a finished script, they never really stood a chance, as sets and stars had already been built and cast. A difficult high profile shoot was put under further pressure from overseas concerns and interference, as well as the imminent arrival of the studio's watchdog. With life imitating art, the shoot soon became a race against time before Twentieth Century–Fox came to perform a surgical strike of their own — one which involved splicing a rough draft and taking the entire production back to Hollywood.

horror movie,"[87] the director has since commented how "at a certain point [Fox] cut the balls off the thing."[88] In Roth's defense, *Alien 3* all but defied classic scares in favor of dramatic tension, with a beleaguered Ripley forced to acknowledge her fate as a Queen embryo leeched its way towards maturity. In such cases, financiers have been grossly inconsistent with regard to their support of these directors, their previously approved scripts and the future of the Hollywood horror franchise.

Attempting to create a more satisfying and traditional horror film for mainstream audiences, Artisan disliked the cerebral shocks and subtext of Berlinger's *Blair Witch* sequel and opted for what the director deemed "cheesy gore."[89] An afterthought from within Artisan's marketing department, these scenes and images were actually shot in the back of Berlinger's house five weeks prior to release. Indeed, it could be argued that these have been almost randomly inserted into the film, despite the director's repeated protestations that such scenes affected the ambiguous tone he had strived for. Shot with Berlinger's cooperation but against his wishes, this insertion of graphically violent scenes in an outsider's film during post-production accurately echoed Rick Rosenthal's experiences on *Halloween II*.

As another first-time director under the pressure of a Halloween release date, Rosenthal's rough-cut was supplanted with additional footage and violent scenes directed by co-writer/producer Carpenter, who felt audiences were looking for a faster pace and more gore after *Friday the 13th*. Whereas Jack Sholder and Dwight H. Little were similarly directed to include more blood and guts in *Nightmare 2* and *Halloween 4*, Jonathan Demme's mainstream reluctance to "pander to ... sado-voyeurs"[90] with *The Silence of the Lambs* was overruled by preview audiences whose feedback forced the director to "restore some of the discarded gore"[91] he had fortuitously overshot.

To further satisfy audiences' alleged need for standard horror conventions and clichés, Berlinger was directed to shoot even more footage within the truncated post-production period. This was intended to support Artisan's representation of Josh as an already imbalanced individual with a history of mental health issues, and therefore capable of the crimes that take place. Fond of these scenes in isolation, the director nevertheless felt that their inclusion in the film, as flashbacks at irregular intervals, was once again at the expense of any ambiguity he had created.

Rather than shoot additional footage, some directors were forced to delete subplots and specific scenes to appease studio concerns. Peter Medak, for example, was directed to simplify events and focus on the effects in *Species 2*. Understandably puzzled as to "why studios don't decide to take something out at the appropriate time rather than after all the time, effort and money,"[92]

Medak followed instructions, altering the film at the expense of plot coherence via the addition of an unexplainable yet timely "blood and monster"[93] scene. Similarly, Fincher was forced to excise an entire subplot in *Alien 3* depicting Golic's intense yet deluded fascination with the Alien. Preferring to contradict themselves and undermine these outsiders rather than risk alienating audiences, studios and production companies increasingly departed from approved scripts in favor of simplistic and streamlined approaches to the Hollywood horror franchise.

After splicing Josh's asylum scenes and additional gore footage into Berlinger's film, Artisan also restructured it to "deliver the scares earlier."[94] This decision drastically altered Berlinger's original ending in which an eight minute interrogation sequence revealed the guilt of the film's core characters as opposed to anything supernatural. As far as the director was concerned, the inter-cutting of these confessionals throughout the film gave away the ending and ambiguity of the very film they had approved — one designed to be "a light-hearted romp in the woods"[95] before taking "a deadly turn towards the end."[96] Indeed, endings were a major source of contention for many outsiders committed to providing audiences with closure or a set-up for future installments.

Fincher was equally unsuccessful at petitioning Fox to open *Alien 3* with Ripley's suicide, a conclusion adopted at the insistence of star Weaver, and present the film in flashback. A major cause of concern for the studio, particularly in light of similarities to *Terminator 2*, *Alien 3*'s final scenes became a key point of friction and infighting. This culminated in an enforced compromise shot two weeks before the film's release that left neither party happy or particularly proud of the end result.[97] After entrusting the future of the Hollywood horror franchise to talented outsiders, studios and production companies, with the support of selected audiences, frequently sought to safeguard the property by withdrawing their support during these final stages.

As franchise outsiders, directors often deferred to previous installments for a fitting conclusion. *Jaws 2*, for example, followed the first film's pattern. Other sequels, however, not only adopted an open-ended conclusion but also brought the franchise full circle to a new beginning.[98] Although a little more subtle than the staple shock epilogue, cliffhangers at the final fade out denied directors and audiences alike an opportunity for closure. Part marketing ploy and part additional incentive for audiences to return with anticipation, the cliffhanger conclusion was eschewed by many outsiders in favor of some narrative closure. After *Damien: Omen II*'s relatively poor box office showing, for example, Fox reworked its initial franchise strategy and planned a third, and reportedly final, installment in the *Omen* saga entitled *The Final Conflict*, with producer Bernhard proclaiming that "audiences really want to see the s.o.b. die."[99]

Similarly, the death and seemingly total destruction of the antagonist was also a key feature of *Child's Play 3* and *Stepfather 3*, both of which shredded their franchise stars in the final scenes. In search of an equally audience-pleasing finale, franchisers behind sequels to *Species, Candyman* and *Night of the Demons* provided directors Peter Medak, Bill Condon and Brian Trenchard-Smith with additional funding to shoot extended special effects–laden finales. With the feedback from test screenings allowing for this additional financing, audiences were once again responsible for directing the Hollywood horror franchise.

Having witnessed a series of changes and additions to *Blair Witch 2* during post-production, Berlinger was also required to add a title card at the film's opening which "went against one of the basic tenets"[100] of a sequel by acknowledging the first film as a fiction. Besides being allowed to keep the previously agreed and intentionally ironic *Book of Shadows* appellation[101] as part of the film's title, few traces of Berlinger's satirical tone remain. This situation was further reflected in the removal of Frank Sinatra's "Witchcraft" as the opening title track in favor of the Artisan-approved Marilyn Manson song "Disposable Teens."

A commercially cynical attempt to appeal to the target audience, this musical move was in keeping with their revised attitude towards the film. A similar event occurred on Joseph Zito's *Friday the 13th Part 4*, which had an extended introductory prologue imposed upon it by Paramount's Frank Mancuso Jr. that focused on previous kill scenes and Jason's folkloric status. In this respect, outsiders were often guided by studio appointed executives, temporary trustees or franchisers whose main concern was keeping the commercial side of the Hollywood horror franchise intact and ideally broadening its mainstream appeal.

Just as Berlinger intended to follow in the footsteps of the first film by relying on suggestion and the audience's imagination, many outsiders sought to deliver more cerebral scares. With *Hannibal* a noteworthy exception,[102] outsiders who attempted to return the franchise to its darker origins nevertheless continued to face opposition from the MPAA, with *Species II, Alien 3* and Stephen Hopkin's *A Nightmare on Elm Street 5: The Dream Child* standing as three such notable casualties.[103] Although it had never been Hopkins' "intention to throw all kinds of blood and guts up on the screen"[104] in *Nightmare 5*, the director nevertheless recalls the way in which New Line and the MPAA "cut the guts out of it completely"[105] to meet an August release date.

After attempting to play down his film's franchise origins and sequel

status, Berlinger also distanced his film from the horror genre, which he equated with the most clichéd aspects of the slasher film. Such an inherent prejudice and contradiction in his attitude and approach to the Hollywood horror franchise was representative of the majority of outsiders.[106] Such efforts at reclassification and re-branding saw the more marketable term psychological thriller substituted for horror. With such a biased and narrow-minded opinion arguably shared by mainstream audiences, this charade in which horror films are reclassified and publicized is perpetuated through marketing and publicity, and is evident in the numerous interviews conducted and press packets issued to promote these films.

Many outsider-directed sequels have forgone expensive advertising campaigns on account of their dwindling budgets. However, Berlinger's follow-up was afforded a nationwide theatrical release and therefore subjected to additional interference — with the marketing department an ongoing cause for concern. Indeed, both Berlinger and Fincher have since expressed serious concerns that "the marketing of the movie has driven creative decisions in a way that's typical of Hollywood"[107] — to the extent that *Blair Witch 2* was (mis)represented and sold to audiences as another true story. This involved Artisan, who had fully exploited the potential of the Internet to create an unprecedented level of hype for the first film, saturating the market in a similar fashion for Berlinger's sequel.[108]

Over at Universal, Gus Van Sant was also dissatisfied with their marketing department, who played "into the [audience's] expectations of [the *Psycho* remake] being slicker and gorier"[109] than Hitchcock's first film, misleading potential viewers as to the true nature and content of the movie. Outsiders criticized franchisers for their miscommunication and audience dissatisfaction after the fact,[110] and New Line's disgruntled *Freddy's Dead* director, Rachel Talalay,[111] openly criticized the company for the part it played in the relative failure of Hopkins' *Nightmare 5*. In reference to this she cited their greed,

Opposite: A Nightmare on Elm Street 5: The Dream Child (Stephen Hopkins, 1989). Freddy (Robert Englund) catches Alice (Lisa Wilcox) off guard after his demise in part four. After the pop culture mishmash of Renny Harlin's *Dream Master*, Australian import Stephen Hopkins came on board wanting to drag Freddy back into the shadows. However, with the *Rosemary's Baby*-esque *Dream Child* mandate in place, and competing scripts travelling back and forth, the production once again degenerated into a high-pressure race against time to meet an ambitious release date. With the second series of *Freddy's Nightmares* also airing on television between installments, New Line's eagerness to expand the family threatened to saturate the market, and, as such, the project was in some ways destined to be stillborn.

market saturation and "horrible job of marketing"[112] the film to audiences as key causes.

Having expressed dissatisfaction with the way in which their films were governed and promoted, directors were also forced to take onboard feedback from test-screenings. Unable to draw upon any previous association with the franchise, or an impressive enough back catalogue to defend their cut, outsiders were often at the mercy of the results gleaned from scorecards and focus groups. Fincher in particular was frustrated at Fox's decision to restructure and reedit his film based on the opinions of "16-year-old kids in Long Beach."[113] Although Berlinger and the majority of outsiders were unable to prevent their films from undergoing this additional scrutiny, John Boorman was allowed to release *Exorcist II* without such measures being imposed. However, after an unprecedented wide release[114] and impressive opening weekend gross, Warners flew Boorman back to try and salvage their collective reputations after reading highly critical reviews and receiving numerous reports of negative audience reactions. Warners withdrew the film from theaters while Boorman attempted to restructure his poorly received sequel by making a series of extensive changes[115] to "find a horror film that was never there,"[116] a task similarly assigned to Fincher and Berlinger.

Consequently, test screenings have been employed by studios as just one of several preventative tools to improve a film's potential for success in an increasingly crowded marketplace. Far less costly and inconvenient than withdrawing a film and attempting to re-cut it, the process has also impacted a film's allocated prints and advertising costs. As the first outsider, Boorman allowed the test-screening process to gain greater currency in the eyes of anxious studio executives. Indeed, it became a pivotal reference point for studios and affected the way in which future outsiders, like Berlinger, were allowed to direct the Hollywood horror franchise.

Judgment Day

Blair Witch 2 was released on October 27, 2000, fifteen months after the first film and in the wake of numerous parodies and spoofs (from animation to soft-core porn).[117] The film debuted with a $13 million opening weekend before doubling this amount by the end of its theatrical run. Constituting an 80 percent drop in comparison to the success of the first film, and $60 million less than industry insiders expected, the film's box office was far from impressive by industry standards, despite its comparatively low budget.[118]

In terms of reception, New Line's first *Elm Street* sequel was similarly

Hannibal (Ridley Scott, 2000). Although novelist Thomas Harris' controversial text failed to entice Jodie Foster and Jonathan Demme as star and director, Anthony Hopkins agreed to return in the titular role. Here the director, Ridley Scott, right, and Hopkins take a break in filming to discuss the mechanics of the story. With Julianne Moore now cast as Clarice Starling, the difficult task of shepherding the eagerly awaited sequel fell to Scott, who, with the assistance of experienced screenwriters Steven Zaillian and David Mamet, attempted to reach a conclusion that would please and appease all parties. Despite all these cooks, reconciling audiences with the novel's quasi-romantic conclusion was still a contentious decision, with the director carefully selecting the right tone to translate these final pages onto the screen.

criticized for contradicting the first film's rules and internal logic. However, director Jack Sholder has since highlighted how his sequel out-performed its predecessor, set the tone for future installments and contradicted the law of diminishing returns. Following director Jonathan Demme's and star Jodie Foster's departures due to the novel's content, critics were more forgiving of Ridley Scott's *Hannibal*, a film which became the highest grossing R-rated film at that time, with the majority of critics tracing this film's problems back to the book's Grand Guignol excess and failure to conform to structure or expectations. With Lecter brought center stage—from film title to screen time—*Hannibal* fell in line with the established franchise tradition of cautiously rewarding audiences with a meatier role for its icons and antagonists.

In his decision to question the very existence of the Blair Witch, on the other hand, Berlinger made an unprecedented move which audiences and critics failed to anticipate or accept.

Left alone by studios and producers, Van Sant and Boorman were not so easily acquitted by audiences and critics keen to point out discrepancies and the affects of recasting.[119] In isolation of studio and audience concerns, Van Sant rejected prevalent ideology in favor of his own vision — a move that confused audiences and outraged critics. Having adapted a franchise to suit his own theological and thematic concerns, Boorman portrayed himself as a victim of audience expectations on *Exorcist II*. In a series of confessional interviews, the director explained that his only sin as sequel director had been to deny the audience "what they wanted in terms of horror"[120] — a sentiment later echoed by Berlinger and Fincher with respect to their franchise entries. Depicting the audience as "this wild beast out there,"[121] Boorman has since remarked that his failure creating an *Exorcist* sequel was not throwing "enough Christians to it."[122]

Fincher's *Alien 3* similarly disappointed audiences expecting an action-orientated film in keeping with Cameron's sequel and the franchise's afterlife in comic book form. With the primary love interest Hicks and adopted daughter Newt killed off within the first few minutes, it is easy to concur with Thompson that "audiences are not accustomed to being so vanquished, or undermined in a credit sequence."[123] Echoing Boorman's sentiments, Fincher later explained how if "we failed to do one thing in this film, and we failed to do many things, it was to take people out of their everyday lives. It's not a scary scare movie but a queasy scare movie and I think people resent that."[124] Indeed, by eschewing mainstream sensibilities and genre-specific clichés in favor of a more fitting narrative "conclusion" more in keeping with Scott's film, Fincher's feature failed to satisfy the masses.

Supported by friends and colleagues, Berlinger concluded that his sequel was grossly mistreated and fundamentally misunderstood by critics on account of its sequel status. The director even accused them of collectively poisoning audiences against the film with their cynicism and dismissive approach. However, Berlinger has claimed to be all the more shocked and disturbed by the personal criticism he received within their scathing reviews. A far cry from the praise bestowed upon him as documentarian, critics saw fit to question his apparent betrayal, lack of morality, and, perhaps most damaging, the accuracy and authenticity of his previous works — a situation that left the director feeling unduly persecuted.

Having found what he later described as "a world-wide microscope waiting to rip the movie apart,"[125] Berlinger also had to contend with the disapproval of first film directors Myrick and Sanchez, who disliked the sequel's script and direction.[126] Although Chapter 2 highlighted Wes Craven's candor with regard to the *Elm Street* franchise, and James Cameron considers *Alien Resurrection* to be the one "with the rubbish monster,"[127] William Friedkin remains the most indiscrete and damning offender of subsequent entries in the *Exorcist* franchise. This ranges from his prophetic statement that Schrader's prequel would become the cinematic equivalent of a "15 car pile-up"[128] with "bodies all over the place"[129] to his dismissal of Boorman's film as "a stupid mess by a dumb guy."[130] Having survived the studios, audiences and critics to varying degrees of success, outsiders also faced unsolicited criticism from previous directors.

Facing similar accusations of betrayal and dishonesty from audiences and critics, the directors of *Nightmare 2*, *Hellraiser 5* and *Friday the 13th Part V: A New Beginning* all came under attack from fans for being too radical in their reassessment of the franchise. On the other hand, the directors of *Jaws 2*, *Poltergeist II* and the remaining installments of Paramount's *Friday the 13th* sequels were equally criticized for being clichéd and commercial with their repetitively formulaic follow-ups. Indeed, Berlinger's metaphorical description of the *Blair Witch 2* project as a "poisoned chalice"[131] pointed out such a paradox at the outset. Having taken the creatively ambitious option that ran the risk of alienating the first film's fans, Berlinger clearly preferred Boorman's flawed *Exorcist* follow-up to Szwarc's fundamentally safe *Jaws* sequel. (In his defense, Szwarc has been reluctant to take any directorial responsibility for a film he later referred to as a hugely collaborative "mop-up operation."[132]) Furthermore, Berlinger's sequel dovetailed effectively into his previous and subsequent work as a filmmaker and documentarian.

Forever cast as the first franchise outsiders, Boorman and Szwarc, however, continue to epitomize opposing approaches to the franchise. As such, the appropriately titled *Exorcist II: The Heretic* and ritually simplistic *Jaws 2* could, and should, be held up as preexisting templates for potential directors tempted to access Hollywood though the horror franchise.

In their attempts to explain or justify what went wrong, outsiders have singled out specific departments within the studio's corporate structure, and implicated audiences and critics in a system that left many of them dissatisfied with the process and end result. On the cusp of walking off the film in protest, Berlinger was ultimately persuaded to remain and publicly support the studio's final cut in the press after being warned that if "you walk off your first studio feature you'll never work again."[133]

Similarly aware that walking out on *Alien 3* would be "more detrimental"[134] to his filmmaking career in the long term, Fincher also saw the project through to the bitter end, but withdrew from Fox's international marketing machine. As a first time director with no proven track record to fall back on, Fincher's attitude and experience accurately predicted Berlinger's, with the director describing the experience as "hellish"[135] and "the worst thing that ever happened to"[136] him. Indeed, Fincher has since responded to criticism by acknowledging that, although "a lot of people hated *Alien 3* ... no one hated it more than I did,"[137] and to this day he feels physically "sick [at] all the concessions"[138] he had to make along the way. *Howling II* director Philippe Mora also found his franchise film "murder from day one."[139] Berlinger, however, on account of his harrowing and heartbreaking experiences as a documentary filmmaker, has bucked this trend by describing *Blair Witch 2* as "a giant vacation in comparison."[140]

Having blamed negative press for audiences' alleged failure to engage with what was left of the satirical subtext and social commentary he had

Hellbound: Hellraiser II (Tony Randel, 1988). In this scene from Randel's gory sequel, an institutionalized Kirsty (Ashley Lawrence) mistakenly identifies this skinless corpse as her father. Exhausted, bloodied and in dire need of help, the figure presented in this waking nightmare is perhaps an accurate visual representation of many outsiders' experience of the Hollywood horror franchise.

attempted to instill in his sequel, Berlinger relished the opportunity to (re)present the film on DVD. Here, an accompanying booklet and feature length commentary track single-handedly seeks to redress the balance by answering the critics. Berlinger also explains the alternative interpretations and versions of a film that Artisan "just hacked ... to death in the twelfth hour."[141] Six months after the release of Renny Harlin's *Exorcist: The Beginning*, Morgan Creek allowed Paul Schrader to return to *The Exorcist* franchise to fine-tune (on a very limited budget) his previously discarded prequel. Following a series of select screenings at several international film festivals, Schrader's film has been released on DVD as a unique companion piece to Harlin's film and an integral part of a unique franchise.

Likewise, the DVD release of the *Alien Quadrilogy* in 2003 saw Fox reinstate a great deal of deleted and alternative material from Fincher's preferred cut, thereby allowing audiences a chance to glimpse what Fincher had intended within the constraints of the fraught production. Indeed, the growing importance and lucrative nature of DVD releases and re-releases, with their capacity for the inclusion of deleted scenes, alternative endings and director commentaries, has provided an invaluable opportunity for outsiders like Medak, Derrickson and Berlinger to respond to their critics and address their fans.

Although willing to return to the franchise for this purpose, Berlinger has dismissed any possibility of remaining part of the franchise family; and it's equally unlikely that Artisan would want this director to return, in any case. Other studios and production companies, however, were keen to retain their outsiders for *Psycho III*, *Halloween 5* and *Friday the 13th Part 5*.

Indeed, some outsiders were persuaded to remain with or return to the franchise.[142] *Howling II* director Philippe Mora even went the extreme route of persuading franchiser (and executive producer) Stephen Lane to let Mora write and direct a third film after single-handedly setting up the financing and a distribution deal. Supposedly based on Brandner's third *Howling* novel, Mora's second attempt has been the most absurd departure to date — one in which Communism, oppression, immigration and genocide collide with Australia's Aboriginal ancestry as a means of exploring the genetic origins of werewolves. Eclectic and oddly enthralling, this sequel also featured a film-within-a-film (entitled *Shape-Shifters Part 8*) subplot, a misogynistic Hitchcock clone, and an unholy trinity of lycanthropic nuns sent to Sydney to bring back a runaway bride. Subtitled *The Marsupials*, the film featured romance, inter-breeding, and the birth of a new generation, and certainly proved that "there are more things in heaven and earth than you can shake a boomerang at."[143] This was a far cry from the commercial approach to

Halloween: Resurrection, which Rick Rosenthal (of *Halloween II* fame) returned to as "a second chance to make a similar but in some ways different movie"[144] after a seventeen year absence from the franchise.

Whereas some outsiders optimistically carried on their association with the franchise, and other low-budget directors disappeared from the industry without a trace, a great many more returned to the relative security of previous positions within the film or television industry, sometimes permanently. In this respect, Berlinger entered into a period of profound inactivity, one described by the director as "two months on the floor of my office in the fetal position,"[145] convinced his career was over. Full of regret regarding the choices and compromises he made, Berlinger's situation mirrored that of Fincher's. The director found the industry unflinchingly unforgiving of *Alien 3*'s poor reception to such an extent that it "affected [his] reputation for a long time."[146]

Although Medak and Van Sant returned to television and experimental independent filmmaking, and Boorman retreated to Ireland, less established directors were able to secure the necessary support for their own first films within the genre. Just as Dwight Little and Scott Derrickson graduated from *Halloween 4* and *Hellraiser 5* to *The Phantom of the Opera* and *The Exorcism of Emily Rose*, Bill Condon followed up his *Candyman 2* debut with the Academy Award–winning *Gods and Monsters* and *Kinsey*, scripting the successful adaptation of *Chicago* in between. Based on this evidence, and these directors' ability to sustain and develop their careers, it is clear that an outsider's decision to direct the Hollywood horror franchise can translate into a higher profile and establish the necessary studio support to move on to other commercially viable projects.

As others' career prospects languished in various stages of "Development Hell," some outsiders turned their attention to more personal projects. These required less funding and resulted in more creative control, as demonstrated by Jean-Pierre Jeunet's welcome return to French cinema with the critically-acclaimed *Amelie*. Channeling whatever effects of post-franchise depression they felt into abating a growing pressure for critical and commercial success, directors such as Fincher, Boorman and Berlinger bounced back from their experiences as franchise outsiders with such acclaimed projects as *Se7en*, *Excalibur* and the award-wining documentary *Metallica: Some Kind of Monster*.

A project supportively resurrected by Berlinger's previous collaborator Bruce Sinofsky at the ailing director's suggestion, the Metallica documentary was the very antithesis of his franchise filmmaking experience. Lacking the constraints of an evolving script and punishing release schedule, this return to familiar territory was made with the full cooperation of the band, and without any media backlash or insurmountable wall of audience expectation to climb. With creative control and final cut signed over, studio interference was completely removed once the band single-handedly bought back the rights to the footage to avoid becoming a syndicated heavy metal pastiche of *The Osbournes*. Since the successful release and reception of this documentary, Berlinger has not only completed *Gray Matter*,[147] but also begun orchestrating his return to feature filmmaking with an adaptation of Edward Bunker's autobiography *Education of a Felon*.

Despite having no prior creative or financial connection with the franchise, established and aspiring directors alike were hired from a variety of different backgrounds. Once in the hands of these studios and production companies who had previously owned, assimilated or purchased the rights to a particular title, franchises were often exploited without a realistic schedule or long-term franchise agenda. The role of director was often filled late in the production process, and this further diminished their potential for involvement or success.

Indeed, few outsiders shared Ridley Scott's overwhelmingly positive experience on *Hannibal* prior to the test-screening process and the subsequent onslaught of audiences and critics well versed in sequel traditions. Insatiable and divisive, audiences have been more content to embrace mediocrity and regurgitation than innovation and an individual voice, despite repetitive complaints of dissatisfaction and a lack of originality with regard to each successive installment.

Keen to exploit the frustration and ambition of fledgling and experienced filmmakers alike, the Hollywood horror franchise has the potential to nurture or annihilate the creative talent involved. In spite of such stringent controls and restrictions, however, directors have attempted to actively participate in and shape this process through a range of experimental and unexpected approaches, ranging from faint facsimiles to the thoughtfully blasphemous. As a means of asserting themselves and inserting their own ideas and thematic concerns into the material, directors have been reactionary, revisionist and returned to first principals. Subject to mixed messages, mis-marketing and the specter of mainstream audiences, many films' earning potential and popularity have been affected by buyer's remorse.

In spite of all this, by successfully courting controversy and raising their individual profiles, franchise filmmakers have created a number of undoubtedly flawed yet fascinating pieces of contemporary cinema that collectively address the pitfalls of the production process and demonstrate the inherent potential of outsiders working within the Hollywood horror franchise.

5

Jeff Burr

Divided We Fall

"Horror films have become so corporate and franchised ... right now I'm part of the problem, rather than the solution but I hope to change that."[1]

— Jeff Burr

As demonstrated in Chapter 4, studios and production companies deferred to the franchise outsider in lieu of a first film director or suitable member of the franchise family with mixed results. The growth of the Hollywood horror franchise has seen many filmmakers direct sequels in two or more different franchises, an unavoidable outcome given the genre's development over the last twenty years. As has been established, the majority of trends and approaches to franchise filmmaking originated with classic Universal and Hammer horror films.

Defined as any filmmaker who has directed at least two follow-ups in two different franchises, the sequel director also arose with classic Universal honor, since the genre's first sequel-maker was Erle C. Kenton, helmer of Universal's *Ghost of Frankenstein*, *House of Frankenstein* and *House of Dracula*. Following the critical and commercial success of *Island of Lost Souls*[2] in 1933, Kenton's shift from slapstick comedy to Universal's horror franchises saw him take over from first film directors Tod Browning and James Whale just prior to Abbott and Costello's introduction to Universal's monsters. Steeped in franchise folklore, Kenton's films combined characters and cast members with increasingly preposterous yet entertaining narratives of redemption or revenge. Similarly, cinematographer Freddie Francis temporarily took over Hammer's *Dracula* and *Frankenstein* franchises with *The Evil of Frankenstein* and *Dracula Has Risen from the Grave* to create striking visuals that cemented his abilities behind the camera.³ Likewise, Roy Ward Baker directed both the third entry in the *Quatermass* franchise in 1967 and the sixth of Hammer's *Dracula* films in 1970.

With the concept of sequel director firmly established within the Hollywood horror franchise, this final chapter examines an alleged ghetto of franchise filmmaking and the experiences of the sequel directors apparently trapped within it. As the director of *Stepfather 2, Leatherface: The Texas Chainsaw Massacre III, Puppet Master 4* and *5* and *Pumpkinhead 2: Blood Wings*, Jeff Burr became the definitive franchise filmmaker over the course of an intense five year period from 1989 to 1994, and this chapter focusses on his relationship with the franchise.

Although fledgling companies like Trimark and Blue Rider also relied upon tried and tested talent after acquiring the rights to first films,⁴ Dimension experimented with first-time directors before financing their own ideas.⁵ This chapter also considers the extent to which, first, sequel-makers have delivered films in keeping with their attitudes and, second, the films are deemed satisfying by the established jury of studios, stars, censors and audiences. In order to achieve this objective I contrast Burr's experiences with those of sequel-makers James Cameron, Mick Garris, Renny Harlin, Anthony Hickox, Tommy Lee Wallace, Steve Miner, Brian Yuzna and Ronny Yu, each of whom has earned the title of sequel-maker. Finally, this chapter evaluates the success of these sequel-makers in relation to their subsequent and/or intervening careers outside of the Hollywood horror franchise.

Corman's Children

With an ongoing legacy of almost three hundred films as producer or director, genre-giant Roger Corman is one of Hollywood's most renowned living legends. His impact on the industry, and consequently the Hollywood horror franchise, is both far-reaching and profound. Starting off as a messenger for Fox, Corman became a story analyst before producing his first feature in 1954, the appropriately titled *Monster from the Ocean Floor*. As a key participant in what eventually became American International Pictures, Corman created genre movies based on market research and catchy titles with pre-conceived ad campaigns. By responding to audience tastes, Corman flourished in the fifties by maximizing budgets through a seemingly endless series of cost-effective tricks and techniques.[6]

In this respect, Corman secured his reputation by exploiting the ambition and inexperience of first generation film school graduates keen to break into Hollywood by any means necessary. With a canny eye for fresh talent, and a virtual open door policy as employer, Corman has been instrumental in providing such figures and future sequel-makers as Irvin Kerschner and Francis Ford Coppola with their directorial debuts.[7] Furthermore, Corman has been credited with launching the careers of directors Jonathan Demme, Ron Howard, Peter Bogdanovich and Martin Scorsese; therefore, his impact on modern cinema has been inevitable and is indisputable.

As an independent filmmaker in competition with television and big-budget Hollywood films, Corman was nevertheless frustrated by studio interference prior to distribution and the disproportionate allocation of profits thereafter. Consequently, he created New World Pictures in 1970. His second attempt at managing a production and distribution company (after Filmcorp in the 1960s), New World gave Corman complete control over all aspects of feature film production. After announcing his retirement from directing less than a year later, the full-time producer simultaneously championed the New Wave of cine-literate directors and an endless series of European auteurs whose films he picked up for distribution.

Achieving success with audiences, critics and the Academy, Corman can also be credited as the inspiration behind Bob Shaye and the Weinsteins. Indeed, New World's in-house approach to directors and the pursuit of a successful formula has been successfully appropriated by New Line and Miramax's Dimension Films, each playing a pivotal role in the selection of sequel directors for the Hollywood horror franchise.[8] As full-time producer and company director, Corman provided his future competitors with an effective foundation upon which to build their own empires.

After experimenting with Super-8 in his teenage years, the Ohio-born but Georgian-raised Jeff Burr enrolled at an L.A. film school. After dropping out during his undergraduate training, Burr nevertheless secured a position working in Corman's advertising department on the back of his student film *Divided We Fall*. Similarly inexperienced and ambitious, James Cameron was another aspiring filmmaker who convinced the company of his potential on the basis of a show reel he had apparently put together with dentists' money. Whereas Cameron began as a model builder[9] on the *Star Wars*–inspired *Battle Beyond the Stars*, a certified Corman classic of clichés and incoherency, Burr remained in the advertising department working on potential campaigns and concepts.

Roger Corman. From AIP to New Horizons, Roger Corman has been a permanent fixture within the Hollywood film industry for almost fifty years. His role in recruiting and exploiting new talent, concepts and themes has secured his place in the footnotes of many directors' careers — James Cameron included. With low budget, exploitation and imitation at the heart of his tried and tested philosophy, Corman is a key progenitor of the Hollywood horror franchise and its founders.

Reportedly inspired by George A. Romero and Sam Raimi, Burr left Corman's company to work on his own independent horror film. The project was produced by Darin Scott and Burr's brother, who also raised the necessary financing for the film, and designed as an EC comics–inspired anthology in the style of Romero's *Creepshow* and sequel director Roy Ward Baker's *Vault of Horror*. Created as a showcase for Burr's talents, the film starred horror icon Vincent Price as the sinister interviewee responsible for the four tales.[10]

The Offspring, or *From a Whisper to a Scream*, follows the familiar pattern set down by sequel-maker Jack Sholder, whose *Alone in the Dark* starred Donald Pleasance in 1982; while this same style was later adopted by Anthony Hickox for *Waxwork*—an homage to the pantheon of classic monsters, crammed with references and in-jokes. As director, co-writer and co-producer of *The Offspring*, Burr had an opportunity to develop ideas surrounded by an established support network. By strip-mining horror's rich heritage and filling their low-budget debuts with an abundance of references and eye-catching cameos, directors such as Sholder, Burr and Hickox demonstrated their dedication and commitment to the genre in these first films, which, although flawed, found a receptive audience on video.

Although James Cameron and Jim Wynorski adopted Corman as an unofficial mentor, others openly acknowledged the way in which previous professional and personal relationships were instrumental in securing them their first franchise film. Mick Garris, for example, infiltrated the industry as a publicist and celebrity interviewer for Channel Z's *Fantasy Film Festival* before accepting a job as a publicist at Universal. Here he made a series of invaluable contacts, including David Cronenberg, who would later recommend him as a writer for *The Fly II*, and Steven Spielberg, who hired Garris as a writer and then director on *Amazing Stories*. Such progression saw New Line offer Garris *Critters 2* as a writing/directing package.

Similarly, *Waxwork*'s Hickox exploited his association with Vestron to raise the financing for his vampire western spoof *Sundown: The Vampire in Retreat* before directing a *Waxwork* sequel.[11] Irrespective of their origins, and often in conjunction with such figures, companies and connections as Corman, Vestron and Spielberg, these and other future sequel-makers were targeted and stereotyped by the industry from the outset.

Released in 1987, the same year as Burr's first film (and eight months prior to its nearest contemporary companion piece, *Fatal Attraction*), Joseph Ruben's *The Stepfather* was an effective thriller and cutting edge satire of Reaganism, traditional family values and one man's disillusionment with the American Dream. Written by mystery writer Donald Westlake, the film was loosely based on the case of John List, the New Jersey killer who murdered his own family. Despite accusations of mis-marketing and a lukewarm response at the U.S. box office, the film was a sleeper hit, thereby prompting ITC to begin work on a sequel after convincing Terry O'Quinn to resume the title role.

Burr was approached by ITC on account of his debut feature and accepted the assignment, with his brother once again onboard. Predominantly a thematic and narrative retread of Ruben's first film, Burr's sequel nevertheless exploited the inherent black comedy of the scenario without detracting from the suspense. After a rushed yet relatively straightforward 25-day shoot, Burr delivered an effective follow-up that expanded on the first film without any form of desecration.

Scheduled to coincide with the release of Universal's *Jaws* sequel, Joe Dante's *Piranha* was Corman's exploitative cash-in on the Hollywood blockbuster, and one that came under Spielberg's protection when Universal considered legal action. Convinced he was "making the worst movie in history,"[12] Dante intentionally doused the film with comedy, adhering to the producer's guidelines regarding the timing of attacks and gratuitous nudity. Successful enough to warrant a sequel, Corman agreed to distribute a follow-up after Dante's departure,[13] and offered *Piranha II: The Spawning* to James Cameron as his first directing job, in light of his progress and special effects background.

According to Cameron, his first sequel experience lasted two and a half weeks on a shoot characterized by a lack of finance, organization and communication. Repeatedly under attack as an outsider from Ovidio G. Assonitis, the film's executive producer (and director of the 1977 *Jaws* imitation *Tentacles*), Cameron was fired and flew back to Los Angeles, with the picture completed in his absence.

Cast somewhere between Burr's and Cameron's first sequel experiences, Hickox's *Hellraiser III* had a troubled pre-production history that impacted upon the film.[14] Hickox's belated arrival was the beginning of a demanding shoot in which an ambitious script, deprived of an appropriate budget, forced the filmmakers to rely on traditional cheats and limited choices when it came to individual set-ups.

Burr shot his *Stepfather* sequel in December and delivered it to ITC in time for a scheduled April release date. However, the company was impressed enough to consider giving the film a brief theatrical run. After selling theatrical rights to Miramax, the producers subjected the film to a series of test screenings before approaching Burr with their findings and suggestions for improvement. As Miramax's first franchise acquisition, *Stepfather II* received the now standard pre-distribution procedure in which "Harvey Scissorhands"[15] removed around eight minutes of character development in favor of additional gore sequences, replacing the TV broadcast scenes and re-shooting one of the film's key sequences — the hanging of Caroline Williams' character Matty. With Burr already occupied on his second sequel, such changes were completed without the director's participation or approval.

Miramax's attempts to make a roller coaster ride out of Burr's slow-building sequel were to the detriment of the film but in keeping with standard slasher conventions and clichés. Rendered "20 percent less effective"[16] from Burr's perspective, *Stepfather II* nevertheless benefited from O'Quinn's riveting performance, a vital ingredient recognized by the director in his

Piranha II: The Spawning (James Cameron, 1982). In this creature feature sequel, Cameron saw to it that the monsters evolved in order to offer audiences something fresh to feast their eyes upon. In this shot here, one of the film's many flying killers feasts on a victim's eye. Indeed, when Cameron's spawn served up fish with wings, and such kitsch set pieces as a full-on beach attack and gratuitous nudity, audiences were at least compensated for their time (so long as they didn't look too closely). For the director, this first filmmaking experience marked the beginning of his own battle to make the films he wanted — and this meant teaming up with a supportive producer.

publicity for the film and cited as the only reason behind his decision to direct the Hollywood horror franchise.

Having since stated that "if there's a theme to the movies we make, it's about the outsider who can come in and change things,"[17] Harvey Weinstein's philosophy was also applied to Hickox's *Hellraiser III*, the company's second sequel purchase prior to the creation of Dimension Films. Similarly acquired after completion, this second case of postproduction interference involved the initially reticent return of first film director Clive Barker. The author/director had disapproved of Hickox's selection and was dissatisfied with aspects of the finished film. Described by screenwriter Peter Atkins as both a sequel and prequel to *Hellbound* that completed the trilogy, the narrative dragged Pinhead's duality center stage for a target audience of American teens in terms of look, location and soundtrack.

Keen to promote the film with a "Clive Barker Presents" prefix, however, Miramax agreed to Barker's terms of "total control ... to remake the picture the way I wanted it."[18] This arrangement saw a significant amount of restructuring, re-shoots and additional effects sequences as Barker temporarily reclaimed the franchise and proclaimed the film a "50/50 split between"[19] his and Hickox's vision. Innovative in its early use of CGI, the film represented an uneasy compromise that suffered two further indignities at the hands of the MPAA.[20] Nevertheless, it highlighted studios' preference for first film directors and their endorsement as a means of promoting the Hollywood horror franchise

Prior to Miramax's involvement with these first sequels, Cameron could not afford to abandon his first film, and faced a far worse scenario on *Piranha II*.[21] According to Cameron in subsequent interviews, his response to such overwhelming interference was to break into the editing room after dark and reconstruct the film the way he wanted it. The experience made the director "mistrustful of other people who have creative power on a film."[22] Refusing to abandon his first film despite such opposition, Cameron's determination differed from that of many other outsiders who had begun work on other projects during such extended post-production periods.

With less creative, financial and emotional investment in either the project or the franchise's longevity, outsiders were easily distanced and dissuaded from any further involvement out of economic necessity and a lack of contractually negotiated creative control. However, in refraining from any public disputes with the producers and distributors in order to further their respective careers and protect their reputations within the industry, outsiders such as Hickox and Burr reinforced the negative stereotype of sequel directors as "hacks" and confirmed it in subsequent films.

The Stepfather Franchise

Whether symptomatic of their outsider status or the franchiser's perception of their limited role in the filmmaking process, varying levels of dissatisfaction have been expressed by filmmakers. However, their association with a franchise has often elicited interest from other studios keen to exploit ownership of specific titles and the experience of these franchise filmmakers. In other words, despite their previous outsider status on first sequels, directors with franchise associations are valued by marketing departments attempting to secure pre-sales. Greg Spence and Brian Trenchard Smith, for example, were offered sequels to *The Prophecy* and *Leprechaun* by the same companies for which they had recently made *Children of the Corn IV* and *Night of the Demons 2*.

Similarly, Trimark approached established sequel directors Hickox and Brian Yuzna to resurrect their recently acquired titles *Warlock* and *Return of the Living Dead*. Indeed, New Line Cinema applied this stringent career stereotyping when approaching Jeff Burr as a potential candidate to direct *The Texas Chainsaw Massacre III* after screening a preview tape of *Stepfather 2*. By accepting the job (in spite of his prior experiences) Burr also bought into this process of mutual exploitation.

However, not all sequel-makers made two franchise films in such quick succession. Both Steve Miner and Renny Harlin made belated returns to the genre and the franchise with *Halloween H20* and *Exorcist: The Beginning* fifteen years after their first sequels.[23] Miner, who had worked with Jamie Lee Curtis on *Forever Young*, and directed several genre films since his *Friday the 13th* origins, was approached by the actress after her attempts to secure John Carpenter's return were unsuccessful. Harlin, on the other hand, was one of several directors invited to comment on Schrader's prequel as a result of his prior associations with Warner Bros. and prequel star Stellan Skarsgard.[24]

Indeed, studios and producers have characteristically deferred to sequel directors and previous collaborators to take over a franchise during the production process. *Omen* producer Harvey Bernhard, for example, turned to close personal friend and *Escape from the Planet of the Apes* director Don Taylor for *Damien: Omen II* after firing initial selection Mike Hodges three weeks into the shoot.[25] This was after proclaiming to *Variety* that Hodges "must have seen [*The Omen*] 15 or 20 times to make sure he'll keep the sequel in line with it."[26] Although Taylor was Bernhard's first choice replacement, Burr recalls how he was "probably the 50th choice"[27] for *Leatherface: Texas Chainsaw Massacre III*, based on the reports and reception he received from those outside and inside the industry.

Reports have indeed described how the *Chainsaw* sequel was offered to outsiders John McNaughton and Peter Jackson, who had impressed New Line with their debut films *Henry: Portrait of a Serial Killer* and *Bad Taste*. Moreover, New Line's selection of these two talented yet wildly different directors was indicative of their indecisive attitude towards the material. Having vetoed special effects artist Tom Savini, a strategy covered in Chapter 4 and later explored on *Freddy vs. Jason* (until conflicts over the film's budget prompted Rob Bottin's departure), New Line eventually hired Jonathan Beutel for *Leatherface*. However, reported contractual obligations on the *Alien Nation* TV series saw the deal fall through and the project thrown into development hell. It was at this point that Burr cautiously stepped into the breach on the understanding that he could rework some elements of the script.

Since *Leatherface*, New Line has continued this strategy of hiring sequel-makers, from James Isaac on *Jason X*, an appointment rooted in the director's long-standing relationship with Sean Cunningham, to Ronny Yu's *Freddy vs. Jason*. Whereas some sequel-makers were approached by studios, others actively pursued such projects on account of the production's profile and potential for career development, with the most famous example being James Cameron's supposed act of "career suicide"[28] on *Aliens*.

After *Piranha II*, Cameron salvaged his directorial career by writing an original script[29] suited to his special effects background and potential budgetary allowance. Insofar as *Piranha II* played a part in this process, Cameron only used the credit, for want of a better word, to get his second film off the ground. Afterwards *Piranha II* was all but dropped from his resume (in much the same way that the director has disassociated himself from his *Rambo: First Blood Part II* script).

With the unwavering support and loyalty of fledgling producer and fellow New World alumnus Gale Ann Hurd, *The Terminator* was tailored to Cameron's talents and interests as a filmmaker. After two years the project found a home at Hemdale, with a deal that saw Cameron sign away the sequel rights and Hurd resist Hollywood's attempts to buy the script without Cameron attached.[30] Having extensively prepped the film, the director nevertheless faced interference and a lack of support from distributor Orion during postproduction.[31] *The Terminator*'s success allowed Cameron to negotiate his way into the *Aliens* director chair—a decision with "absolutely no logic to it"[32] other than the fact that the director "thought it would be cool."[33] Intimidated and seduced by the idea of directing a sequel to Ridley Scott's "vicious shocker,"[34] Cameron inadvertently became modern horror's first sequel-maker. Indeed, what has continued to distinguish this director from his contemporaries is his capacity to commit fully to a project and its potential, despite the risks involved.

The future and success of many franchise films has been determined by the production company behind it and reflected in the allocated budget and intended method of distribution. Prior to the current fondness for big-budget remakes designed to resurrect a Hollywood horror franchise from the seventies,[35] several sequels had been commissioned on the understanding that they would be released directly to video/DVD, whereas others, such as *Omen IV* and *The Birds II*, were to be screened on network or cable television channels.

This latter category also included Mick Garris' *Psycho IV*, a sequel the director actively campaigned for on the back of John Landis' personal recommendation and promise of on-screen participation. The film was commissioned by Universal's Sid Sheinberg as the "ideal high profile low risk production"[36] to publicize the studio's new Florida theme park. New Line hoped Burr's *Leatherface* would resurrect the *Texas Chainsaw* franchise and take over from the recently ailing *Elm Street* films as the company's most profitable commodity. Under the influence of such high expectations internally, this project was subjected to intense round table scrutiny prior to Burr's arrival.

In direct contrast to Burr's pressure-fuelled inauguration, Cameron was reportedly taken aback yet relieved that *Aliens* hardly seemed to register on Fox's radar — the studio was preoccupied with its high profile summer release *Space Camp*. Whether cynical, shrewd or half-hearted, the origins of franchise films often exposed a lack of long-term insight or forethought on behalf of franchisers whose motives and ambitions were only infrequently backed up by adequate resources, understanding or experience.

Burr graduated from the comparatively low-key *Stepfather* franchise and entered New Line's all-too-literal *Texas Chainsaw Massacre* as an outsider late in the pre-production process. Cameron, however, had the benefit of recently acquired clout afforded to him by the success of *The Terminator*. Consequently, when the creative team of Cameron and Hurd experienced an unfortunate reversal of fortune during negotiations, in that Fox was not happy with Hurd on board as producer, Cameron was able to fight in her corner and persuade the studio to back down. Hurd the producer was not one of Hollywood's many "frustrated directors"[37] and did not interfere on set or in the editing room.

In contrast to Hurd's collaborative approach, producer Bernhard continued to hire and fire directors of *The Omen* franchise. *Halloween 5*'s Dominique Othenin-Girard became a casualty after two weeks of shooting on *Omen IV: The Awakening*, discovering too late that the "*Omen* road shows ... were a one man operation,"[38] with Bernhard "used to full control."[39] Similarly, New Line's increasingly corporate structure relegated Burr as a franchise outsider from the start. Far from being in a strong position to assert his authority during an endless series of rewrites on the *Leatherface* script, the

Aliens (James Cameron, 1986). As franchise outsiders, writer-director James Cameron and producer Gale Ann Hurd, pictured together, presented a united front to both the studio, who attempted to come between them for a second time, and the sequel's British crew. Furthermore, when it came to the cast, Cameron also had to cajole star Sigourney Weaver into adopting a Rambo-esque persona for Ripley in preparation for the final showdown between her and the Alien Queen. However, geographical distance and relatively low expectations kept Fox executives out of the process once the film entered production.

director was isolated and unable to direct the Hollywood horror franchise in keeping with his ideas.

Often allocated lower budgets than their predecessors, sequel directors have either been unable to secure the participation of previous franchise actors or forced to cast relative unknowns. Consequently, producers have also shrewdly employed actors with recognizable genre credentials, on account of their appearance or musical background, to attract audiences.[40] Accordingly, New Line exploited Ken Foree's *Dawn of the Dead* and *From Beyond* connection, and arranged a brief cameo by *Chainsaw 2*'s final girl as an intrepid reporter in search of the cannibal clan in the opening scenes of *Leatherface*.[41] However, Burr was unable to secure Gunnar Hansen for the title role on account of New Line's reluctance to pay above scale, given the limited budget.

In conjunction with this approach to casting, directors often retained their favorite (affordable) cast and crew members as a means of ensuring some continuity and quality control. Hickox, for example, recast *Hellraiser III*'s Paula Marshall for *Warlock: Armageddon*, and Burr contacted R.A. Mihailoff to take on *Leatherface* after working with the actor on his student film. Much like it has the sequel director, the Hollywood horror franchise has also heralded the rise of the sequel actor. Affordable and marketable to target audiences, stars such as Foree and Lance Henriksen have been equally stereotyped by the industry and recast by directors and franchisers throughout their careers.

The narrative departure of Burr's film preempted many casting issues and the subsequent need for negotiations. Cameron, on the other hand, who completed his *Aliens* screenplay based on Fox's assurance that Sigourney Weaver was already attached, later discovered the actress was unaware of the project. In response, an increasingly studio-savvy Cameron orchestrated a series of events guaranteed to ensure Fox's support and readiness to meet the actress' asking price. The return of increasingly expensive franchise stars Anthony Perkins, Jamie Lee Curtis and Robert Englund has been integral to the plots and potential success of *Psycho IV*, *Halloween H20* and *Freddy vs. Jason*. Their cooperation and creative input was secured and appeased by financial incentives — often at the expense of the sequel director.

However, on Miner's *Halloween H20* the franchise family was fiercely divided. With franchiser Malek Akkad on one side as the self-proclaimed "protector of the franchise,"[42] and star Curtis proudly on the other as both "an unbilled executive producer"[43] and "Laurie Strode's guardian angel,"[44] Miramax was caught in the middle. In siding with Curtis, Miner found a mutually supportive ally, just as Mick Garris agreed with returning screenwriter Joseph Stefano in wanting Perkins to tone down his performance for

Psycho IV.[45] Indeed, with various parties to please in terms of profit participation and production personnel, sequel scripts for high profile films were revised innumerable times in accordance with a franchise family's conflicting viewpoints.

The Franchise Family Massacre

Although James Cameron had to court Brandywine Productions' approval during preproduction, his *Aliens* script was, according to Sammon, based on the remnants of the gutted *Rambo* screenplay and "a pre-existing story ... Cameron had created years earlier ... originally titled *E.T.*"[46] and then *Mother*. As previously established, grafting elements of an existing treatment, script or film into or onto a franchise has been increasingly adopted by companies like Dimension,[47] and seen in rejected proposals for *Psycho IV* and *Jason X* with regard to *Spellbound* and *The Shining*.

Whereas Cameron was *Aliens*' scriptwriter from the outset, Burr was an unwelcome outsider on the *Leatherface* project whose late arrival and revisionist intentions were largely unwanted and seldom incorporated. For example, Burr's interest in developing a "sick juxtaposition"[48] between the Final Girl's dysfunctional family and the warped interactions of the Leatherface clan was rejected. Similarly, his suggestion to shoot on 16mm in Texas to increase the film's authenticity was swiftly discarded. In contrast, Renny Harlin, in his role of studio-appointed savior, had to ensure his *Exorcist* prequel adhered to a mutually agreed checklist of franchise ingredients seemingly drawn up in accordance with perceived audience expectations.

Eschewing such authenticity, Burr's follow-up was filmed on the outskirts of Hollywood, next door to the Magic Mountain theme park. Although this location was an improvement over Garris' locale on *Psycho IV*, where the shoot also served as a tourist attraction, the production was in close proximity to New Line's offices and subjected to unwelcome set visits from studio executives. Alternatively, shooting *Aliens* at London's Pinewood Studios saw Cameron and Hurd free from impromptu studio visits by Fox executives throughout principal photography. However, Cameron has since revealed that in the absence of a strong studio presence he was faced with a "scornful British crew that was convinced it was working on a crappy sequel to a great [British-directed] thriller."[49] This led to his firing the cinematographer, and Hurd extending that threat to others when the potential for mutiny surfaced.

For Cameron, it was Sigourney Weaver's politics that proved most problematic, with her anti-gun stance seeming somewhat absurd in light of his action-packed screenplay. Moreover, the director has since characterized their relationship by describing himself as the throttle and Weaver as the brakes.[50] Since the majority of low-budget projects are now being shot in Vancouver or Eastern Europe to reduce costs, Burr's Hollywood shoot has become more the exception than the rule. Although this has reduced the opportunity for set visits, it has, unfortunately, also increased the potential for studio dissatisfaction and interference during post-production.

Although Weaver strongly disapproved of *Aliens'* apparent glorification of gun violence, Cameron's authority as director was never called into question. Burr, on the other hand, was reportedly fired after five weeks of filming by New Line's appointed second in command, who, according to the director, "hated the movie, hated the script, [and] hated the idea of making it."[51] (Burr was quickly re-hired.) As a replacement sequel director on *Leatherface*, Burr was isolated from his familiar support group for the first time. Moreover, he had to come to terms with Hollywood's corporate structure and "a gauntlet of people you had to run through to make a decision"[52] over the course of an ambitious thirty-day shoot. For the director, this sequel's downfall can be traced back to its elevated status, mainstream aspirations as New Line's latest potential cash cow, and its roots as an independent horror film.

In direct contrast to Burr's isolationist experience on *Leatherface*, James Isaac, an established special effects artist and surviving sequel director, was attached to *Jason X* from the start. With a pitch to producer Cunningham and distributor New Line that involved trading on previous working relationships and twenty years of experience in the industry, Isaac promised to "put together a team of talented people ... who wouldn't normally work on Jason part 10."[53] Furthermore, he helped develop the script with screenwriter Todd Farmer, brought in his own crew, and personally hired everyone on the project for the Toronto-based shoot.

Despite continuing the franchise's fondness for unscrupulous authority figures, promiscuous teens and creative deaths, Isaac's *Jason X* avoided Camp Crystal Lake in all but one scene.[54] Instead, the film substituted scares for science fiction[55] via such staple plot devices as an exploding ship and malfunctioning airlock. Prior to this combination of science fiction and splatter, Cameron had distanced his *Alien* sequel from its predecessor via a generic shift and action-orientated "Vietnam analogy."[56] Just as Cameron's *Piranha II* featured genetically modified piranhas with wings, *Aliens* ditched Scott's claustrophobic scare tactics and allegedly "stupid concept"[57] of having humans transform into eggs in favor of a termite-esque approach and grandiose egg-laying Queen. Although Cameron's sequels epitomized this approach of slipping into other established formats and sub-genres, directors Brian

Trenchard-Smith and Brian Yuzna, with *Leprechaun 3* and *Return of the Living Dead Part 3*, have also demonstrated that science fiction, comedy and romance can resuscitate a franchise. However, this was only possible so long as the frequency and potency of the special effects sequences remained intact, and the central conceits of the script and franchise were adhered to.[58]

Scripted by David J. Schow, *Leatherface* was an intense and visceral bloodbath that was developed by New Line and Burr as a return to the suspense of the first film. After criticizing the script for being "a gore-a-thon,"[59] the director ironically focused on the skewed family interactions and the importance of a tag line appropriated from the previous film, "Saw is Family."[60] In contrast, Tobe Hooper's earlier sequel, *The Texas Chainsaw Massacre 2*, boldly departed from the first film's "through the looking glass" approach to drag audiences down the rabbit hole to meet the circus-like horrors and rotting sideshows of an "American Dream gone sour."[61] With its underground labyrinth resembling an intestinal tract littered with partially digested degenerates, Hooper's second Sawyer clan no longer operated outside society.

Interpreted by Hanke as "a blistering indictment of Reaganism and the 'Me' generation,"[62] *Chainsaw 2* controversially made implicit sexual connotations explicit and combined them with an EC comics approach. Targeted at those audiences that had not "appreciated or understood"[63] the first film, Hooper wanted to solicit "guilty laughter"[64] at the outrageous effects, and reveled in such disparate sub-genres as the rape revenge film and culture clash comedy through biting satire. Burr "absolutely despised"[65] this film, and his follow-up was a reactionary departure from it and comparable to Hickox's approach on *Hellraiser III*. Both *The Texas Chainsaw Massacre 2* and *Hellbound: Hellraiser II* were awkward marriages of commercialism and cinematic sadism culminating in a Final Girl's extended fight for survival.

Whereas Tommy Lee Wallace's *Fright Night* retread, *Fright Night Part 2*, substituted vampire Jerry Dandridge for an avenging sister and her acolytes, both Cameron and Miner took this approach one step further in *Aliens* and *Halloween H20*, with their tales of redemption and revenge. These films revolved around returning characters Ripley and Laurie Strode, whose transformations from final girls to fiercely protective mothers struck a crowd-pleasing chord with audiences. In contrast, by denying the Final Girl any emotional depth or backstory, Burr's *Leatherface* was hindered by a lack of audience investment in the protagonist. This absence detracts from our ability to root for her revenge and survival.

Under strict studio directives to break from Hooper's narrative and not contact the director, Burr was brought on board to create a film that would focus on the titular character (at the expense of overexposure). Consequently,

Burr's film featured an adoptive family, in keeping with the first movie, at the expense of continuity, innovation and emotional investment. This selective approach towards previous installments was often dictated by a perceived audience response, and also fed into New Line's stipulation that *Jason X* should disregard the redundant resolutions of previous entries yet accommodate *Freddy vs. Jason*.

In a reversal of the events affecting Burr's sequel, Ronnie Yu drew on his marketing experience to dispute New Line's demands for sufficient protagonist backstories in *Freddy vs. Jason*. Appealing to basic expectations, Yu included the stereotypical characters and clichés associated with each franchise. From post-coital slaughters and shower scenes to surrealistic deaths,[66] the director was shepherded through the process by aficionado (and executive producer) Robert Shaye to ensure he pleased and appeased fans of both franchises.[67]

With a deep respect for John Carpenter's film and blatant disregard for all that came after, Steve Miner also directed *Halloween H20* "like I'm the audience."[68] In doing so he married such clichés as introductory voice-overs, the early dispensing of returning characters and an uncommonly judicious use of nightmarish flashbacks to enough references, reversals and in-jokes to appeal to the post–*Scream* audience in an economical yet suspenseful account of a Final Girl's revenge. Taking the narrative forward and pushing for a character-based resolution, Miner's sequel reaped the benefits of narrative continuity, returning characters and a contemporary High School setting to create a contemporary classic of the Hollywood horror franchise.

However, the direction of a franchise and the level of respect, fidelity and continuity afforded previous installments has been subject to studio agendas. United in their much-publicized decision to direct the franchise with respect for the first film, sequel directors empathized with fans throughout the publicity trail as a means of endearing their projects to them. With the potential for genuine scares somewhat restricted by an unfamiliar African landscape and post–World War II setting, Renny Harlin's *Exorcist* prequel was further constrained by its characters and thematic content. By echoing shots, sounds and images from the first film, Harlin slavishly combined the iconography of Pazuzu and Captain Howdy with a standard case of cinematic misdirection. Furthermore, the final act evoked all the stereotypes associated with William Friedkin's original film.[69]

However, both Harlin and *Psycho IV*'s Mick Garris could not compete with the first film in terms of impact. Indeed, with over thirty years of parodies, clichés and spoofs to soften the suspense or shock impact, some sequel directors could only aspire to acceptability insofar as audiences were concerned. Nevertheless, Garris felt protected by the existence of previous entries, Stefano's script[70] and Perkins' presence, all of which gave the film an air of authenticity. In this respect, later sequel directors have been less intimidated on account of their previous experience and the reception of previous entries.

Post-production frequently exposed the inconsistencies of a studio's approach and highlighted their lack of focus and direction — at sequel directors' expense. Conclusions and shock epilogues were often the first elements to be altered after test-screenings and first film comparisons. Although James Cameron created one of the greatest confrontations in franchise, if not cinematic, history with *Aliens*, the director nevertheless fell back onto Ridley Scott's original resolution in which the Alien is jettisoned into space. A closing shot of not one but two sleeping beauties brought the narrative full circle, as the faint sound of a rogue face hugger slithered over the final credits.

Similarly, *Jason X*, *Halloween H20*, and many others cannibalized this template and concluded with an iconic shot and/or sequel-friendly set-up, be it Jason returning to a teen-infested campground or Laurie Strode maniacally standing over her brother's decapitated corpse. Furthermore, the prequels *Red Dragon* and *Exorcist: The Beginning* simultaneously achieved narrative closure and a definite link to the first film through choice dialogue and location.

Whereas Garris shot multiple endings for *Psycho IV* as part of a bid to preserve the mystery and, more importantly, generate publicity, New Line subjected Burr and Yu to endless re-shoots and alternative endings on *Leatherface* and *Freddy vs. Jason*. With shock epilogues and sequel set-ups shot then discarded on a regular basis, directors were charged with ending their sequel narrative on a satisfying note. Reportedly left alone during the initial editing period, Burr's post-production problems on *Leatherface* escalated after the first test-screening, attended by New Line's foreign and domestic department heads. Their response led to the removal of many objectionable sequences from the original negative. Furthermore, an ongoing dispute over the film's conclusion necessitated re-shoots, both with and without Burr's involvement, that rendered the film increasingly incoherent as characters were resurrected and sequences rewritten to accommodate an audience/franchise–friendly finale. Trapped between making a mainstream movie and an independent horror film, Burr faced a difficult situation that fostered conflict and mutual dissatisfaction.[71] Nevertheless, *Leatherface* fell under New Line's jurisdiction, and therefore the film had to fall in line with its corporate sensibilities prior to feedback from the MPAA.

Producers of the Hollywood horror franchise have undoubtedly reaped the benefits of high profile productions and exploited genre history through publicity and marketing. Many directors, however, have argued that first film reputations and current release strategies have adversely affected their film's treatment by the ratings board. Though kowtowing to the MPAA is viewed by *Return of the Living Dead Part 3*'s Brian Yuzna as a necessary business decision (so "long as there are some unrated festival prints and an unrated video around"[72]), the MPAA has repeatedly been criticized by filmmakers on account of its alleged double standards and enduring memory.

For example, Burr and New Line executive Mike De Luca cited Cannon's unrated release of *The Texas Chainsaw Massacre 2* as the reason behind the board's negative attitude towards *Leatherface*. They also bemoaned the inadequacy of the current system and the commercial suicide of the X-rating, and accused the board of being "harder on independents like New Line than on major companies."[73] A war of attrition that totaled a record-breaking eleven resubmissions[74] cost the company their December release date but raised the publicity and profile of the film in the press. Since *Leatherface*, New Line's franchises have benefited from a corporate structure more adept at anticipating ratings problems.[75] As gritty as it was grounded, Burr's film made few concessions to the video-gaming generation, yet was penalized for its realistic portrayal of violence in contrast to the comic book fantasy approach of other films.

Together, New Line and the censor rendered Burr's film "incoherent ... a hideous compromise,"[76] and one De Luca has accepted some responsibility for.[77] Moreover, the director has since conceded that his fatal mistake was in trying to make the film his own when it "can never be yours ... [and] never could be."[78] This admission that a fatal flaw was rooted in his own approach saw the director attempt to have his name "taken off the movie."[79]

Although Burr was unsuccessful, sequel director Rick Rosenthal took a stand and formally disowned his second sequel by successfully petitioning the DGA to have his name taken off *The Birds II: Lands End*. Rosenthal represents the most extreme case of rejection that often characterized the sequel director's reflections and audience responses. Just as *Jason X*'s James Isaac appealed to audiences to enter "theaters with an open mind,"[80] Burr has since described *Leatherface* as a "missed opportunity"[81] that "everyone was really primed to not like"[82] on account of its sequel status and Hooper's absence. From first mistakes to final regrets, Burr's involvement with New Line and the *Texas Chainsaw Massacre* franchise came at an important turning point in their respective histories, with the director retrospectively noting the irony that "the film I'm probably least proud of ... is the film that most people will see."[83]

Although Yu's *Freddy vs. Jason* shied away from William Castle's *Mr. Sardonicus* gimmick of letting the audience decide a character's fate,[84] the Hollywood horror franchise has increasingly courted the affirmation of audiences following the advent of cable, video and DVD. DVD in particular has provided many first films and follow-ups with a profitable afterlife. From Cameron's *Aliens: Special Edition* to the release of Schrader's *Dominion: Prequel to the Exorcist*, this additional source of revenue has allowed increasingly media-savvy audiences to pass judgment on alternative and extended cuts. In this way, studios and production companies have encouraged fans to "buy into" the postproduction nightmares of these films in retrospect. Just as Harlin passionately defended *Exorcist: The Beginning*,[85] Burr's *Leatherface* has undergone a similar reinvestigation and re-release — with New Line's financial support. Given the opportunity to critique his own work, the director has provided a subjective insight into the circumstances that surrounded the film's production after fourteen years and several other experiences with the Hollywood horror franchise.

Straight Into Darkness

James Cameron capitalized on *Aliens'* success by maintaining his relationship and funding arrangement with Fox on his next project — an ambitious underwater fantasy. *The Abyss* continued Cameron's fondness for science fiction and kick-started an obsession with underwater technologies. Burr, on the other hand, made a reactionary retreat from studio and genre-based filmmaking with *Eddie Presley*, a character-driven comedy-drama based on writer/star Duane Whitaker's play. The film was a definite return to Burr's humble beginnings following a brief but ironically appropriate association with the TV series *Land of the Lost*. Characteristically featuring genre stalwarts in supporting and cameo roles, *Eddie Presley* was about, for and by independent industry outsiders. Directors Burr and Yu both subsequently found work as independent filmmakers, temporarily escaping industry stereotyping and the trappings of franchise association. However, many sequel-makers were either unable to find projects or were restricted to a combination of TV series and occasional features before similar offers materialized.

Whereas Miner and Isaac exploited their genre associations and moved from slasher films to monster movies,[86] others embarked upon a more surreptitious return to the Hollywood horror franchise. *Return of the Living Dead Part 3*'s Yuzna, for example, started his own serial killer franchise with *The*

Dentist in 1996 after trading on his *Re-Animator* connection as a contributor to the Lovecraft anthology *Necronomicon*. Similarly, Wallace shot a relatively successful yet tepid and under-funded adaptation of King's *IT* after his successful *Fright Night* retread before returning to franchise filmmaking with *Vampires: Los Muertos* in 2002.

However, it was Garris who most effectively sidestepped the franchise. Following a brief return to *Amazing Stories* before developing *Hocus Pocus* for Disney, Garris established a long-running association with Stephen King on *Sleepwalkers* that continued through TV-bound adaptations of *The Stand*, *The Shining*, and *Desperation*.[87] This attachment to King, however, belies a more stereotyped and widespread sensibility at work as directors often traded on reputations and relationships by attaching themselves to another established brand name, literary or otherwise. Evident in the careers of Stuart Gordon and more recently Don Coscarelli, the industry has allowed sequel directors to work in a similar vein as a means of exploiting their association with the Hollywood horror franchise.

Similarly, Burr's follow-up to *Eddie Presley* grew out of his shared history with low-budget mogul Charles Band, which began with meetings over *Ghost Town*—a horror Western hybrid Empire pictures had been developing in the late eighties.[88] Whereas Garris deliberately avoided any further direct association with the Hollywood horror franchise, Band persuaded Burr to direct *Puppet Master 4* and *5* back to back, a cost-effective approach previously adopted for the company's *Subspecies* and *Trancers* franchises. Although these films were originally conceived by Band as Full Moon's first theatrical venture that Band himself would direct, the script was split in two and rewritten as a pair of direct-to-video sequels.

Despite his negative experiences on *Leatherface* and, to a lesser extent, *Stepfather 2*, Burr not only returned to the Hollywood horror franchise, but also accepted this *Puppet Master* assignment as a replacement director with only two weeks' preparation time. Whether born of desperation, dedication or career-based masochism, Burr's apparent willingness to reprise a familiar role under similar circumstances once again came with a mainstream mandate. Having explored time travel in its third entry, *Toulon's Revenge*, this franchise's sequel scripts set up a new story arc to attract a wider audience, and carried over iconic puppets and moments from previous entries. By lessening the horrific elements in favor of a more light-hearted approach, these back-to-back projects saw a switch in the puppets' allegiance, and the introduction of new villains and puppets alike. Following Full Moon's directives to the best of his ability, Burr fulfilled his clearly defined role without the problems that plagued his previous attempts. Without the pressure of a high profile or weighty audience expectations, Burr thrived in this arena of financially restrictive autonomy.

Arguably the director was attracted to the fantastic elements of the franchise and the opportunity to become a part of the Full Moon family. Burr's decision to return to the Hollywood horror franchise, with its financial security, was not an isolated one, since *Leprechaun 3*'s Brian Trenchard-Smith signed on for a science fiction-esque *Leprechaun in Space*. Likewise, despite having his name removed from *The Birds II*, Rick Rosenthal directed *Halloween: Resurrection* (aka *Halloween 8*) almost twenty years after his first *Halloween* sequel (*Halloween II*). However, he soon found an alternate and extended, yet no less involved, *Halloween* franchise family in place. Contradicted and forced to solicit approval, Rosenthal clashed with star Jamie Lee Curtis and producer Akkad throughout the production process, highlighting how little had changed in the intervening years since *Part II*.

Although Tommy Lee Wallace was a third returning director with *Vampires: Los Muertos*, his involvement was more on account of his long-standing friendship with Carpenter, whose Storm King Productions co-produced the direct-to-video sequel. Nevertheless, each of these cases reflects the way in which franchise production companies and directors mutually exploited one another in the search for success.

As such, the Motion Picture Corporation of America approached sequel directors Anthony (*Waxwork*) Hickox and Tony (*Hellraiser II*) Randel for the follow-up to Winston's *Pumpkinhead*.[89] However, when Randel left the project, Burr stepped back into the breach with only three weeks of pre-production remaining. This time, however, the director ensured previous collaborator Will Huston was on board to help flesh out the script. After loyally placing a positive spin on the original film's low budget and status as a 50s "B movie in the best sense"[90] during interviews, Burr attacked Winston's first film for being slow and "little more than a slasher movie."[91] Having criticized the pacing and content, Burr's *Pumpkinhead II: Blood Wings* fell back on uncomfortable clichés and failed to capture the atmosphere for which its predecessor had been praised. With the inclusion of a black and white prologue, which insufficiently expanded the Pumpkinhead mythos, the film appeared amateurish and ineffective. Arguably more interested in developing the franchise away from feature films and into an accompanying video game, the Motion Picture Corporation of America employed Burr on the basis of his sequel-directing reputation. Without the necessary budget, backing or guidance from Band, Burr's fifth franchise film was a half-hearted and ill-thought-out enterprise that failed to make an impact.

Despite this setback, Burr was finally given the opportunity to help *create* a horror franchise with Republic Picture's *Night of the Scarecrow*. His first genre film without a number since 1987's *The Offspring*, the movie was far more effective than *Pumpkinhead II*. Both featured a Midwest setting and examined the origins and vengeful spirits of American folklore, but this second slice of dark Americana was atmospheric and engaging, with actual scares and solid acting. Rather than wallowing in the constraints and clichés of the genre, this time around the director exploited the concept and limited production values to his advantage. Shepherded and supported by veteran horror/franchise producer Barry Bernardi[92] on this occasion, Burr wove a more compelling narrative, complete with creative deaths, before concluding with a relatively satisfying finale. However, despite Burr's intentions and the concept's potential, *Night of the Scarecrow* has yet to warrant a follow-up. Consequently, the director returned to the Full Moon fold, making more palatable pictures for the family market—*Johnny Mysto: Boy Wizard* and *The Werewolf Reborn*.

Following these family-orientated features, Burr once again adopted a reactionary approach by making a second break from Full Moon to direct *Spoiler*. A futuristic prison-set action film, the script's focus was an innocent (every)man's struggle to re-establish a connection with his family against all odds. With a narrative liberally borrowed from such films as *Demolition Man*, *Total Recall* and Stuart Gordon's *Fortress*, the actual production was, according to Burr, appropriately shot for around half a million dollars in eighteen days "using cannibalized sets from two other movies."[93] Downbeat in execution and littered with Burr's fondness for cameo players, the film showed some promise, particularly in relation to key sequences, yet faltered in its overall effect. In his defense, the director has since revealed that he was removed from the film right after shooting. Furthermore, he alleges a producer who wanted to direct the movie in post-production prevented him from putting together a first cut of the film. Disenfranchised once more, the director adopted the pseudonym Cameron Van Daacke and distanced himself from the film. In this respect, Burr's career echoes Cameron's early experiences on *Piranha II*, with producers and directors clashing over creative control and final cut.

After experiencing early success and a sustained involvement with the Hollywood horror franchise, Burr's career descended into a dependable yet creatively dissatisfying on/off relationship with Full Moon entertainment. This began with back-to-back sequels and culminated in family-orientated fairy tales targeted at the *Harry Potter/Goosebumps* audience. With the financial security of Full Moon replacing the Hollywood horror franchise, Burr returned to Band's company after *Spoiler* to make *The Boy with the X-Ray Eyes* and *Phantom Town*—a light-hearted version of Band's *Ghost Town* featuring an array of impressive sequences and references. In many ways superior to *Ghost Town*, and innovative in its use of Romanian locations, Burr's horror/Western hybrid is one of the few Full Moon entries to feature likable protagonists, some pitch-perfect scares and appeal to the *Pulse Pounders* preteen audience. However, during this period, Burr drew together the right creative team to make a successful break from his franchise/Full Moon past to produce an independent film for a different audience demographic.

Shot in Romania, Burr's 2004 film *Straight Into Darkness* was the direct result of his association with director of photography Viorel Gergevicij, who offered to co-finance the project through his recently established Silver Bullet production company. To secure his share of the funding, the director relied on previous supporters and collaborators and put together a dedicated creative team that included his brother Mark Hannah from *The Offspring*, and Chuck Williams and Will Huston from *Eddie Presley*. Written by Burr for Romanian actors and actual locations in close proximity to Band's multipurpose set, the director referenced a number of documentary and cinematic sources to create an ambitious yet achievable epic set during World War II.

A stark yet sumptuous story of two U.S. soldiers forced to navigate their way through the Nazi heartland, *Straight Into Darkness* effectively showcased Burr's talents. Furthermore, he exploited his previous genre experience to maximum effect, particularly in a number of disturbing sequences and encounters with cannibal priests and feral children playing at being freedom fighters. Indeed, Burr received an unprecedented amount of critical acclaim with a film that was tonally in keeping with his features outside of the Full Moon/franchise arena. Clearly afforded artistic license and creative control on account of his supportive financiers and dual role of writer and director, Burr benefited from being an integrated part of the production process from the outset. As such, this film presents a more accurate representation of his cumulative talents—which only highlights the restrictive nature of the Hollywood horror franchise and the industry it has come to represent.

Following *Straight Into Darkness*, Burr used the positive press attention to firmly reposition himself alongside his fellow independent filmmakers. In replicating Berlinger's return to documentary success, the director has also attempted to re-establish his credibility by drawing a very clear distinction between those films deserving of a "Jeff Burr Picture" credit and those that do not.[94] In a similar vein to Spielberg, Burr has begun to exploit an area of compromise wherein he may soon be able to alternate between personal pet projects and those commercially viable compromises for which he has become renowned.

The director's association with the Hollywood horror franchise has been resurrected on a number of occasions with his fleeting attachment to a pair of *Monster Man* sequels for Lion's Gate and the star-studded *The Demons 5*—characteristically featuring a plethora of veteran horror actors. Prior to these commercial enterprises, Burr homaged Coscarelli and Tarantino/Rodriguez with *Mil Mascaras vs. the Aztec Mummy* and *The Devil's Den*—a film whose synopsis cannibalizes *From Dusk Till Dawn* and *Underworld*. Having worked for both Corman and Band during the course of his twenty-year career, Burr has used imitation and the franchise to forge ahead in an increasingly difficult market. With numerous sequels, setbacks and self-penned projects, he has consistently proven his resilience and ensured his career longevity with juxtaposing ventures.

In an industry notorious for stereotyping its stars and product, the sequel-makers have fought with, for and against the Hollywood horror franchise. From chronologically correct continuations to comedies and spoofs, these directors have collectively addressed and challenged the franchise's complex needs. As a late and sometimes unwelcome addition to the franchise family, these seasoned outsiders were often relegated to the role of a vessel through which a studio, star or producer's version of the Hollywood horror franchise had to be filtered and preserved.

Indeed, this final chapter has clearly demonstrated the way in which sequel directors, like their franchise films, were frequently disrespected throughout the production process. Seduced by a myriad of push and pull factors, these directors fought against a diminishing role and the difficult responsibility of reconciling contractual obligations with their own ambitions and concerns. As a result, the Hollywood horror franchise has frequently seen these filmmakers, with the unique exception of James Cameron, enjoy and endure an ambivalently addictive relationship that shows no sign of ending.

Conclusions

"The film medium has always been parasitic and vampiric ... the movies are always interested in adapting."[1]
— David Cronenberg.

"I'm going to keep making this over until I get it right."[2]
— Sean S. Cunningham.

"Films aren't made, they're remade."[3]
— Irving Thalberg.

As part of the Hollywood horror franchise, filmmakers are immersed within a microcosm that encapsulates the cyclical nature of Hollywood film genres. They are also assimilated into the reigning studio system. Much like the classic genre system, the franchise expands upon the foundations of a tripartite system of production, distribution and consumption to seamlessly match concept and consumer as a means of ensuring financial success.

As a cultural and economic cash cow, the horror franchise's popularity is the result of notoriety, prejudice and predictability, and these are signposts for audiences, critics and censors alike. Supported by brand identities and fuelled by an effective combination of audience anticipation and corporate greed, it is a process of adaptation and mutual exploitation. Directors, studios and independents have consistently manipulated and mined the profitability of the Hollywood horror franchise through synergy, merchandising and any other method imaginable.

Bound by studios and audiences to replicate a film's success, irrespective of their relationship to it, filmmakers have consistently courted success and encountered pressure to adjust their own expectations. Throughout a process of collaboration and compromise they have attempted to reconcile the paradoxical need for conformity with a sense of innovation. For David Fincher in particular, "the lesson to be learned is that you can't take on an enterprise of this size and scope if you don't have a *Terminator* or *Jaws* behind you,"[4] especially as a first-time feature filmmaker working for Fox on *Alien 3*. In other words, the vast majority of directors, discounting the phenomenal success and autonomy afforded to James Cameron and Steven Spielberg, have been required to all but abandon an auteur-based fantasy in favor of a more realistic approach through their affiliation with the Hollywood horror franchise.

The Franchise Director

Directors' assimilation mirrored that of many independent production companies and distributors in that they were either bought up by the industry conglomerates or simply were unable to compete with them. For the Hollywood horror franchise, this shift to studio financing and control often impacted upon the way in which returning directors were allowed to redress the perceived inadequacies of a first installment, and the extent to which they could depart from its proven formula. Although many first films are representative of directors' attitudes towards filmmaking at that time, their involvement in sequels was sometimes devoid of personal attachment.

Indeed, some bore all the hallmarks of a standard business decision designed to ingratiate them with the studios and ensure their professional development. Rather than work against or outside Hollywood, directors such as Sam Raimi even sought acceptance and absolution from the very controversy they had initially courted. As a consequence, directors produced more palatable follow-ups to ensure an R-rating. Nevertheless, there were others who pioneered new ideas and reflected prior concerns, and even continued to challenge audience expectations and MPAA rulings.

Initially cautious to answer the collective cry of "What happened next?" few directors have been able to resist those push and pull factors designed to ensure loyalty and career longevity. Some directors cited contractual or moral obligations, whereas others did so out of industry coercion, frustration or simply the opportunity to direct another feature film. However, after a dissatisfying studio experience, filmmakers found the additional funding, increased autonomy and higher profile of a franchise film a shrewd decision. Indeed, Steven Spielberg, George Lucas and Francis Ford Coppola are indebted to the franchise and were followed by the likes of Richard Donner and Robert Zemeckis into the mainstream.[5] Seduced by its relative security, directors were drawn to the franchise by bigger names, budgets and backers.

For genre directors such as George A. Romero, Sam Raimi and Wes Craven, the opportunity to explore new themes and expand the mythos of the first film also paved the way for academic analysis, and a swifter elevation to auteur status and increased academic attention. This also applies to Larry Cohen and Frank Henenlotter, whose *It's Alive* and *Basket Case* trilogies have not only allowed them to develop characters, concepts and themes over a sustained period but also opened up the financing for other projects. There are tangible benefits.

In this respect, only David Cronenberg has notably avoided the franchise in favor of literary adaptations, sidestepping such industry trappings

Day of the Dead (George A. Romero, 1985). This iconic shot of Romero on the set of his third *Dead* film is an accurate metaphor for the director's place in the zombie sub-genre. Central to its evolution, and surrounded by imitations, Romero walked away from the franchise as director to focus on *Monkey Shines* and a number of stalled projects with various studios — including work on *Resident Evil*. Like one of his own creations, Romero returned to the franchise after a resurgence in the sub-genre made *Land of the Dead* a definite possibility. With *Diary of the Dead* marking his fifth unofficial entry in his franchise, the director nevertheless faces an army of associated prequels, remakes and sequels in an already crowded genre.

despite an overwhelming number of offers.[6] Rather than a titular association, Cronenberg's body of work is often canonized under the thematic term and almost burgeoning sub-genre of "body horror." Fundamentally concerned with the process of bodily evolution, transformation and disintegration, his focus ranges from the individual to society as a whole. Thematically consistent and challenging in his choice of material in which medicine, science and the media are fused with sexuality and self-destruction, this director's filmography, under the auspicious banner of body horror, has nevertheless benefited from this association after the early success of *Shivers* and *Rabid*.

Whereas audiences identify Cronenberg with "body horror" and controversial adaptations of Burroughs and Ballard, Dario Argento's association with the giallo[7] and self-proclaimed "Three Mothers" trilogy has seen the Italian auteur develop an identifiable brand name with which to penetrate the American and international markets, and potentially raise the necessary financing for future films. Indeed, the commonality shared by those directors who eschewed the Hollywood horror franchise is the support of established producers. Moreover, there has been a perceived marketable strength in the source material, literary or otherwise, based on previous successes with which they have become identified.

Although numerous installments of variable quality in a particular franchise could potentially tarnish all those associated with the franchise, in many cases the appearance of numerous sequels has only served to elevate the alleged originality and effectiveness of first films. What is more, these first film directors and literary inspirations are often held in higher esteem than their contemporary competitors' best efforts to work within the constraints of the medium and an unforgiving media.

United in their decision to begin careers within the controversial commerciality of the horror genre, Stuart Gordon, Don Coscarelli and Wes Craven have each made a significant impact upon audiences. With Hollywood in search of fresh ideas, these and other such directors were readily assimilated into a system of supply and demand in which the Hollywood horror franchise emerged as a preferred route. However, such generic stereotyping also played an important role by way of industrial relegation, with directors unable to secure financing for personal projects. For example, both Gordon and Coscarelli have primarily been relegated to the low-budget independent arena on account of their preferred material, industry stereotyping and limited professional relationships.

Craven, on the other hand, has repeatedly broken out of the exploitation market in search of a mainstream audience and worked with the majority of Hollywood's studios and corporations (to varying degrees of personal satisfaction and commercial success). However, such opportunities were only made available on account of his commitment to the Hollywood horror franchise and a level of commercial success that exceeded the $100 million mark. Furthermore, his significantly higher profile has led to tabloid controversy, increased media scrutiny and pressure — a poisoned chalice of success.

Despite differing relationships with the Hollywood horror franchise, directors' first film experiences shaped their subsequent careers. Indeed, those professional relationships formed during a first film were resurrected and revisited through similarly themed projects and conceptual spin-offs. Many shrewdly exploited their success to solicit studio interest or raise the requisite amount of financing for future films. Similarly, publicity departments reminded audiences of such accomplishments throughout various teasers, trailers and press materials at the crux of their marketing campaigns. Whether adopted as leverage or dismissed as history in accordance with their current industry standing, directors' attitudes towards these films clearly varied.

However, the names and reputations of first film directors are irrevocably entwined with the franchise's subsequent successes and failures, in much the same way that authors are attached to adaptations of their work. Indeed, the franchise is equal with other forms of adaptation, literary or otherwise, even in the eyes the Academy. In other words, directors remain connected to their landmark first films, and therefore the franchise, in the collective minds of studios, audiences and, to a lesser extent, censors.

This investigation into the franchise has shown that an established directorial hierarchy is at work within the Hollywood system — one that places the adaptation, and more recently, even the remake, above the horror film. For directors such as Coscarelli, the role of sequel director is a significant step down in terms of career progression, despite the opportunities and exposure it can potentially provide. In this respect, Hollywood's hierarchical attitude and approach to genre-based filmmaking, and franchise filmmaking in particular, is clearly exposed.

Moreover, the inherent hypocrisy of the industry is illustrated by the studios' attitude towards the genre, in spite of the commercial success it affords them.[8] Unfortunately, such feeling has also infiltrated the collective consciousness of directors, who are equally deserving of such an indictment in light of their exploitation of the genre and the Hollywood horror franchise. Consequently, even though literary adaptations have legitimacy and respectability, the traditional view of the Hollywood horror franchise is one that sees it residing somewhere below the line of professional respectability, especially if the first film director is no longer attached.

First film directors often nominated close friends, acquaintances and first film colleagues to take over sequel chores. This modern mentoring system began with Sean Cunningham and John Carpenter in the early eighties, as they preferred to shoulder producing responsibilities and/or receive passive payments. This relationship with the franchise was later adopted by George A. Romero and Clive Barker, who fulfilled their obligation to studio demands and supported key members of a production team. More recently, Wes Craven's editor, Patrick Lussier, was promoted to the director's chair for Dimension's *Dracula 2000*, a film heavily promoted and released under an all-too-familiar "Wes Craven Presents" banner.[9]

However, several filmmakers remained involved or were seduced back to the franchise on account of their status as franchisers and professional mentors to new talent. In this respect, a further level of exploitation was afforded to these filmmakers, allowing directors such as Steve Miner and Tommy Lee Wallace a chance to kick-start their careers. Therefore, the Hollywood horror franchise has placed first film directors in the enviable position, previously epitomized by Roger Corman and Charles Band, of being able to offer ambitious yet relatively inexperienced individuals the opportunity to prove themselves as directors in their own right. Provided with a structured platform from which to experiment and develop, the Hollywood horror franchise has proven to be a fertile training ground from the beginning.

Deliberately echoing this farming out of the franchise based on a director's recommendations, studios and production companies also promoted key figures from within a first film's cast and crew. Employing them not only as a means of ensuring continuity, fidelity and commitment, studios also exploited such associations in marketing campaigns. Rather than forgo their involvement and see the franchise taken in a direction they felt was inappropriate, writers, production assistants, stars and special effects artists also claimed the sequel as an invaluable training ground.

Rewarded for their franchise loyalty, screenwriters in particular have exploited their literary connections and used their knowledge of its genre codes and conventions to maneuver the franchise back to their original concerns. The most recent examples of this growing trend have been Don Mancini and David S. Goyer on *Seed of Chucky* and *Blade: Trinity*, respectively. Consequently, filmmakers such as these (including William Peter Blatty) have challenged audiences' notions of fidelity by seeking to put their own personal stamp on the material as members of the franchise family and, in some respects, reclaim it in line with their own original intentions.

Franchise families are headed by a franchiser who usually controls the rights and profits. Inspired by commercially successful follow-ups, the franchiser or licensor has exploited established titles and acquired the rights to others. As self-appointed guardians with a vested interest, these companies and individuals exerted creative control from initial concept to final cut. *House* and *Friday the 13th* producer Sean S. Cunningham has described how, "an active producer ... [is] responsible for everything from the time the idea is hatched to the time the film reaches theaters.... He produces the film [even though] the industry, however, doesn't perceive producers as filmmakers."[10] Such a stance detracts from the role, responsibilities and definition of a director, and certainly has implications for auteurist approaches.

Indeed, with producers Robert Shaye, Malek Akkad and Harvey Bernhard scrutinizing and shepherding sequels to *A Nightmare on Elm Street*, *Halloween* and *The Omen*, critics and audiences have understandably, yet mistakenly, attributed the success or blame to the film's director. As *Hellraiser*'s Clive Barker has since pointed out, "when the reviews come out, nobody ever criticizes the producer ... it's always the director or the writer, or both who get it in the neck."[11] Nevertheless, at its most positive and productive, the role of the franchiser is not a self-serving guardian but an intermediary between outsider and audience. The main issue is that this restricted view leads them to "direct" the tone and content from a position of relative safety. This, in turn, means an economically motivated temptation to abandon experimentation and edginess in favor of formula and cliché.

For outsiders, franchise families were often obstacles to achieving professional satisfaction. Recruited on account of their prior genre experience in TV or film, or independent credentials, such directors were preferable for production companies keen to promote an ongoing franchise. Many of these second- or third-time filmmakers hoping to follow in Romero's and Hooper's footsteps regarded the Hollywood horror franchise as an isolated yet fairly established route to bigger-budgeted studio-based filmmaking. Impressionable yet enthusiastic, and with comparatively less experience, directors in this third category were a great deal more affordable than their absent predecessors.

However, such a recruitment strategy, whether adopted through necessity or choice, opened up many franchises to criticisms that centered on the relative obscurity of their directors.[12] Nevertheless, the notion of contributing to what many industry insiders have deemed to be a destructive force has seen studios consistently recruit from outside Hollywood. By importing up-and-coming talent from across the globe, the Hollywood horror franchise has been a showcase for new talent,[13] with Alexandre Aja's *Haute Tension* most recently precipitating his selection and approval as the director of the disturbing *The Hills Have Eyes* remake.

A popular point of entry for filmmakers with little studio experience, the Hollywood horror franchise has also served as an intermediate training ground for directors caught between television and a first film of their own. As demonstrated in Chapter 5, the sequel-makers' prior knowledge, experience and, to some extent, acclaim in relation to the Hollywood horror franchise saw them subjected to industry stereotyping. Whether willing victims or seasoned survivors, their involvement with various sequels further ghettoized the genre director into a sub-category.

Attitudes and Approaches

The demands placed upon franchise directors are inherently paradoxical. Their attitude and approach must be conservative yet innovative, and geared towards preempting industry and audience expectations. Herein lies the challenge for the franchise filmmaker — to walk the tightrope between these two arenas. With the support and cooperation of the franchiser, the director's objective is to meet or exceed expectations while keeping faith with his or her creative concerns.

Whereas returning directors traded autonomy for advancement, outsiders were frequently stifled by a studio's lack of financial support. Directors such as Scott Spiegel on *From Dusk Till Dawn 2* were charged with the duplicitous task of transforming the property into a marketable commodity on a fraction of the first film's budget. As such, they struggled to maintain quality and continuity, with their ability to secure key cast members and adequate special effects firmly capped.

Commissioning sequels purely for the direct-to-video/DVD or cable markets, after the theatrical release of previous entries, demonstrates the reluctance of companies like Dimension, Trimark and Lion's Gate to reinvest in a franchise and uphold the quality behind it. This denies sequel directors the opportunity to continue or compete with the first film's content.[14] Consequently, this corporate choice to take advantage of the new developments in distribution damages a director's ability to do any follow-up justice, and diminishes the reputation of the title and every franchise. Furthermore, it duly exposes the dismissive attitude and approach of companies towards the Hollywood horror franchise.

Whether timed to capitalize on the recent impact of previous entries or commemorate a first film's anniversary, the relationship of a sequel to its ancestors fluctuated according to a director's mandate. In following a linear and logical approach to narrative, several erred on the side of caution by adhering to a first film's conceit. As writers and co-writers of a first film, others sought to expand it in line with their own creative vision. Indeed, with franchise film criticism dominated by notions of fidelity, sequels are subjected to an extensive process of comparison — at the expense of any objective assessment. However, by promoting films with a numerical or titular association, studios have invited this instinctive form of appraisal. With the process reframed as an additional form of adaptation, some directors have taken into account the way in which a preexisting text has shaped and sharpened audience expectations. However, audiences and critics alike have to overcome the aforementioned hierarchy and hypocrisy surrounding the Hollywood horror franchise.

Cannibalism within and between genres is a cinematic constant, and it has spread throughout the microcosmic confines of the Hollywood horror franchise. Faced with the fusion of disparate elements and demands, many directors succumbed to pressure and took the easier option of shamelessly recreating a first film, with slight alterations, as in Jeannot Szwarc's *Jaws 2*. In other words, this pressure led to increasingly imitative and desperate approaches, with first film narratives adopted but not updated. Whether designed as a shot-for-shot remake or slight variation on a theme, reproduction has remained central to many directors' approach.

Indeed, the temptation to succumb to imitation as a form of cinematic flattery by producing a facsimile of a first film without any real thought has become a genre staple. Whereas first sequel directors were challenged and intimidated by the idea of a follow-up, subsequent directors benefited from some necessary distance. To this end, later directors exploited the participation of franchise family members to not only legitimize their entry, but also to justify the dramatic license they had taken with it. In many respects, those directors who embraced a form of playful reverence that, for the most part, eschewed any elements of parody have experienced the greatest success.

Trapped between audiences' expectations and preserving enigmatic antagonists, directors seldom shied away from dragging them center stage by a third film. This need for further installments to theorize, rationalize and research an antagonist's origin has been a legitimate cause for concern. This satisfying of our collective curiosity as to how and why such people or events occur in society is a key function of the Hollywood horror franchise. It perpetuates a need to explore what Robin Wood has referred to as the "return of the repressed,"[15] with sequels detracting from the intensity of the genre and its potentially cathartic nature. With the exception of Craven's *Scream* franchise, directors have placed their faith in "the Other" and diminished the extent to which they must rely upon returning cast members.[16] In these and other cases, the Hollywood horror franchise has exerted its supremacy over

Hollywood's star system, with actors written out, written off or simply replaced in future installments.

Horror's interdependent relationship with comedy has provided many sequel directors with a seemingly easy option. Many opted to dilute the intensity by shifting into parody as means of securing success. However, any modicum of achievement in this respect has been overshadowed by atrocious second installments in the *C.H.U.D.* and *Return of the Living Dead* franchises, produced by ineffective companies with little understanding of the material. Moreover, the collapse of these and other such production companies and distributors, coupled with a first film director's desire to break into Hollywood, saw the rights to many third entries revert to studios and individuals only willing to finance a successful formula. One such company was Trimark, who wisely entrusted the resurrection of the *Return of the Living Dead* franchise to Brian Yuzna five years later.

Whether recovering from a poorly received first sequel or strengthened by a second film's success, directors of third films often found themselves compelled to introduce gimmicks as an incentive to potential audiences. In other words, the success or failure of a second film dictated the extent to which directors were allowed to experiment. Nevertheless, a healthy resistance to convention has been demonstrated by many filmmakers eager to embark upon a variety of shifts into various other genres. In this respect, the Hollywood horror franchise has not been as conservative a cash cow as first suspected, and has, on occasion, demonstrated its potential to successfully subvert previous entries.

In light of the stigma associated with directing the Hollywood horror franchise, filmmakers often followed a deliberate process of distancing their film from both its predecessors and the genre as a whole. These public denials and misleading marketing campaigns are damaging to the film and the franchise. It also mirrors the industry's denial of a film's belonging to the horror genre, with Craven being a repeat offender on this charge in regard to the initial publicity for *A Nightmare on Elm Street* and *Scream*.[17] Rather than broaden the working definition and audience's understanding of the horror film, this unsavory hallmark of the Hollywood horror franchise further detracts from any respectability it may aspire to.

Indeed, the industry has actively encouraged directors and publicists to transcend the genre. Within this artificial artistic hierarchy, films have attempted to buy their way out of the genre with big budgets, studio backing or a stellar cast. From *Arachnophobia*'s marketing as a "thrillomedy" to *Fangoria* magazine's studio-savvy "It's Not a Horror Film" feature coverage in the early nineties, ambitious directors and demographic-conscious studios

Halloween III: Season of the Witch (Tommy Lee Wallace, 1983). Wallace's sequel had no connection to the tone and content of the previous two entries. In its exploration of pseudo–Celtic myths and the mass murder of America's children, the film had potential; but it disappointed audiences expecting Curtis, Loomis and the Shape to be the focus. Indeed, this one-sheet poster for the film exposes the extent to which Wallace's film was mismarketed to expectant audiences back in 1983.

sought to broaden their mainstream appeal — at the genre's expense. Consequently, the horror genre has been afforded an increasingly narrow definition that wallowed in the worst aspects of exploitation cinema.

Despite such complications and first sequel directors' adherence to successful formulas, subsequent directors saw fit to question the essence of the first film and explore alternatives. Besides excursions into unfamiliar genres and frequent hybrids, directors adopted a series of revisionist and post-modern approaches to the franchise, particularly in relation to issues of gender, stereotypes and genre clichés, as seen in Tom Savini's *Night of the Living Dead* remake. Rather than aggressively challenge or abandon a franchise in all but its brand name value, others faithfully recreated a series of memorable moments with delicate shifts in location and logic.

However, as the Hollywood horror franchise has evolved, several directors have deliberately subverted the established conventions and audience expectations by blending familiarity with innovation in the scripting process. Savini and James Cameron, for example, have highlighted the importance of a filmmaker's interest in, affection for and inside knowledge of the genre and a particular franchise. In this respect, the Hollywood horror franchise has been able to develop in line with a judicious approach to cultural development and the introduction of new technologies.

As demonstrated by Cameron and John Boorman in particular, genre experimentation and stylistic shifts have not been uncommon. Such experimentation has ranged from the slight to the severe in terms of content and success. By adopting an antagonistic stance towards their audiences and predecessors, some directors challenged the very concepts and characters upon which a first film was based. Choosing instead to work against the studio system, they embraced all manner of anarchic approaches and issued a challenge to the Hollywood establishment.

As Joe Berlinger found with *Blair Witch 2*, drastic departures and contradictory concepts have often been regarded as a form of betrayal by fans, and inconsistent by critics. Including only the most negligible of references to previous installments, some sequels required audiences and critics to discard their formulaic expectations and attachments to a stand-alone film. In light of such unwelcome departures, directors of the Hollywood horror franchise have often utilized the promotional aspect of their role to appeal to audiences and request that they approach their film with an open mind as a means of preempting potential criticism and any such adverse reactions.

Filming the Franchise

The Hollywood horror franchise has produced a disproportionate number of troubled shoots stemming from pre-production problems and miscommunication. Although returning directors and franchise family members were far from spared with regard to such conflicts and limitations, outsiders and sequel-makers were subjected to inordinate levels of interference from the outset on account of their status and lack of previous involvement. The majority of uninitiated sequel directors were replacements for first film or franchise family directors who had declined to participate.

Therefore, their pre-production relationship with a project was often last minute, chaotic and focused on solving a myriad of problems under increasing levels of pressure, with Jeff Burr's *Texas Chainsaw Massacre III* tribulations being a classic example. Shooting scripts came under additional scrutiny from directors wanting to make their mark on the film, sometimes at the expense of the original writer, first film director or both. Whether seduced by the salary, a significantly high profile release, or the opportunity to work with specific cast and crew members, directors addressed the challenging nature of the franchise, and an apparent love and respect for the first film, throughout their publicity trails and press junkets. With little evidence of such sentiments discernible in the finished film, directors were often ill prepared for the potentially negative impact and consequences the Hollywood horror franchise could have on their careers.

Directors accepted a sequel assignment on the understanding that there would be alterations to the script in line with their own attitude and approach. Indeed, a sequel's pre-production period often heralded changes in direction and director, with several replaced and creative differences cited as the overriding factor. Consequently, many expectations were left unfulfilled, and unforeseen circumstances affected schedules, budgets and the temperamental nature of studio-backing. Furthermore, directors had to contend with the contributions of executives, producers and returning stars — each of whom had their own take on the material.

However, some directors found themselves at the opposite end of the creative spectrum, given free reign to explore alternative approaches as writers and directors. In this respect, the Hollywood horror franchise has facilitated directors' creative freedom. Even so, completed scripts and treatments were subject to approval, revisions and rewrites throughout the production process, one seldom free from budgetary restrictions and punishing schedules to meet a previously arranged release date in the wake of test-screenings and MPAA approval.

As facilitators of the franchise, sequel directors were charged with delivering a successful addition, and providing the necessary link and narrative sustenance for future films. Consequently, a plethora of climaxes, cliffhangers and shock epilogues were often invoked — at the franchiser's insistence — to provide an adequate source of closure and/or potential for the omnipresent threat of future films. However, such standardized conclusions were contentious and a prime source of disagreement. With many filmmakers entering the franchise without the benefit of a big-budget blockbuster or firmly established track record, their powers of persuasion were significantly reduced, and so were unable to solicit creative support. Despite second, third and fourth units shooting simultaneously, many directors entered the post-production phase under intense scrutiny from studios and production companies eager to see a return on their investment.

Without the right to final, or sometimes even first, cut, some directors underwent the ironic process of being disenfranchised at this stage. As has been demonstrated, the multiple forms of interference inflicted upon directors included alternative endings, additional effects sequences and structural overhaul. Wary of taxing the attention span of the lowest common denominator, subplots, expositional sequences and character-enhancing backstories were also cast aside by distributors and production companies in consideration of a more profitable and audience-friendly running time.

Although low-budget independent franchises could not afford to embark upon a costly test-screening process, directors of higher profile, box office-bound sequels like *The Exorcist III* and *Alien 3* were routinely subjected to this stringent yet far from scientific process. Just as positive reactions have comforted directors during post-production, negative comments and test scores have seen studios release additional funding and shift release dates to maximize earning potential. However, this process has also demanded that directors adhere closer to the rules of the previous films, and adequately satisfy audiences' demands for additional violence and those clichés for which the Hollywood horror franchise has been criticized.

By demanding the inclusion of various clichés and stereotypes, audiences have reinforced studios' narrow approach to the genre. Indeed, the pivotal role of audiences in the production and proliferation of the Hollywood horror franchise cannot be ignored. This is evidenced by Coscarelli's mindful online dialogue and interest in fan-sites prior to scripting the next installment in his *Phantasm* franchise, and seen in Barker and Cunningham's alternate views of where the *Hellraiser* and *Friday the 13th* franchises should continue in a narrative sense.[18] In this respect, directors' original intentions have frequently been superseded by those of the franchise fan-base.

Once released, the franchise belongs to an audience that has the option to accept or reject future installments. Therefore, audiences' masochistic mainstream sensibilities and unwillingness to embrace innovation within the franchise have directed franchise content. In other words, far from being passive or innocent victims in this process, audiences have, through a unique combination of Internet forums and fan-sites, influenced the direction and directors of the Hollywood horror franchise.

As is often the case with horror films, success and scandal are intrinsically linked. Rising box office figures have often led to an unfortunate yet anticipated controversy and backlash from newspapers, pressure groups, critics and sections of the community. Accusations of copycat killers have seen condemnation fuel the cultural impact of these first features, and the topic of censorship become a political cause celebre — an approach propagated by the media and groups dedicated to denigrating the genre. Although this further complicates Hollywood's exploitation of the franchise, the franchise filmmaker is inevitably caught up in the minefield, with the MPAA caught in the middle.

Interpreted as proactive or reactive, depending upon your point of view, the Classifications and Ratings Administration (CARA) has been subjected to criticism from both sides. Craven, for example, has described how "the trick with scary material is to break through the audience's complacency"[19] by challenging their adjusted sensibilities and crossing a hypothetical line in terms of tone and intensity. That said, the director, like so many others working within the genre, has found that "the first line you cross is the ratings line."[20] In carrying out its self-regulatory role for the Hollywood film industry, the board has been demonized by directors. Moreover, accusations of favoritism and unfair play have further diminished the genre's relationship with the MPAA.

The MPAA has been portrayed as biased, corrupt and vindictive with regard to specific franchises and directors. Such films and filmmakers have either courted controversy or previously abstained from the ratings process in favor of the less profitable alternative; consequently, they have paid the price for such rebellion or abstention. Both hypocritical and mysterious in its methods, advice and judgments, the board's inner workings are, for most, confusing if not thoroughly inconsistent.[21] In response to such accusations, the board has repeatedly stressed its impartiality towards all films and filmmakers, irrespective of their background, backing or budget.

Although the ratings board is not a legal requirement, and the introduction of an NC-17 rating has, at least on the surface, provided filmmakers an additional option with regard to releasing their films with an approved rating, studios have continued to insist that directors contractually deliver an R-rated film. Indeed, the alternative continues to be perceived as the equivalent of commercial suicide. By imposing the more profitable R-rating, studios and production companies have inadvertently prevented directors from competing with their predecessors on a visceral level, or even simply maintaining the standard set down in previous films. As such, a sense of disappointment has characterized directors' and audiences' experiences of the Hollywood horror franchise.

To fulfill their contractual obligations, directors had to work within this system for the purposes of a theatrical release. In this respect, studios and key members of the production team are an integral part of the self-regulatory process. As self-appointed supervisors, producers such as Paramount's Frank Mancuso Jr. on the *Friday the 13th* franchise have explicitly advised directors to shoot alternate takes of specific scenes, ranging from the bloodless to the bloody. Expected to push the boundaries and provide a visually satisfying follow-up while providing distributors with an R-rated feature, directors have adapted and adopted a range of well-publicized techniques to ensure that certain shots remain in the film.

From Hitchcock's use of misdirection and deliberate inclusion of outrageous footage as a bargaining tool in *Psycho*, through to Romero's most recent and judicious use of green screen zombies and CGI gore to dilute the impact of particular single-take scenes in *Land of the Dead*, directors have engaged in preemptive strikes. Moreover, their publicity and promotion for a franchise film has led to the exploitation of such experiences as a means of demonstrating their affection for the genre and affinity with the audience against the MPAA. As an external scapegoat for sequel directors, the board has given credibility back to the Hollywood horror franchise and enhanced its marketable reputation as controversial and capable of returning to its independent roots.

Directors have similarly criticized the misleading marketing strategies adopted by distributors to either cover up or over-emphasize a sequel's numerical history and genre association. Furthermore, an over-reliance on and pandering to the profitable youth market has contributed to their concerns. Wallace and Blatty, for example, would have preferred their films be publicized without the use of *Halloween* or *The Exorcist* in the title.

The reality of the situation, from a studio standpoint at least, is that such pictures would never have been commissioned at all without such marketable associations. Keen to distance themselves from the stigma of horror sequels, directors have also had their genre denials plastered across the pages of industry magazines, using alternative terms to either disguise or impose franchise history. Nevertheless, an accepted hierarchy in which the slasher film, epitomized by the *Friday the 13th* franchise in the minds of many, is regarded as a vastly inferior and unsavory label in comparison to the psychological thriller, further complicates the current standing of the Hollywood horror franchise.

With marketing campaigns subject to studio endorsement and direction, filmmakers were often trapped between internal pressures and external expectations. A staple of cinema since its Universal and independent origins, horror films have been marketed as cinematic endurance tests. With spectacular warnings and promises scrawled across posters, horror movie publicity has been specifically designed to goad audiences into attending. Indeed, the genre has traditionally functioned as a parentally forbidden rite of passage and quintessential "date movie."

To intensify the experience and similar such associations, marketing

Conclusions 173

departments behind *The Exorcist*, *The Omen* and *The Blair Witch Project*, for example, have also exploited a story's origins and supernatural connotations, and propagated fictional curses. Following the creation of a cult classic or cultural phenomenon, sequel directors have been trapped under the burden of media hype and experienced an audience backlash.[22] In response to such circumstances, directors have incorporated William Castle-esque gimmicks and exploited new technologies to solicit critical and commercial success, with the increasingly successful *Saw* franchise sponsoring an annual Blood Drive[23] as part of its pre-release publicity campaign.

This reliance on hoaxes, hyperbole and media hype has seen subsequent entries accused of being ineffective and lacking innovation by critics for whom the genre holds little fascination or merit. Although positive comments from critics played a pivotal role in raising the profile of a first film like *The Evil Dead*, virulent reviews have equally enabled directors to reach their target audiences more efficiently than could ever have been hoped for. Whereas Hitchcock solicited critical support for *Psycho*, directors such as Romero, with *Night of the Living Dead*, duly exploited the controversy and supposedly negative comments and bore them as an unexpected seal of approval to fuel the marketing fire.

Sequel directors, however, had to face critics who sometimes adopted a nostalgic or revisionist stance to the first film in their condemnation, and comments from openly disappointed first film directors. Friedkin, in particular, has been a strong critic of *Exorcist* sequel directors. As cinematic underdogs derided and dismissed by the critics and their predecessors, directors of the Hollywood horror franchise have nevertheless endured and enjoyed a sustained existence due to the devotion of fans and dogged determination of franchisers to exploit their interest.

Directing the Hollywood Horror Franchise

From conception to reception, the Hollywood horror franchise could be characterized as a cinema of creative dissatisfaction for all concerned, with its directors often displaced. Nevertheless, it is an invaluable point of entry for those seeking career progression and planning to infiltrate the industry through a widely recognized product. Relatively inexperienced directors, drafted into the sequel and promoted from outside a first film, and with only a few features behind them or some episodic TV experience, found it to be a challenging training ground.

The experience has also been complicated by franchise families, a situation successfully avoided by Jonathan Demme on *The Silence of the Lambs*, the most successful sequel thus far. By importing their own production teams and trusted personnel, and sometimes even recasting certain characters, directors cut down on the potential for miscommunication. For those operating on a significantly lower budget, the freedom to experiment within the framework of the franchise proved vital in securing directors' first assignments and, more often than not, their most financially successful film to date.

Hollywood's hypocrisy, hierarchies and greed are the three key barriers limiting the potential of the horror franchise. Production companies and franchisers have begun to take advantage of new technologies but without sufficiently investing in research and development during pre-production. Unprecedented access to audience responses and tastes through online forums and fan-sites has the potential to be overwhelming and contradictory insofar as impacting the direction taken. Franchisers have been unclear of established parameters and in their expectations of what could and should realistically be expected from filmmakers working within an allocated schedule and budget. Without minimizing the potential for miscommunication, studios and production companies have hampered directors' attempts to adapt and adopt these concepts.

With regard to the test-screening process, studios have yet to adopt a realistic and genre-sensitive approach in keeping with the target audience. That said, feedback from national and international film festivals, in addition to those comments made on fan-sites and such forums, is increasingly having an impact on production.[24] As with the marketing campaign, directors should neither mislead an audience nor set the finished film up to fail. Test audiences, however, have been stoic in their expectations and support, and as such must take responsibility for a lack of product that dares to challenge the established codes and conventions.

Undeniably a creative and commercial asset for these directors to exploit, the Hollywood horror franchise has the potential to be as empowering as it is castrating, with the end result a trade off between autonomy and advancement. Based on their experiences, directors have shown a limited awareness of the benefits and pitfalls associated with it, and the vast potential for conflict, confusion and compromise. Describable in retrospect as a Faustian pact in which ambitious directors are seduced by the studios, the Hollywood horror franchise has seen directors adopt a number of roles with respect to their sequel involvement. Whether presented as victims, survivors or co-conspirators, it must be understood that each has been a willing participant and paid employee with creative objectives and an ambitious career-driven agenda.

In terms of career progression, directors such as Berlinger and Burr have made a less profitable yet personally more rewarding return to their roots. For example, *Some Kind of Monster* and *Straight Into Darkness* have since showcased their skills and post-franchise potential. Similarly, both Gordon and Craven have made effective bids for the mainstream with *Edmond* and *Red Eye*, which, although far more prestigious in terms of the recognizable talent in front of and behind the camera, continue to bear a close relation to the tone and content of their franchise films. Both filmmakers have also continued to highlight the links between the franchise, theater and adaptation by participating in upcoming anthology series and the development of similarly themed projects for the stage.

Further proof that the franchise is conducive, if not essential, to a long career can be found in Coscarelli's plans to adapt and direct a prequel to *Bubba Ho-Tep*, entitled *Bubba Nosferatu*, and his plans to further exploit his connection to the *Phantasm* franchise, which is back in development at New Line. By addressing familiar themes and issues throughout their careers, irrespective of their franchise involvement, the core content of directors' films has supported Renoir's claim that "all directors make the same film over and over again."[25] United by their established support networks and fruitful professional relationships, these filmmakers are all industry survivors for whom numerous sequels have elevated their status and potential for success.

On a par with the theatrical and literary adaptation, and with its origins firmly rooted in both realms, the Hollywood horror franchise is a frustrating and fascinating form of cinema. From formulaic to innovative, the paradoxical nature of the franchise is further constrained by audiences' clichéd expectations. Furthermore, Hollywood's hierarchy infects its reputation and informs the studios' frequent mishandling and misappropriation of it. With the agenda for change set down, directors can begin to challenge attitudes towards the genre and the franchise from the inside through their own production companies and ability to set up distribution deals.

In adopting the mentoring system on an industry-wide basis, directors such as Barker and Raimi, with Midnight Pictures and Ghost House Pictures, have adopted Carpenter's, Craven's and Cunningham's approaches. Similarly, Garris' *Masters of Horror* anthology series for Showtime has been an overdue genre breakthrough in format, freedom and execution.[26] In light of this, directors may no longer have to use the franchise as a negotiable asset or be tempted to return purely for commercial reasons. Alternatively, they may willingly explore the concepts and themes of a first film on their own creative terms as just one of the options available rather than the only route remaining open to them.

However, much like the genre itself, the Hollywood horror franchise is currently perceived by many filmmakers as a first step or foundation. Many would prefer to embark upon an unrelated project or first film, but the industry is geared towards the risk reduction strategy of franchise filmmaking. From Spielberg and Schumacher to Craven and Coscarelli, the franchise is a guaranteed form of career advancement that has been exploited by these and all subsequent directors through a judicious approach to their careers and the projects they support. Guillermo Del Toro's *Blade II* success, for example, guaranteed the necessary support to allow him to direct *Hellboy* with his chosen cast, and lessened the level of interference faced throughout production.

Indeed, directors of the Hollywood horror franchise have always been indebted to receptive audiences, regardless of intent, content or fidelity, and been subject to their discerning approval or rejection. Directors have therefore cannibalized their predecessors and contemporaries to create a medium that has become increasingly self-referential and intertextual. With Newman previously describing how "few arenas of cinema depend so on the loyalty and inside knowledge of their audiences,"[27] the Hollywood horror franchise has expanded the genre's cinematic scope and cyclical nature.

In providing an examination of the Hollywood horror franchise from the filmmakers' perspective, this text has demonstrated the sheer diversity of directors' experiences and identified the strands which tie them together. Whether approached from an historical perspective or thematic analysis, the contextual foundation of the Hollywood horror franchise makes it obvious that many of these films are overdue for critical reassessment. Further research could allow for comparative analysis from alternate perspectives, including the writer, producer and star. Also, there still remains the potential for an investigation into the franchise with regard to reception, since several of the films addressed here have divided audiences and critics.

As for the future ... the rise of the video game film has arguably displaced the Hollywood horror franchise as the worst form of adaptation within the current climate. Director Uwe Boll, for example, has excelled in this arena to an even greater extent than the sequel-maker, with an output set to rival that of Roger Corman and Ed Wood combined.[28] Moreover, such figures as King, Barker, Romero and Carpenter are further exploiting this form of adaptation in various forms. Elsewhere, the popular trend of softening mainstream studio horrors, as epitomized by their profitable and proud PG-13 ratings, in the form of domestic and international remakes has intensified and been fuelled by the stars of the WB network. Cementing the genre's status as the ideal "date movie," and specifically targeting young women through their films' protagonists, studios and production companies have adopted a Lewton-esque approach to their frequently supernatural tales and evoked the harmless feel of the traditional campfire ghost story.[29]

Fortunately, a reactionary renaissance of the realistic horrors first celebrated in the seventies has simultaneously occurred. By testing the boundaries, breaking taboos and being far more forceful in both their intentions and sheer intensity, several filmmakers have begun to redress the balance of genre-related product on the market following the impressive advancements made in international markets. From Eli Roth's *Hostel* franchise to Greg McLean's *Wolf Creek* and Neil Marshall's *The Descent* (from Australia and the U.K. respectively), this revival has made a significant impact at the box office, and such projects have been actively supported by Lions Gate[30] and other studios keen to exploit this trend.

With the advent of the Laser Disc and DVD, directors have finally been given a forum to begin addressing, redressing and discussing the reception of a finished film in contrast to their original intentions. Increasingly exploited by studios, franchisers and production companies through a seemingly endless process of re-releases and retrospectives, this revolutionary new format offers audiences and critics additional insight into the production process via publicity materials and multiple commentaries. The inclusion of deleted scenes and alternative endings also allows audiences to make their own judgments by offering a more holistic, but by no means complete, account of film production. Taking full advantage of this newfound freedom to communicate both technically and thematically with their intended audiences on an unprecedented level, directors have justified their decisions and pinpointed those that were made for them.

Although a film's fidelity or illegitimacy has traditionally been exposed upon its release, and extensively commented upon by audiences and critics, directors' intentions and experiences have often remained buried in the past. However, through a comparative understanding of their contributions and considered reflections, and the mechanics of filmmaking, audiences are now far better equipped to reconcile and reassess alternative interpretations as the Hollywood horror franchise continues to develop in spite of its critical reputation.

Hollywood Horror Series Filmography

Alien (1979)
Director: Ridley Scott; *Writers*: Dan O'Bannon, Ronald Shussett; *Producers*: Gordon Carroll, David Giler, Walter Hill; *Cast*: Sigourney Weaver, Tom Skerrit, Ian Holm; *Production Companies*: Twentieth Century–Fox, Brandywine Productions; *Distributor*: Twentieth Century–Fox; *Runtime*: 117 minutes / 116 minutes; *Rating*: R / 18

Aliens (1986)
Director: James Cameron; *Writers*: James Cameron, David Giler, Walter Hill; *Producer*: Gale Ann Hurd; *Cast*: Sigourney Weaver, Lance Henriksen, Michael Biehn; *Production Companies*: Twentieth Century–Fox, Brandywine Productions; *Distributor*: Twentieth Century–Fox; *Runtime*: 137 minutes / 154 minutes; *Rating*: R / 18

Alien 3 (1992)
Director: David Fincher; *Writers*: Vincent Ward, David Giler, Walter Hill and Larry Ferguson; *Producers*: Gordon Carroll, David Giler, Walter Hill; *Cast*: Sigourney Weaver, Lance Henriksen, Charles Dance; *Production Companies*: Twentieth Century–Fox, Brandywine Productions; *Distributor*: Twentieth Century–Fox; *Runtime*: 114 minutes / 145 minutes; *Rating*: R / 18

Alien Resurrection (1997)
Director: Jean-Pierre Jeunet; *Writer*: Joss Whedon; *Producers*: Gordon Carroll, David Giler, Walter Hill, Bill Badalato; *Cast*: Sigourney Weaver, Winona Ryder, Dan Hedaya; *Production Companies*: Twentieth Century–Fox, Brandywine Productions; *Distributor*: Twentieth Century–Fox; *Runtime*: 109 minutes/ 116 minutes; *Rating*: R / 18

Alien vs. Predator (2004)
Director: Paul W.S. Anderson; *Writer*: Paul W.S. Anderson; *Producers*: Gordon Carroll, David Giler, Walter Hill, John Davis; *Cast*: Sanaa Lathan, Raoul, Bova, Lance Henriksen; *Production Companies*: Twentieth Century–Fox, Davis Entertainment, Impact Pictures, Charenton Productions Limited, Inside Track Films, Zweite Babelsberg Film GmbH, Brandywine Productions; *Distributor*: Twentieth Century–Fox; *Runtime*: 101 minutes / 108 minutes; *Rating*: PG-13 / 15

Alligator (1980)
Director: Lewis Teague; *Writers*: John Sayles, Frank Ray Perilli; *Producer*: Brandon Chase; *Cast*: Robert Forster, Robin

Riker, Michael V. Gazzo; *Production Company*: Alligator Inc.; *Distributor*: Group 1 International Distribution Organization Ltd.; *Runtime*: 89 minutes; *Rating*: R / 15

Alligator II: The Mutation (1991)

Director: Jon Hess; *Writer*: Curt Allen; *Producers*: Brandon Chase, Cary Glieberman; *Cast*: Joseph Bologna, Dee Wallace-Stone, Richard Lynch; *Production Company*: Golden Hawk Entertainment; *Distributors*: New Line Cinema, American Broadcasting Company (ABC); *Runtime*: 92 minutes; *Rating*: PG-13 /15

American Psycho (2000)

Director: Mary Harron; *Writers*: Bret Easton Ellis, Mary Harron, Guinevere Turner; *Producers*: Edward Pressman, Christian Halsey Solomon, Chris Hanley; *Cast*: Christian Bale, Chloe Sevigny, Willem Dafoe; *Production Companies*: Edward R. Pressman Film Corporation, Lions Gate Films, Muse Productions, P.P.S. Films, Quadra Entertainment, Universal Pictures; *Distributors*: Amuse Pictures Inc, Lions Gate Films; *Runtime*: 101 minutes; *Rating*: R / 18

American Psycho 2: All American Girl (2002)

Director: Morgan J. Freeman; *Writers*: Alex Sanger, Karen Craig; *Producer*: Ernie Barbarash; *Cast*: Mila Kunis, William Shatner, Robin Dunne; *Production Company*: Lions Gate Films; *Distributors*: Studio Home Entertainment, Lions Gate Films; *Runtime*: 88 minutes; *Rating*: R / 18;

The Amityville Horror (1979)

Director: Stuart Rosenberg; *Writers*: Jay Anson, Sandor Stern; *Producers*: Elliot Geisinger, Ronald Saland; *Cast*: James Brolin, Margot Kidder, Rod Steiger; *Production Companies*: American-International Pictures, Cinema 77, Professional Films; *Distributor*: American-International Pictures; *Runtime*: 117 minutes; *Rating*: R / 15

Amityville II: The Possession (1982)

Director: Damiano Damiani; *Writers*: Hans Holzer, Tommy Lee Wallace; *Producers*: Ira N. Smith, Stephen R. Greenwald, Dino De Laurentiis; *Cast*: James Olsen, Burt Young; *Production Companies*: Dino De Laurentiis, Media Transactions; *Distributor*: Orion Pictures; *Runtime*: 100 minutes; *Rating*: R / 18

Amityville 3-D (1983)

Director: Richard Fleischer; *Writer*: William Wales; *Producer*: Stephen F. Kesten; *Cast*: Tony Roberts, Tess Harper, Meg Ryan; *Production Company*: De Laurentiis Entertainment Group (DEG); *Distributor*: Orion Pictures Corporation; *Runtime*: 105 minutes; *Rating*: PG / 15

Amityville 4: The Evil Escapes (1989)

Director: Sandor Stern; *Writers*: John G. Jones, Sandor Stern; *Producers*: Kenneth Atchity, Barry Bernardi; *Cast*: Patty Duke, Jane Wyatt; *Production Company*: NBC; *Distributors*: NBC, Vidmark Entertainment; *Runtime*: 95 minutes; *Rating*: R / 18

The Amityville Curse (1990)

Director: Tom Berry; *Writers*: Hans Holzer, Michael Krueger, Doug Olsen, Norvelle Rose, Micheal Krueger; *Producer*: Franco Battista; *Cast*: Kim Coates, Dawna Wightman, Helen Hughes; *Production Company*: Allegro Films; *Distributors*: Vidmark Entertainment, Les Films René Malo, Lions Gate Films Home Entertainment, Trimark Video; *Runtime*: 91 minutes; *Rating*: R / 18

Amityville 1992: It's About Time (1992)

Director: Tony Randel; *Writers*: John G. Jones, Chris DeFaria and Antonio Toro; *Producer*: Christopher DeFaria; *Cast*: Stephen Macht, Shawn Weatherly, Megan Ward; *Production Company*: VPS; *Distributor*:

Republic Pictures Corporation; *Runtime*: 91 minutes; *Rating*: R / 18

Amityville: A New Generation (1993)

Director: John Murlowski; *Writers*: Chris DeFaria, Antonio Toro; *Producer*: Chris DeFaria; *Cast*: David Naughton, Ross Partridge, Julia Nickson-Soul; *Production Company*: Republic Pictures Corporation; *Distributor*: Republic Pictures Corporation; *Runtime*: 90 minutes; *Rating*: R / 18

Amityville: Dollhouse (1996)

Director: Steve White; *Writer*: Joshua Michael Stern; *Producers*: Steve White, Mark Yellen, Zane W. Levitt; *Cast*: Robin Thomas, Starr Andreeff; *Production Companies*: Promark Entertainment Group, Spectacor Films, Zeta Entertainment Ltd.; *Distributor*: Republic Entertainment Inc.; *Runtime*: 93 minutes; *Rating*: R / 18

The Amityville Horror (2005)

Director: Andrew Douglas; *Writers*: Jay Anson, Sandor Stern, Scott Kosar; *Producers*: Michael Bay, Andrew Form; *Cast*: Ryan Reynolds, Melissa George, Philip Baker Hall; *Production Companies*: MGM, Dimension Films, Radar Pictures Inc., Platinum Dunes, United Artists; *Distributors*: Sony Pictures Entertainment, MGM; *Runtime*: 90 minutes; *Rating*: R / 15

Anaconda (1997)

Director: Luis Llosa; *Writers*: Hans Bauer, Jim Cash, Jack Epps Jr.; *Producers*: Verna Harrah, Carole Little, Leonard Rabinowitz; *Cast*: Jennifer Lopez, Ice Cube, Jon Voight; *Production Companies*: Cinema Line Film Corporation, Columbia Pictures Corporation, Iguana Producciones, Middle Fork Productions, Skylight Cinema Foto Art Ltd., St. Tropez Films; *Distributor*: Columbia Pictures; *Runtime*: 89 minutes; *Rating*: PG-13 / 15

Anacondas: The Hunt for the Blood Orchid (2004)

Director: Dwight H. Little; *Writers*: John Claflin, Daniel Zelman, Michael Miner, Edward Neumeier; *Producer*: Verna Harrah; *Cast*: Johnny Messner, KaDee Strickland, Matthew Marsden; *Production Companies*: Screen Gems, Middle Fork Productions; *Distributors*: Sony Pictures Releasing, Screen Gems; *Runtime*: 97 minutes; *Rating*: PG-13 / 12

Basket Case (1982)

Director: Frank Henenlotter; *Writer*: Frank Henenlotter; *Producer*: Edgar Ievins; *Cast*: Kevin Van Hentenryck, Terri Susan Smith, Beverly Bonner; *Production Company*: Basket Case Productions; *Distributors*: Analysis Film Releasing Corporation, Media Home Entertainment; *Runtime*: 91 minutes; *Rating*: R / 18

Basket Case 2 (1990)

Director: Frank Henenlotter; *Writer*: Frank Henenlotter; *Producer*: Edgar Ievins; *Cast*: Kevin Van Hentenryck, Annie Ross, Heather Rattray; *Production Company*: Shapiro-Glickenhaus Entertainment; *Distributor*: Shapiro-Glickenhaus Home Video; *Runtime*: 90 minutes; *Rating*: R / 18

Basket Case 3: The Progeny (1992)

Director: Frank Henenlotter; *Writers*: Frank Henenlotter, Robert Martin; *Producer*: Edgar Ievins; *Cast*: Kevin Van Hentenryck; *Production Company*: Shapiro-Glickenhaus Entertainment; *Distributors*: Shapiro-Glickenhaus Home Video, MCA/Universal Home Video; *Runtime*: 90 minutes; *Rating*: R / 18;

The Birds (1963)

Director: Alfred Hitchcock; *Writers*: Daphne Du Maurier, Evan Hunter; *Producer*: Alfred Hitchcock; *Cast*: Tippi Hedren, Rod

Taylor, Jessica Tandy; *Production Companies*: Alfred J. Hitchcock Productions, Universal Pictures; *Distributor*: Universal Pictures; *Runtime*: 119 minutes; *Rating*: PG-13 / 15

The Birds II: Land's End (1994)

Director: Alan Smithee (Rick Rosenthal); *Writers*: Daphne Du Maurier, Ken Wheat, Jim Wheat, Robert Eisele; *Producer*: Ted Kurdyla; *Cast*: Brad Johnson, Chelsea Field, Tippi Hedren; *Production Company*: MTE; *Distributors*: Showtime, MCA; *Runtime*: 87 minutes; *Rating*: R / 15

Blade (1998)

Director: Stephen Norrington; *Writer*: David S. Goyer; *Producers*: Robert Engelman, Peter Frankfurt, Wesley Snipes; *Cast*: Wesley Snipes, Stephen Dorff, Kris Kristofferson; *Production Companies*: Amen Ra Films, Imaginary Forces, Marvel Enterprises, New Line Cinema; *Distributor*: New Line Cinema; *Runtime*: 120 minutes; *Rating*: R / 18

Blade II (2002)

Director: Guillermo del Toro; *Writer*: David S. Goyer; *Producers*: Peter Frankfurt, Patrick J. Palmer, Wesley Snipes; *Cast*: Wesley Snipes, Kris Kristofferson, Ron Perlman; *Production Companies*: Amen Ra Films, Imaginary Forces, Justin Pictures, Linovo Productions GmbH & Co. KG, Marvel Enterprises, Milk & Honey, New Line Cinema, Pacific Title and Art Studio; *Distributor*: New Line Cinema; *Runtime*: 117 minutes; *Rating*: R / 18

Blade: Trinity (2004)

Director: David S. Goyer; *Writer*: David S. Goyer; *Producers*: David S. Goyer, Lynn Harris, Wesley Snipes; *Cast*: Wesley Snipes, Jessica Biel, Ryan Reynolds; *Production Companies*: New Line Cinema, Shawn Danielle Productions Ltd., Marvel Enterprises, Amen Ra Films, Imaginary Forces; *Distributor*: New Line Cinema; *Runtime*: 113 minutes / 124 minutes; *Rating*: R / 15

The Blair Witch Project (1999)

Directors: Daniel Myrick, Eduardo Sánchez; *Writers*: Daniel Myrick, Eduardo Sánchez; *Producers*: Robin Cowie, Gregg Hale; *Cast*: Heather Donahue, Joshua Leonard, Michael C. Williams; *Production Company*: Haxan Films; *Distributor*: Artisan Entertainment; *Runtime*: 86 minutes; *Rating*: R / 15

Book of Shadows: Blair Witch 2 (2000)

Director: Joe Berlinger; *Writers*: Dick Beebe, Joe Berlinger; *Producer*: Bill Carraro; *Cast*: Kim Director, Jeffrey Donovan, Erica Leerhsen; *Production Companies*: Artisan Entertainment, Haxan Films; *Distributor*: Artisan Entertainment; *Runtime*: 90 minutes; *Rating*: R / 15

Blood Feast (1963)

Director: Herschell Gordon Lewis; *Writer*: Allison Louise Downe; *Producer*: David F. Friedman; *Cast*: William Kerwin, Mal Arnold, Connie Mason; *Production Company*: Friedman-Lewis Productions Inc.; *Distributor*: Box Office Spectaculars; *Runtime*: 67 minutes; *Rating*: Unrated / 18

Blood Feast 2: All U Can Eat (2002)

Director: Herschell Gordon Lewis; *Writer*: W. Boyd Ford; *Producer*: Jacky Lee Morgan; *Cast*: John McConnell, Mark McLachlan, Melissa Morgan; *Production Companies*: Indie Productions, Queso Grande Productions Inc.; *Distributor*: Queso Grande Productions Inc.; *Runtime*: 99 minutes; *Rating*: R / 18

The Boogeyman (1980)

Director: Ulli Lommel; *Writers*: Ulli Lommel, David Herschel, Suzanna Love;

Producer: Ulli Lommel; *Cast*: Suzanna Love, Ron James, John Carradine; *Production Company*: Jerry Gross Org.; *Distributors*: Jerry Gross Org., Magnum Video, Wizard Video, Hollywood Home Ent.; *Runtime*: 82 minutes; *Rating*: R / 18

Boogeyman II (1983)

Director: Bruce Starr; *Writers*: Ulli Lommel, Suzanna Love; *Producers*: Mark Balsam, Ulli Lommel; *Cast*: Suzanna Love, Shannah Hall, John Carradine; *Production Company*: Unknown; *Distributor*: VCI Home Video; *Runtime*: 79 minutes; *Rating*: R

Return of the Boogeyman (1994)

Director: Deland Nurse; *Writer*: Jack Smight; *Producer*: Edward Oleschak; *Cast*: Kelly Galindo, Omar Kaczmarczyk, Richard Quick; *Production Companies*: Simitar Entertainment, Hollywood Home Vision; *Distributors*: Simitar Entertainment, Hollywood Home Vision; *Runtime*: 76 minutes; *Rating*: Not listed

Candyman (1992)

Director: Bernard Rose; *Writers*: Clive Barker, Bernard Rose; *Producers*: Steve Golin, Alan Poul, Sigurjon Sighvatsson; *Cast*: Virginia Madsen, Tony Todd, Kasi Lemmons; *Production Companies*: Polygram Filmed Entertainment, Propaganda Films; *Distributor*: Tri-Star Pictures; *Runtime*: 99 minutes; *Rating*: R / 18

Candyman: Farewell to the Flesh (1995)

Director: Bill Condon; *Writers*: Clive Barker, Rand Ravich, Mark Kruger; *Producers*: Sigurjon Sighvatsson, Greg Fienberg; *Cast*: Tony Todd, Kelly Rowan, William O'Leary; *Production Companies*: Polygram Filmed Entertainment, Propaganda Films; *Distributor*: Gramercy Pictures; *Runtime*: 93 minutes; *Rating*: R / 18

Candyman: Day of the Dead (1999)

Director: Turi Meyer; *Writers*: Turi Meyer, Al Septien; *Producers*: William Stuart, Al Septien; *Cast*: Tony Todd, Donna D'Errico, Alexia Robinson; *Production Company*: Artisan Entertainment; *Distributor*: Artisan Entertainment; *Runtime*: 93 minutes; *Rating*: R / 18

Carnosaur (1993)

Director: Adam Simon; *Writers*: John Brosnan, Adam Simon; *Producer*: Mike Elliott; *Cast*: Diane Ladd, Raphael Sbarge, Jennifer Runyon; *Production Company*: New Horizon Picture Corp.; *Distributor*: New Horizons; *Runtime*: 83 minutes; *Rating*: R / 15

Carnosaur 2 (1995)

Director: Louis Morneau; *Writer*: Michael Palmer; *Producer*: Roger Corman; *Cast*: John Savage, Cliff De Young, Rick Dean; *Production Companies*: Concorde-New Horizons, New Horizon Picture Corp.; *Distributor*: Concorde-New Horizons; *Runtime*: 83 minutes; *Rating*: R

Carnosaur 3: Primal Species (1996)

Director: Jonathan Winfrey; *Writer*: Rob Kerchner (story); *Producer*: Roger Corman; *Cast*: Scott Valentine, Stephen Lee, Janet Gunn; *Production Company*: Concorde-New Horizons; *Distributor*: New Horizons; *Runtime*: 85 minutes; *Rating*: R / 15

Carrie (1976)

Director: Brian De Palma; *Writers*: Stephen King, Lawrence D. Cohen; *Producers*: Brian De Palma, Paul Monash; *Cast*: Sissy Spacek, Piper Laurie, Amy Irving; *Production Company*: Redbank Films; *Distributor*: United Artists; *Runtime*: 98 minutes; *Rating*: R / 18

The Rage: Carrie II

Director: Katt Shea; *Writer:* Rafael Moreu; *Producer:* Paul Monash; *Cast:* Emily Bergl, Jason London, Amy Irving; *Production Companies:* Red Bank Films, United Artists; *Distributors:* Redbus Film Distribution, United Artists; *Runtime:* 104 minutes; *Rating:* R / 15

Carrie (2002)

Director: David Carson; *Writers:* Stephen King, Bryan Fuller; *Producer:* David Livingston; *Cast:* Angela Bettis, Patricia Clarkson, Rena Sofer; *Production Companies:* MGM Television, Trilogy Entertainment Group; *Distributors:* National Broadcasting Company (NBC), Chum Television, MGM/UA Television; *Runtime:* 132 minutes; *Rating:* Not Rated

☆ ☆ ☆

Children of the Corn (1984)

Director: Fritz Kiersch; *Writers:* Stephen King, George Goldsmith; *Producers:* Donald P. Borchers, Terence Kirby; *Cast:* Linda Hamilton, John Franklin, Peter Horton; *Production Companies:* Angeles Entertainment Group, Cinema Group, Gatlin, Inverness Productions, Hal Roach Studios Inc.; *Distributor:* New World Pictures; *Runtime:* 93 minutes; *Rating:* R / 18

Children of the Corn II: The Final Sacrifice (1993)

Director: David Price; *Writers:* Gilbert Adler, A.L. Katz; *Producers:* Scott A. Stone, David G. Stanley; *Cast:* Terence Knox, Ryan Bollman, Paul Scherrer; *Production Companies:* Corn Cobb Productions, Dimension Films, Fifth Avenue Entertainment; *Distributors:* Paramount Pictures, Dimension Films; *Runtime:* 92 minutes; *Rating:* R / 18

Children of the Corn III (1995)

Director: James D.R. Hickox; *Writer:* Dode B. Levenson; *Producers:* Brad Southwick, Gary Depew; *Cast:* Jim Metzler, Daniel Cerny, Nancy Grahn; *Production Companies:* Park Avenue Productions, Trans Atlantic Entertainment; *Distributors:* Dimension Films, Buena Vista Pictures; *Runtime:* 92 minutes; *Rating:* R / 18

Children of the Corn IV: The Gathering (1996)

Director: Greg Spence; *Writers:* Stephen Berger, Greg Spence; *Producer:* Gary Depew; *Cast:* Naomi Watts, Karen Black, Mark Salling; *Production Company:* Dimension Films; *Distributors:* Dimension Films, Buena Vista Home Video; *Runtime:* 85 minutes; *Rating:* R / 18

Children of the Corn V: Fields of Terror (1998)

Director: Ethan Wiley; *Writer:* Ethan Wiley; *Producers:* Jeff Geoffrey, Walter Josten; *Cast:* Alexis Arquette, David Carradine, Stacey Gallina; *Production Company:* Blue Rider Pictures; *Distributors:* New Films International, Dimension Films, Buena Vista Home Video; *Runtime:* 83 minutes; *Rating:* R / 18

Children of the Corn 666: Isaac's Return (1999)

Director: Kari Skogland; *Writers:* John Franklin, Tim Sulka; *Producers:* Jeff Geoffrey, Bill Berry, Walter Josten; *Cast:* John Franklin, Nancy Allen, Stacy Keach; *Production Company:* Blue Rider Pictures; *Distributors:* Buena Vista Home Video, Highlight Video; *Runtime:* 82 minutes; *Rating:* R / 18

Children of the Corn: Revelation (2001)

Director: Guy Magar; *Writer:* S.J. Smith; *Producers:* Joel Soisson, Michael Leahy; *Cast:* Claudette Mink, Michael Ironside, Kyle Cassie; *Production Company:* Neo Art & Logic; *Distributors:* Dimension Films, Buena Vista Home Video; *Runtime:* 82 minutes; *Rating:* R / 15

☆ ☆ ☆

Child's Play (1988)
Director: Tom Holland; *Writers*: Don Mancini, John Lafia, Tom Holland; *Producer*: David Kirschner; *Cast*: Brad Dourif, Chris Sarandon, Alex Vincent; *Production Company*: United Artists; *Distributor*: MGM/UA; *Runtime*: 87 minutes; *Rating*: R / 15

Child's Play 2 (1990)
Director: John Lafia; *Writer*: Don Mancini; *Producer*: David Kirschner; *Cast*: Brad Dourif, Jenny Agutter, Alex Vincent; *Production Company*: Universal Pictures; *Distributor*: Universal Pictures; *Runtime*: 84 minutes; *Rating*: R / 15

Child's Play 3 (1991)
Director: Jack Bender; *Writer*: Don Mancini; *Producer*: Robert Latham Brown; *Cast*: Justin Whalin, Perrey Reeves, Brad Dourif; *Production Company*: Universal Pictures; *Distributor*: Universal Pictures; *Runtime*: 90 minutes; *Rating*: R / 18

Bride of Chucky (1998)
Director: Ronny Yu; *Writer*: Don Mancini; *Producers*: David Kirschner, Grace Kilroy; *Cast*: Brad Dourif, Jennifer Tilly, John Ritter; *Production Company*: Midwinter Productions Inc., Universal Pictures; *Distributor*: Universal Pictures; *Runtime*: 89 minutes; *Rating*: R / 18

Seed of Chucky (2004)
Director: Don Mancini; *Writer*: Don Mancini; *Producers*: David Kirschner, Corey Sienega; *Cast*: Brad Dourif, Jennifer Tilly, Billy Boyd; *Production Companies*: Rogue Pictures, David Kirschner Productions, Castel Film Romania, La Sienega Productions; *Distributor*: Rogue Pictures; *Runtime*: 87 minutes; *Rating*: R / 15

C.H.U.D. (1984)
Director: Douglas Cheek; *Writers*: Shepard Abbott, Parnell Hall; *Producer*: Andrew Bonime; *Cast*: John Heard, Daniel Stern, Christopher Curry; *Production Companies*: C.H.U.D. Productions, New World Pictures; *Distributor*: New World Pictures; *Runtime*: 88 minutes / 96 minutes; *Rating*: R / 18

C.H.U.D. II: Bud the C.H.U.D. (1989)
Director: David Irving; *Writer*: Ed Naha; *Producer*: Jonathan D. Krane; *Cast*: Tricia Leigh Fisher, Gerrit Graham, Robert Vaughn; *Production Company*: M.C.E.G. Virgin Home Entertainment; *Distributors*: Lightning Pictures Inc., Vestron Video; *Runtime*: 84 minutes; *Rating*: R / 15

Class of 1984 (1982)
Director: Mark L. Lester; *Writers*: Mark L. Lester, John C.W. Saxton, Tom Holland; *Producer*: Arthur Kent; *Cast*: Perry King, Merrie Lynn Ross, Roddy McDowall; *Production Company*: Guerilla High Productions; *Distributor*: United Film Distribution Company (UFDC); *Runtime*: 98 minutes; *Rating*: R / 18

Class of 1999 (1990)
Director: Mark L. Lester; *Writers*: Mark L. Lester, C. Courtney Joyner; *Producer*: Mark L. Lester; *Cast*: Bradley Gregg, Malcolm McDowell, Stacy Keach; *Production Companies*: Lightning Pictures, Original Pictures, Vestron Pictures Ltd.; *Distributor*: Taurus Entertainment Company; *Runtime*: 99 minutes; *Rating*: R / 18

Class of 1999 II: The Substitute (1994)
Director: Spiro Razatos; *Writer*: Mark Sevi; *Producer*: Russell D. Markowitz; *Cast*: Sasha Mitchell, Caitlin Dulany, Nick Cassavetes; *Production Companies*: Grey Matter Entertainment, Trimark Pictures; *Distributor*:

Vidmark Entertainment; *Runtime*: 87 minutes; *Rating*: R / 18

Creepshow (1982)

Director: George A. Romero; *Writer*: Stephen King; *Producer*: Richard P. Rubinstein; *Cast*: Adrienne Barbeau, Leslie Nielsen, E.G. Marshall; *Production Companies*: Creepshow Films Inc., Laurel Entertainment Inc., Warner Bros. Pictures, Laurel-Show Inc.; *Distributor*: Warner Bros. Pictures; *Runtime*: 120 minutes; *Rating*: R / 15

Creepshow 2 (1987)

Director: Michael Gornick; *Writers*: Stephen King, George A. Romero; *Producer*: David Ball; *Cast*: Domenick John, Tom Savini, George Kennedy; *Production Companies*: Laurel Entertainment Inc., Laurel-Show Inc., New World Pictures; *Distributor*: New World Pictures; *Runtime*: 92 minutes; *Rating*: R / 18

Creepshow 3 (2006)

Directors: Ana Clavell, James Glenn Dudelson; *Writers*: Alex Ugelow, Ana Clavell, James Glenn Dudelson, Scott Frazelle, Pablo C. Pappano; *Producers*: Ana Clavell, James Glenn Dudelson; *Cast*: A.J. Bowen, Kris Allen, Stephanie Pettee; *Production Companies*: Creepy Film Production, Taurus Entertainment Company; *Distributor*: Taurus Entertainment Company; *Runtime*: 110 minutes; *Rating*: R

Critters (1986)

Director: Stephen Herek; *Writers*: Dominic Muir, Stephen Herek, Don Keith Opper; *Producers*: Barry Opper, Rupert Harvey; *Cast*: Dee Wallace-Stone, M. Emmet Walsh, Billy Zane; *Production Companies*: New Line Cinema, Sho Films, Smart Egg Pictures; *Distributors*: New Line Cinema, Columbia Tri-Star; *Runtime*: 82 minutes; *Rating*: PG-13 / 12

Critters 2: The Main Course (1988)

Director: Mick Garris; *Writers*: David Twohy, Mick Garris; *Producer*: Barry Opper; *Cast*: Don Keith Opper, Cynthia Garris, Scott Grimes; *Production Companies*: New Line Cinema, Sho Films; *Distributors*: New Line Cinema, MCA, RCA/Columbia; *Runtime*: 93 minutes; *Rating*: PG-13 / 12

Critters 3 (1991)

Director: Kristine Peterson; *Writers*: Rupert Harvey, Barry Opper, David J. Schow; *Producers*: Rupert Harvey and Barry Opper; *Cast*: Don Keith Opper, Aimee Brooks, Leonardo DiCaprio; *Production Companies*: New Line Cinema, OH Films; *Distributor*: New Line Home Video; *Runtime*: 86 minutes; *Rating*: PG-13 / 12

Critters 4 (1991)

Director: Rupert Harvey; *Writers*: Rupert Harvey, Barry Opper, Joseph Lyle, David J. Schow; *Producers*: Rupert Harvey, Barry Opper; *Cast*: Don Keith Opper, Angela Bassett, Brad Dourif; *Production Companies*: New Line Cinema, OH Films; *Distributor*: New Line Home Video; *Runtime*: 100 minutes; *Rating*: PG-13 / 15

☆ ☆ ☆

The Dentist (1996)

Director: Brian Yuzna; *Writers*: Dennis Paoli, Stuart Gordon, Charles Finch; *Producer*: Pierre David; *Cast*: Corbin Bernsen, Linda Hoffman, Ken Foree; *Production Company*: Pierre David; *Distributor*: Trimark Pictures; *Runtime*: 92 minutes; *Rating*: R / 18

The Dentist II (1998)

Director: Brian Yuzna; *Writer*: Richard Dana Smith; *Producers*: Pierre David, Bruce David Eisen; *Cast*: Corbin Bernsen, Jillian

McWhirter, Jeff Doucette; *Production Companies*: Pierre David, Trimark Pictures; *Distributors*: Trimark Pictures, Home Box Office (HBO); *Runtime*: 100 minutes; *Rating*: R / 18

Dracula 2000 (2000)
Director: Patrick Lussier; *Writers*: Joel Soisson, Patrick Lussier; *Producers*: Joel Soisson, W.K. Border; *Cast*: Gerard Butler, Christopher Plummer, Jonny Lee Miller; *Production Companies*: Carfax Productions Ltd., Dimension Films, Neo Art & Logic, Wes Craven Films; *Distributors*: Dimension Films, Miramax Films; *Runtime*: 99 minutes; *Rating*: R / 15

Dracula II: Ascension (2003)
Director: Patrick Lussier; *Writers*: Joel Soisson, Patrick Lussier; *Producers*: Joel Soisson, W.K. Border; *Cast*: Craig Sheffer, Stephen Billington, Jason Scott-Lee; *Production Companies*: Castel Film Romania, Neo Art & Logic; *Distributor*: Buena Vista Home Video; *Runtime*: 85 minutes; *Rating*: R / 15

Dracula III: Legacy (2005)
Director: Patrick Lussier; *Writers*: Joel Soisson, Patrick Lussier; *Producers*: Joel Soisson, W.K. Border; *Cast*: Jason Scott-Lee, Rutger Hauer, Diane Neal; *Production Companies*: Castel Film Romania, Buena Vista Pictures, Miramax Films, Neo Art & Logic; *Distributors*: Buena Vista Home Video, Dimension Films; *Runtime*: 90 minutes; *Rating*: R

The Evil Dead (1981)
Director: Sam Raimi; *Writer*: Sam Raimi; *Producer*: Robert G. Tapert; *Cast*: Bruce Campbell, Ellen Sandweiss, Betsy Baker; *Production Company*: Renaissance Pictures; *Distributor*: New Line Cinema; *Runtime*: 85 minutes; *Rating*: Unrated/NC-17 / 18

Evil Dead II: Dead by Dawn (1987)
Director: Sam Raimi; *Writers*: Sam Raimi, Scott Speigel; *Producer*: Robert G. Tapert; *Cast*: Bruce Campbell, Dan Hicks, Sarah Berry; *Production Companies*: Renaissance Pictures, DEG; *Distributor*: Rosebud Releasing Corporation; *Runtime*: 85 minutes; *Rating*: Unrated/R / 18

Army of Darkness (Evil Dead III) (1992)
Director: Sam Raimi; *Writers*: Sam Raimi, Ivan Raimi; *Producer*: Robert Tapert; *Cast*: Bruce Campbell, Embeth Davidtz, Marcus Gilbert; *Production Companies*: Dino de Laurentiis Corporation, Renaissance Pictures, Introvision International, Universal Pictures; *Distributor*: Universal Pictures; *Runtime*: 81minutes (96 minutes); *Rating*: R / 15

The Exorcist (1973)
Director: William Friedkin; *Writer*: William Peter Blatty; *Producer*: William Peter Blatty; *Cast*: Max Von Sydow, Jason Miller, Linda Blair; *Production Companies*: Hoya Productions, Warner Bros. Pictures; *Distributor*: Warner Bros.; *Runtime*: 122 minutes (132 minutes); *Rating*: R / 18

Exorcist II: The Heretic (1977)
Director: John Boorman; *Writer*: William Goodheart; *Producers*: John Boorman, Richard S. Lederer; *Cast*: Max Von Sydow, Linda Blair, Louise Fletcher; *Production Company*: Warner Bros. Pictures; *Distributor*: Warner Bros.; *Runtime*: 118 minutes; *Rating*: R / 18

The Exorcist III: Legion (1990)
Director: William Peter Blatty; *Writer*: William Peter Blatty; *Producer*: Carter DeHaven; *Cast*: Jason Miller, George C Scott, Brad Dourif; *Production Company*: Morgan Creek Productions; *Distributor*: Twentieth Century–Fox Film Corporation; *Runtime*: 110 minutes; *Rating*: R / 15

Exorcist: The Beginning (2004)
Director: Renny Harlin; *Writers*: William Wisher Jr., Caleb Carr, Alexi Hawley; *Producers*: James G. Robinson, William Raee; *Cast*: Stellan Skarsgård, Izabella Scorupco, James D'Arcy; *Production Companies*: Dominion Productions, Morgan Creek Productions; *Distributor*: Warner Bros.; *Runtime*: 114 minutes; *Rating*: R / 15

Dominion: Prequel to the Exorcist (2005)
Director: Paul Schrader; *Writers*: William Wisher Jr., Caleb Carr; *Producer*: James G. Robinson; *Cast*: Stellan Skarsgård, Gabriel Mann, Billy Crudup; *Production Company*: Morgan Creek International; *Distributor*: Warner Bros.; *Runtime*: 117 minutes; *Rating*: R / 15

Final Destination (2000)
Director: James Wong; *Writers*: Glen Morgan, James Wong, Jeffrey Reddick; *Producers*: Glen Morgan, Craig Perry, Warren Zide; *Cast*: Devon Sawa, Ali Larter, Kerr Smith; *Production Companies*: Hard Eight Pictures, New Line Cinema, Zide-Perry Productions; *Distributor*: New Line Cinema; *Runtime*: 98 minutes; *Rating*: R / 15

Final Destination 2 (2003)
Director: David R. Ellis; *Writers*: J. Mackye Gruber, Eric Bress, Jeffrey Reddick; *Producers*: Craig Perry, Warren Zide; *Cast*: Ali Larter, A.J. Cook, Michael Landes; *Production Companies*: New Line Cinema, Zide-Perry Productions; *Distributor*: New Line Cinema; *Runtime*: 90 minutes; *Rating*: R / 15

Final Destination 3 (2006)
Director: James Wong; *Writers*: Glen Morgan, James Wong; *Producers*: Glen Morgan, Craig Perry, James Wong, Warren Zide; *Cast*: Mary Elizabeth Winstead, Ryan Merriman, Kris Lemche; *Production Companies*: New Line Cinema, Hard Eight Pictures, Kumar Mobiliengesellschaft mbH & Co. Projekt Nr. 1 KG, Matinee Pictures, Practical Pictures, Zide-Perry Productions; *Distributor*: New Line Cinema; *Runtime*: 93 minutes; *Rating*: R / 15

Firestarter (1984)
Director: Mark L. Lester; *Writers*: Stephen King, Stanley Mann; *Producer*: Frank Capra Jr.; *Cast*: Drew Barrymore, Martin Sheen, George C. Scott; *Production Companies*: Dino De Laurentiis Productions, Universal Pictures; *Distributor*: Universal Pictures; *Runtime*: 114 minutes; *Rating*: R / 15

Firestarter Rekindled (2002)
Director: Robert Iscove; *Writer*: Philip Eisner; *Producer*: Jeffrey Morton; *Cast*: Marguerite Moreau, Malcolm McDowell, Dennis Hopper; *Production Companies*: USA Films, Traveler's Rest Films, USA Cable Network; *Distributor*: The Sci-Fi Channel; *Runtime*: 168 minutes; *Rating*: PG / 15

The Fly (1986)
Director: David Cronenberg; *Writers*: George Langelaan, Charles Edward Pogue, David Cronenberg; *Producer*: Stuart Cornfeld; *Cast*: Jeff Goldblum, Geena Davis, John Getz; *Production Company*: Brooksfilms; *Distributor*: Twentieth Century–Fox Film Corporation; *Runtime*: 95 minutes; *Rating*: R / 18

The Fly II (1989)
Director: Chris Walas; *Writers*: Mick Garris, Jim Wheat, Ken Wheat, Frank Darabont; *Producer*: Steven-Charles Jaffe; *Cast*: Eric Stoltz, Daphne Zuniga, Lee Richardson; *Production Company*: Brooksfilms; *Distributor*: Twentieth Century–Fox Film

Corporation; *Runtime*: 105 minutes; *Rating*: R / 18

☆ ☆ ☆

Friday the 13th (1980)

Director: Sean S. Cunningham; *Writer*: Victor Miller; *Producer*: Sean S. Cunningham; *Cast*: Adrienne King, Kevin Bacon, Betsy Palmer; *Production Companies*: Georgetown Productions Inc., Sean S. Cunningham Films, Paramount Pictures; *Distributor*: Paramount Pictures; *Runtime*: 95 minutes; *Rating*: R / 18

Friday the 13th Part 2 (1981)

Director: Steve Miner; *Writer*: Ron Kurz; *Producer*: Steve Miner; *Cast*: Adrienne King, Amy Steel, John Furey; *Production Companies*: Paramount Pictures, Georgetown Productions Inc., Greengrass Productions; *Distributor*: Paramount Pictures; *Runtime*: 87 minutes; *Rating*: R / 18

Friday the 13th Part 3 (1982)

Director: Steve Miner; *Writers*: Martin Kitrosser, Carol Watson; *Producer*: Frank Mancuso Jr.; *Cast*: Dana Kimmell, Richard Brooker, Paul Kratka; *Production Companies*: Paramount Pictures, Jason Productions, Georgetown Productions Inc.; *Distributor*: Paramount Pictures; *Runtime*: 95 minutes; *Rating*: R / 18

Friday the 13th: The Final Chapter (1984)

Director: Joseph Zito; *Writers*: Bruce Hidemi Sakow, Barney Cohen; *Producer*: Frank Mancuso Jr.; *Cast*: Kimberley Beck, Corey Feldman, Erich Anderson; *Production Companies*: Paramount Pictures, Georgetown Productions Inc.; *Distributor*: Paramount Pictures; *Runtime*: 90 minutes; *Rating*: R / 18

Friday the 13th: A New Beginning (1985)

Director: Danny Steinmann; *Writers*: Martin Kitrosser, David Cohen, Danny Steinmann; *Producer*: Timothy Silva; *Cast*: John Shepherd, Melanie Kinneman, Todd Bryant; *Production Companies*: Paramount Pictures, Terror Inc., Georgetown Productions Inc.; *Distributor*: Paramount Pictures; *Runtime*: 92 minutes; *Rating*: R / 18

Friday the 13th Part VI: Jason Lives (1986)

Director: Tom McLoughlin; *Writer*: Tom McLoughlin; *Producer*: Don Behrns; *Cast*: Thom Matthews, Jennifer Cooke, Tony Goldwyn; *Production Companies*: Paramount Pictures, Terror Films Inc.; *Distributor*: Paramount Pictures; *Runtime*: 86 minutes; *Rating*: R / 15

Friday the 13th Part VII: The New Blood (1988)

Director: John Buechler; *Writers*: Daryl Haney, Manuel Fidello; *Producer*: Iain Paterson; *Cast*: Lar Park Lincoln, Kevin Spirtas, Kane Hodder; *Production Companies*: Friday Four Films Inc., Paramount Pictures; *Distributor*: Paramount Pictures; *Runtime*: 90 minutes; *Rating*: R / 18

Friday the 13th Part VIII: Jason Takes Manhattan (1989)

Director: Rob Hedden; *Writer*: Rob Hedden; *Producer*: Randy Cheveldave; *Cast*: Jensen Daggett, Scott Reeves, Kane Hodder; *Production Companies*: Horror Films, Paramount Pictures; *Distributor*: Paramount Pictures; *Runtime*: 100 minutes; *Rating*: R / 18

Jason Goes to Hell: The Final Friday (1993)

Director: Adam Marcus; *Writers*: Jay Huguely, Adam Marcus, Dean Lorey; *Producer*: Sean S. Cunningham; *Cast*: John D LeMay, Kane Hodder, Kari Keegan; *Production Companies*: Sean S. Cunningham Films, New Line Cinema; *Distributor*: New Line Cinema; *Runtime*: 87 minutes; *Rating*: R / 18

Jason X (2001)

Director: James Isaac; *Writer*: Todd Farmer; *Producer*: Noel B. Cunningham; *Cast*: Kane Hodder, Lexa Doig, Lisa Ryder; *Production Companies*: Friday X Productions, New Line Cinema, Crystal Lake Entertainment Inc.; *Distributor*: New Line Cinema; *Runtime*: 93 minutes; *Rating*: R / 15

☆ ☆ ☆

Fright Night (1986)

Director: Tom Holland; *Writer*: Tom Holland; *Producer*: Herb Jaffe; *Cast*: Roddy McDowell, Chris Sarandon, William Ragsdale; *Production Companies*: Columbia Pictures Corporation, Delphi IV Productions, Vistar Films; *Distributor*: Columbia Pictures; *Runtime*: 106 minutes; *Rating*: R / 18

Fright Night Part II (1988)

Director: Tommy Lee Wallace; *Writers*: Tim Metcalfe, Miguel Tejada-Flores, Tommy Lee Wallace; *Producers*: Herb Jaffe, Mort Engelberg, Miguel Tejada-Flores; *Cast*: Roddy McDowell, Julie Carmen, William Ragsdale; *Production Companies*: TriStar Pictures, Vista Organization; *Distributor*: New Century Vista Film Company; *Runtime*: 104 minutes; *Rating*: R / 18

☆ ☆ ☆

From Dusk Till Dawn (1995)

Director: Robert Rodriguez; *Writers*: Robert Kurtzman, Quentin Tarantino; *Producers*: Meir Teper, Gianni Nunnari; *Cast*: George Clooney, Harvey Keitel, Quentin Tarantino; *Production Companies*: A Band Apart, Dimension Films, Los Hooligans Productions, Miramax Films; *Distributor*: Dimension Films; *Runtime*: 108 minutes; *Rating*: R / 18

From Dusk Till Dawn 2: Texas Blood Money (1999)

Director: Scott Spiegel; *Writers*: Scott Spiegel, Boaz Yakin, Duane Whittaker; *Producers*: Gianni Nunnari, Meir Teper, Michael S. Murphy; *Cast*: Robert Patrick, Danny Trejo, Bo Hopkins; *Production Companies*: A Band Apart, Dimension Films, Los Hooligans Productions; *Distributor*: Dimension Home Video; *Runtime*: 88 minutes; *Rating*: R / 18

From Dusk Till Dawn 3: The Hangman's Daughter (2000)

Director: P.J. Pesce; *Writers*: Robert Rodriguez, Alvaro Rodriguez; *Producers*: Gianni Nunnari, Meir Teper, Michael S. Murphy; *Cast*: Sonia Braga, Danny Trejo, Rebecca Gayheart; *Production Companies*: A Band Apart, Dimension Films, Los Hooligans Productions; *Distributor*: Dimension Home Video; *Runtime*: 94 minutes; *Rating*: R / 18

☆ ☆ ☆

The Gate (1987)

Director: Tibor Takács; *Writer*: Michael Nankin; *Producer*: John Kemeny; *Cast*: Stephen Dorff, Christa Denton, Louis Tripp; *Production Companies*: Alliance Entertainment, Gate Productions, New Century Entertainment Corporation, The Vista Organization Ltd.; *Distributors*: New Century Vista Film Company, Vestron Video; *Runtime*: 85 minutes; *Rating*: PG-13 / 15

The Gate II (1992)

Director: Tibor Takács; *Writer*: Michael Nankin; *Producer*: András Hámori; *Cast*: Louis Tripp, Simon Reynolds, James Villemaire; *Production Companies*: Alliance Entertainment, Epic Productions Inc., New Century Vista Film Company, Vision PDG; *Distributors*: New Century Vista Film Company, Sony Video; *Runtime*: 90 minutes; *Rating*: PG-13 / 15

☆ ☆ ☆

Ghoulies (1985)

Director: Luca Bercovici; *Writers*: Luca Bercovici, Jefrey Levy; *Producer*: Jefrey

Levy; *Cast*: Peter Liapis, Lisa Pelkian, Jack Nance; *Production Company*: Empire Pictures; *Distributor*: Empire Pictures; *Runtime*: 81 minutes; *Rating*: PG-13 / 15

Ghoulies II (1987)

Director: Albert Band; *Writers*: Charlie Dolan, Dennis Paoli; *Producer*: Albert Band; *Cast*: Damon Martin, Phil Fondacaro, Kerry Remsen; *Production Company*: Empire Pictures; *Distributor*: Empire Pictures; *Runtime*: 89 minutes; *Rating*: PG-13 / 15

*Ghoulies III:
Ghoulies Go to College* (1991)

Director: John Carl Buechler; *Writer*: Brent Olsen; *Producer*: Iain Paterson; *Cast*: Jason Scott Lee, Kevin McCarthy, John Johnston; *Production Company*: Unknown; *Distributor*: Vestron Video. Taurus Entertainment Company, Live HomeVideo; *Runtime*: 94 minutes; *Rating*: R / 15

Ghoulies IV (1994)

Director: Jim Wynorski; *Writer*: Mark Sevi; *Producer*: Gary Schmoeller; *Cast*: Barbara Alyn Woods, Bobby Di Cicco, Stacie Randall; *Production Company*: Cinetel Films Inc.; *Distributor*: Unknown; *Runtime*: 84 minutes; *Rating*: R / 12

☆ ☆ ☆

Ginger Snaps (2000)

Director: John Fawcett; *Writers*: Karen Walton, John Fawcett; *Producers*: Karen Lee Hall, Steven Hoban; *Cast*: Emily Perkins, Katharine Isabelle, Mimi Rogers; *Production Companies*: Copper Heart Entertainment, Water Pictures, Motion International, Lions Gate Films, Unapix Entertainment Inc., Canadian Television Fund, Téléfilm Canada, Space: The Imagination Station, The Movie Network (TMN), Oddbod Productions Inc., TVA International; *Distributor*: Artisan Home Entertainment; *Runtime*: 108 minutes; *Rating*: Unrated / 18

Ginger Snaps: Unleashed (2004)

Director: Brett Sullivan; *Writer*: Megan Martin; *Producers*: Grant Harvey, Steven Hoban; *Cast*: Emily Perkins, Tatiana Maslany, Eric Johnson; *Production Companies*: 49th Parallel Productions, Combustion Inc.; *Distributor*: Lions Gate Films; *Runtime*: 94 minutes; *Rating*: R / 18

Ginger Snaps: The Beginning (2004)

Director: Grant Harvey; *Writers*: Stephen Massicotte, Christina Ray; *Producers*: Paula Devonshire, Grant Harvey, Steven Hoban; *Cast*: Katharine Isabelle, Emily Perkins, Nathaniel Arcand; *Production Company*: Combustion Inc.; *Distributor*: Lions Gate Films; *Runtime*: 94 minutes; *Rating*: R / 18

☆ ☆ ☆

The Grudge (2004)

Director: Takashi Shimizu; *Writers*: Takashi Shimizu, Stephen Susco; *Producers*: Sam Raimi, Takashige Ichise; *Cast*: Sarah Michelle Gellar, Jason Behr, William Mapother; *Production Companies*: Senator International, Ghost House Pictures, Vertigo Entertainment, Renaissance Pictures, Fellah Pictures; *Distributors*: Sony Pictures Entertainment, Columbia Pictures; *Runtime*: 92 minutes; *Rating*: PG-13 / 15

The Grudge 2 (2006)

Director: Takashi Shimizu; *Writers*: Takashi Shimizu, Stephen Susco; *Producers*: Robert G. Tapert, Takashige Ichise; *Cast*: Sarah Michelle Gellar, Amber Tamblyn, Edison Chen; *Production Companies*: Columbia Pictures Corporation, Ghost House Pictures, Mandate Pictures, Vertigo Entertainment; *Distributors*: Sony Pictures Entertainment, Columbia Pictures; *Runtime*: 92 minutes; *Rating*: PG-13 / 15

☆ ☆ ☆

Halloween (1978)

Director: John Carpenter; *Writers*: John

Carpenter, Debra Hill; *Producer*: Debra Hill; *Cast*: Jamie Lee Curtis, Donald Pleasance, P.J. Soles; *Production Company*: Compass International Pictures, Falcon Films; *Distributor*: Compass International Pictures; *Runtime*: 91 minutes; *Rating*: R / 18

Halloween II (1981)

Director: Rick Rosenthal; *Writers*: John Carpenter, Debra Hill; *Producers*: John Carpenter, Debra Hill; *Cast*: Jamie Lee Curtis, Donald Pleasance, Charles Cyphers; *Production Companies*: Dino De Laurentiis Productions, Universal Pictures; *Distributor*: Universal Pictures; *Runtime*: 92 minutes; *Rating*: R / 18

Halloween III: Season of the Witch (1983)

Director: Tommy Lee Wallace; *Writers*: Nigel Kneale, Tommy Lee Wallace; *Producers*: Debra Hill, John Carpenter; *Cast*: Tom Atkins, Stacey Nelkinm, Dan O' Herlihy; *Production Companies*: Dino De Laurentiis Productions, Universal Pictures; *Distributor*: Universal Pictures; *Runtime*: 96 minutes; *Rating*: R / 15

Halloween 4: The Return of Michael Myers (1988)

Director: Dwight H. Little; *Writers*: Danny Lipsius, Larry Rattner, Ben Ruffner, Alan McElroy; *Producer*: Paul Freeman; *Cast*: Donald Pleasance, Danielle Harris, Kathleen Kinmont; *Production Company*: Trancas International Films; *Distributor*: Galaxy International Releasing; *Runtime*: 88 minutes; *Rating*: R / 18

Halloween 5: The Revenge of Michael Myers (1989)

Director: Dominique Othenin-Girard; *Writers*: Shem Bitterman, Michael Jacobs, Dominique Othenin-Girard; *Producer*: Ramsey Thomas; *Cast*: Donald Pleasance, Danielle Harris, Ellie Cornell; *Production Companies*: The Return of Myers, Trancas International Films, Magnum Pictures Inc.; *Distributor*: Galaxy International Releasing; *Runtime*: 96 minutes; *Rating*: R / 18

Halloween: The Curse of Michael Myers (1995)

Director: Joe Chappelle; *Writer*: Daniel Ferrands; *Producer*: Paul Freeman; *Cast*: Donald Pleasance, Paul Rudd, Kim Darby; *Production Companies*: Halloween VI Productions, Nightfall, Miramax Films; *Distributor*: Dimension Films; *Runtime*: 88 minutes; *Rating*: R / 18

Halloween H20: 20 Years Later (1998)

Director: Steve Miner; *Writers*: Robert Zappia, Matt Greenburg; *Producer*: Paul Freeman; *Cast*: Jamie Lee Curtis, Michelle Williams, Josh Hartnett; *Production Companies*: Dimension Films, Nightfall Productions; *Distributor*: Dimension Films; *Runtime*: 87 minutes; *Rating*: R / 18

Halloween: Resurrection (2002)

Director: Rick Rosenthal; *Writers*: Larry Brand, Sean Hood; *Producers*: Paul Freeman, Michael Leahy; *Cast*: Bianca Kajilich, Busta Rhymes, Jamie Lee Curtis; *Production Companies*: Dimension Films, Nightfall Productions, Trancas International Films; *Distributors*: Miramax Films, Dimension Films; *Runtime*: 94 minutes; *Rating*: R / 15

Hellraiser (1987)

Director: Clive Barker; *Writer*: Clive Barker; *Producer*: Christopher Figg; *Cast*: Doug Bradley, Ashley Lawrence, Claire Higgins; *Production Companies*: Cinemarque Entertainment BV, Film Futures, Rivdel Films; *Distributor*: New World Pictures; *Runtime*: 94 minutes; *Rating*: R / 18

Hellbound: Hellraiser II (1988)

Director: Tony Randel; *Writers*: Peter Atkins, Clive Barker; *Producer*: Christopher Figg; *Cast*: Doug Bradley, Ashley Lawrence,

Claire Higgins; *Production Companies*: Film Futures, New World Pictures, Troopstar; *Distributor*: New World Pictures; *Runtime*: 97 minutes; *Rating*: R / 18

Hellraiser III: Hell on Earth (1992)

Director: Anthony Hickox; *Writers*: Peter Atkins, Tony Randel; *Producers*: Christopher Figg, Lawrence Mortoff; *Cast*: Doug Bradley, Terry Farrell, Paula Marshall; *Production Companies*: Fifth Avenue Entertainment, Trans Atlantic Entertainment; *Distributors*: Miramax Films, Paramount Pictures; *Runtime*: 93 minutes (97 minutes); *Rating*: R / 18

Hellraiser: Bloodline (1996)

Director: Alan Smithee (Kevin Yagher); *Writer*: Peter Atkins; *Producer*: Nancy Rae Stone; *Cast*: Doug Bradley, Bruce Ramsay, Valentina Vargas; *Production Companies*: Dimension Films, Miramax Films, Trans Atlantic Entertainment; *Distributors*: Dimension Films, Miramax Films; *Runtime*: 86 minutes; *Rating*: R / 18

Hellraiser: Inferno (2000)

Director: Scott Derrickson; *Writers*: Scott Derrickson, Paul Harris Boardman; *Producers*: W.K. Border, Joel Soisson; *Cast*: Doug Bradley, Craig Sheffer, James Remar; *Production Companies*: Dimension Films, Miramax Films, Neo Art & Logic; *Distributors*: Dimension Films, Buena Vista Home Video; *Runtime*: 99 minutes; *Rating*: R / 18

Hellraiser: Hellseeker (2002)

Director: Rick Bota; *Writers*: Carl V. Dupre, Tim Day; *Producers*: Michael Leahy, Ron Schmidt; *Cast*: Doug Bradley, Ashley Lawrence, Dean Winters; *Production Companies*: Dimension Films, Miramax Films, Neo Art & Logic, Cold Day Ltd.; *Distributor*: Buena Vista Home Video; *Runtime*: 89 minutes; *Rating*: R / 18

Hellraiser: Deader (2005)

Director: Rick Bota; *Writers*: Neal Marshall Stevens, Tim Day; *Producers*: David S. Greathouse, Ron Schmidt; *Cast*: Doug Bradley, Kari Wuhrer, Paul Rhys; *Production Companies*: Castel Film Romania, Dimension Films, Miramax Films, Neo Art & Logic; *Distributors*: Buena Vista Home Video, Dimension Films, Miramax Films; *Runtime*: 88 minutes; *Rating*: R

Hellraiser: Hellworld (2005)

Director: Rick Bota; *Writers*: Joel Soisson, Carl V. Dupre; *Producer*: Ron Schmidt; *Cast*: Doug Bradley, Lance Henriksen, Kateryn Winnick; *Production Companies*: Castel Film Romania, Dimension Films, Miramax Films; *Distributor*: Buena Vista Home Video; *Runtime*: 91minutes; *Rating*: R

☆ ☆ ☆

The Hills Have Eyes (1977)

Director: Wes Craven; *Writer*: Wes Craven; *Producer*: Peter Locke; *Cast*: Susan Lanier, Robert Houston, Dee Wallace-Stone; *Production Company*: Blood Relations Co.; *Distributor*: Vanguard; *Runtime*: 89 minutes; *Rating*: R / 18

The Hills Have Eyes Part II (1985)

Director: Wes Craven; *Writer*: Wes Craven; *Producer*: Peter Locke; *Cast*: Robert Houston, Janus Blythe, Michael Berryman; *Production Company*: VTC; *Distributors*: Castle Hill Productions, Vestron Video; *Runtime*: 86 minutes; *Rating*: R / 18

The Hills Have Eyes (2006)

Director: Alexandre Aja; *Writers*: Wes Craven, Alexandre Aja, Grégory Levasseur; *Producers*: Wes Craven, Peter Locke, Marianne Maddalena; *Cast*: Aaron Stanford, Kathleen Quinlan, Ted Levine; *Production Companies*: Craven-Maddalena Films, Dune Entertainment, Major Studio Partners; *Distributor*: Fox Searchlight Pictures; *Runtime*: 107 minutes; *Rating*: R / 18

The Hills Have Eyes 2 (2007)
Director: Martin Wesiz; *Writers*: Jonathan Craven, Wes Craven; *Producers*: Wes Craven, Peter Locke, Marianne Maddalena; *Cast*: Michael McMillian, Jessica Stroup, Daniella Alonso; *Production Companies*: Craven-Maddalena Films, Dune Entertainment, Major Studio Partners; *Distributor*: Fox Atomic; *Runtime*: Unknown; *Rating*: R / 18

The Hitcher (1986)
Director: Robert Harmon; *Writer*: Eric Red; *Producers*: Kip Ohman, David Bombyk; *Cast*: C. Thomas Howell, Rutger Hauer, Jennifer Jason Leigh; *Production Companies*: HBO Pictures, Silver Screen Partners, TriStar Pictures; *Distributor*: TriStar Pictures; *Runtime*: 97 minutes; *Rating*: R / 18

The Hitcher II: I've Been Waiting (2003)
Director: Louis Morneau; *Writers*: Molly Meeker, Charles R. Meeker, Leslie Scharf; *Producers*: Alfred Haber, Oliver G. Hess, Kevin M. Kallberg, Charles R. Meeker; *Cast*: Kari Wuhrer, Jake Busey, C. Thomas Howell; *Production Company*: Universal Home Entertainment Productions; *Distributor*: Universal Studios Home Video; *Runtime*: 93 minutes; *Rating*: R / 15

The Hitcher (2007)
Director: Dave Meyers; *Writers*: Eric Red, Jake Wade Wall, Eric Bernt; *Producers*: Michael Bay, Andrew Form, Bradley Fuller, Alfred Haber, David Linde, Charles R. Meeker; *Cast*: Sean Bean, Sophia Bush, Zachary Knighton; *Production Companies*: Intrepid Pictures, Platinum Dunes; *Distributor*: Rogue Pictures; *Runtime*: 83 minutes; *Rating*: R

House (1986)
Director: Steve Miner; *Writers*: Fred Dekker, Ethan Wiley; *Producer*: Sean S. Cunningham; *Cast*: William Katt, George Wendt, Kay Lenz; *Production Company*: New World Pictures; *Distributor*: New World Pictures; *Runtime*: 93 minutes; *Rating*: R / 15

House II: The Second Story (1987)
Director: Ethan Wiley; *Writer*: Ethan Wiley; *Producer*: Sean S. Cunningham; *Cast*: John Ratzenberger, Arye Gross, Lar Park-Lincoln; *Production Company*: New World Pictures; *Distributor*: New World Pictures; *Runtime*: 88 minutes; *Rating*: PG-13 / 15

House III: The Horror Show (1989)
Director: James Isaacs; *Writers*: Alan Smithee (Allyn Warner), Leslie Bohem; *Producer*: Sean S. Cunningham; *Cast*: Lance Henriksen, Brian James, Rita Taggert; *Production Company*: Sean S. Cunningham Films; *Distributor*: United Artists; *Runtime*: 95 minutes; *Rating*: R / 18

House IV (1992)
Director: Lewis Abernathy; *Writers*: Geof Miller, Deirdre Higgins, Jim Wynorski, R.J. Robertson; *Producers*: Sean S. Cunningham, Debbie Hayn-Cass; *Cast*: Terri Treas, Melissa Clayton, William Katt; *Production Company*: Sean S. Cunningham Films; *Distributor*: New Line Home Video; *Runtime*: 94 minutes; *Rating*: R / 15

House of 1,000 Corpses (2003)
Director: Rob Zombie; *Writer*: Rob Zombie; *Producer*: Andy Gould; *Cast*: Sid Haig, Bill Mosely, Karen Black; *Production Company*: Universal Pictures; *Distributor*: Lions Gate Films; *Runtime*: 89 minutes; *Rating*: R / 18

The Devil's Rejects (2005)
Director: Rob Zombie; *Writer*: Rob Zombie; *Producers*: Mike Elliott, Andy Gould, Marco Mehlitz, Michael Ohoven, Rob Zombie; *Cast*: Sid Haig, Bill Mosely, Sheri Moon Zombie; *Production Companies*: Lions Gate Films, Cinerenta Medienbeteiligungs KG,

Devil's Rejects Inc., Firm Films, Entache Entertainment, Creep Entertainment International; *Distributor*: Lions Gate Films; *Runtime*: 109 minutes; *Rating*: R / 18

The Howling (1981)

Director: Joe Dante; *Writers*: Gary Brandner, John Sayles, Terence H. Winkless; *Producers*: Michael Finnell, Jack Conrad; *Cast*: Dee Wallace, Patrick MacNee, Dick Miller; *Production Companies*: AVCO Embassy Pictures, International Film Investors, Wescom Productions; *Distributor*: AVCO Embassy Pictures; *Runtime*: 91 minutes; *Rating*: R / 18

The Howling II: Your Sister Is a Werewolf (1985)

Director: Philippe Mora; *Writers*: Robert Sarno, Gary Brandner; *Producer*: Steven Lane; *Cast*: Christopher Lee, Sybil Danning, Annie McEnroe; *Production Companies*: Cinema 86, Euro Film Fund, Granite, Thorn EMI Screen Entertainment; *Distributor*: Hemdale Film Corporation; *Runtime*: 91 minutes; *Rating*: R / 18

Howling III: The Marsupials (1987)

Director: Philippe Mora; *Writer*: Philippe Mora; *Producers*: Charles Waterstreet, Philippe Mora; *Cast*: Barry Otto, Imogen Annesley, Leigh Biolos; *Production Company*: Bancannia Holdings Pty. Ltd.; *Distributors*: Square Pictures, Vista Home Video; *Runtime*: 94 minutes; *Rating*: PG-13 / 18

Howling IV: The Original Nightmare (1988)

Director: John Hough; *Writers*: Freddie Rowe, Clive Turner; *Producer*: Harry Alan Towers; *Cast*: Romy Windsor, Michael Weiss, Anthony Hamilton; *Production Companies*: Allied Entertainments Group PLC, Allied Vision Ltd.; *Distributor*: International Video Entertainment (IVE); *Runtime*: 94 minutes; *Rating*: R / 18

Howling V: The Rebirth (1989)

Director: Neal Sundstrom; *Writers*: Freddie Rowe, Clive Turner; *Producer*: Clive Turner; *Cast*: Victoria Catlin, Philip Davis, Ben Cole; *Production Companies*: Allied Vision Ltd., Lane Pringle Productions; *Distributor*: International Video Entertainment (IVE); *Runtime*: 96 minutes; *Rating*: R / 15

Howling VI: The Freaks (1991)

Director: Hope Perello; *Writer*: Kevin Rock; *Producer*: Robert Pringle; *Cast*: Brendan Hughes, Michele Matheson, Bruce Payne; *Production Companies*: Allied Entertainments Group PLC, Allied Vision Ltd.; *Distributor*: Image Entertainment; *Runtime*: 102 minutes; *Rating*: R / 18

Howling: New Moon Rising (1995)

Director: Clive Turner; *Writer*: Clive Turner; *Producer*: Clive Turner; *Cast*: John Ramsden, Ernest Kester, Clive Turner; *Production Companies*: Allied Entertainments Group PLC, Allied Vision Ltd.; *Distributors*: New Line Home Video, Park Entertainment; *Runtime*: 90 minutes; *Rating*: R / 15

I Know What You Did Last Summer (1997)

Director: Jim Gillespie; *Writers*: Lois Duncan, Kevin Williamson; *Producers*: Stokely Chaffin, Erik Feig, Neal H. Moritz; *Cast*: Jennifer Love Hewitt, Freddie Prinze Jr., Sarah Michelle Gellar; *Production Companies*: Columbia Pictures Corporation, Mandalay Entertainment, Summer Knowledge LLC; *Distributors*: Columbia Pictures, Sony Pictures Entertainment; *Runtime*: 100 minutes; *Rating*: R / 15

I Still Know What You Did Last Summer (1998)

Director: Danny Cannon; *Writer*: Trey Callaway; *Producers*: William S. Beasley, Stokely Chaffin, Erik Feig, Neal H. Moritz; *Cast*:

Jennifer Love Hewitt, Freddie Prinze Jr., Mekhi Phifer; *Production Companies*: Mandalay Entertainment, Summer Knowledge LLC; *Distributors*: Columbia Pictures, Sony Pictures Entertainment; *Runtime*: 100 minutes; *Rating*: R / 18

I'll Always Know What You Did Last Summer (2006)

Director: Sylvain White; *Writer*: Michael D. Weiss; *Producers*: Amanda Cohen, Erik Feig, Nancy Kirhoffer, Neal H. Moritz; *Cast*: Brooke Nevin, Ben Easter, Torrey DeVitto; *Production Companies*: Screen Gems Inc., Sony Pictures Entertainment; *Distributors*: Screen Gems Inc., Sony Pictures Entertainment; *Runtime*: 92 minutes; *Rating*: R / 15

Interview with the Vampire (1994)

Director: Neil Jordan; *Writer*: Anne Rice; *Producers*: David Geffen, Stephen Woolley; *Cast*: Tom Cruise, Brad Pitt, Kirsten Dunst; *Production Company*: Geffen Pictures; *Distributor*: Warner Bros. Pictures; *Runtime*: 123 minutes; *Rating*: R / 18

Queen of the Damned (2002)

Director: Michael Rymer; *Writers*: Anne Rice, Scott Abbott, Michael Petroni; *Producer*: Jorge Saralegui; *Cast*: Aailyah, Stuart Townsend, Vincent Perez; *Production Companies*: Material, NPV Entertainment, Village Roadshow Pictures, WV Films LLC, Warner Bros. Pictures; *Distributor*: Warner Bros. Pictures; *Runtime*: 101 minutes; *Rating*: R / 15

It's Alive (1974)

Director: Larry Cohen; *Writer*: Larry Cohen; *Producer*: Larry Cohen; *Cast*: John P. Ryan, Andrew Duggan, James Dixon; *Production Companies*: Warner Bros. Pictures, Larco Productions Inc.; *Distributor*: Warner Bros. Pictures; *Runtime*: 91minutes; *Rating*: PG / 15

It Lives Again (1978)

Director: Larry Cohen; *Writer*: Larry Cohen; *Producer*: Larry Cohen; *Cast*: Frederic Forest, Andrew Duggan, John P. Ryan; *Production Company*: Larco Productions Inc.; *Distributor*: Warner Bros. Pictures; *Runtime*: 91 minutes; *Rating*: R / 15

It's Alive III: Island of the Alive (1987)

Director: Larry Cohen; *Writer*: Larry Cohen; *Producers*: Paul Stada, Paul Kurta; *Cast*: Michael Moriarty, Karen Black, Laurene Landon; *Production Company*: Larco Productions Inc.; *Distributor*: Warner Bros. Pictures; *Runtime*: 95 minutes; *Rating*: R / 15

Jaws (1975)

Director: Steven Spielberg; *Writers*: Peter Benchley, Carl Gottlieb; *Producers*: Richard D. Zanuck, David Brown; *Cast*: Roy Scheider, Richard Dreyfuss, Robert Shaw; *Production Companies*: Universal Pictures, Zanuck/Brown productions; *Distributor*: Universal Pictures; *Runtime*: 124 minutes; *Rating*: PG / PG

Jaws 2 (1978)

Director: Jeannot Szwarc; *Writers*: Howard Sackler, Carl Gottlieb; *Producers*: Richard D. Zanuck, David Brown; *Cast*: Roy Scheider, Lorraine Gary, Murray Hamilton; *Production Company*: Universal Pictures; *Distributor*: Universal Pictures; *Runtime*: 116 minutes; *Rating*: PG / PG

Jaws 3-D (1983)

Director: Joe Alves; *Writers*: Guerdon Trueblood, Richard Matheson, Carl Gottlieb, Michael Kane; *Producer*: Rupert Hitzig; *Cast*: Dennis Quaid, Bess Armstrong, Lou Gossett Jr.; *Production Companies*: Alan Landsburg

Productions, MCA Theatricals, Universal Pictures; *Distributor*: Universal Pictures; *Runtime*: 99 minutes; *Rating*: PG / 12

Jaws: The Revenge (1987)

Director: Joseph Sargent; *Writer*: Michael De Guzman; *Producer*: Joseph Sargent; *Cast*: Lorraine Gary, Michael Caine, Lance Guest; *Production Company*: Universal Pictures; *Distributor*: Universal Pictures; *Runtime*: 89 minutes; *Rating*: PG / 12

Jeepers Creepers (2001)

Director: Victor Salva; *Writer*: Victor Salva; *Producers*: Tom Luse, Barry Opper; *Cast*: Gina Phillips, Justin Long, Jonathan Breck; *Production Companies*: Cinerenta Medienbeteiligungs KG, VCL Communications GmbH, American Zoetrope, Cinerenta-Cinebeta; *Distributor*: MGM/UA Distribution Company; *Runtime*: 90 minutes; *Rating*: R / 15

Jeepers Creepers 2 (2003)

Director: Victor Salva; *Writer*: Victor Salva; *Producer*: Tom Luse; *Cast*: Jonathan Breck, Eric Nenninger, Ray Wise; *Production Companies*: American Zoetrope, Jeepers Creepers II LLC, Myriad Pictures Inc.; *Distributor*: MGM/UA Distribution Company; *Runtime*: 104 minutes; *Rating*: R / 15

Jurassic Park (1993)

Director: Steven Spielberg; *Writers*: Michael Crichton, David Koepp; *Producers*: Kathleen Kennedy, Gerald R. Molen; *Cast*: Sam Neill, Laura Dern, Jeff Goldblum; *Production Companies*: Universal Pictures, Amblin Entertainment; *Distributor*: Universal Pictures; *Runtime*: 127 minutes; *Rating*: PG-13 / PG

The Lost World: Jurassic Park (1997)

Director: Steven Spielberg; *Writers*: Michael Crichton, David Koepp; *Producers*: Gerald R. Molen, Colin Wilson; *Cast*: Jeff Goldblum, Julianne Moore, Pete Postlethwaite; *Production Companies*: Universal Pictures, Amblin Entertainment; *Distributor*: Universal Pictures; *Runtime*: 129 minutes; *Rating*: PG-13 / PG

Jurassic Park III

Director: Joe Johnston; *Writers*: Peter Buchman, Alexander Payne, Jim Taylor; *Producers*: Larry J. Franco, Kathleen Kennedy; *Cast*: Sam Neill, William H. Macy, Téa Leoni; *Production Companies*: Universal Pictures, Amblin Entertainment; *Distributor*: Universal Pictures; *Runtime*: 92 minutes; *Rating*: PG-13 / PG

Leprechaun (1993)

Director: Mark Jones; *Writer*: Mark Jones; *Producer*: Jeffrey B. Mallian; *Cast*: Warwick Davis, Jennifer Aniston, Ken Olandt; *Production Company*: Trimark Pictures; *Distributor*: Trimark Pictures; *Runtime*: 92 minutes; *Rating*: R / 15

Leprechaun 2 (1994)

Director: Rodman Flender; *Writers*: Turi Meyer, Al Septien; *Producer*: Donald P. Borchers; *Cast*: Warwick Davies, Charlie Heath, Sandy Baron; *Production Company*: Trimark Pictures; *Distributor*: Trimark Pictures; *Runtime*: 85 minutes; *Rating*: R / 18

Leprechaun 3 (1995)

Director: Brian Trenchard-Smith; *Writer*: David DuBos; *Producers*: Jeff Geoffray, Walter Josten, Henry Seggerman; *Cast*: Warwick Davis, John Gatins, Lee Armstrong; *Production Company*: Blue Rider Productions; *Distributor*: Trimark Pictures; *Runtime*: 90 minutes; *Rating*: R / 15

Leprechaun 4: In Space (1997)

Director: Brian Trenchard-Smith; *Writer*: Dennis A. Pratt; *Producers*: Jeff Geoffray, Walter Josten; *Cast*: Warwick Davies,

Debbie Dunning, Rebekah Carlton; *Production Company*: Blue Rider Productions; *Distributor*: Trimark Pictures; *Runtime*: 95 minutes; *Rating*: R / 15

Leprechaun in the Hood (2000)

Director: Rob Spera; *Writers*: Doug Hall, John Huffman, Alan Reynolds, Rob Spera, William Wells; *Producers*: Bruce David Eisen, Darin Spillman, Mike Upton; *Cast*: Warwick Davis, Ice-T, Coolio; *Production Company*: Trimark Pictures; *Distributor*: Trimark Pictures; *Runtime*: 90 minutes; *Rating*: R / 15

Leprechaun: Back to the Hood (2003)

Director: Steven Ayromlooi; *Writer*: Steven Ayromlooi; *Producer*: Mike Upton; *Cast*: Warwick Davis, Tangi Miller, Laz Alonso; *Production Company*: Lions Gate Entertainment; *Distributor*: Lions Gate Films; *Runtime*: 90 minutes; *Rating*: R

The Mangler (1995)

Director: Tobe Hooper; *Writers*: Stephen King, Tobe Hooper, Stephen David Brooks, Harry Alan Towers; *Producer*: Anant Singh; *Cast*: Robert Englund, Ted Levine, Daniel Matmor; *Production Companies*: Allied Film Production, Distant Horizons, Filmex Pty. Ltd, New Line Cinema; *Distributor*: New Line Cinema; *Runtime*: 106 minutes; *Rating*: R / 18

The Mangler 2 (2001)

Director: Michael Hamilton-Wright; *Writer*: Michael Hamilton-Wright; *Producer*: Glen Tedham; *Cast*: Lance Henriksen, Chelse Swain, Philippe Bergeron; *Production Companies*: Banana Brothers Entertainment Inc., Barnholtz Entertainment; *Distributor*: Artisan Entertainment; *Runtime*: 97 minutes; *Rating*: R / 15

The Mangler Reborn (2005)

Directors: Matt Cunningham, Erik Gardner; *Writers*: Matt Cunningham, Erik Gardner; *Producers*: Mark Burman, Scott Pearlman; *Cast*: Aimee Brooks, Reggie Bannister, Weston Blakesley; *Production Companies*: Assembly Line Studios, Barnholtz Entertainment, MEB Entertainment, Mangler Reborn Productions LLC; *Distributors*: Lions Gate Films, Barnholtz Entertainment; *Runtime*: 84 minutes; *Rating*: R

Manhunter (1986)

Director: Michael Mann; *Writers*: Thomas Harris, Michael Mann; *Producers*: Dino De Laurentiis, Richard Roth; *Cast*: William L. Petersen, Joan Allen, Brian Cox; *Production Companies*: De Laurentiis Entertainment Group (DEG), Studio Canal, Red Dragon Productions S.A.; *Distributor*: De Laurentiis Entertainment Group (DEG); *Runtime*: 119 minutes / 124 minutes; *Rating*: R / 18

The Silence of the Lambs (1991)

Director: Jonathan Demme; *Writers*: Thomas Harris, Ted Tally; *Producers*: Ronald M. Bozman, Edward Saxon, Kenneth Utt; *Cast*: Jodie Foster, Anthony Hopkins, Scott Glenn; *Production Companies*: Orion Pictures Corporation, Strong Heart/Demme Production; *Distributor*: Orion Pictures Corporation; *Runtime*: 118 minutes; *Rating*: R / 18

Hannibal (2001)

Director: Ridley Scott; *Writers*: Thomas Harris, David Mamet, Steven Zaillian; *Producers*: Dino De Laurentiis, Martha Schumacher, Ridley Scott; *Cast*: Julianne Moore, Anthony Hopkins, Gary Oldman; *Production Companies*: Dino De Laurentiis Productions, Metro-Goldwyn-Mayer (MGM), Scott Free Productions, Universal Pictures; *Distributor*: Metro-Goldwyn-Mayer (MGM); *Runtime*: 131 minutes; *Rating*: R / 18

Red Dragon (2002)

Director: Brett Ratner; *Writers*: Thomas Harris, Ted Tally; *Producers*: Dino De Laurentiis,

Martha Schumacher; *Cast*: Anthony Hopkins, Edward Norton, Ralph Fiennes; *Production Companies*: Dino De Laurentiis Company (DDLC), Metro-Goldwyn-Mayer (MGM), Mikona Productions GmbH & Co. KG, Scott Free Productions, Universal Pictures; *Distributor*: Universal Pictures; *Runtime*: 124 minutes; *Rating*: R / 15

Hannibal Rising (2007)

Director: Peter Webber; *Writer*: Thomas Harris; *Producers*: Tarak Ben Ammar, Dino De Laurentiis, Martha Schumacher; *Cast*: Gaspard Ulliel, Li Gong, Helena Lia Tachovska; *Production Companies*: De Laurentiis Productions, Young Hannibal Productions Ltd., Carthago Films S.a.r.l., Dino de Laurentiis Corporation, Ingenious Film Partners, Quinta Communications USA Inc., Zephyr Films Ltd.; *Distributors*: The Weinstein Company, Metro-Goldwyn-Mayer (MGM); *Runtime*: 117 minutes; *Rating*: R / 18

Maniac Cop (1988)

Director: William Lustig; *Writer*: Larry Cohen; *Producer*: Larry Cohen; *Cast*: Bruce Campbell, Tom Atkins, Laurene Landon; *Production Company*: Shapiro-Glickenhaus Home Video; *Distributor*: Shapiro-Glickenhaus Home Video; *Runtime*: 85 minutes; *Rating*: R / 18

Maniac Cop 2 (1990)

Director: William Lustig; *Writer*: Larry Cohen; *Producer*: Larry Cohen; *Cast*: Bruce Campbell, Robert Davi, Robert Z'Dar; *Production Company*: Medusa Pictures; *Distributor*: Vestron Video; *Runtime*: 90 minutes; *Rating*: R / 18

Maniac Cop 3: Badge of Silence (1993)

Directors: William Lustig, Joel Soisson; *Writer*: Larry Cohen; *Producers*: Larry Cohen, Michael Leahy, Joel Soisson; *Cast*: Robert Davi, Robert Z'Dar, Gretchen Becker; *Production Companies*: Neo Motion Pictures, First Look Pictures; *Distributor*: Home Box Office (HBO); *Runtime*: 85 minutes; *Rating*: NC-17/R / 18

Mimic (1997)

Director: Guillermo del Toro; *Writers*: Donald A. Wollheim, Matthew Robbins, Guillermo del Toro; *Producers*: Ole Bornedal, B.J. Rack, Bob Weinstein; *Cast*: Mira Sorvino, Jeremy Northam, Alexander Goodwin; *Production Companies*: Dimension Films, Miramax Films; *Distributors*: Dimension Films, Miramax Films; *Runtime*: 105 minutes; *Rating*: R / 15

Mimic 2 (2001)

Director: Jean de Segonzac; *Writer*: Joel Soisson; *Producers*: Mike Leahy, Joel Soisson; *Cast*: Alix Koromzay, Bruno Campos, Will Estes; *Production Companies*: Dimension Films, Neo Art & Logic; *Distributors*: Dimension Home Video, Miramax Films; *Runtime*: 82 minutes; *Rating*: R / 15

Mimic: Sentinel (2003)

Director: J.T. Petty; *Writer*: J.T. Petty; *Producers*: W.K. Border, Ron Schmidt; *Cast*: Karl Geary, Alexis Dziena, Keith Robinson; *Production Companies*: Dimension Films, Neo Art & Logic; *Distributors*: Buena Vista Home Video, Dimension Films; *Runtime*: 77 minutes; *Rating*: R / 15

Night of the Demons (1987)

Director: Kevin Tenney; *Writer*: Joe Augustyn; *Producer*: Joe Augustyn; *Cast*: Alvin Alexis, Allison Barron, Lance Fenton; *Production Companies*: Meridian Productions, Paragon Arts International, Republic Pictures Corporation; *Distributor*: International Film Marketing; *Runtime*: 90 minutes; *Rating*: R / 18

Night of the Demons 2 (1994)
Director: Brian Trenchard-Smith; *Writers*: Joe Augustyn, James Penzi; *Producers*: Jeff Geoffray, Walter Josten; *Cast*: Cristi Harris, Darin Heames, Robert Jayne; *Production Company*: Blue Rider Productions; *Distributor*: Republic Pictures Corporation; *Runtime*: 96 minutes; *Rating*: R / 18

Night of the Demons 3 (1996)
Director: Jim Kaufman; *Writer*: Kevin Tenney; *Producer*: Claudio Castravelli; *Cast*: Larry Day, Amelia Kinkade, Kristen Holden-Ried; *Production Company*: Blue Rider Productions; *Distributors*: Fries Film Group, Republic Entertainment Inc.; *Runtime*: 85 minutes; *Rating*: R / 18

Night of the Living Dead (1968)
Director: George A Romero; *Writers*: John A. Russo, George A. Romero; *Producers*: Russell Streiner, Karl Hardman; *Cast*: Duane Jones, Karl Hardman, Russell Streiner; *Production Companies*: Image Ten, Laurel Group, Market Square Productions, Off Color Films; *Distributors*: Walter Reade Organization, Continental Motion Pictures; *Runtime*: 96 minutes; *Rating*: R / 18

Dawn of the Dead (1978)
Director: George A. Romero; *Writer*: George A. Romero; *Producers*: Dario Argento, Richard P. Rubinstein; *Cast*: Ken Foree, David Emge, Scott H. Reiniger; *Production Company*: Laurel Group; *Distributor*: United Film Distribution Company (UFDC); *Runtime*: 128 minutes / 139 minutes; *Rating*: Unrated / 18

Day of the Dead (1985)
Director: George A. Romero; *Writer*: George A. Romero; *Producer*: Richard P. Rubinstein; *Cast*: Howard Sherman, Lori Cardille, Terry Alexander; *Production Companies*: Dead Films Inc., Laurel Entertainment Inc., Laurel-Day Inc.; *Distributor*: United Film Distribution Company (UFDC); *Runtime*: 102 minutes; *Rating*: Unrated / 18

Night of the Living Dead (1990)
Director: Tom Savini; *Writers*: John A. Russo, George A. Romero; *Producer*: John A. Russo; *Cast*: Tony Todd, Patricia Tallman, Tom Towles; *Production Companies*: 21st Century Film Corporation, Columbia Pictures Corporation; *Distributor*: Columbia Pictures; *Runtime*: 88 minutes; *Rating*: R / 18

Children of the Living Dead (2001)
Director: Tor Ramsey; *Writer*: Karen L. Wolf; *Producer*: Karen L. Wolf; *Cast*: Tom Savini, Marty Schiff, Damien Luvara; *Production Company*: Westwood Artists International Inc.; *Distributor*: Spartan Home Entertainment; *Runtime*: 90 minutes; *Rating*: R / 15

Dawn of the Dead (2004)
Director: Zack Snyder; *Writers*: George A. Romero, James Gunn; *Producers*: Marc Abraham, Eric Newman, Richard P. Rubinstein; *Cast*: Sarah Polley, Ving Rhames, Jake Weber; *Production Companies*: Strike Entertainment, New Amsterdam Entertainment Inc., Metropolitan Filmexport, Toho-Towa; *Distributor*: Universal Pictures; *Runtime*: 100 minutes / 109 minutes; *Rating*: R / 18

Day of the Dead 2: Contagium (2005)
Directors: Ana Clavell, James Glenn Dudelson; *Writer*: Ana Clavell; *Producer*: James Glenn Dudelson; *Cast*: Laurie Baranyay, Steve Colosi, John Freedom Henry; *Production Company*: Taurus Entertainment Company; *Distributors*: Taurus Entertainment Company, Anchor Bay Entertainment; *Runtime*: 103 minutes; *Rating*: R / 18

Land of the Dead (2005)
Director: George A. Romero; *Writer*: George A. Romero; *Producers*: Mark Canton, Bernie

Goldmann, Peter Grunwald; *Cast*: Simon Baker, John Leguizamo, Dennis Hopper; *Production Companies*: Atmosphere Entertainment MM, Aurora Entertainment Corporation, Exception Wild Bunch, Laurel Entertainment Inc., Romero-Grunwald Productions; *Distributor*: Universal Pictures; *Runtime*: 93 minutes / 97 minutes; *Rating*: R / 15

Night of the Living Dead 3-D (2006)

Director: Jeff Broadstreet; *Writers*: George A. Romero, John A. Russo, Robert Valding; *Producer*: Jeff Broadstreet; *Cast*: Brianna Brown, Joshua DesRoches, Sid Haig; *Production Companies*: Lux Digital Pictures, The Horrorworks; *Distributors*: Midnight Movies, Lux Digital Pictures; *Runtime*: 80 minutes; *Rating*: R

☆ ☆ ☆

A Nightmare on Elm Street (1984)

Director: Wes Craven; *Writer*: Wes Craven; *Producer*: Robert Shaye; *Cast*: Heather Langenkamp, John Saxon, Robert Englund; *Production Companies*: The Elm Street Venture, Media Home Entertainment, Smart Egg Productions, New Line Cinema; *Distributor*: New Line Cinema; *Runtime*: 91 minutes; *Rating*: R / 18

A Nightmare on Elm Street 2: Freddy's Revenge (1985)

Director: Jack Sholder; *Writer*: David Chaskin; *Producer*: Robert Shaye; *Cast*: Robert Englund, Kim Meyers, Mark Patton; *Production Companies*: Heron Communications, Media Home Entertainment, New Line Cinema, Second Elm Street Venture, Smart Egg Pictures; *Distributor*: New Line Cinema; *Runtime*: 87 minutes; *Rating*: R / 18

A Nightmare on Elm Street 3: Dream Warriors (1987)

Director: Charles Russell; *Writers*: Wes Craven, Bruce Wagner, Charles Russell, Frank Darabont; *Producer*: Robert Shaye; *Cast*: Robert Englund, Heather Langenkamp, John Saxon; *Production Companies*: Heron Communications, New Line Cinema, Smart Egg Pictures; *Distributor*: New Line Cinema; *Runtime*: 96 minutes; *Rating*: R / 18

A Nightmare on Elm Street 4: The Dream Master (1988)

Director: Renny Harlin; *Writers*: William Kotzwinkle, Brian Helgeland, Jim and Ken Wheat; *Producer*: Robert Shaye; *Cast*: Robert Englund, Lisa Wilcox, Tuesday Knight; *Production Companies*: Heron Communications, New Line Cinema, Smart Egg Pictures; *Distributor*: New Line Cinema; *Runtime*: 99 minutes; *Rating*: R / 15

A Nightmare on Elm Street 5: The Dream Child (1989)

Director: Stephen Hopkins; *Writers*: John Skipp, Craig Spector, Leslie Bohem; *Producer*: Robert Shaye; *Cast*: Robert Englund, Lisa Wilcox, Danny Hassle; *Production Companies*: Fourth New Line Heron Joint Venture, New Line Cinema; *Distributor*: New Line Cinema; *Runtime*: 89 minutes; *Rating*: R / 18

Freddy's Dead: The Final Nightmare (1991)

Director: Rachel Talalay; *Writers*: Rachel Talalay, Michael De Luca; *Producers*: Robert Shaye, Aron Warner; *Cast*: Robert Englund, Lisa Zane, Yaphet Kotto; *Production Company*: New Line Cinema; *Distributor*: New Line Cinema; *Runtime*: 89 minutes; *Rating*: R / 18

Wes Craven's New Nightmare (1994)

Director: Wes Craven; *Writer*: Wes Craven; *Producer*: Marianne Maddalena; *Cast*: Heather Langenkamp, John Saxon, Robert Englund; *Production Company*: New Line Cinema; *Distributor*: New Line

Cinema; *Runtime*: 112 minutes; *Rating*: R / 18

☆ ☆ ☆

976-EVIL (1989)

Director: Robert Englund; *Writers*: Brian Helgeland, Rhet Topham; *Producer*: Lisa M. Hansen; *Cast*: Robert Picardo, Stephen Geoffreys, Patrick O'Bryan; *Production Companies*: Cinetel Films Inc., Horrorscope Productions; *Distributor*: New Line Cinema; *Runtime*: 92 minutes; *Rating*: R / 18

976-EVIL 2: The Astral Factor (1992)

Director: Jim Wynorski; *Writers*: Erik Anjou, Rick Glassman; *Producer*: Paul Hertzberg; *Cast*: Debbie James, René Assa, Patrick O'Bryan; *Production Company*: Cinétel; *Distributor*: Live Home Video; *Runtime*: 93 minutes; *Rating*: R / 18

☆ ☆ ☆

The Omen (1976)

Director: Richard Donner; *Writer*: David Seltzer; *Producer*: Harvey Bernhard; *Cast*: Gregory Peck, Lee Remick, David Warner; *Production Company*: 20th Century–Fox; *Distributor*: Twentieth Century–Fox Film Corporation; *Runtime*: 111 minutes; *Rating*: R / 18

Damien: Omen II (1978)

Director: Don Taylor; *Writers*: Harvey Bernhard, Stanley Mann, Mike Hodges; *Producer*: Harvey Bernhard; *Cast*: William Holden, Lee Grant, Jonathan Scott-Taylor; *Production Companies*: 20th Century–Fox, Industrie Cinematografiche Italiane (ICI); *Distributor*: Twentieth Century–Fox Film Corporation; *Runtime*: 107 minutes; *Rating*: R / 18

The Final Conflict: Omen III (1981)

Director: Graham Baker; *Writer*: Andrew Birkin; *Producer*: Harvey Bernhard; *Cast*: Sam Neill, Don Gordon, Lisa Harrow; *Production Company*: 20th Century–Fox; *Distributor*: Twentieth Century–Fox Film Corporation; *Runtime*: 108 minutes; *Rating*: R / 18

Omen IV: The Awakening (1991)

Directors: Jorge Montesi, Dominique Othenin-Girard; *Writers*: Harvey Bernhard, Brian Taggert; *Producer*: Harvey Bernhard; *Cast*: Faye Grant, Michael Lerner, Asia Vieira; *Production Company*: FNM Films; *Distributor*: Fox Network; *Runtime*: 97 minutes; *Rating*: Unrated / 15

The Omen (2006)

Director: John Moore; *Writer*: David Seltzer; *Producers*: John Moore, Glen Williamson; *Cast*: Live Schreiber, Julia Stiles, Mia Farrow; *Production Companies*: 11:11 Mediaworks, Twentieth Century–Fox Film Corporation; *Distributor*: Twentieth Century–Fox Film Corporation; *Runtime*: 110 minutes; *Rating*: R / 15

☆ ☆ ☆

Pet Sematary (1989)

Director: Mary Lambert; *Writer*: Stephen King; *Producer*: Richard P. Rubinstein; *Cast*: Dale Midkiff, Fred Gwynne, Denise Crosby; *Production Companies*: Laurel Productions, Paramount Pictures; *Distributor*: Paramount Pictures; *Runtime*: 103 minutes; *Rating*: R / 18

Pet Sematary 2 (1992)

Director: Mary Lambert; *Writer*: Richard Outten; *Producer*: Ralph S. Singleton; *Cast*: Edward Furlong, Anthony Edwards, Clancy Brown; *Production Companies*: Columbus Circle Films, Paramount Pictures; *Distributor*: Paramount Pictures; *Runtime*: 100 minutes; *Rating*: R / 18

☆ ☆ ☆

Phantasm (1979)

Director: Don Coscarelli; *Writer*: Don Coscarelli; *Producer*: Don Coscarelli; *Cast*:

A. Michael Baldwin, Reggie Bannister, Angus Scrimm; *Production Company*: New Breed Productions Inc.; *Distributor*: Avco-Embassy Pictures; *Runtime*: 88 minutes; *Rating*: R / 18

Phantasm II (1988)

Director: Don Coscarelli; *Writer*: Don Coscarelli; *Producer*: Roberto A. Quezada; *Cast*: James LeGros, Reggie Bannister, Angus Scrimm; *Production Companies*: Spacegate Productions, Starway International Inc., Universal Pictures; *Distributor*: Universal Pictures; *Runtime*: 97 minutes; *Rating*: R / 18

Phantasm III: Lord of the Dead (1994)

Director: Don Coscarelli; *Writer*: Don Coscarelli; *Producer*: Don Coscarelli; *Cast*: A. Michael Baldwin, Reggie Bannister, Angus Scrimm; *Production Company*: Starway International Inc.; *Distributor*: Universal Home Entertainment; *Runtime*: 91 minutes; *Rating*: R / 18

Phantasm IV: Oblivion (1998)

Director: Don Coscarelli; *Writer*: Don Coscarelli; *Producer*: Don Coscarelli; *Cast*: A. Michael Baldwin, Reggie Bannister, Angus Scrimm; *Production Company*: Silver Sphere Corporation; *Distributors*: Silver Sphere Corporation, Warner Bros. Pictures; *Runtime*: 90 minutes; *Rating*: R / 15

Piranha (1978)

Director: Joe Dante; *Writers*: Richard Robinson, John Sayles; *Producer*: Jon Davison; *Cast*: Bradford Dillman, Heather Menzies, Kevin McCarthy; *Production Company*: New World Pictures; *Distributor*: New World Pictures; *Runtime*: 94 minutes; *Rating*: R / 15

Piranha II: The Spawning (1981)

Director: James Cameron; *Writer*: H.A. Milton; *Producers*: Chako van Leeuwen, Jeff Schechtman; *Cast*: Tricia O'Neil, Steve Marachuk, Lance Henriksen; *Production Companies*: Brouwersgracht Investments, Chako Film Company; *Distributors*: Columbia Pictures, Embassy Home Entertainment, Nelson Entertainment, Saturn International; *Runtime*: 84 minutes / 94 minutes; *Rating*: R / 15

Piranha (1995)

Director: Scott P. Levy; *Writers*: Richard Robinson, John Sayles, Alex Simon; *Producers*: Mike Elliott, Chako van Leeuwen; *Cast*: William Katt, Alexandra Paul, Monte Markham; *Production Companies*: Concorde-New Horizons, Showtime Networks; *Distributors*: Concorde Pictures, Concorde-New Horizons, Showtime Networks; *Runtime*: 89 minutes; *Rating*: R / 15

Poltergeist (1982)

Director: Tobe Hooper; *Writers*: Steven Spielberg, Michael Grais, Mark Victor; *Producers*: Steven Spielberg, Frank Marshall; *Cast*: Craig T. Nelson, JoBeth Williams, Heather O'Rourke; *Production Companies*: Metro-Goldwyn-Mayer (MGM), SLM Production Group; *Distributor*: MGM/UA Entertainment Company; *Runtime*: 114 minutes; *Rating*: PG / 15

Poltergeist 2 (1986)

Director: Brian Gibson; *Writers*: Michael Grais, Mark Victor; *Producers*: Michael Grais, Mark Victor; *Cast*: Craig T. Nelson, JoBeth Williams, Heather O'Rourke; *Production Company*: Metro-Goldwyn-Mayer (MGM); *Distributor*: Metro-Goldwyn-Mayer (MGM); *Runtime*: 91 minutes; *Rating*: PG-13 / 15

Poltergeist III (1988)

Director: Gary Sherman; *Writers*: Gary Sherman, Brian Taggert; *Producer*: Barry Bernardi; *Cast*: Heather O'Rourke, Zelda Rubinstein, Tom Skerritt; *Production Company*: Metro-Goldwyn-

Mayer (MGM); *Distributor*: Metro-Goldwyn-Mayer (MGM); *Runtime*: 98 minutes; *Rating*: PG / 15

☆ ☆ ☆

Prom Night (1980)
Director: Paul Lynch; *Writer*: Robert Guza Jr.; *Producers*: Peter R. Simpson, Robert Simpson; *Cast*: Leslie Nielsen, Jamie Lee Curtis, Casey Stevens; *Production Companies*: Quadrant Trust Company, Simcom Limited; *Distributor*: AVCO Embassy Pictures; *Runtime*: 90 minutes; *Rating*: R / 18

Hello Mary Lou: Prom Night II (1987)
Director: Bruce Pittman; *Writer*: Ron Oliver; *Producer*: Peter R. Simpson; *Cast*: Michael Ironside, Lisa Scharge, Wendy Lyon; *Production Company*: Simcom Limited; *Distributor*: Samuel Goldwyn Company; *Runtime*: 97 minutes; *Rating*: R / 18

Prom Night III: The Last Kiss (1990)
Directors: Ron Oliver, Peter R. Simpson; *Writer*: Ron Oliver; *Producers*: Peter R. Simpson, Ray Sager; *Cast*: Tim Conlon, Cyndy Preston, Courtney Taylor; *Production Company*: Simcom Limited; *Distributor*: International Video Entertainment (IVE); *Runtime*: 97 minutes; *Rating*: R / 18

Prom Night IV: Deliver Us from Evil (1992)
Director: Clay Borris; *Writer*: Richard Beattie; *Producer*: Ray Sager; *Cast*: Nicole de Boer, J.H. Wyman, Joy Tanner; *Production Company*: Unknown; *Distributor*: Live America Inc.; *Runtime*: 115 minutes; *Rating*: R / 18

☆ ☆ ☆

The Prophecy (1995)
Director: Gregory Widen; *Writer*: Gregory Widen; *Producer*: Joel Soisson; *Cast*: Christopher Walken, Elias Koteas, Virginia Madsen; *Production Companies*: First Look Pictures Releasing, NEO Motion Pictures, Overseas Film Group; *Distributors*: Dimension Films, Miramax Films; *Runtime*: 98 minutes; *Rating*: R / 18

The Prophecy II (1998)
Director: Greg Spence; *Writers*: Matt Greenberg, Greg Spence; *Producers*: W.K. Border, Joel Soisson; *Cast*: Christopher Walken, Eric Roberts, Brittany Murphy; *Production Company*: NEO Motion Pictures; *Distributors*: Buena Vista Home Video, Dimension Films; *Runtime*: 87 minutes; *Rating*: R / 18

The Prophecy 3: The Ascent (2000)
Director: Patrick Lussier; *Writers*: Carl V. Dupré, Joel Soisson; *Producer*: Joel Soisson; *Cast*: Christopher Walken, Vincent Spano, Dave Buzzotta; *Production Company*: Dimension Films; *Distributors*: Buena Vista Home Video, Dimension Films; *Runtime*: 84 minutes; *Rating*: R / 15

The Prophecy: Uprising (2005)
Director: Joel Soisson; *Writers*: John Sullivan, Joel Soisson; *Producer*: Ron Schmidt; *Cast*: John Light, Sean Pertwee, Kari Wuhrer; *Production Companies*: Dimension Films, Neo Art & Logic; *Distributors*: Buena Vista Home Video, Dimension Films; *Runtime*: 88 minutes; *Rating*: R

The Prophecy: Forsaken (2005)
Director: Joel Soisson; *Writers*: John Sullivan, Joel Soisson; *Producer*: Ron Schmidt; *Cast*: Kari Wuhrer, Jason Scott Lee, John Light; *Production Companies*: Castel Film Romania, Dimension Films; *Distributors*: Buena Vista Home Video, Dimension Films; *Runtime*: 75 minutes; *Rating*: R

☆ ☆ ☆

Psycho (1960)
Director: Alfred Hitchcock; *Writers*: Robert Bloch, Joseph Stefano; *Producer*: Alfred

Hitchcock; *Cast*: Anthony Perkins, Janet Leigh, Vera Miles; *Production Company*: Shamley Productions; *Distributors*: Paramount Pictures, Universal Pictures (re-release); *Runtime*: 109 minutes; *Rating*: R / 15

Psycho II (1983)

Director: Richard Franklin; *Writer*: Tom Holland; *Producer*: Hilton A. Green; *Cast*: Anthony Perkins, Vera Miles, Robert Loggia; *Production Companies*: Oak, Universal Pictures; *Distributor*: Universal Pictures; *Runtime*: 113 minutes; *Rating*: R / 18

Psycho III (1986)

Director: Anthony Perkins; *Writer*: Charles Edward Pogue; *Producer*: Hilton A. Green; *Cast*: Anthony Perkins, Diana Scarwid, Jeff Fahey; *Production Company*: Universal Pictures; *Distributor*: Universal Pictures; *Runtime*: 93 minutes; *Rating*: R / 15

Psycho IV: The Beginning (1990)

Director: Mick Garris; *Writer*: Joseph Stefano; *Producers*: Les Mayfield, George Zaloom; *Cast*: Anthony Perkins, Olivia Hussey, Henry Thomas; *Production Companies*: Smart Money Productions, Universal Television; *Distributor*: MTE (MCA Television Entertainment); *Runtime*: 96 minutes; *Rating*: R / 18

Psycho (1998)

Director: Gus VanSant; *Writers*: Robert Bloch, Joseph Stefano; *Producers*: Brian Grazer, Gus VanSant; *Cast*: Vince Vaughn, Anne Heche, Julianne Moore; *Production Companies*: Imagine Entertainment, Universal Pictures; *Distributors*: MCA/Universal Pictures, United International Pictures (UIP); *Runtime*: 105 minutes; *Rating*: R / 15

☆ ☆ ☆

Pumpkinhead (1989)

Director: Stan Winston; *Writers*: Ed Justin, Mark Patrick Carducci, Stan Winston, Richard Weinman; *Producers*: Howard Smith, Richard Weinman; *Cast*: Lance Henriksen, Jeff East, John D'Aquino; *Production Companies*: De Laurentiis Entertainment Group (DEG), Lion Films; *Distributors*: Metro-Goldwyn-Mayer (MGM), United Artists; *Runtime*: 86 minutes; *Rating*: R / 18

Pumpkinhead II: Blood Wings (1994)

Director: Jeff Burr; *Writers*: Constantine Chachornia, Ivan Chachornia; *Producers*: Brad Krevoy, Steven Stabler; *Cast*: Andrew Robinson, Ami Dolenz, Soleil Moon Frye; *Production Companies*: Live Entertainment, Motion Picture Corporation of America (MPCA); *Distributors*: Live Home Entertainment, Motion Picture Corporation of America (MPCA); *Runtime*: 88 minutes; *Rating*: R / 18

Pumpkinhead: Ashes to Ashes (2006)

Director: Jake West; *Writers*: Barbara Werner, John Werner, Jake West; *Producers*: Brad Krevoy, Donald Kushner, Pierre Spengler; *Cast*: Doug Bradley, Douglas Roberts, Lisa McAllister; *Production Companies*: Motion Picture Corporation of America (MPCA), Castel Film Romania, Clubdeal; *Distributor*: Sony Pictures Home Entertainment; *Runtime*: 91 minutes; *Rating*: R

☆ ☆ ☆

Puppet Master (1989)

Director: David Schmoeller; *Writers*: Charles Band, Kenneth J. Hall, David Schmoeller; *Producer*: Hope Perello; *Cast*: William Hickey, Irene Miracle, Robin Frates; *Production Companies*: Empire Pictures, Full Moon Entertainment; *Distributors*: Empire Pictures, JGM Enterprises, Paramount Pictures; *Runtime*: 90 minutes; *Rating*: R / 18

Puppet Master II (1990)

Director: Dave Allen; *Writers*: Charles Band, David Pabian; *Producers*: David DeCoteau,

John Schouweiler; *Cast*: Elizabeth Maclellan, Collin Bernsen, Michael Kenney; *Production Company*: Full Moon Entertainment; *Distributors*: Paramount Pictures, Full Moon Entertainment; *Runtime*: 88 minutes; *Rating*: R / 18

Puppet Master III: Toulon's Revenge (1991)

Director: David DeCoteau; *Writers*: Charles Band, C. Courtney Joyner; *Producers*: David DeCoteau, John Schouweiler; *Cast*: Guy Rolfe, Richard Lynch, Ian Abercrombie; *Production Company*: Full Moon Entertainment; *Distributor*: Paramount Home Video; *Runtime*: 86 minutes; *Rating*: R / 18

Puppet Master 4 (1993)

Director: Jeff Burr; *Writers*: Douglas Aarniokoski, Steven E. Carr, Jo Duffy, Todd Henschell, Keith S. Payson; *Producer*: Charles Band; *Cast*: Gordon Currie, Chandra West, Ash Adams; *Production Company*: Full Moon Entertainment; *Distributor*: Paramount Home Video; *Runtime*: 79 minutes; *Rating*: R / 15

Puppet Master 5: The Final Chapter (1994)

Director: Jeff Burr; *Writers*: Douglas Aarniokoski, Steven E. Carr, Jo Duffy, Todd Henschell, Keith S. Payson; *Producer*: Keith S. Payson; *Cast*: Gordon Currie, Chandra West, Ian Ogilvy; *Production Company*: Full Moon Entertainment; *Distributor*: Paramount Home Video; *Runtime*: 82 minutes; *Rating*: R / 15

Curse of the Puppet Master (1998)

Director: David DeCoteau; *Writer*: Benjamin Carr; *Producer*: Kirk Edward Hansen; *Cast*: George Peck, Emily Harrison, Josh Green; *Production Company*: Full Moon Entertainment; *Distributor*: Full Moon Entertainment; *Runtime*: 90 minutes; *Rating*: R / 18

Retro-Puppet Master (1999)

Director: David DeCoteau; *Writers*: Charles Band, Benjamin Carr; *Producers*: Kirk Edward Hansen, Vlad Paunescu; *Cast*: Greg Sestero, Brigitta Dau, Stephen Blackehart; *Production Company*: Kushner-Locke Company; *Distributor*: Full Moon Entertainment; *Runtime*: 90 minutes; *Rating*: PG-13 / 15

Puppet Master: The Legacy (2003)

Director: Charles Band; *Writer*: C. Courtney Joyner; *Producer*: Kurt Iswarienko; *Cast*: Jacob Witkin, Kate Orsini, Ian Abercrombie; *Production Companies*: Shadow Entertainment, Shadow Films; *Distributor*: Shadow Entertainment; *Runtime*: 80 minutes; *Rating*: Not Rated

Puppet Master vs. Demonic Toys (2004)

Director: Ted Nicolaou; *Writers*: C. Courtney Joyner, Ted Nicolaou; *Producers*: Bob Perkis, Jörg Westerkamp; *Cast*: Corey Feldman, Vanessa Angel, Danielle Keaton; *Production Companies*: ApolloProScreen GmbH & Co. Filmproduktion KG, Jeff Franklin Productions; *Distributors*: Anchor Bay Entertainment, The Sci-Fi Channel; *Runtime*: 88 minutes; *Rating*: TV-14

☆ ☆ ☆

Re-Animator (1985)

Director: Stuart Gordon; *Writers*: H.P. Lovecraft, Dennis Paoli, William Norris, Stuart Gordon; *Producer*: Brian Yuzna; *Cast*: Jeffrey Combs, Bruce Abbott, Barbara Crampton; *Production Companies*: Empire Pictures, Re-Animator Productions Inc.; *Distributor*: Empire Pictures; *Runtime*: 86 minutes; *Rating*: Unrated / 18

Bride of Re-Animator (1990)

Director: Brian Yuzna; *Writers*: H.P. Lovecraft, Rick Fry, Woody Keith, Brian Yuzna; *Producer*: Brian Yuzna; *Cast*: Jeffrey Combs, Bruce Abbott, David Gale; *Production Company*: Wild Street; *Distributor*: 50th Street Films; *Runtime*: 96 minutes; *Rating*: R / 18

Beyond Re-Animator (2003)
Director: Brian Yuzna; *Writers:* José Manuel Gómez, Miguel Tejada-Flores; *Producers:* Brian Yuzna, Julio Fernández; *Cast:* Jeffrey Combs, Tommy Dean Musset, Jason Barry; *Production Companies:* Castelao Producciones S.A., Fantastic Factory, Filmax, Vía Digital; *Distributor:* Lions Gate Films; *Runtime:* 95 minutes; *Rating:* R / 18

Resident Evil (2002)
Director: Paul W.S. Anderson; *Writer:* Paul W.S. Anderson; *Producers:* Paul W.S. Anderson, Jeremy Bolt, Bernd Eichinger, Samuel Hadida; *Cast:* Milla Jovovich, Michelle Rodriguez, Eric Mabius; *Production Companies:* Constantin Film Produktion GmbH, Davis-Films, Impact Pictures, New Legacy; *Distributor:* Sony Pictures Entertainment; *Runtime:* 100 minutes; *Rating:* R / 15

Resident Evil: Apocalypse (2004)
Director: Alexander Witt; *Writer:* Paul W.S. Anderson; *Producers:* Jeremy Bolt, Don Carmody, Paul W.S. Anderson; *Cast:* Milla Jovovich, Sienna Guillory, Oded Fehr; *Production Companies:* Constantin Film Produktion GmbH, Screen Gems Inc., Davis-Films, Impact Pictures, Constantin Film Ltd.; *Distributors:* Sony Pictures Entertainment, Screen Gems Inc.; *Runtime:* 94 minutes; *Rating:* R / 15

Return of the Living Dead (1985)
Director: Dan O'Bannon; *Writer:* Dan O'Bannon; *Producer:* Tom Fox; *Cast:* Clu Galager, Linnea Quigley, James Karen; *Production Companies:* Hemdale Film Corporation, Fox Films Ltd., Cinema 84; *Distributor:* Orion Pictures Corporation; *Runtime:* 91 minutes; *Rating:* R / 18

Return of the Living Dead Part 2 (1988)
Director: Ken Wiederhorn; *Writer:* Ken Wiederhorn; *Producers:* Tom Fox, Eugene C. Cashman, William S. Gilmore; *Cast:* James Karen, Dana Ashbrook, Thom Matthews; *Production Company:* Greenfox; *Distributor:* Lorimar Film Entertainment; *Runtime:* 89 minutes; *Rating:* R / 15

Return of the Living Dead Part 3 (1993)
Director: Brian Yuzna; *Writer:* John Penney; *Producers:* Gary Schmoeller, Brian Yuzna; *Cast:* Mindy Clarke, James T. Callahan, Melinda Clarke; *Production Companies:* Bandai Visual Co., Ozla Productions; *Distributors:* Trimark Pictures, Vidmark Entertainment; *Runtime:* 97 minutes; *Rating:* R / 18

Return of the Living Dead: Necropolis (2005)
Director: Ellory Elkayem; *Writers:* William Butler, Aaron Strongoni; *Producers:* Anatoly Fradis, Steve Scarduzio; *Cast:* Aimee-Lynn Chadwick, Cory Hardrict, Peter Coyote; *Production Companies:* Denholm Trading Inc., Aurora Entertainment Corporation, Castel Film Romania; *Distributor:* Denholm Trading Inc.; *Runtime:* 88 minutes; *Rating:* R

Return of the Living Dead: Rave to the Grave (2005)
Director: Ellory Elkayem; *Writers:* William Butler, Aaron Strongoni; *Producers:* Anatoly Fradis, Steve Scarduzio; *Cast:* Aimee-Lynn Chadwick, Cory Hardrict, Peter Coyote; *Production Companies:* Denholm Trading Inc., Aurora Entertainment Corporation, Castel Film Romania; *Distributor:* Denholm Trading Inc.; *Runtime:* 86 minutes; *Rating:* R

The Ring (2002)
Director: Gore Verbinski; *Writers:* Kôji Suzuki, Hiroshi Takahashi, Ehren Kruger;

Producers: Laurie MacDonald, Walter F. Parkes; *Cast*: Naomi Watts, Martin Henderson, Brian Cox; *Production Companies*: DreamWorks SKG, MacDonald/Parkes Productions, BenderSpink, Vertigo Entertainment; *Distributor*: DreamWorks Distribution; *Runtime*: 115 minutes; *Rating*: PG-13 / 15

The Ring Two (2005)

Director: Hideo Nakata; *Writers*: Kôji Suzuki, Hiroshi Takahashi, Ehren Kruger; *Producers*: Laurie MacDonald, Walter F. Parkes; *Cast*: Naomi Watts, Simon Baker, David Dorfman; *Production Companies*: DreamWorks SKG, MacDonald/Parkes Productions, BenderSpink, Vertigo Entertainment; *Distributor*: DreamWorks Distribution; *Runtime*: 110 minutes; *Rating*: PG-13 / 15

Rosemary's Baby (1968)

Director: Roman Polanski; *Writers*: Ira Levin, Roman Polanski; *Producer*: William Castle; *Cast*: Mia Farrow, John Cassavetes, Ruth Gordon; *Production Company*: William Castle Productions; *Distributor*: Paramount Pictures; *Runtime*: 136 minutes; *Rating*: R / 18

Look What's Happened to Rosemary's Baby (1976)

Director: Sam O'Steen; *Writer*: Anthony Wilson; *Producer*: Anthony Wilson; *Cast*: Stephen McHattie, Patty Duke, Ruth Gordon; *Production Companies*: Paramount Television, The Culzean Corporation; *Distributor*: American Broadcasting Company (ABC); *Runtime*: 110 minutes; *Rating*: Unrated / 15

Salem's Lot (1979)

Director: Tobe Hooper; *Writers*: Stephen King, Paul Monash; *Producer*: Richard Kobritz; *Cast*: David Soul, James Mason, Lance Kerwin; *Production Company*: Warner Bros. Television; *Distributors*: CBS Television, Warner Bros. Pictures; *Runtime*: 183 minutes; *Rating*: PG / 15

A Return to Salem's Lot (1987)

Director: Larry Cohen; *Writer*: Larry Cohen; *Producer*: Paul Kurta; *Cast*: Michael Moriarty, Ricky Addison Reed, Samuel Fuller; *Production Company*: Larco Productions Inc.; *Distributor*: Warner Home Video; *Runtime*: 101 minutes; *Rating*: R / 18

'Salem's Lot (2005)

Director: Mikael Salomon; *Writers*: Stephen King, Peter Filardi; *Producer*: Brett Popplewell; *Cast*: Rob Lowe, Andre Braugher, Donald Sutherland; *Production Companies*: Coote Hayes Productions, The Wolper Organization, Warner Bros. Television; *Distributor*: Turner Network Television (TNT); *Runtime*: 181 minutes; *Rating*: TV-14 / 15

Saw (2004)

Director: James Wan; *Writers*: James Wan, Leigh Whannell; *Producers*: Mark Burg, Gregg Hoffman, Oren Koules; *Cast*: Leigh Whannell, Cary Elwes, Danny Glover; *Production Companies*: Evolution Entertainment, Saw Productions Inc., Twisted Pictures; *Distributor*: Lions Gate Films; *Runtime*: 103 minutes; *Rating*: R / 18

Saw II (2005)

Director: Darren Lynn Bousman; *Writers*: Leigh Whannell, Darren Lynn Bousman; *Producers*: Mark Burg, Gregg Hoffman, Oren Koules; *Cast*: Tobin Bell, Shawnee Smith, Donnie Wahlberg; *Production Companies*: Twisted Pictures, Got Films; *Distributor*: Lions Gate Films; *Runtime*: 93 minutes; *Rating*: R / 18;

Saw III (2006)

Director: Darren Lynn Bousman; *Writers*: James Wan, Leigh Whannell; *Producers*: Mark

Burg, Oren Koules; *Cast*: Tobin Bell, Shawnee Smith, Bahar Soomekh; *Production Companies*: Lions Gate Films, Twisted Pictures; *Distributor*: Lions Gate Films; *Runtime*: 107 minutes / 113 minutes; *Rating*: R / 18

☆ ☆ ☆

Scanners (1981)
Director: David Cronenberg; *Writer*: David Cronenberg; *Producer*: Claude Héroux; *Cast*: Jennifer O'Neill, Stephen Lack, Patrick McGoohan; *Production Companies*: Canadian Film Development Corporation (CFDC), Filmplan, Victor Solnicki Productions; *Distributor*: AVCO Embassy Pictures; *Runtime*: 103 minutes; *Rating*: R / 18

Scanners II: The New Order (1991)
Director: Christian Duguay; *Writer*: B.J. Nelson; *Producers*: Pierre David, René Malo; *Cast*: David Hewlett, Deborah Raffin, Yvan Ponton; *Production Company*: Malofilm; *Distributors*: Triton Pictures, Fox Video; *Runtime*: 104 minutes; *Rating*: R / 18

Scanners III: The Takeover (1992)
Director: Christian Duguay; *Writer*: B.J. Nelson; *Producers*: Irene Litinsky, René Malo; *Cast*: Liliana Komorowska, Valérie Valois, Steve Parrish; *Production Companies*: Lance Entertainment, Malofilm; *Distributor*: Republic Pictures Corporation; *Runtime*: 101 minutes; *Rating*: R / 18

Scanner Cop (1994)
Director: Pierre David; *Writers*: John Bryant, Pierre David, George Saunders; *Producer*: Pierre David; *Cast*: Daniel Quinn, Darlanne Fluegel, Richard Grove; *Production Companies*: Republic Entertainment Inc., The Image Organization; *Distributor*: Republic Pictures Home Video; *Runtime*: 95 minutes; *Rating*: R / 18

Scanner Cop II (1995)
Director: Steve Barnett; *Writer*: Mark Sevi; *Producer*: Pierre David; *Cast*: Daniel Quinn, Patrick Kilpatrick, Khrystyne Haje; *Production Company*: Showdown Productions; *Distributor*: Republic Pictures Corporation; *Runtime*: 95 minutes; *Rating*: R / 18

☆ ☆ ☆

Scream (1996)
Director: Wes Craven; *Writer*: Kevin Williamson; *Producers*: Cathy Konrad, Cary Woods; *Cast*: Neve Campbell, Courtney Cox, David Arquette; *Production Companies*: Woods Entertainment, Dimension Films; *Distributor*: Dimension Films; *Runtime*: 111 minutes; *Rating*: R / 18

Scream 2 (1997)
Director: Wes Craven; *Writer*: Kevin Williamson; *Producers*: Marianne Maddalena, Cathy Konrad; *Cast*: Neve Campbell, Courtney Cox, David Arquette; *Production Companies*: Craven-Maddalena Films, Dimension Films, Konrad Pictures, Maven Entertainment, Miramax Films; *Distributors*: Miramax Films, Dimension Films; *Runtime*: 120 minutes; *Rating*: R / 18

Scream 3 (2000)
Director: Wes Craven; *Writer*: Ehren Kruger; *Producers*: Kevin Williamson, Cathy Konrad, Marianne Maddalena; *Cast*: Neve Campbell, Courtney Cox, David Arquette; *Production Companies*: Craven-Maddalena Films, Dimension Films, Konrad Pictures; *Distributors*: Miramax Films, Dimension Films; *Runtime*: 116 minutes; *Rating*: R / 18

☆ ☆ ☆

Shark Attack (1999)
Director: Bob Misiorowski; *Writers*: Scott Devine, William Hooke; *Producer*: Mandy Branch; *Cast*: Cordell McQueen, Chris Olley, Jacob Makgoba; *Production Companies*: Martien Holdings A.V.V., Nu Image Films, Sharky Productions; *Distributor*: Trimark Video; *Runtime*: 100 minutes; *Rating*: R / 15

Shark Attack 2 (2001)
Director: David Worth; *Writers*: Scott Devine, William Hooke; *Producers*: Marlow De Mardt, Danny Lerner, Brigid Olen, David Varod; *Cast*: Thorsten Kaye, Nikita Ager, Daniel Alexander; *Production Companies*: Do Productions, Martien Holdings A.V.V, Nu Image Films, Nu World Services; *Distributor*: Martien Holdings A.V.V.; *Runtime*: 93 minutes; *Rating*: R / 15

Shark Attack 3: Megalodon (2002)
Director: David Worth; *Writers*: Scott Devine, William Hooke; *Producers*: Boaz Davidson, Danny Lerner, David Varod; *Cast*: John Barrowman, Jenny McShane, Ryan Cutrona; *Production Companies*: Martien Holdings A.V.V., Nu Image Films; *Distributor*: Studio Home Entertainment; *Runtime*: 94 minutes; *Rating*: R / 15

☆ ☆ ☆

Silent Night, Deadly Night (1984)
Director: Charles E. Sellier Jr.; *Writers*: Paul Caimi, Michael Hickey; *Producer*: Ira Richard Barmak; *Cast*: Robert Brian Wilson, Linnea Quigley; *Production Company*: Slayride Inc.; *Distributor*: TriStar Pictures; *Runtime*: 79 minutes; *Rating*: R

Silent Night, Deadly Night Part 2 (1987)
Director: Lee Harry; *Writers*: Joseph H. Earle, Lee Harry, Lawrence Appelbaum, Dennis Patterson; *Producer*: Lawrence Appelbaum; *Cast*: Jean Miller, Eric Freeman, James Newman; *Production Company*: Silent Night Releasing Corporation; *Distributors*: Silent Night Releasing Corporation, International Video Entertainment (IVE); *Runtime*: 88 minutes; *Rating*: R / Rejected

Silent Night, Deadly Night 3: Better Watch Out! (1989)
Director: Monte Hellman; *Writers*: Steven Gaydos, Richard N. Gladstein, Monte Hellman, Carlos Lazlo; *Producer*: Arthur Gorson; *Cast*: Richard Beymer, Bill Moseley, Samantha Scully; *Production Company*: Quiet Films Inc.; *Distributor*: International Video Entertainment (IVE); *Runtime*: 90 minutes; *Rating*: R

Initiation: Silent Night, Deadly Night 4 (1990)
Director: Brian Yuzna; *Writers*: Arthur Gorson, Woody Keith, S.J. Smith, Brian Yuzna; *Producer*: Richard N. Gladstein; *Cast*: Reggie Bannister, Clint Howard, Neith Hunter; *Production Company*: Silent Films Inc.; *Distributor*: Live Video; *Runtime*: 90 minutes; *Rating*: R / 18

Silent Night Deadly Night 5: The Toy Maker (1992)
Director: Martin Kitrosser; *Writers*: Martin Kitrosser, Brian Yuzna; *Producers*: Richard N. Gladstein, Brian Yuzna; *Cast*: Clint Howard, Mickey Rooney, Neith Hunter; *Production Company*: Still Silent Films Inc.; *Distributor*: International Video Entertainment (IVE); *Runtime*: 90 minutes; *Rating*: R

☆ ☆ ☆

Sleepaway Camp (1983)
Director: Robert Hiltzik; *Writer*: Robert Hiltzik; *Producers*: Jerry Silva, Michele Tatosian; *Cast*: Felissa Rose, Jonathan Tiersten, Karen Fields; *Production Company*: American Eagle; *Distributors*: Media Home Entertainment, United Film Distribution Company (UFDC), Video Treasures; *Runtime*: 88 minutes; *Rating*: R / 15

Sleepaway Camp II: Unhappy Campers (1988)
Director: Michael A. Simpson; *Writer*: Fritz Gordon; *Producers*: Jerry Silva, Michael A. Simpson; *Cast*: Pamela Springsteen, Renée Estevez, Tony Higgins; *Production Company*: Double Helix Films; *Distributor*: Nelson Entertainment; *Runtime*: 80 minutes; *Rating*: R / 18

Sleepaway Camp III (1989)
Director: Michael A. Simpson; *Writer*: Fritz Gordon; *Producers*: Krishna Shah, Jerry Silva, Michael A. Simpson; *Cast*: Pamela Springsteen, Tracy Griffith, Michael J. Pollard; *Production Company*: Double Helix Films; *Distributor*: Nelson Entertainment; *Runtime*: 80 minutes; *Rating*: R / 18

Sometimes They Come Back (1991)
Director: Tom McLoughlin; *Writers*: Stephen King, Lawrence Konner, Mark Rosenthal; *Producer*: Michael S. Murphey; *Cast*: Tim Matheson, Brooke Adams, Robert Rusler; *Production Company*: Paradise Films; *Distributor*: Vidmark Entertainment; *Runtime*: 97 minutes; *Rating*: R / 15

Sometimes They Come Back ... Again (1996)
Director: Adam Grossman; *Writers*: Guy Riedel, Adam Grossman; *Producer*: Michael L. Meltzer; *Cast*: Michael Gross, Alexis Arquette, Hilary Swank; *Production Company*: Trimark Pictures; *Distributor*: Trimark Pictures; *Runtime*: 98 minutes; *Rating*: R / 18

Sometimes They Come Back ... For More (1999)
Director: Daniel Zelik Berk; *Writers*: Adam Grossman, Darryl Sollerh; *Producers*: Daniel Zelik Berk, Diana Zahn; *Cast*: Clayton Rohner, Faith Ford, Max Perlich; *Production Company*: Trimark Pictures; *Distributor*: Trimark Pictures; *Runtime*: 89 minutes; *Rating*: R / 15

Species (1995)
Director: Roger Donaldson; *Writer*: Dennis Feldman; *Producers*: Dennis Feldman, Frank Mancuso Jr.; *Cast*: Ben Kingsley, Michael Madsen, Alfred Molina; *Production Company*: Metro-Goldwyn-Mayer (MGM); *Distributor*: MGM/UA Distribution Company; *Runtime*: 108 minutes; *Rating*: R / 18

Species II (1998)
Director: Peter Medak; *Writer*: Chris Brancato; *Producer*: Frank Mancuso Jr.; *Cast*: Michael Madsen, Natasha Henstridge, Marg Helgenberger; *Production Companies*: Metro-Goldwyn-Mayer (MGM), FGM Entertainment; *Distributor*: Metro-Goldwyn-Mayer Distributing Corporation (MGM); *Runtime*: 93 minutes; *Rating*: R / 18

Species III (2004)
Director: Brad Turner; *Writer*: Ben Ripley; *Producer*: David Dwiggins; *Cast*: Robin Dunne, Robert Knepper, Amelia Cooke; *Production Companies*: Metro-Goldwyn-Mayer (MGM), FGM Entertainment; *Distributor*: MGM Home Entertainment; *Runtime*: 111 minutes; *Rating*: R / 15

The Stepfather (1987)
Director: Joseph Ruben; *Writers*: Donald E. Westlake, Carolyn Lefcourt, Brian Garfield; *Producer*: Jay Benson; *Cast*: Terry O'Quinn, Jill Schoelen, Shelley Hack; *Production Company*: Incorporated Television Company (ITC); *Distributor*: New Century Vista Film Company; *Runtime*: 89 minutes; *Rating*: R / 18

Stepfather 2 (1989)
Director: Jeff Burr; *Writer*: John Auerbach; *Producers*: William Burr, Darin Scott; *Cast*: Terry O'Quinn, Meg Foster, Carloine Williams; *Production Company*: Incorporated Television Company (ITC); *Distributors*: Millimeter Films, Miramax Films; *Runtime*: 93 minutes; *Rating*: R / 18

The Stepfather III: Father's Day (1992)
Director: Guy Magar; *Writers*: Guy Magar, Marc B. Ray; *Producers*: Guy Magar, Paul Moen; *Cast*: Robert Wightman, Priscilla

Barnes, Season Hubley; *Production Company*: Incorporated Television Company (ITC); *Distributors*: ITC Entertainment Group, Starlight, Vidmark Entertainment; *Runtime*: 110 minutes; *Rating*: R / 18

Subspecies (1991)

Director: Ted Nicolaou; *Writers*: Charles Band, Jackson Barr, David Pabian; *Producer*: Ion Ionescu; *Cast*: Angus Scrimm, Laura Tate, Michelle McBride; *Production Company*: Full Moon Entertainment; *Distributor*: Full Moon Entertainment; *Runtime*: 90 minutes; *Rating*: R / 18

Bloodstone: Subspecies II (1993)

Director: Ted Nicolaou; *Writer*: Ted Nicolao; *Producers*: Oana Paunescu, Vlad Paunescu; *Cast*: Anders Hove, Denice Duff, Kevin Spirtas; *Production Company*: Full Moon Entertainment; *Distributor*: Full Moon Entertainment; *Runtime*: 107 minutes; *Rating*: R / 18

Bloodlust: Subspecies III (1993)

Director: Ted Nicolaou; *Writer*: Ted Nicolaou; *Producers*: Oana Paunescu, Vlad Paunescu; *Cast*: Anders Hove, Denice Duff, Kevin Spirtas; *Production Company*: Full Moon Entertainment; *Distributors*: Paramount Home Video, Full Moon Entertainment; *Runtime*: 83 minutes; *Rating*: R / 18

Subspecies 4: Bloodstorm (1998)

Director: Ted Nicolaou; *Writer*: Ted Nicolaou; *Producers*: Kirk Edward Hansen, Vlad Paunescu; *Cast*: Anders Hove, Denice Duff, Jonathon Morris; *Production Company*: Castel Film Romania; *Distributor*: Full Moon Entertainment; *Runtime*: 85 minutes; *Rating*: R / 18

The Texas Chain Saw Massacre (1974)

Director: Tobe Hooper; *Writers*: Tobe Hooper, Kim Henkel; *Producers*: Tobe Hooper, Lou Peraino; *Cast*: Marilyn Burns, Gunnar Hansen, Jim Siedow; *Production Company*: Vortex; *Distributor*: Bryanston Distributing; *Runtime*: 83 minutes; *Rating*: R / 18

The Texas Chainsaw Massacre 2 (1986)

Director: Tobe Hooper; *Writer*: L.M. Kit Carson; *Producers*: Menahem Golan, Yoram Globus; *Cast*: Dennis Hopper, Caroline Williams, Jim Siedow; *Production Company*: Canon Films; *Distributor*: Cannon Film Distributors; *Runtime*: 89 minutes / 100 minutes; *Rating*: Unrated / 18

Leatherface: Texas Chainsaw Massacre III (1990)

Director: Jeff Burr; *Writer*: David J. Schow; *Producer*: Robert Engelman; *Cast*: Kate Hodge, Ken Foree. R.A. Mihailoff; *Production Company*: New Line Cinema; *Distributor*: New Line Cinema; *Runtime*: 81 minutes; *Rating*: R / 18

The Return of the Texas Chainsaw Massacre (1994)

Director: Kim Henkel; *Writer*: Kim Henkel; *Producers*: Kim Henkel, Robert Kuhn; *Cast*: Matthew McConaughey, Renee Zelwegger, Robert Jacks; *Production Companies*: Genre Pictures, Return Productions, River City Films, Ultra Muchos Productions; *Distributors*: New Line Cinema, Genre Pictures International; *Runtime*: 86 minutes; *Rating*: R / 18

The Texas Chainsaw Massacre (2003)

Director: Marcus Nispel; *Writers*: Kim Henkel, Tobe Hooper, Scott Kosar; *Producers*: Michael Bay, Mike Fleiss; *Cast*: Jessica Biel, Jonathan Tucker, Erica Leerhsen; *Production Companies*: New Line Cinema, Focus Features, Radar Pictures Inc., Platinum Dunes, Next Entertainment, Chainsaw Productions LLC; *Distributor*: New

Line Cinema; *Runtime*: 98 minutes; *Rating*: R / 18

Texas Chainsaw Massacre: The Beginning (2006)
Director: Jonathan Liebesman; *Writers*: Sheldon Turner, David J. Schow; *Producers*: Michael Bay, Mike Fleiss, Andrew Form, Bradley Fuller, Kim Henkel, Tobe Hooper; *Cast*: Jordana Brewster, R. Lee Ermey, Andrew Bryniarski; *Production Companies*: New Line Cinema, Texas Chainsaw Productions, Platinum Dunes, Next Entertainment, Vortex/Henkel/Hooper; *Distributor*: New Line Cinema; *Runtime*: 91 minutes; *Rating*: R / 18

Tremors (1990)
Director: Ron Underwood; *Writers*: Ron Underwood, S.S. Wilson, Brent Maddock; *Producers*: S.S. Wilson, Brent Maddock; *Cast*: Kevin Bacon, Fred Ward, Michael Gross; *Production Companies*: No Frills Film Production, Universal Pictures; *Distributor*: Universal Pictures; *Runtime*: 96 minutes; *Rating*: PG-13 / 15

Tremors II: Aftershocks (1996)
Director: S.S. Wilson; *Writers*: S.S. Wilson, Brent Maddock; *Producers*: Christopher DeFaria, Nancy Roberts; *Cast*: Fred Ward, Helen Shaver, Michael Gross; *Production Companies*: Stampede Entertainment, Universal Pictures; *Distributor*: MCA/Universal Pictures; *Runtime*: 100 minutes; *Rating*: PG-13 / 12

Tremors 3: Back to Perfection (2001)
Director: Brent Maddock; *Writers*: S.S. Wilson, Brent Maddock, Nancy Roberts, John Whelpley; *Producers*: Nancy Roberts, S.S. Wilson; *Cast*: Michael Gross, Shawn Christian, Susan Chuang; *Production Company*: Stampede Entertainment; *Distributor*: Universal Studios Home Video; *Runtime*: 104 minutes; *Rating*: PG / 12

Tremors 4: The Legend Begins (2004)
Director: S.S. Wilson; *Writers*: S.S. Wilson, Brent Maddock, Nancy Roberts, Scott Buck; *Producer*: Nancy Roberts; *Cast*: Michael Gross, Sara Botsford, Billy Drago; *Production Company*: Stampede Entertainment; *Distributor*: Universal Studios Home Video; *Runtime*: 101 minutes; *Rating*: PG-13 / 12

The Unborn (1991)
Director: Rodman Flender; *Writers*: John D. Brancato, Michael Ferris; *Producers*: Roger Corman, Rodman Flender; *Cast*: Brooke Adams, Brad Blaisdell, K. Callan; *Production Company*: Concorde-New Horizons; *Distributor*: Concorde Pictures; *Runtime*: 83 minutes; *Rating*: R / 18

The Unborn II (1994)
Director: Rick Jacobson; *Writers*: Rob Kerchner, Daniella Purcell, Mark Evan Schwartz; *Producers*: Roger Corman, Mike Elliott; *Cast*: Michele Greene, Robin Curtis, Scott Valentine; *Production Company*: Concorde-New Horizons; *Distributor*: New Horizon Picture Corp; *Runtime*: 83 minutes; *Rating*: R / 18

Underworld (2003)
Director: Len Wiseman; *Writers*: Kevin Grevioux, Len Wiseman, Danny McBride; *Producers*: Gary Lucchesi, Tom Rosenberg, Richard S. Wright; *Cast*: Kate Beckinsale, Scott Speedman, Michael Sheen; *Production Companies*: Lakeshore Entertainment, Laurinfilm Ltd., Subterranean Productions LLC, Subterranean Productions UK Ltd., Underworld Produktions GmbH; *Distributors*: Screen Gems, Lakeshore International; *Runtime*: 121 minutes / 133 minutes; *Rating*: R / 15

Underworld: Evolution (2006)
Director: Len Wiseman; *Writers*: Len Wiseman, Danny McBride; *Producers*: David

Coatsworth, Gary Lucchesi, Tom Rosenberg, Richard S. Wright; *Cast*: Kate Beckinsale, Scott Speedman, Derek Jacobi; *Production Companies*: Lakeshore Entertainment, Screen Gems; *Distributor*: Screen Gems; *Runtime*: 106 minutes; *Rating*: R / 18

The Unnamable (1988)

Director: Jean-Paul Ouellette; *Writers*: H.P. Lovecraft, Jean-Paul Ouellette; *Producers*: Jean-Paul Ouellette, Dean Ramser; *Cast*: Mark Kinsey Stephenson, Alexandra Durrell, Laura Albert; *Production Company*: Unknown; *Distributors*: Image Entertainment, Vidmark Entertainment; *Runtime*: 87 minutes; *Rating*: R / 18

The Unnamable II: The Statement of Randolph Carter (1988)

Director: Jean-Paul Ouellette; *Writers*: H.P. Lovecraft, Jean-Paul Ouellette; *Producer*: Jean-Paul Ouellette; *Cast*: Mark Kinsey Stephenson, Charles Klausmeyer, Maria Ford; *Production Companies*: Lions Gate Films, The Unnamable Productions Co., Yankee Classic Pictures; *Distributor*: Prism Pictures; *Runtime*: 104 minutes; *Rating*: R / 18

Urban Legend (1998)

Director: Jamie Blanks; *Writer*: Silvio Horta; *Producers*: Gina Matthews, Michael McDonnell, Neal H. Moritz; *Cast*: Jared Leto, Alicia Witt, Rebecca Gayheart; *Production Companies*: Canal+ Droits Audiovisuels, Original Film, Phoenix Pictures; *Distributor*: TriStar Pictures; *Runtime*: 99 minutes; *Rating*: R / 18

Urban Legends: Final Cut (2000)

Director: John Ottman; *Writers*: Paul Harris Boardman, Scott Derrickson; *Producers*: Gina Matthews, Neal H. Moritz, Richard Luke Rothschild; *Cast*: Jennifer Morrison, Matthew Davis, Hart Bochner; *Production Companies*: Original Film, Phoenix Pictures; *Distributors*: Sony Pictures Entertainment, Columbia Pictures; *Runtime*: 97 minutes; *Rating*: R / 15

Urban Legends: Bloody Mary (2005)

Director: Mary Lambert; *Writers*: Michael Dougherty, Dan Harris; *Producers*: Aaron Merrell, Scott Messer, Louis Phillips; *Cast*: Kate Mara, Robert Vito, Tina Lifford; *Production Company*: NPP Productions Inc.; *Distributors*: Sony Pictures Entertainment, Columbia Pictures; *Runtime*: 93 minutes; *Rating*: R / 15

★ ★ ★

Vampires (1998)

Director: John Carpenter; *Writers*: John Steakley, Don Jakoby; *Producer*: Sandy King; *Cast*: James Woods, Daniel Baldwin, Sheryl Lee; *Production Companies*: Film Office, JVC Entertainment, Largo Entertainment, Spooky Tooth Productions, Storm King Productions; *Distributors*: Sony Pictures Entertainment, Columbia Pictures; *Runtime*: 108 minutes; *Rating*: R / 18

Vampires: Los Muertos (2002)

Director: Tommy Lee Wallace; *Writer*: Tommy Lee Wallace; *Producer*: Jack Lorenz; *Cast*: Jon Bon Jovi, Cristián de la Fuente, Natasha Gregson Wagner; *Production Companies*: Screen Gems, Storm King Productions; *Distributors*: Screen Gems, Sony Pictures Entertainment; *Runtime*: 93 minutes; *Rating*: R / 15

Vampires: The Turning (2005)

Director: Marty Weiss; *Writers*: D.B. Farmer, Andy Hurst; *Producers*: Scott Einbinder, Carol Kottenbrook; *Cast*: Patrick Bauchau, Nophand Boonyai, Stephanie Chao; *Production Companies*: Living Films, Sandstorm Films; *Distributor*: Sony Pictures Home Entertainment; *Runtime*: 84 minutes; *Rating*: R / 15

Warlock (1989)
Director: Steve Miner; *Writer*: David Twohy; *Producer*: Steve Miner; *Cast*: Julian Sands, Lori Singer, Richard E. Grant; *Production Company*: New World Pictures; *Distributors*: Trimark Pictures, Vidmark Entertainment; *Runtime*: 103 minutes; *Rating*: R / 15

Warlock: The Armageddon (1993)
Director: Anthony Hickox; *Writers*: Kevin Rock, Sam Bernard; *Producers*: Peter Abrams, Robert L. Levy; *Cast*: Julian Sands, Chris Young, Paula Marshall; *Production Companies*: Tapestry Films, Trimark Pictures; *Distributors*: Trimark Pictures, Vidmark Entertainment; *Runtime*: 98 minutes; *Rating*: R / 18

Warlock III: The End of Innocence (1999)
Director: Eric Freiser; *Writers*: Pierce Milestone, Bruce David Eisen, Eric Freiser; *Producer*: Bruce David Eisen; *Cast*: Bruce Payne, Ashley Laurence, Paul Francis; *Production Company*: Trimark Pictures; *Distributor*: Trimark Pictures; *Runtime*: 94 minutes; *Rating*: R / 18

Watchers (1988)
Director: Jon Hess; *Writers*: Dean R. Koontz, Bill Freed, Damian Lee; *Producers*: Damian Lee, David Mitchell; *Cast*: Michael Ironside, Corey Haim, Duncan Fraser; *Production Companies*: Canadian Entertainment Investors II, Carolco Pictures Inc., Centaur Films, Company Limited Partnership, Concorde Pictures, Rose & Ruby Productions; *Distributor*: MCA/Universal Pictures; *Runtime*: 91 minutes; *Rating*: R / 18

Watchers II (1990)
Director: Thierry Notz; *Writers*: John D. Brancato, Michael Ferris; *Producer*: Roger Corman; *Cast*: Timothy Marlowe, Marc Singer, Tracy Scoggins; *Production Company*: Concorde; *Distributor*: Concorde Pictures; *Runtime*: 101 minutes; *Rating*: R / 18

Watchers III (1994)
Director: Jeremy Stanford; *Writer*: Michael Palmer; *Producer*: Luis Llosa; *Cast*: Wings Hauser, Gregory Scott Cummins, Daryl Keith Roach; *Production Company*: Iguana Producciones; *Distributor*: Concorde Pictures; *Runtime*: 80 minutes; *Rating*: R / 15

Watchers Reborn (1998)
Director: John Carl Buechler; *Writer*: Sean Dash; *Producer*: Darin Spillman; *Cast*: Mark Hamill, Lisa Wilcox, Stephen Macht; *Production Companies*: Concorde Pictures, Manga Films; *Distributor*: Concorde Pictures; *Runtime*: 90 minutes; *Rating*: R / 15

Waxwork (1988)
Director: Anthony Hickox; *Writer*: Anthony Hickox; *Producers*: Staffan Ahrenberg, Eyal Rimmon; *Cast*: Zach Galligan, Deborah Foreman, Michelle Johnson; *Production Companies*: HB Filmrullen, Palla; *Distributor*: Vestron Pictures Ltd.; *Runtime*: 95 minutes; *Rating*: R / 18

Waxwork II: Lost in Time (1992)
Director: Anthony Hickox; *Writer*: Anthony Hickox; *Producer*: Nancy Paloian; *Cast*: Zach Galligan, Monika Schnarre, Martin Kemp; *Production Company*: Unknown; *Distributor*: Lions Gate Films; *Runtime*: 104 minutes; *Rating*: R / 15

White Noise (2005)
Director: Geoffrey Sax; *Writer*: Niall Johnson; *Producers*: Shawn Williamson, Paul Brooks; *Cast*: Michael Keaton, Chandra West, Deborah Kara Unger; *Production Companies*: Brightlight Pictures, Endgame Entertainment, Gold Circle Films, Universal

Pictures, White Noise UK Ltd.; *Distributor*: Universal Pictures; *Runtime*: 101 minutes; *Rating*: PG-13 / 15

White Noise: The Light (2007)

Director: Patrick Lussier; *Writer*: Matt Venne; *Producer*: Shawn Williamson; *Cast*: Nathan Fillion, Katee Sackhoff, Ed Anders; *Production Companies*: Gold Circle Films, Brightlight Pictures; *Distributor*: Rogue Pictures; *Runtime*: 99 minutes; *Rating*: PG-13 / 15

Wishmaster (1997)

Director: Robert Kurtzman; *Writer*: Peter Atkins; *Producers*: Pierre David, Clark Peterson, Noël A. Zanitsch; *Cast*: Tammy Lauren, Andrew Divoff, Robert Englund; *Production Company*: Pierre David; *Distributor*: Live Film & Mediaworks Inc.; *Runtime*: 90 minutes; *Rating*: R / 18

Wishmaster 2: Evil Never Dies (1999)

Director: Jack Sholder; *Writer*: Jack Sholder; *Producer*: Tony Amatullo; *Cast*: Andrew Divoff, Paul Johansson, Holly Fields; *Production Company*: Artisan Entertainment; *Distributor*: Artisan Pictures Inc.; *Runtime*: 96 minutes; *Rating*: R / 18

Wishmaster 3: Beyond the Gates of Hell (2001)

Director: Chris Angel; *Writer*: Alex Wright; *Producers*: Gary Howsam, Craig Nicholls, Gilles Paquin; *Cast*: John Novak, A.J. Cook, Tobias Mehler; *Production Companies*: Overseas Film Group, Artisan Entertainment, Blue Rider Pictures, GFT Entertainment, Paquin Entertainment Group, Pendle View (WM) Limited; *Distributor*: Artisan Entertainment; *Runtime*: 90 minutes; *Rating*: R / 15

Wishmaster 4: The Prophecy Fulfilled (2002)

Director: Chris Angel; *Writer*: John Benjamin Martin; *Producers*: Gary Howsam, Gilles Paquin; *Cast*: Tara Spencer-Nairn, Michael Trucco, Jason Thompson; *Production Companies*: Overseas Film Group, Artisan Entertainment, Blue Rider Pictures, GFT Entertainment, Paquin Entertainment Group, Pendle View (WM) Limited; *Distributor*: Artisan Entertainment; *Runtime*: 90 minutes; *Rating*: R / 18

Witchboard (1986)

Director: Kevin Tenney; *Writer*: Kevin Tenney; *Producer*: Gerald Geoffray; *Cast*: Todd Allen, Clare Bristol, Gloria Hayes; *Production Company*: Paragon Arts International; *Distributors*: Cinema Group, Magnum Entertainment; *Runtime*: 98 minutes; *Rating*: R / 15

Witchboard 2: The Devil's Doorway (1993)

Director: Kevin Tenney; *Writer*: Kevin Tenney; *Producers*: Jeff Geoffray, Walter Josten; *Cast*: Ami Dolenz, Chris Michael Moore, Laraine Newman; *Production Companies*: Blue Rider Pictures, Witchboard Partners; *Distributors*: Blue Rider Pictures, Republic Pictures Home Video; *Runtime*: 98 minutes; *Rating*: R / 15

Witchboard III: The Possession (1995)

Director: Peter Svatek; *Writers*: Kevin Tenney, Jon Ezrine; *Producer*: Robin Spry; *Cast*: David Nerman, Locky Lambert, Cedric Smith; *Production Companies*: Telescene Film Group Productions, Vista Street Entertainment; *Distributor*: Republic Entertainment Inc.; *Runtime*: 93 minutes; *Rating*: R / 18

Witchcraft (1988)

Director: Rob Spera; *Writer*: Jody Savin; *Producer*: Yoram Barzilai; *Cast*: Anat Topol, Gary Sloan, Mary Shelley; *Production

Company: Vista Street Entertainment; *Distributor*: Academy Entertainment Inc.; *Runtime*: 95 minutes; *Rating*: R / 18

Witchcraft II: The Temptress (1990)
Director: Mark Woods; *Writers*: Jim Hanson, Sal Manna; *Producers*: Megan Barnett, Jerry Feifer, Renza Mizbani; *Cast*: Charles Solomon, Delia Sheppard, David Homb; *Production Company*: Vista Street Entertainment; *Distributor*: Academy Entertainment Inc.; *Runtime*: 88 minutes; *Rating*: R / 18

Witchcraft III: The Kiss of Death (1991)
Director: Rachel Feldman; *Writer*: Jerry Daly; *Producer*: Holly MacConkey; *Cast*: Charles Solomon, Lisa Toothman, Domonic Luciana; *Production Company*: Vista Street Entertainment; *Distributor*: Academy Entertainment Inc.; *Runtime*: 95 minutes; *Rating*: R

Witchcraft IV: The Virgin Heart (1992)
Director: James Merendino; *Writers*: Michael Paul Girard, James Merendino; *Producers*: Stephen Lieb, Holly MacConkey; *Cast*: Charles Solomon, Julie Strain, Clive Pearson; *Production Company*: Vista Street Entertainment; *Distributor*: Academy Entertainment Inc.; *Runtime*: 92 minutes; *Rating*: R

Witchcraft V: Dance with the Devil (1993)
Director: Talun Hsu; *Writers*: James Merendino, Steve Tymon; *Producers*: Michael Feifer, Drew Peloso; *Cast*: Marklen Kennedy, Carolyn Taye-Loren, Nicole Sassaman; *Production Company*: Vista Street Entertainment; *Distributor*: Academy Entertainment Inc.; *Runtime*: 94 minutes; *Rating*: R / 18

Witchcraft VI (1994)
Director: Julie Davis; *Writers*: Julie Davis, Peter E. Fleming; *Producers*: Jerry Feifer, Michael Feifer, Robyn Mellen; *Cast*: Jerry Spicer, Debra K. Beatty, Shannon McLeod; *Production Company*: Vista Street Entertainment; *Distributor*: Unknown; *Runtime*: 88 minutes; *Rating*: R

Witchcraft VII: A Taste for Blood (1995)
Director: Michael Paul Girard; *Writers*: Jerry Feifer, Peter E. Fleming; *Producer*: Michael Feifer; *Cast*: David Byrnes, April Breneman, Loren Schmalle; *Production Company*: Vista Street Entertainment; *Distributor*: A-Pix Entertainment Inc.; *Runtime*: 90 minutes; *Rating*: R

Witchcraft VIII: Salem's Ghost (1996)
Director: Joseph John Barmettler; *Writer*: Joseph John Barmettler; *Producer*: Michael Feifer; *Cast*: Lee Grober, Kim Kopf, Tom Overmyer; *Production Company*: Vista Street Entertainment; *Distributor*: A-Pix Entertainment Inc.; *Runtime*: 90 minutes; *Rating*: R

Witchcraft IX: Bitter Flesh (1997)
Director: Michael Paul Girard; *Writer*: Stephen Downing; *Producer*: Michael Feifer; *Cast*: Landon Hall, David Byrnes, Julius Antonio; *Production Company*: Vista Street Entertainment; *Distributor*: Vista Street Entertainment; *Runtime*: 92 minutes; *Rating*: R

Witchcraft X: Mistress of the Craft (1998)
Director: Elisar Cabrera; *Writer*: Elisar Cabrera; *Producers*: Jon Blay, Elisar Cabrera; *Cast*: Wendy Cooper, Eileen Daly, Kerry Knowlton; *Production Company*: Armadillo Films; *Distributor*: Vista Street Entertainment; *Runtime*: 90 minutes; *Rating*: R

Witchcraft XI: Sisters in Blood (2000)
Director: Ron Ford; *Writer*: Ron Ford; *Producer*: David S. Sterling; *Cast*: Miranda Odell, Lauren Ian Richards, Kathleen St. Lawrence; *Production Company*: Vista Street Entertainment; *Distributor*: Brentwood

Video; *Runtime*: 90 minutes; *Rating*: Not Rated

Witchcraft XII: In the Lair of the Serpent (2004)

Director: Brad Sykes; *Writer*: Brad Sykes; *Producer*: David S. Sterling; *Cast*: Janet Keijser, Bruce Blauer, Monika Wild; *Production Company*: Vista Street Entertainment; *Distributor*: Vista Street Entertainment; *Runtime*: 88 minutes; *Rating*: Unrated

Witchcraft 13: Blood of the Chosen (2007)

Director: Mel House; *Writers*: Jeffrey Wolinski, Michael Wolinski; *Producer*: Shaun Fox; *Cast*: Tim Wrobel, Cesar Castillo, Anjanette Clewis; *Production Company*: Tripod Films LLC; *Distributor*: Vista Street Entertainment; *Runtime*: Unknown; *Rating*: Unknown

Witchouse (1999)

Director: David DeCoteau; *Writer*: Matthew Jason Walsh; *Producers*: Kirk Edward Hansen, Vlad Paunescu; *Cast*: Ariauna Albright, Matt Raftery, Monica Serene Garnich; *Production Companies*: Castel Film Romania, Full Moon Pictures; *Distributor*: Full Moon Entertainment; *Runtime*: 72 minutes; *Rating*: R / 15

Witchouse 2: Blood Coven (2000)

Director: J.R. Bookwalter; *Writer*: Douglas Snauffer; *Producers*: Vlad Paunescu, Gary Schmoeller; *Cast*: Ariauna Albright, Elizabeth Hobgood, Nicholas Lanier; *Production Companies*: Castel Film Romania, Full Moon Pictures; *Distributor*: Full Moon Entertainment; *Runtime*: 77 minutes; *Rating*: R / 15

Witchouse 3: Demon Fire (2001)

Director: J.R. Bookwalter; *Writers*: J.R. Bookwalter, Matthew Jason Walsh; *Producers*: Charles Band, J.R. Bookwalter; *Cast*: Debbie Rochon, Tanya Dempsey, Tina Krause; *Production Company*: Tempe Video; *Distributor*: Full Moon Entertainment; *Runtime*: 77 minutes; *Rating*: R / 15

Xtro (1983)

Director: Harry Bromley Davenport; *Writers*: Harry Bromley Davenport, Iain Cassie, Michel Parry, Robert Smith; *Producer*: Mark Forstater; *Cast*: Philip Sayer, Bernice Stegers, Danny Brainin; *Production Company*: Amalgamated Film Enterprises; *Distributor*: New Line Cinema; *Runtime*: 84 minutes; *Rating*: R / 18

Xtro 2: The Second Encounter (1990)

Director: Harry Bromley Davenport; *Writers*: John A. Curtis, Edward Kovach, Stephen Lister, Robert Smith; *Producer*: Lloyd A. Simandl; *Cast*: Jan-Michael Vincent, Paul Koslo, Tara Buckman; *Production Companies*: Excalibur Pictures, North American Pictures; *Distributor*: New Line Home Video; *Runtime*: 92 minutes; *Rating*: R / 18

Xtro 3: Watch the Skies (1995)

Director: Harry Bromley Davenport; *Writer*: Daryl Haney; *Producer*: Harry Bromley Davenport; *Cast*: Robert Culp, Andrew Divoff, Daryl Haney; *Production Company*: Harry Bromley Davenport; *Distributor*: Dorian Inc.; *Runtime*: 90 minutes; *Rating*: R / 18

Chapter Notes

Preface

1. Quote from Whale's *Bride of Frankenstein* (1935).

Introduction

1. Mendik, Xavier. "Logic, Creativity and (Critical) Misinterpretations: An Interview with David Cronenberg," in Grant, Michael (ed.). *The Modern Fantastic: The Films of David Cronenberg*. Trowbridge, Wilts: Flicks Books, 2000, p. 117.
2. McDonagh, Maitland. *Filmmaking on the Fringe: The Good, the Bad, and the Deviant Directors*. New York: Carol, 1995, p. 93.
3. Spoken by Stuart "Stu" Macher, who, along with his dominant partner Billy Loomis, was one of the slasher-inspired serial killers in Wes Craven's *Scream* (1996).
4. For a detailed production history of what is regarded as Whale's greatest achievement see James Curtis. *James Whale: A New World of Gods and Monsters*. Boston and London: Faber and Faber, 1998, pp. 233–254.
5. However, Whale's celebrated sequel came two years after Schoedsack's less successful *Son of Kong* (1933), a family friendly follow-up which was hastily constructed and failed to inspire audiences in the same way its predecessor had done earlier that year.
6. Jancovich, Mark (ed.). *Horror: The Film Reader*. London: Routledge, 2001, p. 9.
7. Wood, Robin, and Richard Lippe (eds.). *American Nightmare: Essays on the Horror Film*. Toronto Festival of Festivals, 1979, p. 13.
8. For example, Skal, David. J. *The Monster Show: A Cultural History of Horror*. New York: Norton, 1993; Tudor, Andrew. *Monsters and Mad Scientists: A Cultural History of the Horror Movie*. London: Blackwell, 1989; Wood, Robin. *Hollywood from Vietnam to Reagan*. New York and Surrey: Columbia University Press, 1986; and Newman, Kim. *Nightmare Movies: A Cultural History of the Horror Film 1968–88*. London: Bloomsbury, 1988.
9. Clarens, Carlos. *Horror Movies: An Illustrated Survey*. London: Secker & Walburg, 1968; and Wells, Paul. *The Horror Genre: From Beelzebub to Blair Witch*. London: Wallflower, 2000. Other generic and historical approaches to horror can be seen in Butler, Ivan. *Horror in the Cinema*. London: Barnes, 1979; Prawer, S.S. *Caligari's Children*. Oxford: Oxford University Press, 1980; Quackenbush, Robert. *Movie Monsters and their Masters: The Birth of the Horror Film*. Chicago: Albert, Whitman, 1980; Twitchell, James B. *Dreadful Pleasures: An Anatomy of Modern Horror*. New York and Oxford: Oxford University Press, 1985; Hardy, Phil. *Horror Films*. London: Aurum Press, 1986; Underwood, Tim, Chuck Miller and Jeff Conner. *Nightmare Movies: A Critical History of the Horror Film*. New York: New American Library, 1987; Carroll, Noel. *The Philosophy of Horror*. New York: Routeledge, 1990; King, Geoff. *New Hollywood Cinema: An Introduction*. London: I.B. Tauris, 2002; Soren, David. *The Rise and Fall of the Horror Film*. Baltimore, MA: Midnight Marquee Press, 1997; and Humphries, Reynold. *The American Horror Film: An Introduction*. Edinburgh: Edinburgh University Press, 2002.
10. Neale has consistently written on and revised his notions regarding the definition of genre.
11. Naremore, James. *More Than Night: Film Noir in Its Contexts*. Berkeley, CA: University of California Press, 1998, pp. 9–39.

12. Russell, David. J. "Monster Roundup: Reintegrating the Horror Genre," in Browne, Nick (ed.). *Refiguring American Film Genres: Theory and History.* Berkeley: University of California Press, 1998.
13. Jancovich, 2001: 9.
14. Ibid.
15. Clover, Carol J. *Men, Women and Chainsaws: Gender in the Modern Horror Film.* London: British Film Institute, 1992, p. 5.
16. Clover sets this up in her Introduction to *Men, Women and Chainsaws* (Clover, 1992: 5).
17. For example, classic scenes were selected and analyzed in Crane, Jonathan Lake. *Terror and Everyday Life: Singular Moments in the History of the Horror Film.* Thousand Oaks: Sage, 1994; as well as by Sternfield, Jonathan. *The Look of Horror: Scary Moments from Scary Movies.* New York: Moore & Moore, 1990.
18. Dettmann, B., and M. Bedford. *The Horror Factory: The Horror Films of Universal 1931–1955.* New York: Gordon Press, 1976; John Soister, John. *Of Gods and Monsters: A Critical Guide to Universal Studio's Science Fiction, Horror and Mystery Films.* Jefferson, NC, and London: McFarland, 1999.
19. Coubro, Gerry. *Hammer and Horror: Bad Taste and Popular British Cinema.* Sheffield: Pavic, 1991; Hutchings, Peter. *Hammer and Beyond: The British Horror Film.* Manchester: Manchester University Press, 1993; and Jonathan Rigby, Jonathan. *English Gothic: A Century of Horror Cinema.* London: Reynolds & Hearn, 2000.
20. See Dyson, Jeremy. *Bright Darkness: The Lost Art of the Supernatural Horror Film.* London and Washington: Cassell, 1997; McCarty, John. *Splatter Movies: Breaking the Last Taboo Off the Screen.* Bromley, Kent: Columbus Books, 1984; and McCarty, John. *The Official Splatter Movie Guide.* New York: St. Martin's Press, 1989. There has also been Dika, Vera. *Games of Terror: Halloween, Friday the 13th and Films of the Stalker Cycle.* New Jersey and London: Associated University Press, 1990.
21. Simpson, Philip L. *Psychopaths: Tracking the Serial Killer Through Contemporary Fiction and Film.* Illinois: Southern Illinois University Press, 2000.
22. Paul, W. *Laughing Screaming: Modern Hollywood Horror and Comedy.* Columbia: Columbia University Press, 1994.
23. McBride, Joseph. *Steven Spielberg.* London: Faber and Faber, 1997, p. 240.
24. Ibid, p. 241.
25. As reported by Richard Finney on page 58 of his article "Nanny and the Possessor: The Guardian," *Fangoria* 91, April 1990, pp. 30–33 and 58.
26. See Williams (1984); Berenstein, R.J. *Attack of the Leading Ladies: Gender and Spectatorship in Classic Horror Cinema.* Columbia: Columbia University Press, 1996; Grant, Barry Keith (ed.). *The Dread of Difference: Gender and Horror.* Austin, Texas: University of Texas Press, 1996; Pinedo, I.C. *Recreational Terror: Women and the Pleasures of Horror Film Viewing.* New York: State University of New York Press, 1997; and Cherry, Brigid, in Jancovich, 2001.
27. Benshoff, Harry M. *Monsters in the Closet: Homosexuality and the Horror Film.* Manchester: Manchester University Press, 1997.
28. Creed, Barbara. *The Monstrous-Feminine: Film, Feminism and Psychoanalysis.* London: Routledge, 1993.
29. See Bussing, Sabine. *Aliens in the Home: The Child in Horror Fiction.* New York: Greenwood Press, 1987; and Westfahl, G., and G. Slusser. *Nursery Realms: Children in the World of Science Fiction, Fantasy and Horror.* Georgia: University of Georgia Press, 1999.
30. Williams, Tony. *Hearths of Darkness: The Family in the American Horror Film.* New Jersey: Associated University Press, 1996.
31. Weaver, James, and Ron Tanborini. *Horror Films: Current Research on Audience Preferences and Reactions.* Mahwah, New Jersey: Lawrence Erlbaum, 1995.
32. Britton, 1979.
33. Grant, Barry K. (ed.). *Planks of Reason: Essays on the Horror Film.* Metuchen, New Jersey: Scarecrow Press, 1984; and Waller, G.A. (ed.). *American Horrors: Essays on the Modern American Horror Film.* Illinois: Illinois University Press, 1987.
34. These similarly titled surveys of recent and celebrated articles are: Silver, A., and J. Ursini (ed.). *Horror Film Reader.* New York: Limelight Editions, 2000; Gelder, Ken (ed.). *The Horror Reader.* London: Routledge, 2000; and *Horror: The Film Reader* (Jancovich, 2001).
35. The origins of a franchise are numerous, ranging from the literary, as in the case of Conan Doyle's *Sherlock Holmes*, Tolkien's *Lord of the Rings* and Rowling's *Harry Potter* novels, to such alternative but by no means less fruitful sources as comic books, video games or even particular toys. The upcoming resurrection of the *Transformers* franchise highlights this form of media synergy.
36. There are, of course, the unofficial, unlicensed books and other merchandise, not to mention reams of fan-sites and forums, which would not fall under the definition of the franchise, but form an integral part of the franchise's functionality and success. Indeed, an established fan base is a fundamental aspect of a franchise's popularity and longevity.
37. Clover, 1992: 10.
38 Budra, Paul, and Betty R. Schellenberg.

Part Two: Reflections on the Sequel. Toronto, London: Toronto University Press, 1998, p. 7.

39. Ibid.

40. This was actor Sir Ian McKellen responding to criticisms of another *X-Men* film in *X3*. Chitwood, Scott. "*X-Men: The Last Stand.* Set Visit Part 3." *http://www.superherohype.com/news/featuresnews.php?id=3863* (downloaded February 23, 2006).

41. Steven Spielberg speaking in 1975 at the San Francisco film festival in McBride, 1997: 257.

42. Crawley, Tony. "The Sequel$$$ Game." *Photoplay*, Vol. 33, No. 10. October 1982, p. 58.

43. Dupont, David. "It's Only a Movie: Play It Again Sam," *Starburst* 92, April 1986, p. 35.

44. Goldman, William. *Which Lie Did I tell? Or More Adventures in the Screen Trade.* New York: Pantheon, 2000, p. 48.

45. Blandford, Steve, Barry K. Grant and Jim Huillier. *The Film Studies Dictionary.* London: Arnold, 2001, p. 209.

46. One character attempting self-criticism in Craven's *Scream 2* (1997).

47. Braudy's Afterward in Horton, Andrew, and Stuart Y. McDougal (eds.). *Play It Again, Sam: Retakes on Remakes.* London: University of California Press, 1998, p. 329.

48. See Part Two's table of "sequel narrative modes." Budra and Schallenberg, 1998: 12.

49. Budra and Schallenberg, 1998.

50. Horton and McDougal, 1998.

51. Braudy's "Afterward" in Horton and McDougal, 1998: 327.

52. Ibid, p. 329.

53. Ibid, p. 333.

54. Naremore, James (ed.). *Film Adaptation.* London: The Athlone Press, 2000, p. 13.

55. Ibid.

56. Forrest, Jennifer, and Leonard R. Koos (eds.). *Dead Ringers: The Remake in Theory and Practice.* Albany, NY: State University of New York Press, 2002.

57. Milberg, Doris. *Repeat Performances: A Guide to Hollywood Movie Remakes.* New York: Broadway Press, 1990.

58. See Druxman, Michael B. *One Good Film Deserves Another.* London and New York: Barnes, Yoseloff, 1977; Hicken, Mandy E. *Sequels.* London: Association of Assistant Librarians, 1982; Nowlan, Robert A., and Gwendolyn W. Nolan. *Cinema Sequels and Remakes, 1903–1987.* London: McFarland, 1989; and Limbacher, James L. *Haven't I Seen You Somewhere Before: Remakes, Sequels and Series in Motion Pictures Videos and Television 1896–1990.* Michigan: Pierian Press, 1992.

59. Hanke, Ken. *A Critical Guide to Horror Film Series.* New York and London: Garland, 1991.

60. Stell, John. *Psychos, Sickos and Sequels: Horror Films of the 1980s.* Baltimore, Maryland: Midnight Marquee Press, 1998; and Holsten, Kim R., and Tom Winchester. *Science Fiction, Fantasy and Horror Film Sequels, Series and Remakes.* Jefferson, NC: McFarland, 1997.

61. See Newman, Howard. *The Exorcist: The Strange Story Behind the Film.* New York: Pinnacle Books, 1974; Kermode, Mark. *The Exorcist.* London: British Film Institute, 1998; and McCabe, Bob. *The Exorcist: Out of the Shadows.* London: Omnibus, 1999.

62. Rebello, Stephen. *Alfred Hitchcock and the Making of Psycho.* New York: Dembner Books, 1990; and Leigh, Janet, and Chris Nickens. *Psycho: Behind the Scenes of the Classic Chiller.* New York: Harmony Books, 1995.

63. Pallenberg, Barbara. *The Making of Exorcist II: The Heretic.* New York: Warner, 1977; and Loynd, Ray. *The Jaws 2 Log.* New York: Dell, 1978.

64. See Collins, Michael R. *The Films of Stephen King.* Mercer Island, Washington: Starmont Press, 1986; Jones, Stephen. *Creepshows: The Illustrated Stephen King Movie Guide.* London: Titan, 2001; and Underwood, Tim. *Stephen King Goes to Hollywood.* New York: New American Library, 1987.

65. Cooper, Jeffrey. *The Nightmare on Elm Street Companion.* New York: St. Martin's Press, 1987; followed by Schoell, William, and James Spencer. *The Nightmare Never Ends: The Official History of Freddy Kruger and the Nightmare on Elm Street Films.* New York: Carol, 1992.

66. Just a few examples of such texts include: Thompson, David. *The Alien Quartet.* London: Bloomsbury, 1998; Warren, Bill. *The Evil Dead Companion.* London: Titan, 2000; Brosnan, John. *Scream.* London: Boxtree, 2000; O'Brien, Daniel. *The Hannibal Files.* London: Reynolds & Hearn, 2001; and Jaworzyn, Stefan. *The Texas Chainsaw Massacre Companion.* London: Titan, 2003.

67. McDonagh, Maitland. "The State of the Horror Nation," *Fangoria*, no. 103, June 1991, p. 23.

68. Maitland McDonagh Interview. *Scream and Scream Again.* Documentary.

69. Dick, Bernard F. *Anatomy of Film.* New York: St. Martin's Press, 1990, p. 175.

70. Vincendau, Ginette (ed.). *Film/Literature/Heritage: A Sight and Sound Reader.* London: BFI Publishing, 2001, p. xi.

71. Naremore, James (ed.). *Film Adaptation.* London: The Athlone Press, 2000, p. 13.

72. Ibid, p. 4.

73. Ibid, p. 5.

74. Factors that influenced Hollywood's hold over the American cinema-going public included the U.S. Supreme Court's Paramount Decree in 1948, the impact of television and such fundamental sociological shifts as the onset of the baby boom and suburbanization.

75. Rigby, 2000: 41.
76. Ibid, p. 44.
77. Paraphrased from Rigby, 2000: 44.
78. Wood, Robin. *Hitchcock's Films Revisited*. New York: Columbia University Press, 1989, p. 150.
79. Gomery, Douglas. "The Economics of the Horror Film," in Weaver and Tanborini, 1995: 53.
80. Wexman, Virginia Wright. *Roman Polanski*. Boston: Twayne Publishers, 1985, p. 49.
81. McDonagh, Maitland. "The State of the Horror Nation," *Fangoria*, no. 103, June 1991, p. 22.
82. McBride, 1997: 232–3.
83. Ibid, p. 233.
84. McBride, 1997: 239–40.
85. Rice's initial displeasure over Cruise's casting as Lestat is well documented. Salisbury, Mark. "Interview with the Director," *Fangoria* 138, November 1994, pp. 44–50.
86. Naremore, 2000: 3.
87. For example, Robert Bloch's experience with Hitchcock and *Psycho* saw a blind bid of $9000 accepted for the rights to *Psycho* in perpetuity. Consequently, he received nothing from the film's financial success, its sequels or any subsequent merchandising. This was repeated in Stephen King's decision to let Doubleday have all film rights to *Carrie* fifteen years later. After such literary injustices, novelists and their agents have acted in a shrewder manner, insisting on sequel rights, profit participation and even the opportunity for authors to adapt their own stories.
88. Vincendeau, 2001: xi.
89. Ibid, xii.
90. Quackenbush, 1980: 7.
91. Ibid.
92. The politics of fidelity and subsequent rebuttals of its stringent application to film adaptation have been debated at length in both Naremore and Vincendau's collections. However, Naremore concedes that McFairlaine's *Novel to Film* (1996) also attacks this singular strand of film criticism.
93. Goldman, William. *Which Lie Did I Tell? More Adventures in the Screen Trade*. New York: Pantheon, 2000, p. 48.
94. Although a cinematic sequel to Polanski's adaptation appeared in 1976, a Showtime-produced sequel to Hitchcock's *The Birds* finally took off in 1994.
95. Spielberg spared Richard Dreyfuss' character of Hooper in *Jaws* and Attenborough's character of John Hammond in *Jurassic Park*, despite their dramatic deaths at the hands of the authors.
96. McBride, 1997: 244.
97. As described by Randy Meeks in Craven's *Scream* (1996).
98. Survivor Sue Snell takes flowers to the site of the former "White House," only to be ambushed by Carrie's bloodied hand before waking up to discover it was only a dream. Brian De Palma Interview. "Visualising Carrie," *Carrie: Special Edition* DVD.
99. Jancovich, 2001: 6.
100. Harmetz, Aljean. "The Sequel Becomes the New Bankable Film Star." *The New York Times*, 8/7/1985, p. 16.
101. Rowe, Michael. "Dawning of New Dread," *Fangoria*, no. 200, March 2001, p. 50.
102. A common term used to describe this phenomenon with connotations of disease, illness and decay.
103. Leming, Rod. "From *Psycho* to *Asylum*: The Horror Films of Robert Bloch." *http://mgpfeff.home.sprynet.com/leming_interview1.html* (Downloaded: August 15, 2002).
104. Ibid.
105. For a more in-depth examination of the *Elm Street* marketing phenomenon, see Conrich, Ian. "Seducing the Subject: Freddy Kruger," in Silver and Ursini, 2000: 223–35.
106. Although the vast majority of producers and distributors trading in established titles were interested in propagating their own, Embassy and MGM/UA were keen to distance themselves from the growing trend and sold off the rights to *The Howling* and *Child's Play* series, respectively. Needless to say, these two franchises soon found a new home as Hemdale offered *Howling II* producer Stephen Lane the proverbial too good to be true deal and Universal gave *Child's Play's 2* a bigger budget, better marketing and improved distribution.
107. Scapperotti, Dan. "New Line Cinema: The House That Freddy Built," *Cinefantastique*, vol. 20, no. 1 / 2, November 1989, pp. 89 and 124–5.
108. In interim periods, spanning from a few months to several years (if not decades), many franchises were adopted and adapted for the small screen. Repackaged to accommodate dwindling returns and ensure a low level of risk yet a healthy return, episodic TV horror was inspired by the pioneering success of *Alfred Hitchcock Presents*. Such attempts began with Universal's ill-fated pilot for *Bates Motel* in 1987, itself a spin-off from Hitchcock's *Psycho*, with fear franchises *A Nightmare on Elm Street, Friday the 13th, Poltergeist, Tremors* and, most recently, *Blade* all flirting with the television format, with relatively short-term success.
109. Morgan J. Freeman has been quick to praise Lions Gate's similar release strategy for *American Psycho 2*, which saw the film debut with significant store-based promotions and DVD extras.
110. Following its mixed experiences with

Psycho and *The Mummy*, the studio has since released *Dawn of the Dead* and *King Kong*.

111. Consequently, such films as *Freddy vs. Jason*, *Alien vs. Predator* and even proposals for a *Helloween* have strengthened the foundations of the Houses of New Line, Fox, and Dimension. These grudge matches have arguably ushered the franchise into its final stages, with Universal even attempting to recreate *Frankenstein Meets the Wolf Man* in *Van Helsing*.

112. Studio Briefing Report. "The VHS Is Dead (Well Kinda); Long Live the DVD!" March 20, 2003. http://us.imdb.com/StudioBrief/2003/20030320.html#4 (downloaded March 23, 2003).

113. Dick, 1990: 144.

114. Ibid, p. 146.

115. Ibid.

116. "(1) An auteur is technically competent. (2) An auteur has a personality that manifests itself in recurring stylistic traits that become his or her signature. (3) An auteur's films exhibit a tension between the auteur's personality and his or her material." Dick, 1990: 146.

117. Clover, 1992: 11.

118. Ibid.

119. Ibid.

120. See Morris Dickstein's essay on "The Aesthetics of Fright" in Grant, Barry Keith. *Planks of Reason: Essays on the Horror Film*. New Jersey: Scarecrow Press, 1984.

121. Clover, 1992: 11.

122. Jancovich, 2001: 12.

123. Ibid. Quoting Kitses, 1969: 26.

124. For Polanski see Butler, Ivan. *The Cinema of Roman Polanski*. London: A Zwemmer, 1970; as well as Wrexman, 1985; and for DePalma see Bliss, Michael. *Brian De Palma*. London: Scarecrow Press, 1983.

125. In this respect I am referring to the likes of George R. Romero (Gagne, Paul. *The Zombies That Ate Pittsburgh: The Films of George Romero*. New York: Dodd / Mead, 1987; Caruso, Giacomo. *George A. Romero*. Venezia: Comune di Venezia, 1992; and Williams, Tony. *The Cinema of George A. Romero*. Columbia: Columbia University Press, 2003), David Cronenberg (Rodley, Chris. *Cronenberg on Cronenberg*. London: Faber and Faber, 1993; and Beard, William. *The Artist as Monster: The Cinema of David Cronenberg*. London: University of Toronto Press, 2001), Larry Cohen (Williams, Tony. *Larry Cohen: The Radical Allegories of an Independent Filmmaker*. Jefferson, NC: McFarland, 1997), John Carpenter (Cumbow, Robert C. *Order in the Universe: The Films of John Carpenter, Second Edition*. Lanham, MD, and London: Scarecrow Press, 2000; and Muir, John. *The Films of John Carpenter*. Jefferson, NC, and London: McFarland, 2000) and Wes Craven (Muir, John. *Wes Craven: The Art of Horror*. Jefferson, NC, and London: McFarland, 1998; and Robb, Brian J. *Screams and Nightmares: The Films of Wes Craven*. London: Titan, 1998).

126. Examples include: Pye, Michael, and Linda Myles. *The Movie Brats: How the Film Generation Took Over Hollywood*. London: Faber and Faber, 1979; Von Gunden, Kenneth. *Postmodern Auteurs: Coppola, Lucas, De Palma, Spielberg and Scorsese*. Jefferson, NC, and London: McFarland, 1991; Singer, Mark. *A Cut Above: 50 Film Directors Talk About Their Craft*. Los Angeles, California: Lone Eagle, 1998; and Kagan, Jeremy (ed.). *Directors Close-up: Interviews with Directors Nominated for Outstanding Directorial Achievement in a Feature Film by the Directors Guild of America*. Boston and Oxford: Focal Press, 2000.

127. For example: Weaver, Tom. *Attack of the Monster Movie Makers: Interviews with 20 Genre Giants*. Jefferson, NC: McFarland, 1994; Warren, Bill. *Set Visit: Interviews with 32 Horror and Science Fiction Filmmakers*. Jefferson, NC: McFarland, 1997; and Goldberg, Lee, Randy L'Officier and Jean-Marc L'Officier. *The Dreamweavers: Interviews with the Fantasy Filmmakers of the 1980s*. Jefferson, NC: McFarland, 1995.

128. Notable works include: Quarles, Mike. *Down and Dirty: Hollywood's Exploitation Filmmakers and Their Motives*. Jefferson, NC: McFarland, 1993; McCarty, John. *The Sleaze Merchants*. New York: St. Martin's Press, 1995; McCarty, John. *The Fearmakers: The Screens' Directorial Masters of Suspense and Terror*. London: Virgin, 1995.

129. Fischer, Dennis. *Horror Film Directors 1931–1990*. Jefferson, NC: McFarland, 1991.

130. Prawer, 1980: 46.

131. McDonagh, 1992: 23.

Chapter 1

1. McCarty, 1995: 117.

2. While Davenport has directed three *Xtro* films to date, Nicolaou, as part of the Full Moon family, has shot all four entries in the *Subspecies* franchise.

3. McCarty, 1995: 117.

4. Wooley, John. "Saw Man." *Fangoria* 147, October 1995, pp. 48–51.

5. Gallagher, John A. "From Michigan with Blood," *Fangoria's Bloody Best*, no. 6, 1987, p. 5.

6. In Raimi's case, the financing came about as a result of pitching the project to dentists and local businessmen who, upon watching Raimi's show-reel of *Into the Woods*, agreed to contribute towards the film's financing. Will Murray, Will. "Master of the Evil Dead," *Fangoria* 64, June 87, p. 30.

7. Clover, 1992: 10.

8. Similarly, Carpenter's *Halloween* began life as a sequel to Bob Clark's chilling *Black Christmas* before referencing such films as *I Saw What You Did* and *Fright*, while Hickox's *Waxwork* harked back to the heydays of Hammer and Universal, and Henenlotter's *Basket Case* fondly recalled elements of both *Freaks* and *Frankenstein*.

9. *Last House on the Left* Producer Sean S. Cunningham has commented how, "*Blair Witch* is like *Last House* revisited on a huge level." Szulkin, David. "Last House Mates," *Fangoria* 200, March 2001, p. 60.

10. Raimi's first film also showcases the director's fondness for the Three Stooges and Tex Avery cartoons. This, and more, demonstrated his outlandish comic book style and skill with the camera.

11. Doogan, Todd. "Tall Tales: The Man Behind *Phantasm*: An Interview with Don Coscarelli." *http://www.thedigitalbits.com/articles/coscarelli110399.html* (downloaded March 15, 2003).

12. For a more detailed look at Romero and the *Living Dead* franchise, see Chapter 3.

13. This group is comprised of director Sam Raimi, producer Robert Tapert and star Bruce Campbell.

14. McDonagh, 1995: 140.

15. Hayes, Jeff. "The Mysterious Mr. Hiltzig." *http://www.angelfire.com/retro/officialsleepaway2/hiltzik2002.html* (downloaded February 20, 2003).

16. This saw the investors represented by Robert Kuhn, who formed the corporation MAB to ensure that they would receive their initial investment plus a healthy return. In conjunction with Kuhn, co-writer Kim Henkel and Hooper formed Vortex — a separate production company that would control the production funded by the investor corporation. This arrangement saw to it that the creative control remained with Vortex, and that, in theory, the investors would get "their original investments back and after that it was split 50/50." Hooper, Tobe. "*Texas Chainsaw Massacre*: The Shocking Truth.," *Texas Chainsaw Massacre* Special Edition DVD.

17. Doogan, Todd. "Tall Tales: The Man Behind *Phantasm*: An Interview with Don Coscarelli." *http://www.thedigitalbits.com/articles/coscarelli110399.html* (downloaded March 15, 2003).

18. Derry, Charles. *Dark Dreams: A Psychological History of the Horror Film*. New York and London: Barnes and Yoseloff, 1977, p. 118.

19. The film was eventually picked up by Walter Reade's relatively small Continental Films.

20. This type of release by Avco-Embassy with *Phantasm*, and Compass International with *Halloween*, saw limited prints gradually enjoy a successful local release across the country while gathering hype and pre-publicity through positive word of mouth.

21. McDonagh, 1995: 88. Cunningham has stated how "prior to *Friday the 13th* the biggest release you might get would be with something like *Halloween*, where the distributor would go into town with 75 prints, buy some ads and hope for the best before moving on to the next town." Steve Biodrowski, Steve. 'Sean Cunningham: House Keeper," *Gorezone* 21, Spring 1992, p. 9.

22. McCarty, 1990: 103.

23. Roger Ebert quoting Pauline Kael in his review of *Re-Animator*, October 18 1985. *http://rogerebert.suntimes.com/apps/pbcs.dll/article?AID=/19851018/REVIEWS/510180303/1023* (downloaded June 21, 2004).

24. Ferrante, Anthony C. "The Night HE Made History," *Fangoria* 138, November 1994, p. 21.

25. McDonagh, 1995: 36.

26. This promotional tag line accompanied the film's publicity and cemented the interest of Robert Shaye, head of New Line Cinema, in distributing the film. King had traveled to Cannes in order to help promote the film *Creepshow*, his EC-comics-inspired collaboration with George Romero. Worley, Alex. "Dawn of the Deadites," *Shivers* 79, July 2000, p. 10.

27. Ebert, Roger. "*The Blair Witch Project*," *The Chicago-Sun Times*. July 16, 1999. *http://rogerebert.suntimes.com/apps/pbcs.dll/article?AID=/19990716/REVIEWS/907160301/1023* (Downloaded: March 25, 2004).

28. Doogan, Todd. "Tall Tales: The Man Behind *Phantasm*: An Interview with Don Coscarelli." *http://www.thedigitalbits.com/articles/coscarelli110399.html* (downloaded March 15, 2003).

29. Ibid.

30. Ibid.

31. In singling out Siskel and Ebert's television show, the director has reportedly stated that "there's nothing like struggling for a couple years to make a film, collaborating with talented actors and dedicated crew on a project you all believe has some kind of small merit, and then two loud clowns on national TV use your material to sell advertising, and then quickly dismiss you with two thumbs down." Ibid.

32. The deal saw the director agree to deliver five films with the option for more. In return for such a commitment, Hitchcock was awarded a "lavish private compound situated close to the main studio gate." Once securely installed within the Universal studio system, and arguably under its ever-watchful eye, Hitchcock sought to solidify his position by swapping all rights to *Psycho* and his TV series in return for "about 150,000 shares of MCA stock," which placed key facilities

and trusted technical personnel close at hand. Rebello, 1990: 182. Such a shrewd move saw Universal acquire the rights to the title and, in some respects, the director whom they sought to mold into an even more commercially viable brand name. Indeed, Hitchcock has been described as a "franchise" unto himself—an argument at odds with the definition explicitly stated and adopted by this thesis.

33. Howe, David. "Don Coscarelli," *Starburst*, vol. 11, no. 7, March 1989, p. 40.

34. Author Andre Norton was similarly dissatisfied and had her name removed from the credits.

35. Doogan, Todd. "Tall Tales: The Man Behind *Phantasm*: An Interview with Don Coscarelli." *http://www.thedigitalbits.com/articles/coscarelli110399.html* (downloaded March 15, 2003).

36. Ibid.

37. Hughes, David. "David Cronenberg: Hall of Fame — the Maverick Series," *Empire*, no. 164, February 2003, p. 111.

38. Winecoff, Charles. *Split Image: The Life of Anthony Perkins*. New York: Dutton, 1996, p. 451.

39. This was after the star's plan to direct Norman's story had been "flatly rejected" by the studio on account of part three, along with his other suggestion that he and *Psycho II*'s Richard Franklin "co-direct the new installment together." Ibid.

40. Despite attempting to revive these second sequels to *Halloween* and *Jaws* with fresh literary talent, Dante's efforts were diminished as the production process developed to the extent that both Nigel Kneale and Richard Matheson were reportedly dissatisfied with the finished films.

41. Savlov, Marc. "Sphere of Influence," *The Austin Chronicle*, March 31, 2000. *http://www.auschron.com/issues/dispatch/2000-03-31/screens_feature.html* (downloaded April 12, 2003).

42. However, the director has half-jokingly confessed that he's "still hoping they'll throw me an *Alien* sequel someday." Ibid.

43. Rare examples where a director's proposed concept and consequent participation in a sequel has been rejected include John Landis and Neil Marshall with follow-ups to *An American Werewolf in London* and *Dog Soldiers*.

44. For the history behind Whale's sequel, see Curtis, 1998. *Black Lagoon* director Jack Arnold also agreed to direct the film's follow-up, *Revenge of the Creature*.

45. Fischer, 1991: 643.

46. This period included such pictures as *God Told Me To* and *The Private Files of J. Edgar Hoover* for Cohen, and *The Crazies* and *Season of the Witch* for Romero. Romero did, however, release his underrated homage to the vampire film, *Martin*, in 1977, which ranks among his strongest work to date.

47. Savlov, Marc. "Sphere of Influence," *The Austin Chronicle*, March 31, 2000. *http://www.auschron.com/issues/dispatch/2000-03-31/screens_feature.html* (downloaded April 12, 2003).

48. Having achieved fame as the home of Hollywood's famous monsters, Universal has not only developed sequels to *Psycho* and *Jaws*, but also acquired franchises like *Halloween* and *Child's Play*.

49. Ibid.

50. Everitt, David. "The Arresting Saga of *Maniac Cop 2*," *Fangoria* 96, September 1990, p. 25.

51. Ibid, p. 25.

52. In a similar vein, directors such as Tacacs, Oullette and Tenney, from *The Gate*, *The Unnamable* and *Witchboard*, approached the sequel as a chance to "make a better movie," with Tenney, in particular, considering himself "a better director than I was 7 years ago, so in general the film will look better [since] there was a lot I couldn't achieve the first time because of budget, or my lack of knowledge of how to get around that type of budget." Biodrowski, Steve. "*Witchboard 2: The Devil's Doorway*: Board to Death," *Fangoria* 122, May 1993, p. 46.

53. Biodrowski, Steve. "Sam Raimi's *Evil Dead III*," *Cinefantastique*, vol. 22, no. 5, April 1992, p. 4.

54. Nicoll, Gregory. "Two for the Roadkill," *Fangoria* 117, October 1992, p. 47.

55. Hanke, Ken. *Tim Burton: An Unauthorized Biography of the Filmmaker*. Los Angeles: Renaissance, 1999, p. 119.

56. McDonough, 1995: 135.

57. Hanke, 1991: 120.

58. Ibid, p. 132.

59. McDonagh, 1995: 135.

60. McBride, 1997: 258.

61. Wooley, John. "Leatherface in Love: On the Set of *Texas Chainsaw Massacre 2*," *Fangoria* 57, September 1986. *http://www.geocities.com/leatherfacette* (downloaded January 20, 2003).

62. Hasted, Nick. "What a Carve Up," *The Guardian*, September 28, 2001. *http://film.guardian.co.uk/features/featurepages/0,4120,559120,00.html* (downloaded January 27, 2003).

63. Nutman, Philip. "Of Chainsaws, Cuts and Cannon," *Shock Xpress*, vol. 2, no 2, Winter 1987, p. 29.

64. Although Henenlotter fought to separate the new from the old and call *Basket Case 2* "*House of Freaks*" and "sell it as an independent horror film where Dwayne and Belial just happen to be supporting characters," SGE had other ideas, and it was they who controlled the way in which the film would be titled, marketed and distributed. McDonagh, 1995: 37.

65. The film was promoted with this tagline.
66. Howe, David. "Don Coscarelli," *Starburst*, vol. 11, no. 7, March 1989, p. 40.
67. Doogan, Todd. "Tall Tales: The Man Behind *Phantasm*: An Interview with Don Coscarelli." *http://www.thedigitalbits.com/articles/coscarelli110399.html* (Downloaded: March 15, 2003).
68. Brad Pitt originally auditioned for A. Michael Baldwin's role before it went to James LeGross. However, Coscarelli's main regret surrounding the franchise is his failure to stand up to the studio's demands by calling their bluff over Baldwin's return.
69. Howe, David. "Don Coscarelli," *Starburst*, vol. 11, no. 7, March 1989, p. 43.
70. Ibid.
71. Doogan, Todd. "Tall Tales: The Man Behind Phantasm: An Interview with Don Coscarelli." *http://www.thedigitalbits.com/articles/coscarelli110399.html* (downloaded March 15, 2003).
72. Ibid.
73. A policy employed by the franchise-friendly administration at Universal, who, after acquiring the *Child's Play* franchise from United Artists, were allegedly reluctant to continue their association with the killer doll and released *Child's Play 3* less than nine months after their first sequel had been in cinemas.
74. Howe, David. "Don Coscarelli," *Starburst*, vol. 11, No. 7, March 1989, p. 42.
75. Ibid.
76. Ibid.
77. England, Norman. "An Interview with George Romero: Part 2." *http://www2.gol.com/users/noman/interv3.htm* (downloaded February 18, 2002).
78. Internet Movie Database: Dawn of the Dead: Alternate Versions. *http://us.imdb.com/AlternateVersions?0077402* (downloaded May 14, 2002).
79. Hanke, 1991: 240.
80. McCarty, John. *The Modern Horror Film: 50 Contemporary Classics.* London: Carol, 1990. p. 109.
81. While the majority of directors are contractually obliged to deliver the studio or production company an R-rated picture, the alternative is to either accept the prohibitive NC-17 rating or proceed without any legitimate rating. The downside of such a distribution campaign is evident when publications, television stations, theater owners and Blockbuster adopt a policy of not accepting advertisements for, or copies of, any films being released either Unrated or with the NC-17 label.
82. Paraphrased from Rebello, 1990: 145.
83. In the wake of his negative experience with the MPAA over *Evil Dead 2*, the director indicated that there was an inherent bias in the MPAA's attitude and approach to horror. Citing "the fact that DEG was a small company and that I had rubbed the MPAA the wrong way in the past" as having "a great deal to do with the X for *Evil Dead 2*," Raimi felt that it was "not a level playing field" and that the board "might be swayed when they're dealing with multi-million dollar conglomerates where their friends work." McDonagh, 1995: 144.
84. Peter Atkins. *Hellbound: Hellraiser II* DVD Commentary.
85. Ibid.
86. Tony Randel. Ibid.
87. Peter Atkins. Ibid.
88. Peter Atkins. Ibid.
89. Doogan, Todd. "Tall Tales: The Man Behind *Phantasm*: An Interview with Don Coscarelli." *http://www.thedigitalbits.com/articles/coscarelli110399.html* (downloaded March 15, 2003).
90. Floyd, Nigel. "Speak No Evil," *Shock Xpress*, vol. 1, no. 6, Spring 1987, p. 7. Raimi has since stated how audiences and critics have misinterpreted this epilogue as a different story.
91. Halbertsam, Judith. *Skin Shows: Gothic Horror and the Technology of Monsters.* Durham, NC, and London: Duke University Press, 1996, p. 143. Parallels could possibly be drawn between the subversive feminist shift displayed here and the one Tim Burton adopts in the final frames of *Batman Returns* (1992).
92. Savlov, Marc. "*The Texas Chainsaw Massacre*," *The Austin Chronicle.* November 2, 1998. *http://www.filmvault.com/filmvault/austin/t/texaschainsawmass4.html* (downloaded January 6, 2003).
93. Fischer, 1991: 194.
94. Ibid.
95. Ibid.
96. However, Fisher did return for what could be considered parts four and five in Hammer's *Frankenstein* series.
97. Although Hooper and *The Texas Chainsaw Massacre III* is the most significant example, other notable dropouts include Burton on *Batman Forever*, Spielberg on *Jurassic Park III* and Cameron on *Terminator 3*. However, Spielberg did return for *Indian Jones and the Last Crusade*, citing contractual obligations to George Lucas and atonement for the previous entry as his justification.
98. McDonagh, 1995: 143.
99. Ibid.
100. Williams, 1997: 205. Although it took only three years for Morgan Creek and writer/director Blatty to shoot an *Exorcist* sequel, it would be another eighteen years before *House of Wax* would be deemed worthy of an update.
101. Shapiro, Marc. "From Hell to Eternity," *Fangoria* 130, March 1994, p. 43.

102. Ibid.
103. Ibid, p. 44.
104. *Day of the Dead* was first announced under the title *Zombies in the White House* and budgeted at $6.5 million; Romero, however, was resistant to compromise on his script's violent content, and financiers United Film were only willing to offer $3.5 million. Unable to progress to the final stage in his story, Romero ultimately "created an altered script" that "retained many of the basic ideas but was scaled down and [its] emphases were shifted" to take into account the lack of funds available. Fischer, 1991: 651.
105. Shapiro, Marc. "Monster Invasion: Phantasm III," *Fangoria* 125, August 1993, p. 10.
106. Shapiro, Marc. "From Hell to Eternity," *Fangoria* 130, March 1994, p. 45.
107. Ibid, p. 43.
108. Coscarelli explained that he has expanded "on the project a little ... [to] make it a little more apocalyptic and final." Howe, David. "Don Coscarelli," *Starburst*, vol. 11, no. 7, March 1989, p. 43.
109. In which the Tall Man's sphere is buried beneath the Arctic ice Grand Grimoire-style (see Steve Miner's underrated *Warlock*).
110. Warren, Bill. *"Army of Darkness*: They Want You," *Fangoria* 115, August 1992, p. 41.
111. However, an alternate ending depicting Ash versus the Deadites in a Supermarket was also demanded by the producers and used in some versions of the film.
112. Shapiro, Marc. "Monster Invasion: *Phantasm III*," *Fangoria* 125, August 1993, p. 10.
113. McDonagh, 1995: 44.
114. According to the director, the MPAA "went crazy and gave [*Basket Case 3*] an NC-17," while alleging that Heffner, as head of the board, had "called SGE and told them they were going to give the film an S rating. The person at the SGE office said, "S for Sex? And Heffner said, 'No, S for Shit.'" Ibid, pp. 40–41.
115. Jones, Alan. "The Wicker Basket Man," *Shivers* 3, October 1992, p. 18.
116. Ibid, p. 17.
117. McDonagh, 1995: 36.
118. Ibid, p. 43.
119. Ibid.
120. Nicol, Gregory. "Maul in the Family," *Fangoria* 108, December 1991, p. 38.
121. Ibid.
122. Jones, Alan. "The Wicker Basket Man," *Shivers* 3, October 1992, p. 18.
123. McDonagh, 1995: 37.
124. Shapiro, Marc. "From Hell to Eternity," *Fangoria* 130, March 1994, p. 42.
125. Along with co-writer/director Quentin Tarantino, Avery had recently won the Oscar for Best Original Screenplay for *Pulp Fiction*.
126. Bowen, John W. "Look Back in Angus: Confessions of a *Phantasm* Phanboy." http://www.classic-horror.com/articles/lookbackangus.html (downloaded January 12, 2003).
127. Doogan, Todd. "Tall Tales: The Man Behind *Phantasm*. An Interview with Don Coscarelli." http://www.thedigitalbits.com/articles/coscarelli110399.html (downloaded January 15, 2003).
128. Ibid.
129. Bowen, John W. "Look Back in Angus: Confessions of a *Phantasm* Phanboy." http://www.classic-horror.com/articles/lookbackangus.html (downloaded January 12, 2003).
130. Ibid. Following the relatively recent success of such zombie-themed films as *28 Days Later*, *Resident Evil* (to which the director was once attached), the *Dawn of the Dead* remake and *Shaun of the Dead*, George Romero was able to secure the financing and distribution deal for *Land of the Dead*.
131. Shapiro, Marc. "From Hell to Eternity," *Fangoria* 130, March 1994, p. 43.
132. The Tall Man's silver spheres had cornered Reggie, and Mike, having discovered one within his head, had fled into the wilderness to avoid a fatal encounter with his nemesis.
133. Dumars, Denise. *"Phantasm IV,"* *Cinefantastique*, vol. 30, no. 12, January 1999, p. 56.
134. Ibid.
135. Ibid.
136. Robert Shaye playing himself in *Wes Craven's New Nightmare*.
137. Doogan, Todd. "Tall Tales: The Man Behind *Phantasm*. An Interview with Don Coscarelli." http://www.thedigitalbits.com/articles/coscarelli110399.html (downloaded January 15, 2003).
138. Ibid.
139. Ibid.
140. Chute, David. "Bubba Unites Cult Heroes," *LA Times*, February 26, 2003. http://www.bubbahotep.com/reviews/LATimes.htm (downloaded May 17, 2004).
141. Ibid.
142. Anthony Perkins' portrayal of Norman Bates is a particular case in point.

Chapter 2

1. Prawer, 1980: 46–7.
2. Szulkin, David. "The Hills Were Alive," *Fangoria* 132, May 1994, p. 15.
3. Prior to his film career, Craven had been a college humanities teacher and fathered two children. By 1970, however, Craven was separated from his family and working as a taxi driver before his post-production experiences with Cunningham.

4. The film was tested under a number of titles, including *Krug & Company* and *Sex Crime of the Century*, until an experienced "ad man" suggested the unrelated yet effective title *Last House on the Left*.

5. Although Craven had returned to the genre, Cunningham had, up to this point, resisted industry pressure to return to horror. Biodrowski, Steve. "Sean Cunningham: House Keeper," *Gorezone*, 21, Spring 1992, p. 8.

6. Ibid.

7. Ibid, p. 9.

8. Ibid.

9. Kermode, Mark. *Scream and Scream Again: A History of the Slasher film*. Abbott and Leven, 2000.

10. McDonagh, 1995: 91.

11. Biodrowski, Steve. "Sean Cunningham: House Keeper," *Gorezone* 21, Spring 1992, p. 9.

12. McDonagh, 1995: 88. Cunningham has since stated how, "Prior to *Friday the 13th*, the biggest release you might get would be with something like *Halloween*, where the distributor would go into town with 75 prints, buy some ads and hope for the best before moving on to the next town." Biodrowski, Steve. "Sean Cunningham: House Keeper," *Gorezone* 21, Spring 1992, p. 9.

13. Newman, Kim. "The Truth About Zombies," *Shock Xpress*, vol. 2, no. 4, Summer 1988, p. 32.

14. Ibid.

15. Newman, Kim. "Interview: Wes Craven," *Shock Xpress*, vol. 1, no. 2, September/October 1985, p. 2.

16. Ibid.

17. Returning director Hooper echoed this sentiment only a few years later. His much-maligned follow-up fell foul of Cannon's interference, yet depicted a daring shift in tone and content. However, it received a mixed reception from first film fans. Tobe Hooper Interview, "*Texas Chainsaw Massacre*: The Shocking Truth," *Texas Chainsaw Massacre*: Special Edition DVD.

18. Robb, 1998: 66.

19. Taken from interviews with Craven in *Scream and Scream Again*.

20. Iaccino, James F. *Psychological Interpretations on Cinematic Terror*. Westport, CT, and London: Praeger, 1994, p. 173. The character's surname harkened back to the director's first film and the character of Krug Stillo. While Craven drew the forename of this ultimate bad father from his past, the concept dated back to Germanic folklore, and Kermode has rightfully pointed out how we "only have to look at a picture of Heimrich Hoffman's Straw Peter or Long-legged Scissorman to know who Freddy Kruger's parents really are." *Scream and Scream Again: A History of the Slasher Film*. Abbott and Leven, 2000.

21. Disney expressed some interest but wanted to dilute it for a family audience. Paramount Pictures passed on the project due to its similarity to *Dreamscape*— a film they had been developing for director Joe Ruben with writer Chuck Russell. This script bore a striking resemblance to Craven's; and, according to the director, such an experience "hurt me a lot, mentally and financially." Robb, 1998: 67–8.

22. Scapperotti, Dan. "New Line Cinema: The House That Freddy Built," *Cinefantastique*, vol. 20, no 1/2, November 1989, p. 89.

23. Shapiro, Marc. "Is Wes Craven Still Scared?" *Gorezone* 11, January 90, p. 47.

24. The film was shot in 32 days on a budget of under $2 million.

25. Wes Craven, *A Nightmare on Elm Street* commentary.

26. The three endings included Shaye's, with Freddy at the wheel, Craven's apocalyptic original, and "an ending with which we both had toyed, where Nancy's mother is grabbed by Freddy." Schoell and Spenser, 1992: IX.

27. Fischer, 1991: 261.

28. Sean Cunningham interview, *Scream and Scream Again* documentary.

29. Freeman, Royce. "Interview: Victor Miller." http://www.pitofhorror.com/main/miller.html (downloaded May 20, 2002).

30. For example, what were once the *Night of Anubis, Headcheese, The Babysitter Murders, The Never Dead, Book of the Dead, God's Army* and *The Black Hills Project* later became known as *Night of the Living Dead, The Texas Chain Saw Massacre, Halloween, Phantasm, The Evil Dead, Prophecy* and *The Blair Witch Project*.

31. Schoell and Spenser, 1992: ix.

32. Gire, Dan. "Bye, Bye Freddy!" *Cinefantastique*, vol. 18, no. 5, July 1988, p. 11.

33. McDonagh, 1995: 89.

34. Many critics and industry insiders accused Spielberg of taking over the film at Hooper's expense. The Director's Guild awarded Hooper $15,000 in damages, finding that the trailer "denigrated the role of director," and made MGM take full-page ads in three trade publications apologizing to Hooper and the DGA. Spielberg later made his own public apology and confessed how, "I thought I'd be able to turn *Poltergeist* over to a director and walk away; I was wrong," before adding, "I won't put someone else through what I put Tobe through, and I'll be more honest in my contribution to a film." (Paraphrased from McBride: 1997, pp. 338–339)

35. Gire, Dan. "Bye, Bye Freddy!" *Cinefantastique*, vol. 18, no. 5, July 1988, p. 11.

36. Ferrante, Anthony C. "Memoirs of an Invisible Director," *Fangoria* 110, March 1992, p. 45.

37. In this respect, Carpenter had some

success with his ghost story *The Fog* and the action-orientated *Escape from New York*.
  38. Rosenthal had impressed Hill and Carpenter with his short film *The Toyer*, and was offered the assignment after collaborator and protégé Tommy Lee Wallace had turned the director down on the basis of Carpenter's overinvolvement.
  39. Cumbrow, 2000: 68.
  40. During a shoot for additional scenes to create the first film's Television version, Carpenter's scenes and inserts for Rosenthal's sequel included two murders (with a knife and then a hammer) and a close-up of the hypodermic needle murder.
  41. Despite his involvement in the first sequel, Carpenter concurs with star Curtis that the movie stinks and should never have been made.
  42. Crisafulli, Chuck. "Mr. Friday Night," *Cinefantastique*, vol. 24, no. 3/5, October 1993, p. 119.
  43. McDonagh, 1995: 92.
  44. Ibid.
  45. Ibid.
  46. Biodrowski, Steven. "Sean S. Cunningham: House Keeper," *Gorezone* 21, Spring 1992, p. 9.
  47. Wes Craven interview, *Scream and Scream Again* documentary.
  48. Gallagher, John. "I, Director, I Screenwriter, I Madman," *Fangoria* 80, February 1989, p. 45.
  49. Bouzereau, Laruent. "Elm Street: Freddy's Revenge. The Man Behind the Mask; Director Jack Sholder," *L'Ecran Fantastique*, no. 66, March 1986, p. 49.
  50. Newman, Kim. "Englund's Nightmare," *New Musical Express*, November 7, 1987, p. 20.
  51. Robb, 1998: 92.
  52. Newman, Kim. "Englund's Nightmare," *New Musical Express*, November 7, 1987, p. 20. For a detailed examination of this homoerotic reading of the film, see Benshoff, 1997.
  53. McDonagh, 1995: 189.
  54. This was New Line's director of licensing and promotions at the time, Kevin Benson, commenting upon the Kruger phenomenon in Robb, 1998: 83.
  55. Schoell and Spenser, 1992: 199.
  56. Ibid.
  57. Craven has referred to his first studio picture as "one of my worst films." Szulkin, David A. "Last House Mates," *Fangoria* 200, March 2001, p. 98.
  58. Shapiro, Marc. "Is Wes Craven Still Scared?" *Gorezone* 11, January 1990, p. 46.
  59. Gire, Dan. "Bye, Bye Freddy!" *Cinefantastique*, vol. 18, no. 5, July 1988, p. 9.
  60. With the exception being Damiano Damiani's *Amityville II: The Possession* (1982).
  61. Shapiro, Marc. "A Nightmare on Elm Street 3: Dream Warriors," *Fangoria* 62, p. 66.
  62. Ibid.
  63. Gire, Dan. "Bye, Bye Freddy!" *Cinefantastique*, vol. 18, no. 5, July 1988, p. 9.
  64. Shapiro, Marc. "A Nightmare on Elm Street 3: Dream Warriors," *Fangoria* 62, p. 66.
  65. Shapiro, Marc. "Wes Craven's Psycho-Analysis," *Fangoria* 138, p. 35.
  66. The irony of Russell's appointment was not lost on Englund, who remarked, "If you think about it, Wes has always blamed *Dreamscape* for ripping him off and suddenly the writer of that is the director here." Jones, Alan. "A Nightmare on Elm Street 3: Dream Warriors," *Starburst*, vol. 10, no. 3, November 1987, p. 21.
  67. For a clear contrast between Craven and Wagner's script and Russell's film, see the novelization.
  68. Studio interference in terms of a shock epilogue, re-shoots and ratings problems saw this *Frankenstein* story with a *Terminator* twist become an uneven and misleading misadventure at best, with the director's name and association with the *Elm Street* franchise used to mis-market the film.
  69. In retrospect, this second title could be considered a narrow escape, given Cannon's half-hearted approach to the material and the controversy surrounding the finished film.
  70. Shapiro, Marc. "Is Wes Craven Still Scared?" *Gorezone* 11, January 1990, p. 46.
  71. Ibid.
  72. In addition to Paramount's slasher spoof, Craven also turned down Palace Pictures' request he direct *Dream Demon* another *Elm Street* clone.
  73. Warren, 2000: 32.
  74. Carpenter, when filming Stephen King's *Christine* in 1983, had previously exploited this technique.
  75. Clarke, Frederick S. "*A Nightmare on Elm Street*: The Phenomenon," *Cinefantastique*, vol. 18, no. 5, July 1988, p. 6.
  76. Clarke, Frederick S. "New Line Cinema on Working with Wes Craven," *Cinefantastique*, vol. 18, no. 5, July 1988, p. 11. New Line's decision to reject Craven's proposal was by no means the last time a first film director was overruled. Carpenter intended to send Michael Myers into outer space for *Halloween 6*—a concept that seems slightly less absurd, yet no less disastrous, in light of *Leprechaun in Space*, Pinhead in Space (*Hellraiser Bloodline*) and New Line's *Jason X*.
  77. Fischer, Dennis, and Eric Gilmartin, "Halloween 4," *Cinefantastique*, vol. 19, no. 1, January 1989, p. 28.
  78. Schoell and Spenser, 1992: 199.
  79. Ibid.
  80. Televised in 1988, with a pilot directed by Hooper, it was designed as both an introduction

to the series and a prequel to the feature films. *Freddy's Nightmares: A Nightmare on Elm Street, the Series* ran for two seasons over forty four episodes and attracted a wide range of directorial talent, from the aforementioned Hooper to franchise star Englund — who had his directorial demands written into his contract.

81. Doherty, Thomas. "Review: *Freddy's Dead*," *Cinefantastique*, vol. 22, no. 4, February 1992, p. 57.

82. Examples of which include Flynn's *Brainscan*, Smith's *Trick or Treat* and Manny Coto's atrocious *Dr. Giggles* for Universal.

83. Biodrwoski, Steve. "Wes Craven on the Politics of Horror," *Cinefantastique*, vol. 22, no. 5, April 1992, p. 58.

84. Similarly, Carpenter completed his own two-picture deal with Alive Films following the Satanic slime-fest *Prince of Darkness* in 1987 and *They Live* in 1988 (an adaptation of Ray Nelson's short story *Eight o' Clock in the Morning*, which *homaged* the paranoid invasion narratives of the 1950s).

85. Produced by Cunningham, the film was released as *House III* outside the U.S. to capitalize on the franchise's higher profile.

86. The tendency to explicitly approach a first film as a potential franchise also seized Barker's imagination when adapting *Cabal* in 1989. Released in 1990, after a series of additional shoots, under the title *Nightbreed*, Barker's film was somewhat betrayed by a bewildering marketing campaign and truncated running time.

87. Whereas Scott and Verhoeven have indicated a willingness to explore the darker side of the *Alien* and *Robocop* films, respectively, *Halloween: H20*'s driving force and original scream queen Jamie Lee Curtis fought to secure Carpenter's services for her twentieth anniversary return. However, a combination of creative and financial misgivings, in which Dimension were reluctant to sufficiently feather Carpenter's nest and increase the film's budget, prevented the director's return, since he was guaranteed to receive a passive payment irrespective of his participation. Mauceri, Joe. "A Final Halloween," *Shivers* 25, January 1996, p. 28.

88. More recently, Stuart Gordon has been attached to a fourth *Re-Animator* film entitled *House of Re-Animator*. Previously a staunch objector to sequels and returning to the franchise, the director has returned after a twenty-year absence. Complete with the first film cast and crew in attendance, and starring William H. Macy as the President, the project began in true Charles Band fashion — as a one sheet poster featuring a shot of the White House with a telling neon green glow coming from one of the windows.

89. A change of administration at Paramount paved the way for Cunningham to step in on behalf of New Line after dwindling profit margins, the cancellation of the TV series and the poor reception of *Jason Takes Manhattan*.

90. Shapiro, Marc. "Wes Craven's Psycho Analysis," *Fangoria* 138, November 1994, p. 36.

91. Kutzera, Dale. "Wes Craven's New Nightmare," *Cinefantastique*, vol. 25, no. 4, June 1994, p. 6.

92. Shapiro, Marc. "Wes Craven's Psycho Analysis," *Fangoria* 138, November 1994, p. 32.

93. Robb, 1998: 155

94. Ibid.

95. Shapiro, Marc. "Wes Craven's Psycho Analysis," *Fangoria* 138, November 1994, p. 36.

96. Robb, 1998: 157

97. Kutzera, Dale. "Wes Craven's New Nightmare," *Cinefantastique*, vol. 25, no. 4, June 1994, p. 6.

98. Ibid.

99. Shapiro, Marc. "Wes Craven's Psycho Analysis," *Fangoria* 138, November 1994, p. 32.

100. Kutzera, Dale. "Wes Craven's New Nightmare," *Cinefantastique*, vol. 25, no. 4, June 1994, p. 7.

101. Wes Craven interview, *Scream and Scream Again* documentary.

102. King's novel featured a fictional antagonist exacting revenge on those who supposedly created him and then killed him off. With the malevolent entities' desire to enter into our reality providing the narrative backbone, it soon becomes apparent that, in order to achieve their aims, each must attack their detractors at their weakest point — that is, through their families — and partake in the inevitable showdown.

103. Director Wes Craven speaking in *Wes Craven's New Nightmare* (1994).

104. Ibid.

105. Robb, 1998: 162

106. While the film was briefly subtitled *The Real Story*, and Englund wished they'd kept *Freddy Unbound*, Craven wanted to use the number seven and call it "*A Nightmare on Elm Street 7: The Ascension*. However, the director recalls that New Line were shy about using the number and opted to capitalize on his return to the franchise and his fresh approach by calling it *Wes Craven's New Nightmare*.

107. McDonagh, 1995: 189.

108. Robb, 1998: 164

109. Hearing a strange noise and discovering an open window he was sure had been closed, Williamson armed himself with a butcher knife and called his friend Dave on a cordless phone for moral support. Dave's support included phrases such as "Freddy's gonna get you," and "Michael's behind you"; and before long the two were arguing over which killer was the scarier. Thus, the opening sequence of *Scream* was born.

110. French, Lawrence. "Wes Craven's *Scream*," *Cinefantastique*, vol. 28, no. 7, 1997, p. 34.

111. According to producer Marianne Maddalena, Williamson originally expressed interest in directing the film and shot his own screen test based on the bathroom scene, with the killer wearing the mask from *Halloween*. However, in keeping with Hollywood's overall reluctance to allow unproven writers into the director's chair, the studio passed on the proposal. Shapiro, Marc. "Super Secret Scream," *Fangoria* no. 169, p. 22.

112. The virgin Randy is also presented as the film's randy Virgin — a quality that ensures his survival.

113. Kevin Williamson, "*Scream* Commentary," *Scream* Trilogy DVD: Special Edition, 2001.

114. Wes Craven, "*Scream* Commentary," *Scream* Trilogy DVD: Special Edition, 2001.

115. Ibid. Among other minor elements, the board objected to Steve's guts, Tatum's head, and Billy and Stu's lack of control at the movie's climax. Additionally, Kenny's throat slashing and Casey's hanging were also targeted, with the shot of her hanging compressed from real time to 50 percent by removing every other frame. Ignoring the director's letters of protestation and defense, in which *Rambo III* and *Romeo and Juliet* were presented as comparison pieces, the board cited imitability and intensity as their prime concerns and criteria in denying an R-rating.

116. French, Lawrence. "Wes Craven's *Scream*," *Cinefantastique*, vol. 28, no. 7, 1997, p. 46.

117. Throughout his career, Spielberg has supported and sponsored films, to varying degrees of involvement and success, ranging from the infamous case of over-stepping the mark on Hooper's *Poltergeist* through to Dante's *Gremlins*.

118. For example, *John Carpenter's They Live* and *Wes Craven's New Nightmare*.

119. Biodrowski, Steve. "Sean Cunningham: House Keeper," *Gorezone* 21, Spring 1992, p. 11.

120. In addition, James Isaacs not only rescued *House III* following David Blythe's departure, but later directed the special effects-heavy *Jason X*.

121. *Hills Have Eyes* producer Peter Locke originally intended to produce a third film, with Craven directing, using an alien planet setting. Eventually based on a script written by Craven's son Jonathan, and directed by Joe Gayton (with genre veteran Lance Henrickson starring), the film was later titled *The Outpost* before appearing as *Wes Craven Presents Mindripper*.

122. Similarly, Carpenter operates a "John Carpenter Presents" program under the Storm King production banner (which he runs with his wife/long-time producer Sandy King).

123. Put together by Pierre David, the Canadian producer of Cronenberg's early work, *Wishmaster* spawned an Artisan-sponsored franchise of its own.

124. Anderson, Phil. "Wes Craven Interview." http://www.kaos2000.net/interviews/wescraven00.html (downloaded July 12, 2004).

125. Craven's production company later co-produced his son Jonathan Craven's directorial debut, *They Shoot Divas Don't They?* in 2002, with a plot reminiscent of Curtis Hanson's *The Hand That Rocks the Cradle*.

126. Following its acquisition of the film, Dimension's in-house director Rick Bota was brought in and the film re-edited.

127. Lussier worked with Craven as editor, and directed *Dracula 2000*, whereas Mastandrea had been his second assistant director prior to *The Breed*.

128. Ibid.

129. Including *I Know What You Did Last Summer*, *Urban Legend*, *Cherry Falls* and *Valentine*, with the first two later receiving sequels of their own.

130. Rebello, Stephen. "Fear and Trembling," *Movieline*, vol. 10, no. 4, December/January 1999, p. 80.

131. French, Lawrence. "*Scream 2*," *Cinefantastique*, vol. 29, no. 9, Jan 1998, p. 8.

132. However, as John Muir rightfully points out, this presentation of *Scream 2* as the second installment in a proposed trilogy is problematic at best. Rather than leaving the audience suspended on a cliffhanger and deliberately leaving loose ends, as in *Back to the Future II* (1990), *The Empire Strikes Back* (1980) or even *Damien: Omen II* (1979), *Scream 2* "gives no hint of where the third film will lead." (Muir, 1998: 217.)

133. This includes such films as *The Dorm That Dripped Blood*, *The House on Sorority Row*, *Splatter University* and *Sorority House Massacre*.

134. Wes Craven, "*Scream 2* Commentary," *Scream* Trilogy DVD: Special Edition, 2001.

135. Ibid.

136. Clive Barker, "Lost in the Labyrinth" documentary, Hellraiser: Limited Edition DVD.

137. The film's title was eventually changed to the alliterative *Teaching Mrs. Tingle* to avert any potential controversy in a post–Columbine climate.

138. French, Lawrence. "Wes Craven on *Scream 3*," *Cinefantastique*, vol. 31, no. 10, February 2000, p. 12.

139. Winstanley, Cam. "The Final Cut," *Total Film* 40, May 2000, p. 54.

140. French, Lawrence. "Wes Craven on *Scream 3*," *Cinefantastique*, vol. 31, no. 10, February 2000, p. 14.

141. Spelling, Ian. "Joining the Scream Team," *Fangoria* 190, March 2000, p. 21.

142. The most interesting of which saw Emily (*Stab 3*'s Sidney) being in on Roman's plans as his girlfriend and accomplice; but the director apparently couldn't sell this incestuous twist to the studio.

143. When this date was put back to February 4, 2000, Craven seized the opportunity to reshoot and restructure the opening and closing scenes of the film.

144. The *Pulse* remake eventually reached the screen under director Jim Sonzero; and the video game *Alice* has yet to shoot under Marcus Nispel's direction, with Sarah Michelle Gellar in the title role.

145. Wes Craven, *Scream and Scream Again* documentary.

146. A sequel to *Dog Soldiers* was proposed by the producer, and a superior *Ginger Snaps* sequel and average prequel have already been released on DVD.

147. Shapiro, Marc. "The *Cursed* Is Over?" *Fangoria* 241, March 2005, p. 36.

148. In this respect, Dimension is continuing its, and Hollywood's, current appetite for such PG-13 horrors as *The Ring* and its sequel, *The Grudge* and *Boogeyman* by cutting up R-rated films *They*, *Darkness* and now *Cursed*.

149. Although Craven has publicly described *Cursed* as, "a solid little film" with a "terrific" look, the director has vowed that he would not be involved in any form of follow-up. Shapiro, Marc. "The *Cursed* Is Over?" *Fangoria* 241, March 2005, p. 34.

150. The director has since vowed only to consider a return to Dimension and the Weinsteins with the assurance that he would have "final cut [and] a definite budget," and that the studio "would go away and let me make my film." Ibid, p. 38.

151. Ibid, p. 34.

152. McDonagh 1995: 185.

153. Shapiro, Marc. "Wes Craven's Psycho Analysis," *Fangoria* 138, November 1994, p. 33.

Chapter 3

1. Cumbrow, 2000: 68.

2. Previously addressed in Chapter 3, the first film director as mentor to potential new talent has continued to develop.

3. Gilpin, Kris. "Interview: Sean Cunningham," *L'Ecran Fantastique*, no. 67, April 1986, p. 15.

4. Holliss, Richard. "Tommy Lee Wallace on *Halloween III*," *Starburst*, vol. 4, no. 11, July 1983, p. 15.

5. As one of horror's lesser known and even lesser respected sequels, *Look What's Happened to Rosemary's Baby* saw Paramount Pictures promote Sam O'Steen, the Emmy Award-wining editor of the first film, into the director's chair for a 1976 TV-bound follow-up.

6. In this respect, both Perkins, as the iconic star of the *Psycho* franchise, and Joe Alves, as an established production veteran and second unit director of the *Jaws* franchise, exploited their affinity with the source material as means of securing their appointment. Whereas Perkins offered to direct the third installment for free, Alves used his advisory role to recommend the more manageable sea park concept and pitch his idea of shooting the film in 3-D.

7. The result, *Society*, was an outrageously surreal and special effects-laden foray into sex, snobbery, and "shunting" in the suburb of Beverly Hills, courtesy of make-up effects maestro Screaming Mad George.

8. Jones, Alan. "Brian Yuzna and the Fantastic Factory," *Shivers* 73, January 2000, p. 37.

9. Whether crewmembers in charge of special make-up effects should be considered artists or technicians is open to interpretation and derives from whether filmmaking should be considered an art or a science.

10. McDonagh, Maitland. "The State of the Horror Nation," *Fangoria*, no. 103, June 1991, p. 23.

11. The following films also saw special effects artists graduate into the director's chair: John Carl Buechler's *Friday the 13th Part VII: The New Blood*, Chris Walas' *The Fly II*, Jim Isaac's *House III: The Horror Show*, Dave Allen's *Puppet Master II*, Kevin Yagher's *Hellraiser: Bloodline* and, most recently, Phil Tippett's *Starship Troopers 2: Heroes of the Federation*.

12. Other pertinent examples include E. Wiley's *House II*, Stern's *Amityville 4: The Evil Escapes*, Lafia's *Child's Play 2*, Henkel's *Texas Chainsaw Massacre: The Next Generation* and, most recently, Mancini and Goyer with *Seed of Chucky* and *Blade: Trinity*.

13. The evolution of monster make-ups and their creators has been well chronicled from the performer's point of view in Bradley, 1996: 52.

14. A career retrospective of Pierce's work can be found in Doug Norwine's article "Universal's Monster Maker," *Fangoria* 134, July 1994, p. 14.

15. Ibid, p. 15.

16. A detailed study of these Cold War/invasion narratives can be found in Biskind, 1983.

17. This new technique involved rear projection on overlapping miniature screens.

18. And the award went to *Cleopatra*, with Hitchcock's *The Birds* passed over in favor of this all-star remake.

19. As seen with Chaney, and Lewis, the appearance of an eye-catching moniker, self-styled or otherwise, was pivotal in establishing a

specific reputation in Hollywood. Later examples include Craven as "the Sultan of Slash" and Cronenberg as "the King of Venereal Horror."
20. This accolade appears in Waters' *Serial Mom* (1994).
21. Bissette, Stephen R. "Fango's Family Tree," *Fangoria* 100, March 1991, p. 88.
22. Ibid.
23. Hollywood bible *Variety* labeled Romero's first feature "an unrelieved orgy of sadism." McCarty, 1990: 103.
24. Ferrante, Tim. "The Fangoria Hall of Fame: Dick Smith," *Fangoria* 100, March 1991, p. 54.
25. Having established the first make-up department in television at NBC in the 1950s, and aged Marlon Brando in *The Godfather*, Smith was the perfect choice to prematurely age Von Sydow as Father Merrin.
26. McCabe, 1999: 138.
27. McCarty, 1984: 106.
28. Arguably this cycle began when William Castle was persuaded by Robert Evans at Paramount Pictures to pass on the film in favor of Polanski.
29. McCarty, 1984: 106.
30. For a comprehensive discussion regarding the roots and definition of what constitutes a splatter movie, see McCarty, 1984.
31. England, Norman. "An Interview with George Romero Part 3: Press Conference Transcript," http://www2.gol.com/users/noman/interv4.html (downloaded August 21, 2002).
32. Fischer, 1991: 644.
33. Ibid, p. 645.
34. Savini officially began his career in make-up effects working on the Ed Gein-inspired *Deranged* and *Dead of Night* for *Children Shouldn't Play with Dead Things* creator Alan Ormsby.
35. McCarty, 1995: 119.
36. From Conrich's examination of Cronenberg's career in his article "An Aesthetic Sense: Cronenberg and Neo-horror Film Culture" in Grant, 2000: 44.
37. Ferrante, Tim. "The Fangoria Hall of Fame: Dick Smith," *Fangoria* 100, March 1991, p. 54.
38. Tom Savini as interviewed in the documentary *Scream and Scream Again*.
39. Ibid.
40. *Fangoria*'s short-lived sister magazine *Gorezone* increasingly concentrated on foreign films and special effects artists.
41. Kuehls, David. "The Fangoria Hall of Fame: Tom Savini," *Fangoria* 100, March 1991, p. 53.
42. Honorary awards were given to William Tuttle and John Hanbers for their outstanding work on *The 7 Faces of Dr Lao* (1963) and *Planet of the Apes* (1967), respectively.

43. Baker's subsequent credits include *Greystoke, Gorillas in the Mist* and *Planet of the Apes*.
44. Warren, Bill. "The Fangoria Hall of Fame: Rick Baker," *Fangoria* 100, March 1991, p. 44.
45. Ibid.
46. Winston was part of the FX team who won Best Visual Effects for *Aliens* in 1986.
47. Shapiro, Marc. "Chris Walas Works Out the Bugs," *Gorezone* 16, Winter 1990, p. 50.
48. England, Norman. "An Interview with George Romero Part 3: Press Conference Transcript," http://www2.gol.com/users/noman/interv4.html (downloaded August 21, 2002).
49. Ibid.
50. The most recent incarnation is a 3-D reimagining of the film, directed by Jeff Broadstreet.
51. Jones, 2001: 51.
52. Ibid.
53. Savini was also approached by De Laurentiis to direct the heavy metal horror film *Trick or Treat* but lost out to Charles Martin Smith.
54. Yagher was responsible for *Tales from the Crypt*'s Cryptkeeper segments and the episode "Lower Berth."
55. Shapiro, Marc. "The Fangoria Hall of Fame: Kevin Yagher," *Fangoria* 100, March 1991, p. 55.
56. McDonagh, Maitland. *Filmmaking on the Fringe: The Good, the Bad, and the Deviant Directors.* New York: Carol, 1995, p. 106.
57. After receiving partial credit on *Dungeonmaster* (1985) and full credit on the FX-heavy fantasy film *Troll* a year later (the first film to feature a young boy by the name of Harry Potter as its heroic protagonist), Buechler completed *Cellar Dweller* before starting work on *Friday the 13th Part VII*.
58. Apparently, this was because they were in negotiations with New Line to make *Freddy vs. Jason* until substantial disagreements over distribution rights sent the makers of both franchises back to the drawing board. Paramount swapped Freddy for an ESP-wielding Carrie-clone. Freeman, Royce. "Interview John Carl Buechler," http://www.pitofhorror.com/main/buechler.html (downloaded: April 15, 2002).
59. Shapiro, Marc. "Kevin Yagher: Puppetmaster," *Fangoria* 98, November 1990, p. 47.
60. Ibid, p. 49.
61. Niderost, Eric. "*The Fly II*: Chris Walas Gets His Wings," *Fangoria* 81, April 89, p. 23.
62. Jones, Alan. "George Romero Speaks Out," *Starburst*, vol. 12, no. 7, p. 19.
63. The Caretaker. "Tom Savini Interview." http://www.houseofhorrors.com/tsinterview.html (downloaded: June 19, 2002).
64. Jones, Alan. "George A. Romero Speaks Out," *Starburst*, vol. 12, no. 7, March 1990, p. 19.

65. Watt, Mike. "Night of the Living Dead 90," *Cinefantastique*, vol. 34, no. 3/4, June 2002, p. 118.
66. Atkins' lavish script was a self-contained trilogy that covered three distinct generations and explored the origins of the box.
67. Tomlinson, Anthony. "Peter Atkins: Hell's Scribe," *Shivers* 53, May 1998, p. 36.
68. Ibid.
69. This was despite the producer's reassurances. Buechler, John Carl. "Stories from the Director," http://www.johncarlbuechler.com/fl3.html (downloaded April 15, 2002).
70. Niderost, Eric. "*The Fly II*: Chris Walas Gets His Wings," *Fangoria* 81, April 1989, p. 23.
71. Just as Walas was persuaded by Brooks to concede to shoot the studio's movie, Buechler alleges the associate producer in favor of a more conservative and conventional approach repeatedly overruled him. Yagher similarly endured Miramax's retrospective cost-cutting exercises of removing set pieces and pages from the script.
72. Despite an alleged budget of $4.7 million, Savini later discovered that the production manager had made "some deal ... where he'd get a huge bonus if he brought it in for $2 million." Jones, Alan. "Reliving Night of the Living Dead," *Shivers* 4, December 1992, p. 26.
73. Ibid.
74. Watt, Mike. "Night of the Living Dead 90," *Cinefantastique*, vol. 34, no. 3/4, June 2002, p. 119.
75. Frasher, Micheal. "NOTLD: Zombie Director Tom Savini," *Cinefantastique*, vol. 21, no. 3, December 1990, p. 18.
76. Jones, Alan. "George Romero Speaks Out," *Starburst*, vol. 12, no. 7, p. 19.
77. Szebin, Frederick C. "*Night of the Living Dead*," *Cinefantastique*, vol. 21, no. 7, September 1990, p. 8.
78. Ibid.
79. Ibid.
80. Beeler, Micheal. "*Hellraiser IV: Bloodline*," *Cinefantastique*, vol. 26, no. 3, April 1995, p. 35.
81. Szebin, Frederick C. "*Night of the Living Dead*," *Cinefantastique*, vol. 21, no. 7, September 1990, p. 9.
82. Tom Savini, *Night of the Living Dead* commentary.
83. A key cause for concern was the lack of screen time afforded to the franchise front man and icon, Pinhead.
84. Yagher left to focus on his script for *Sleepy Hollow*, an adaptation he was set to direct until the project's high profile saw it become a Tim Burton film.
85. The majority of murder scenes in Buechler's sequel suffered trims and/or deletions by the MPAA.
86. Freeman, Royce. "Interview John Carl Buechler," http://www.pitofhorror.com/main/buechler.html (downloaded April 15, 2002).
87. Buechler, John Carl. "Stories from the director," http://www.johncarlbuechler.com/fl3.html (downloaded April 15, 2002).
88. Shapiro, Marc. "Chris Walas Works Out the Bugs," *Gorezone* 16, Winter 1990, p. 50.
89. Ibid.
90. Jones, Alan. "Reliving *Night of the Living Dead*," *Shivers* 4, December 1992, p. 26.
91. Watt, Mike. "Night of the Living Dead 90," *Cinefantastique*, vol. 34, no. 3/4, June 2002, p. 118.
92. Ibid.
93. Ibid.
94. Savini has taken cameo roles in a number of pictures, including *Ted Bundy* and *Children of the Living Dead*, along with crowd-pleasing cameo in Romero's *Land of the Dead* and the key role of Sex Machine in *From Dusk Till Dawn*.
95. See Chapter 1.
96. Reportedly, Monash wanted to move the location, change the Iraq-set prologue, change Chris McNeil's career and the characterization of Kinderman (the character to whom Blatty was most strongly attached), and drop Merrin completely. McCabe, 1999: 25.
97. The role of Chris MacNeil had allegedly been based on Blatty's close friend and neighbor, Shirley MacLaine, who had tentatively agreed to star in the picture.
98. McCabe, 1999: 36
99. McCabe, 1999: 121.
100. Friedkin recalls that "he didn't do the novel ... I thought the script was frankly terrible and I told Bill that." McCabe, 1999: 37.
101. Both Kermode and McCabe have documented how Friedkin first declined Hermann's suggestions, then rejected Schifrin's composition outright before happening upon Mike Oldfield's Tubular Bells, a track now synonymous with the franchise. Although Friedkin deemed Schifrin's work unsuitable, the score was later adopted by Rosenberg's adaptation of Anson's *The Amityville Horror* in 1979 and nominated for Best Original Score.
102. McCabe, 1999: 126.
103. McCaffrey, Richard. "William Peter Blatty: Novelist and Screenwriter of *The Exorcist*," http://www.bbc.co.uk/films/2000/10/12/william_peter_blatty_interview.shtml (downloaded August 22, 2002).
104. Kermode, Mark. "*Exorcist II*: The Final Cut," *Film Review*, November 2004, Issue 650, p. 72.
105. McCabe, 1999: 79.
106. It may have been "for the good of the film," but surely this goes against Friedkin's assertion that he was making this first and foremost for Blatty. McCabe, 1999: 126.

107. Friedkin's fondness for film adaptation was evident up until his disastrous return to horror with *The Guardian* in 1990.
108. Both Mancini and Lafia, as writers and scriptwriters on *Child's Play*, were equally frustrated by Tom Holland's take on the script.
109. Savolv, Marc. "The Horror, the Horror: An Interview with *Exorcist* Screenwriter and Author William Peter Blatty," *http://www.austin chronicle.com/issues/dispatch/2000-03-24/screens_feature.html* (downloaded June 16, 2001).
110. For King's own frank recollections and review of the film, see *On Writing: A Memoir*, 2000.
111. Nutman, Philip. "Bring on the Monsters: Part 1," *Fangoria* 87, October 1989, p. 32.
112. Maxford, Howard. "Psycho II," *Shivers* 39, April 1997, p. 39.
113. Similarly, both Stern and Henkel ignored the events of previous entries in self-penned sequels to *The Amityville Horror* and *The Texas Chain Saw Massacre*.
114. Despite an acknowledgement that there were "certain very mundane and commercial reasons for going out and making this film," Henkel optimistically argued in press interviews that he "could do justice to the material where others had failed." Wooley, John. "Saw Man," *Fangoria* 147, October 1995, p. 51.
115. Leming, Rod. From Psycho to Asylum: The Horror Films of Robert Bloch. *http://mgpfeff.home.sprynet.com/leming_interview1.html* (Downloaded: July 24 2003).
116. While Universal had the right to option Bloch's story, their disapproval ensured that their cinematic sequel would eschew Bloch's postmodern examination of the genre.
117. The concept of the director's cut, exploited as an additional marketing ploy, nevertheless gained currency with audiences on account of Scott's revisiting *Blade Runner*.
118. Prior to this, Spielberg had sensationally shot additional footage and re-edited his film for a Special Edition of *Close Encounters of the Third Kind*, released theatrically three years after the original in 1980. To a lesser extent, Carpenter shot additional sequences for the televised version of *Halloween* on the set of the sequel.
119. This approach has been integrated into the marketing strategies of big-budget Hollywood blockbusters and the arrival of Ultimate, Platinum and Collector's Editions. Comic book franchises *X-Men* and *Spider-Man* have taken such an approach one step further with the 1.5 and 2.5 editions on DVD.
120. For a full description of Mancini's outline and discussion regarding the project's stalled development at Universal, see Arrow. "Don Mancini Interview Part 2," *http://www.joblo.com/arrow/interview32-2.htm* (downloaded March 30, 2003).

121. McCabe, 1999: 173.
122. This was due to the fact that "the motel, the house, the general surround ... was as strong a part of the tone of the whole thing." Daniels, 1975: 14.
123. As the iconic face of the franchise, Perkins was inextricably linked with both the character and concept to such an extent that he felt suffocated by it. McCarty, 1990: 69.
124. Winecoff, 1996: 426.
125. In constructing his slice of American Gothic, Perkins heightened the themes of conflict, tragedy and guilt to present a paradoxically ambiguous yet explicit tale of redemption and salvation, with a strong sense of satirical black humor. Gross, Edward. "Norman Bates: The Hamlet of Horror Roles," *Fangoria's Bloody Best* 6, 1987, p. 56.
126. McCabe, 1999: 173.
127. Ibid.
128. Hanke, 1991: 258.
129. Scenes were shot with Dourif that not only restaged Karras' final moments from *The Exorcist*, but also included a sequence in which Karras' corpse (Dourif) is examined in a morgue by a pathologist, with Kinderman in attendance.
130. Kermode, Mark. "A Legion of Interference," *Fangoria* 122, May 1993, p. 68.
131. Koetting, Christopher. "Speak of the Devil," *Fangoria* 180, March 1999, p. 69.
132. Davis, Ivor. "Back to Fright," *The Times*, November 20, 1986, p. 16.
133. Winecoff, 1996: 426.
134. Ibid.
135. McCabe, 1999: 174.
136. Ibid.
137. Biodrowski, Steve. "*The Exorcist III: Legion*," *Cinefantastique*, vol. 21, no. 2, September 1990, p. 21.
138. Ibid.
139. Koetting, Christopher. "Speak of the Devil," *Fangoria* 180, March 1999, p. 69.
140. McCabe, 1999: 175.
141. Ibid, p. 174.
142. Koetting, Christopher. "Speak of the Devil," *Fangoria* 180, March 1999, p. 69.
143. Landsburg was known as the producer of such schlock movies of the week as *The Savage Bees*. Ruby, Jack. "An Interview with Carl Gottleib: Part 2," *http://www.13thstreet.com/site/common/view-content.jsp?section=Features&id=ababa-234ad-asdf3-234ad* (downloaded April 15, 2002).
144. Mills, Nancy. "The Live-Action Filming of *Jaws 3-D*," *Cinefantastique*, vol. 13, no. 6, September 1995, p. 62.
145. Ibid.
146. McCabe, 1999: 175.
147. This quote from *Halloween III* antagonist Conal Cochran is a reference to his plan to

kill America's children through a combination of clever merchandising, marketing and advertising.

148. Wildly different in approach and tone to the first two films, and conceived of as the first of many generic anthology films, Wallace's sequel explored the festival's Celtic origins and American commercialism to answer the nursery rhyme that dared to ask what little boys were made of. By simultaneously commenting and capitalizing upon the mass merchandising of cinematic tie-ins, the film's thematic ambivalence effectively complemented Wallace's *Toy Story* (an excursion into murder-mystery territory courtesy of an army of Terminator-esque toys). Halloweenmovies.com. "Interview: Tommy Lee Wallace," http://www.halloweenmovies.com/site/interview_tlw.htm (downloaded February 10, 2003).

149. Holliss, Richard. "Tommy Lee Wallace on *Halloween III*," *Starburst*, vol. 4, no. 11, July 1983, p. 16.

150. Ibid.

151. McCabe, 1999: 175.

152. Whether the result of sheer coincidence or the product of shrewd commercial tactics and studio strategies, many potential conflicts are resolved as stars leave, scripts change and many projects stall or fall apart.

153. Barnes & Noble.com. "William Friedkin: Exorcising Cinematic Demons with *The Version You've Never Seen*," http://video.barnesandnoble.com/search/interview.asp?ctr=599175 (downloaded June 25, 2002).

154. Co-writer Russo re-edited the film and shot additional footage for a heavily criticized 30th Anniversary edition.

155. Kermode, Mark. "*Exorcist III*: The Final Cut," *Film Review*, November 2004, Issue 650, p. 72.

156. Ibid.

157. This included revolving heads, projectile vomit and bouncing beds. Ibid, p. 74.

158. Ibid, p. 71.

159. The Caretaker. "Tom Savini Interview," http://www.houseofhorrors.com/tsinterview.html (downloaded June 19, 2002).

160. Indeed, more recent writer-directors Goyer and Mancini have seen *Blade: Trinity* and *Seed of Chucky* released on video unrated and rated, in keeping with the current marketing trend and demand for alternative versions and footage deleted from the theatrical version.

Chapter 4

1. Beeler, Micheal. "Clive Barker's *Hellraiser IV: Bloodline*," *Cinemafantastique*, vol. 27, no. 2, November 1995, p. 15.

2. Savlov, Marc. "The Making of the *Blair Witch Project*: Into the Woods," http://www.austinchronicle.com/issues/vol18/issue46/screens.blairwitch.html (downloaded September 30, 2002).

3. *Last House on the Left* producer Cunningham has commented how, "*Blair Witch* is like *Last House* revisited on a huge level." Szulkin, David. "Last House Mates," *Fangoria* 200, March 2001, p. 60.

4. Also released within eighteen months of the previous entry were such under-developed sequels as *Amityville 3-D*, *Child's Play 3*, the ironic *Friday the 13th Part V: A New Beginning*, *A Nightmare on Elm Street 5: The Dream Child*, *Halloween 5*, *The Howling V* and Ratner's prequel/remake of *Red Dragon*.

5. See Chapter 4 for a detailed account of his refusal.

6. Once in the very beginning and again following the dismissal of ocean picture veteran John Hancock after three weeks of shooting.

7. See Dempsey, Michael. "The Return of Jaws," *American Film*, vol. 3, no. 8, June 1978, p. 28. Similarly, *Damien: Omen II*, *Pumpkinhead II*, and *The Rage: Carrie II* all saw a last minute switch in the director's chair, with experienced TV or sequel-makers being brought in after Mike Hodges, Tony Randel, and Robert Mandel either quit or had failed to impress the powers that be.

8. McBride, 1997: 258.

9. Thereby adopting a similar approach to Paramount with Sam O'Steen and the sequel to Polanski's *Rosemary's Baby* two years previous.

10. Andrew J. Kuehn created the infamous tag line "Just when you thought it was safe to go back in the water" for the trailer.

11. Dempsey, Micheal. "The Return of Jaws," *American Film*, vol. 3, no. 8, June 1978, p. 29.

12. More recently, Nispel and Snyder have directed well-received remakes of *The Texas Chainsaw Massacre* and *Dawn of the Dead* for New Line and Universal.

13. Hodges, Adrian. "First Chance on Conflict," *Screen International*, no. 241, May 17, 1980, p. 20.

14. Ibid.

15. Both Bill Condon and Gary Sherman were given the opportunity to direct first and second sequels to *Candyman* and *Poltergeist* on account of their previous genre-specific success.

16. Such franchises as Paramount's *Friday the 13th* seemingly preferred this option — in the case of part four and five, with Joseph Zito and Danny Steinmann, respectively.

17. Richard Franklin and Philippe Mora had satisfied Universal's and Hemdale's selection criteria with the Hitchcockian *Road Games* and *The Beast Within*.

18. Jeunet's previous credits included *Delicatessen* and *The City of Lost Children*, whereas

Yu came to Hollywood's attention via *The Bride with White Hair* and its sequel in 1993. Although Yu and Jeunet's first films for Hollywood were as franchise outsiders, international directors Sluzier and Shimzu were invited to direct the U.S.-funded remakes of their films *The Vanishing* and *The Grudge,* respectively. More recently, Hideo Nakata's Hollywood debut was the sequel to a remake of his *Ringu* franchise.

19. However, it was rare yet possible for directors to resist the franchise as a form of Hollywood short-hand, with *Blair Witch* directors Myrick and Sanchez turning down *Exorcist 4,* and *Bad Taste*'s Peter Jackson rejecting New Line's offer of directing *Leatherface: The Texas Chainsaw Massacre III* in favor of his independently financed and produced X-rated puppet extravaganza *Meet the Feebles.*

20. Medak had made *The Changeling* eighteen years earlier, and Schrader had directed an ill-received remake of *Cat People* in 1982.

21. Although Hough's career had spanned over twenty-five years, with credits including the notable *Legend of Hell House,* Sargent's thirty-year career, primarily as a TV director, provided a clear indication of how high Universal regarded the future of the franchise four years after *Jaws 3-D*.

22. Arguably, this was Harris' authorial challenge to traditional Hollywood filmmaking, with a follow-up that touched upon all manner of societal taboos — from pedophilia to incest — and humanized its eponymous character at the expense of the "free range rude" on display.

23. Van Sant has described how the Hollywood studios eagerly picked high-profile, nominated directors off the "Oscar tree" and capitalized on their current hype and popularity. Rebello, Stephen. "Return to the Bates Motel," *Movieline,* vol. 10, no. 4, December/January 1999, p. 70.

24. McCabe, 1999: 158.

25. Boorman considered the widespread reaction to Friedkin's film a "loathsome" example of "child abuse by proxy" in which "audiences were only sickly responding with a kind of vicarious satisfaction at the abuses heaped upon a 12-year-old girl." Hanke, 1991: 254.

26. Ibid.

27. The company originally started off as Creative Thinking International (CTI) in 1989.

28. By this point Berlinger had nominations and awards from Sundance, the New York Film Critics, the DGA and an Emmy.

29. The case in question involved a man who secretly lived in his lover's attic for seventeen years. When the husband finally discovers the man, and the affair, the lover kills the husband and is brought to trial.

30. Crawford, Travis. "Ready or Not, It's *Blair Witch 2: Book of Shadows,*" *Fangoria* 197, October 2000, p. 95.

31. Ibid.

32. Lee, Patrick. "Director Joe Berlinger Casts a New Spell in *Blair Witch 2,*" http://www.scifi.com/sfw/issue183/interview.html (downloaded January 10, 2005).

33. Mottram, James. "*Book of Shadows: Blair Witch 2,*" http://www.bbc.co.uk/films/2000/10/24/joe_berlinger_bw2_interview.shtml (downloaded: January 10, 2005).

34. Flynn, Gillian. "Set Visit: *Blair Witch 2,*" *Entertainment Weekly,* May 7, 2004, http://jeffreydonovanfans.com/articles/ewblairwitch.html (downloaded January 10, 2005).

35. Having already said no to guns, Sigourney Weaver's co-producer credit allowed her to monitor and control the way in which her character was written, and, more importantly, dictate her fate in the final act.

36. Mark Kermode's narration, "Alien Evolution" documentary.

37. To secure their involvement, studios often required directors to defer to or at least incorporate returning stars' ideas, protective of both their characters and reputations. Just as Sigourney Weaver took a co-producer credit and Anthony Perkins ascended to the director's chair, *Elm Street*'s Robert Englund secured additional financial incentives in the form of a profit participation deal, and furthered his career with acting roles outside of the franchise and directing opportunities on the *Freddy's Nightmares* television series.

38. One such example was the tense and turbulent relationship between director Dominique Othenin-Girard and actor Donald Pleasance on the set of *Halloween 5,* wherein the pair were unable to resolve issues over Loomis' characterization and the film's violent content.

39. When Scott was unable to secure Jodie Foster's return for *Hannibal* (on the basis that the actress objected to the way in which her character had been portrayed in Harris' novel), the role was sensationally recast, with fellow Academy Award winner Julianne Moore taking her place, and producer De Laurentiis putting a positive spin on the proceedings.

40. For *The Texas Chainsaw Massacre* remake, director Nispel worked with returning director of photography Daniel Pearl, whose presence constituted a unique selling point and marketable link to Hooper's first film. Consequently, Nispel played up Pearl's participation and input in interviews when describing the way in which he bowed down before "the grandmaster" and "just went along for the ride." Allen, Christine. "*The Texas Chainsaw Massacre* Cuts Again," *Fangoria* 227, p. 21.

41. For example, just as *Psycho II*'s Richard

Franklin kills off Lila Loomis in a wickedly gratuitous homage to Hitchcock towards the end of the second act, first sequels to *The Omen*, *Friday the 13th* and *Candyman* used their returning characters in an extended prologue before killing them off and introducing a whole new set of characters.

42. New Line initially hired Leslie Bohem and Skipp and Spector to come up with competing drafts for the *Dream Child* script, based on an approved outline which read: Alice is pregnant, Freddy wants the baby, and Dan is the first to die.

43. The extent to which a director's input is incorporated into a film's script can be reflected in the WGA's arbitration processes with Schrader and Spence receiving co-screenplay credit for *Exorcist IV* and *Children of the Corn IV*.

44. The scriptwriters in question were Jon Bokenkamp, Neal Stevens, and Robert Parigi.

45. Hasted, Nick. "Hell Hath No Fury Like a Studio Scorned," *The Independent*. August 8 2003, *http://enjoyment.independent.co.uk/film/features/story.jsp?story=431680* (downloaded August 24, 2003).

46. Ibid.

47. Hendrix, Omar. "What Will *'Jaws'* and *'Exorcist'* Do for an Encore?" *New York Times*, June 27, 1976, p. 5.

48. Lee, Patrick. "Director Joe Berlinger Casts a New Spell in *Blair Witch 2*," *http://www.scifi.com/sfw/issue183/interview.html* (downloaded January 10, 2005).

49. Dobson, Dale. "Slings and Arrows: An Interview with Joe Berlinger," *http://www.digitallyobsessed.com/showinterview.php3?ID=14* (downloaded January 10, 2005).

50. Kaufman, Anthony. "Interview: Battling the Blair Witch, Joe Berlinger Takes on Sequels and Studio with Book of Shadows," *http://www.indiewire.com/people/int_Berlinger_Joe_001024.html* (downloaded January 10, 2005).

51. Lee, Patrick. "Director Joe Berlinger Casts a New Spell in *Blair Witch 2*," *http://www.scifi.com/sfw/issue183/interview.html* (downloaded January 10, 2005).

52. Kaufman, Anthony. "Interview: Battling the Blair Witch, Joe Berlinger Takes on Sequels and Studio with Book of Shadows," *http://www.indiewire.com/people/int_Berlinger_Joe_001024.html* (downloaded January 10, 2005).

53. Hanke, 1991: 254.

54. Norton, Bill. "Zealots and Xenomorphs," *Cinefex*, no. 50, May 1992, p. 29.

55. Shapiro, Marc. "The Nightmare Directors," *A Nightmare on Elm Street: The Dream Child Magazine*, August 1989, p. 53.

56. Shapiro, Marc. "Stephen Hopkins: An Englishman on Elm Street," *Gorezone* 10, November 1989, p. 48.

57. Endowed with such standout scenes as an underwater Alien ambush and Ripley's startling discovery, Jeunet's film also included such staples as an artificial person, the face hugger, a graphic chestburster scene and the return of the Alien Queen.

58. Van Sant specifically shot a continuous take for the opening sequence and included an overhead shot of Marion's body at the end of the shower scene to fulfill this objective.

59. Ted Tally, *Red Dragon* DVD commentary.

60. This forms the main title of Barbara Creed's insightful text on the varying representations of women in contemporary horror films.

61. Kaufman., Anthony. "Interview: Battling the Blair Witch, Joe Berlinger Takes on Sequels and Studio with Book of Shadows," *http://www.indiewire.com/people/int_Berlinger_Joe_001024.html* (downloaded January 10, 2005).

62. Ibid.

63. One critic accused Jeannot Szwarc's sequel of looking just like a "Crown International youth picture," complete with its cast of "interchangeable teenagers." An earlier storyline involved the sons of Quint and Brody returning to Amity on the hunt for another killer shark. Szwarc reportedly felt trapped between two choices, but with Universal keen to capture the teen market, the director was encouraged to make "the second mistake" with his commercially viable sequel. Bartholemew, David. *"Jaws 2," Cinefantastique*, vol. 8, no. 1, Winter 1978, p. 18.

64. An approach similarly followed by Boorman and Fincher in their franchise films.

65. Ridley Scott, *Hannibal* DVD commentary.

66. McCabe, 1999: 157.

67. Ibid.

68. Ibid.

69. McCarty, 1989: 118.

70. Berlinger references *Night of the Living Dead* in the owl-eating shot, *The Omen* with the shot of the dogs on the bridge, *The Exorcist* with the backwards playing of the tapes and *Evil Dead 2* via the tree-spinning girl.

71. For a detailed analysis of Hopkins' film see Piston, Jenny. "Parturition and Horror in Stephen Hopkins' *Nightmare on Elm Street 5: The Dream Child*," *http://www.projectorbooth.com/topics/topic.asp?topic=60* (downloaded August 20, 2002).

72. In Robert Bloch's script for *Strait-Jacket*, which the author wrote for William Castle for a picture starring Joan Crawford, an attempt is made to drive a former murderer insane. In Franklin's sequel Vera Miles' Lila Loomis is just one of the three mothers attempting to dominate and ultimately destroy Norman this second time around.

73. Williams, 1997: 33.

74. Newman, Kim. "Larry Cohen: Stuff 'n' Nonsense," *Shock Xpress*, vol. 1, no. 5, August/September 1986, p. 8.
75. Spelling, Ian. "Scripting a Fresh Cut," *Fangoria* 211, April 2002, p. 33.
76. Lee, Patrick. "Director Joe Berlinger Casts a New Spell in *Blair Witch 2*," *http://www.scifi.com/sfw/issue183/interview.html* (downloaded January 10, 2005).
77. Kaufman, Anthony. "Interview: Battling the Blair Witch, Joe Berlinger Takes on Sequels and Studio with Book of Shadows," *http://www.indiewire.com/people/int_Berlinger_Joe_001024.html* (downloaded January 10, 2005).
78. Fischer, Paul. "Interview: Brice Sinofsky and Joe Berlinger: Metallica; Some Kind of Monster," *http://www.darkhorizons.com/news04/metallica.php* (downloaded: January 10, 2005).
79. Aloi, Peg. "Interview with Joe Berlinger: Director and Co-writer, *Book of Shadows: Blair Witch 2*," *http://www.witchvox.com/va/dt_va.html?a=usma&c=media&id=3052* (downloaded January 10, 2005).
80. The financial success of Sholder's *Elm Street* sequel convinced *Sleepaway Camp 2* and *3* director Simpson, and *Bride of Chucky*'s Ronny Yu, that "the teen horror genre was already in danger of becoming a parody of itself." As such, they created their sequels to be "as much a parody of the horror genre itself as a continuation of the" first film. Hayes, Jeff. "Twice Red: An Interview with Michael J. Simpson, Part 1," *http://www.angelfire.com/retro/scfilms/interview_simpson.html* (downloaded November 11, 2002).
81. Dobson, Dale. "Slings and Arrows: An Interview with Joe Berlinger," *http://www.digitallyobsessed.com/showinterview.php3?ID=14* (downloaded January 10, 2005).
82. Ibid.
83. Ibid.
84. Fischer, Paul. "Interview: Brice Sinofsky and Joe Berlinger: Metallica; Some Kind of Monster," *http://www.darkhorizons.com/news04/metallica.php* (downloaded January 10, 2005).
85. According to Fincher, the surgical strike followed the arrival of official "hatchet-man" Jon Landau, who was charged with monitoring progress on the London-based shoot. After a series of escalating confrontations, Landau, on the authority of studio head Joe Roth, decided that it was "more cost-effective to cut the film and then see exactly what was needed" before recommencing the shoot, albeit this time in L.A. under even tighter supervision. Richardson, John H. "Mother from Another Planet," *Premier*, May 1992, p. 70.
86. Ibid.
87. Ibid.
88. Smith, Adam. "Taming the Beast: The Making of the *Alien* Saga," *Empire*, issue 161, November 2002, p. 169.
89. Fischer, Paul. "Interview: Brice Sinofsky and Joe Berlinger: Metallica; Some Kind of Monster," *http://www.darkhorizons.com/news04/metallica.php* (downloaded January 10, 2005).
90. O'Brien, 2001: 105.
91. Ibid. One such shot was a close-up of Raspail's head.
92. Peter Medak, *Species 2* DVD commentary.
93. Ibid.
94. Flynn, Gillian. "Set Visit: *Blair Witch 2*," *Entertainment Weekly*, May 7, 2004. *http://jeffreydonovanfans.com/articles/ewblairwitch.html* (downloaded January 10, 2005).
95. Joe Berlinger, *Blair Witch 2: Book of Shadows* DVD commentary.
96. Ibid.
97. Rather than have Ripley resigned to her final leap of faith, Fincher was forced to incorporate a climactic and crowd-pleasing chest-bursting shot of the Alien Queen as Ripley fell into the furnace. However, both Fincher and Weaver were nevertheless determined to make this violent and bloody explosion from the actress' chest a tender rather than brutal moment of self-sacrifice.
98. Along with *Psycho II*, fourth entries in the *Halloween* and *Friday the 13th* sagas proved particularly effective.
99. Koetting, Christopher. "Speak of the Devil," *Fangoria* 180, March 1999, p. 72.
100. Joe Berlinger, *Blair Witch 2: Book of Shadows* DVD commentary.
101. The title was ironic in that it was intended to simultaneously challenge peoples' stereotypes of witches and refer to the dark side of the character's personalities and subconscious.
102. *Hannibal*'s uncomplicated route to an R-rating was attributed to its status as a big-budget, high-profile studio release rather than Scott's handling of bowel slashing and brain surgery.
103. Fincher, who had "always wanted [*Alien 3*] to be more graphically violent," subsequently regretted the way in which "a lot of stuff also got cut because of censors." Burman, Mark. "David Fincher's Alienation," *Starburst*, vol. 15, no. 8, April 1993, p. 15.
104. Nevertheless, Hopkins' film featured one of the franchise's most graphic dream sequences, in which Freddy force feeds the eating-disordered Greta her own innards. This footage, along with Dan's Cronenbergian fusion of man and machine, was highlighted by the MPAA as problematic. Shapiro, Marc. "Stephen Hopkins: An Englishman on Elm Street," *Gorezone* 10, November 1989, p. 46.
105. Shapiro, Marc. "*Predator 2* Stalks the

Urban Jungle," *Fangoria* 99, December 1990, p. 40.

106. From a background that included working for Hammer films, *Species II* director Medak was a noteworthy exception, since the director embraced his film's status as a horror sequel and left any such attempts at re-branding in the hands of the studio.

107. Kaufman, Anthony. "Interview: Battling the Blair Witch, Joe Berlinger Takes on Sequels and Studio with Book of Shadows," *http://www.indiewire.com/people/int_Berlinger_Joe_001024.html* (downloaded January 10, 2005).

108. Artisan's campaign involved an onslaught of posters, trailers, books and other tie-ins, coupled with a Sci-fi Channel mock investigative report focusing on Donovan's character Jeff that was supported by a 64-hour "webfest" to at least guarantee a strong opening weekend.

109. Ibid.

110. Paramount's misleading yet canny titling and publicity of Hedden's *Friday the 13th Part VIII* is a solid example of this.

111. Talalay had put herself forward to direct *Nightmare 5* but had been passed over.

112. Biodrowski, Steve. "Freddy's Dead," *Cinefantastique*, vol. 22, no. 2, October 1991, p. 10.

113. However, the audience did support the director's logical demand to shoot a scene showing audiences where the Alien had come from, if nothing else. Burman, Mark. "David Fincher's Alienation," *Starburst*, vol. 15, no. 8, April 1993, p. 14.

114. Boorman's *Exorcist II* was afforded the widest release in Warners' cinematic history at that time.

115. Boorman's changes ranged from a reintroduced narration in the opening scenes, to altering the film's climactic scenes in terms of dialogue, story, and structure, to reducing the film's running time by over fifteen minutes.

116. Referred to as *Exorcist III* by Hollywood insiders, Boorman's first attempt at the franchise was finally released in 1988, twenty years after its first appearance. Hanke, 1991: 256.

117. More memorable examples include *The Scooby Doo Project*, *The Erotic Witch Project* and the comedy short *The Blair Bitch Project*, starring Linda Blair.

118. According to box office analyst Tom Borys of ACNielsen EDI, "on average, sequels to $100 million movies drop 40 percent and sequels [to] horror movies drop 45 percent ... you'd expect this to do about $85 million in total." Flynn, Gillian. "Set Visit: *Blair Witch 2*," *Entertainment Weekly*, May 7, 2004, *http://jeffreydonovanfans.com/articles/ewblairwitch.html* (downloaded January 10, 2005).

119. For examples of such comparisons between the two, and the reactions of both critics and audiences, see Schneider, Steven Jay. "A Tale of Two Psychos (Prelude to a Future Reassessment)," *http://www.sensesofcinema.com/contents/00/10/psychos.html* (downloaded June 20, 2002); and Santas, Constantine. "The Remake of *Psycho* (Gus Van Sant, 1998): Creativity or Cinematic Blasphemy?" *http://www.sensesofcinema.com/contents/00/10/psycho.html* (downloaded June 20, 2002).

120. McCabe, 1999: 164.

121. Ibid.

122. Ibid.

123. Fincher's film not only killed off all but one of *Aliens'* surviving characters in its title sequence, but also performed an exploratory autopsy on the deceased Newt later in the film. Thompson, 1998: 106.

124. Burman, Marc. "A Real Horror Show," *The Independent*, August 21, 1992, p. 14.

125. For their 2001 awards ceremony, the organizers behind the Razzies, the antithesis of Hollywood's Academy Awards, introduced the category of "Worst Sequel or Remake," an accolade Berlinger's film walked away with (despite competition from sequels to *Mission Impossible* and *The Flintstones*, and remakes of *The Grinch* and *Get Carter*). Aloi, Peg. "Interview with Joe Berlinger: Director and Co-writer, *Book of Shadows: Blair Witch 2*," *http://www.witchvox.com/va/dt_va.html?a=usma&c=media&id=3052* (downloaded January 10, 2005).

126. However, as estranged executive producers with a vested interest in the success of the franchise and making a third film, the two were reticent to openly criticize the picture prior to or during its release.

127. Dinning, Marc, and Michael O'Neill. "James Cameron Hall of Fame," *Empire* 168, June 2003, p. 112.

128. Interview with William Friedkin, Moviehole, *http://www.moviehole.net/news.php?newsid=649* (downloaded August 24, 2003).

129. Ibid.

130. McCabe, 1999: 165.

131. Lee, Patrick. "Director Joe Berlinger Casts a New Spell in *Blair Witch 2*," *http://www.scifi.com/sfw/issue183/interview.html* (downloaded January 10, 2005).

132. Dempsey, Micheal. "The Return of Jaws," *American Film*, vol. 3, no. 8, June 1978, p. 31.

133. Fischer, Paul. "Interview: Brice Sinofsky and Joe Berlinger: Metallica; Some Kind of Monster," *http://www.darkhorizons.com/news04/metallica.php* (downloaded January 10, 2005).

134. Burman, Mark. "David Fincher's Alienation," *Starburst*, vol. 15, no. 8, April 1993, p. 13.

135. Ibid.

136. Ibid.

137. Brooks, Xan. "Directing Ids Masochism," *The Guardian*, Wednesday April 24, 2002, http://www.guardian.co.uk/arts/story/0,3604,689497,00.html (downloaded September 12, 2003).

138. Vachaud, Laurent. "An Interview with David Fincher: In the Circles of Hell," *Positif*, no. 420, February 1996, p. 83.

139. Jones, Alan. "The Howling Continues..." *Starburst*, vol. 7, no. 6, February 1985, p. 25.

140. Aloi, Peg. "Interview with Joe Berlinger: Director and Co-writer, *Book of Shadows: Blair Witch 2*," http://www.witchvox.com/va/dt_va.html?a=usma&c=media&id=3052 (downloaded January 10, 2005).

141. Fischer, Paul. "Interview: Brice Sinofsky and Joe Berlinger: Metallica; Some Kind of Monster," http://www.darkhorizons.com/news04/metallica.php (downloaded January 10, 2005).

142. Some outsiders were contractually obliged to make at least two sequels in quick succession, with Simpson's *Sleepaway Camp 2* and *3*, and Christina Douguay's *Scanners* sequels being examples.

143. This is just one of the exemplary lines of dialogue from Mora's *Howling III*.

144. Shapiro, Marc. "Monster Invasion: Halloween 8," *Fangoria* 206, September 2001, p. 8.

145. Spence, D. "Interview: Joe Berlinger & Bruce Sinofsky; We Talk to the Directors of the Documentary *Metallica: Some Kind of Monster*," http://filmforce.ign.com/articles/529/529863p1.html (downloaded January 10, 2005).

146. Vachaud, Laurent. "An Interview with David Fincher: In the Circles of Hell," *Positif*, no. 420, February 1996, p. 83.

147. *Gray Matter* is another of Berlinger's investigations into the nature and existence of evil. This time his subject matter begins with the burial of the preserved brains of over seven hundred children murdered at a Nazi "euthanasia" clinic, and continues as the director attempts to track down a man who allegedly participated in these murders.

Chapter 5

1. Crisafulli, Chuck. "*Pumpkinhead II*," *Cinefantastique*, vol. 25, no 3, June 1994, p. 53.

2. An adaptation of H.G. Wells' *The Island of Dr Moreau*.

3. Indeed, Francis later became a multi-award winning cinematographer on such diverse pictures as *Glory*, *The Straight Story* and Scorsese's *Cape Fear* remake.

4. Trimark built their business around sequels to *Warlock* and *Return of the Living Dead*, and Blue Rider bought the sequel rights to *Leprechaun* and *Night of the Demons* before working on the *Children of the Corn* franchise for Dimension.

5. Miramax production executive Greg Spence co-wrote and directed *Children of the Corn IV* and *The Prophecy II*.

6. For a full analysis of Corman's inspirational career, readers should consult his 1990 autobiography, *How I Made a Hundred Movies in Hollywood and Never Lost a Dime*.

7. Kerschner shot *Stakeout on Dope Street* in 1958 whereas Coppola directed *Dementia 13* five years later in 1963.

8. Indeed, they both began as independent distributors and attempted to infiltrate the market through the horror genre. Miramax released its *Halloween/Friday the 13th* clone *The Burning* in 1981, with Bob scripting and Harvey producing, and Shaye wrote the story for Jack Sholder's *Alone in the Dark*.

9. Cameron's role required him to create the first "spaceship with tits." Kenneth Turan, Kenneth. "Interview: James Cameron," *L.A. Times*, August 1991, http://www.terminatorfiles.com/reload.htm?extras/articles/cameron_005.htm (downloaded October 12, 2003).

10. Price relates each of following four stories to an interviewer. The first segment touches on necrophilia, while the second revolves around the secret of eternal life. Burr's third segment combines Browning's *Freaks* with a classic tale of jealousy and revenge, before the film concludes with an alternative take on Stephen King's *Children of the Corn* in a Civil War setting that evoked Burr's student film.

11. *Waxwork II: Lost in Time* featured the same segmented, stylistic approach as the first film, and incorporated classic and contemporary horror images and icons.

12. McDonagh, 1995: 132.

13. Having paid Dante $8,000 for *Piranha*, Corman offered the director the similarly themed *Humanoids from the Deep*, but was rejected in favor of an offer from De Laurentiis to direct a planned *Orca II* for $50,000. Despite the film falling through, Hollywood still had Dante stereotyped, and Universal offered him *Jaws 3*, which at that time was to be a parody of the first two films entitled *Jaws 3 People 0*.

14. After New World collapsed, the rights to the franchise remained with producer Larry Kuppin, despite Barker's attempts to buy them back. With the remnants of this company forming Trans Atlantic Pictures, the project, along with plans for a *Children of the Corn II*, remained in development. However, Randel's reluctance to "become a total hack" in the wake of script changes led to his being fired one month before shooting, and Hickox was recommended to the producers as an emergency replacement by

special effects artist Bob Keen. Jones, Alan. "Hellraiser III: The Politics of Hell," *Cinefantastique*, vol. 23, no. 2/3, October 1992, p. 21.

15. Having edited, restructured and re-shot many films prior to U.S. distribution, Harvey Weinstein earned this cinematic nickname within the industry.

16. Scapperotti. Dan. "Stepfather II: Director Jeff Burr Behind the Scenes," *Cinefantastique*, vol. 20, no. 5, May 1990, p. 53.

17. Biskind, 2004: p. 59.

18. Barker felt excluded by the film's producers throughout the creative process but was approached by Kuppin to offer feedback and endorse Hickox's film in exchange for money. Reluctant to do so, having witnessed "the same old Hickox stew," Barker declined the offer until Miramax, who had purchased the film for distribution, approached him with a better deal. Jones, Alan. "*Hellraiser III* and Me," *Shivers* 3, p. 26.

19. Ibid.

20. After removing almost three minutes of gore footage from the film, Miramax was informed that the character's image was too controversial for the marketing campaign, and Pinhead was effectively banned from the film's poster—despite Miramax's attempts to have the decision overturned. More recently, the MPAA banned Lions Gate's poster for *Saw II*.

21. After being fired during production and replaced by Assonitis, Cameron's name was to remain on the picture for contractual reasons, compelling the first time filmmaker to fly to Rome and confront the executive producer.

22. Richardson, John H. "Iron Jim," *Premier*, August 1994, *http://www.terminatorfiles.com/reload.htm?extras/articles/cameron_005.htm* (downloaded November 26, 2004).

23. Similarly, Artisan approached *Nightmare 2*'s Jack Sholder for their direct-to-video sequel to *Wishmaster*.

24. Harlin had previously worked with the actor on Warners' *Deep Blue Sea*, affectionately known in the industry as *Jurassic Shark*—a film whose ending was rewritten digitally to kill of Saffron Burrows' character after unfavorable test screening responses.

25. Bernhard was reportedly under-whelmed by the footage he was seeing and frustrated by the way in which his feedback was disregarded.

26. Koetting, Christopher. "Speak of the Devil," *Fangoria*, issue 180, p. 69.

27. Burr, Jeff. "The Shocking Truth" documentary, *Texas Chain Saw Massacre* Special Edition DVD.

28. According to the director, he had "some pretty well respected people in Hollywood say: 'This is career suicide, don't do it. If your film is good, they'll attribute it to the first film, and if your film is bad, it'll always be negatively compared to the first film.'" Wootton, Adrian. "Interview: James Cameron," *The Guardian*, Sunday April 13, 2003, *http://film.guardian.co.uk/interview/interviewpages/0,6737,942591,00.html* (downloaded November 26, 2004).

29. Cameron was threatened with legal action by Harlan Ellison, who alleged that Cameron's script was based on several of the episodes he had written for *The Outer Limits*. Without the studio's backing, Cameron conceded in an out of court settlement that saw the writer acknowledged in the film's credits.

30. Cameron has since explained in interviews how he sold Hurd the rights for $1 on the condition that she did not make the film without him.

31. Hemdale chairman John Daly believed the final reel should be removed and the film should end on an explosion. Cameron vehemently felt otherwise. In this case, at least, Cameron triumphed and the film was released as intended. This conflict was followed by Orion disappointing the director with their lack of support for the picture in its advertising, and, according to Cameron, in the way that they "treated me like dogshit." Richardson, John H. "Iron Jim," *Premier*, August 1994, *http://www.terminatorfiles.com/reload.htm?extras/articles/cameron_005.htm* (downloaded November 26, 2004).

32. Wootton, Adrian. "Interview: James Cameron," *The Guardian*, Sunday April 13, 2003, *http://film.guardian.co.uk/interview/interviewpages/0,6737,942591,00.html* (downloaded November 26, 2004).

33. Ibid.

34. Sammon, Paul M. (ed). *Aliens: The Complete Illustrated Screenplay*. London: Orion, 2001, p. 12.

35. More notable examples include *The Texas Chain Saw Massacre*, *The Amityville Horror* and *The Hills Have Eyes*.

36. Biodrowski, Steve. "*Psycho IV*," *Cinefantastique*, vol. 21, no. 3, December 1990, p. 46.

37. Wootton, Adrian. "Interview: James Cameron," *The Guardian*, Sunday April 13, 2003, *http://film.guardian.co.uk/interview/interviewpages/0,6737,942591,00.html* (downloaded November 26, 2004).

38. Jones, Alan. "Harvey Bernhard's Omens," *Starburst* vol. 14, no. 3, November 1991, p. 30.

39. Apparently this is "a right he's always felt compelled to exercise ever since he invented and developed the whole Vegas lounge act institution in the fifties." Ibid.

40. Although good-looking teens are a mandatory selling point for many sequels, *Freddy vs. Jason* and *Halloween: H20* also featured performances from established music stars Kelly Rowland and LL Cool J, respectively.

41. In many respects, such a concept could be

considered a missed opportunity in terms of an alternative approach to the franchise.

42. Halloweenmovies.com. "Interview: Moustapha Akkad," http://www.halloweenmovies.com/site/interview_ma.htm (downloaded December 12, 2002).

43. Halloweenmovies.com. "Interview: Jamie Lee Curtis," http://www.halloweenmovies.com/site/interview_jlc.htm (downloaded December 12, 2002).

44. Ibid.

45. As the screenwriter of Hitchcock's *Psycho*, Stefano publicly derided previous sequels and only consented to returning so long as he could expand the prequel elements in keeping with his own interpretation.

46. Sammon, 2001: 12.

47. In addition to the studio's approach to the *Hellraiser* franchise, Bob Weinstein directed *The Stepfather III*'s Magar to use *The Shining* as a template for *Children of the Corn: Revelation*.

48. Jeff Burr, *Leatherface: The Texas Chainsaw Massacre III* DVD commentary.

49. George Lucas also expressed a sentiment in the same vein, which highlighted the apparent cinematic snobbery of some crewmembers within the British film industry, as a result of his negative experiences directing *Star Wars* at Pinewood almost ten years previous to Cameron's conflicts. Richardson, John H. "Iron Jim," *Premier*, August 1994, http://www.terminatorfiles.com/reload.htm?extras/articles/cameron_005.htm (downloaded November 26, 2004).

50. Paraphrased from an interview with Cameron on the documentary *Alien Evolution*.

51. Burr recalls being fired on a Friday and then rehired late on Sunday night, presumably after New Line were either unable to find a replacement or the producers felt that they had taught the director a valuable lesson. Jeff Burr, "The Saw Is Family: A Documentary," *Leatherface: The Texas Chainsaw Massacre III* DVD.

52. Jeff Burr, *Leatherface: The Texas Chainsaw Massacre III* DVD commentary.

53. Rowe, Michael. "*Jason X*: Kills in Space," *Fangoria* 210, March 2002, p. 46.

54. Although there are no flashbacks, the inclusion of a *Star Trek*-esque "holodeck" allowed the film to pay "homage" to Buechler's *New Blood*. James Isaac. *Jason X* DVD Commentary.

55. Jason's resurrection aptly coincides with a pair of teens copulating—highlighting the unspoken connection that has existed between the two.

56. Sammon, 2001: 18.

57. Ibid, p. 14.

58. Charged with making a clean break from the first film in order to "build a new franchise from the ground up," Hickox directed a teen-orientated follow-up to Miner's *Warlock*.

Biodrowski, Steve. "*Warlock: The Armageddon,*" *Cinefantastique*, vol. 24, no. 3/4, October 1993, p. 120.

59. Ibid. Burr and New Line came under attack from *Leatherface* screenwriter David J. Schow in the pages of *Fangoria* 88 and 89.

60. The line of dialogue in which Cook exclaims that the "Saw is family" appeared in Schow's script as an inscription on the infamous Chainsaw.

61. McCarty, 1990: 151.

62. Hanke, 1991: 268.

63. Savlov, Marc. "The Texas Chainsaw Massacre," *The Austin Chronicle*, November 2, 1998, http://www.filmvault.com/filmvault/austin/t/texaschainsawmass4.html (downloaded January 6, 2003).

64. Hasted, Nick. "What a Carve Up," *The Guardian*, September 28, 2001, http://film.guardian.co.uk/features/featurepages/0,4120,55 9120,00.html (downloaded January 27, 2003).

65. Warren, Bill. "Into the Death Tank with Leatherface," *Gorezone* 11, January 1990, p. 19.

66. Playing on the popular notion of a Prozac Nation, *Freddy vs. Jason* re-emphasized Freddy's history as a lynch-mobbed pederast and child killer, and depicts the dream demon indulging in scenes of rape, incest and necrophilia. Shrouded in a *Candyman*-esque conceit, whereby he must be feared and believed in order to exist, Krueger continues his penchant for surreal transformations and disguises. A similarly vengeful Jason is depicted as the emotionally damaged and disfigured mother's boy who is bullied by his peers and tragically drowned as a direct result of neglect.

67. Designed solely to place the film—and Freddy's motivation—within the context of the *Elm Street* franchise, Yu's introductory prologue also encapsulated the essence of the *Friday the 13th* franchise by allowing a machete-wielding Jason to stalk and slash an attractive bare-breasted girl through the woods at Camp Crystal Lake.

68. Halloweenmovies.com. "Interview: Steve Miner," http://www.halloweenmovies.com/site/lobby.html (downloaded September 12, 2003).

69. The final exorcism featured elaborate versions of the spider-walk sequence, special make-up effects, Mercedes MacCambridge's vocal effects and sexual dialogue.

70. By focusing on Norman's internal struggle and the potential for redemption, Garris wove the past and present together in a pair of parallel narratives exploring the nature vs. nurture debate. By bringing back Dr. Richmond, and lacing the script with dialogue and imagery that marked the first film, Stefano's script was a nostalgic look through the *Psycho* family album.

71. Yu, on the other hand, was vindicated by the *Freddy vs. Jason* test-screening process, in that

audiences rejected the level of human backstory, with the film pared down accordingly.

72. Ferrante, Anthony C. "Director of the Dead," *Fangoria* 128, November 1993, p. 53.

73. As in previous cases, MPAA head Heffner referred to such charges as "bullshit ... foolishness" and merely a variation on "the same old garbage I've heard before." Gire, Dann. "*Texas Chainsaw Massacre III*," *Cinefantastique*, vol. 20, no. 4, March 1990, p. 14.

74. Since *Leatherface*'s battle with the ratings board, rules have been changed to prevent multiple resubmissions within a set time frame.

75. Isaac's *Jason X* switched from backwoods slasher film to action-orientated sci-fi, and Yu's *Freddy vs. Jason* became a comic book fantasy for the video-gaming generation.

76. Jeff Burr, *Leatherface: The Texas Chainsaw Massacre III* DVD commentary.

77. In a somewhat unprecedented move for a studio executive, De Luca has since declared that it was he, and New Line, who "fucked it up." Goldstein, Patricia. "The Rise of Mike De Luca," *Premier*, December 1994, p. 119.

78. Jeff Burr, "The Saw Is Family" documentary, *Texas Chainsaw Massacre III* DVD.

79. Jeff Burr, "The Shocking Truth" documentary, *Texas Chainsaw Massacre* Special Edition DVD.

80. Diabolical Dominion. "Interview: Jim Isaac," http://www.diabolical-dominion.com/Interviews/Isaac/ (downloaded January 20, 2003).

81. Jeff Burr, *Leatherface: The Texas Chainsaw Massacre III* DVD commentary.

82. Jeff Burr, "The Saw Is Family" documentary, *Texas Chainsaw Massacre III* DVD.

83. Ibid.

84. The film was marketed as giving audiences the chance to decide the character's fate. Despite publicizing such a gimmick, Castle had confidently shot only one ending to his film, one in which the character died.

85. This was done with regard to charges of exploitation and dishonesty. Harlin also expressed regret over the film's over-reliance on standard genre clichés, elaborate make-up effects sequences and appallingly inadequate C.G.I.

86. The unexpected success of *Halloween H20* allowed Miner to explore *Tremors* territory and expand his subgenre resume with *Lake Placid*, an affectionate monster of a B movie with a recognizable cast; whereas *Jason X*'s Isaac has recently complete work on Lions Gate's *Skinwalkers*.

87. Having carved out a productive if not prolific niche for himself on account of this, Garris has emerged as one of the key figures in horror — particularly as the driving force behind the *Masters of Horror* format and key contributor to *Nightmares and Dreamscapes*.

88. Richard Governor eventually directed the film.

89. In the wake of bankruptcy proceedings involving DEG and Atlantic, associate producer Jed Weintrob was developing a sequel.

90. In this respect Burr described it as being "tightly constructed, lean, mean and with no frills." Bacal, Simon. "*Pumpkinhead II*," *Shivers*, no. 12, May 1994, p. 10.

91. Ibid.

92. Bernardi began his career as a co-producer on Carpenter's eighties films and the *Halloween* sequels before moving on to the *Amityville* and *Poltergeist* franchises over the past fifteen years. Since his work with Burr on *The Night of the Scarecrow*, Bernardi has infiltrated the mainstream as producer of Disney's *Haunted Mansion*.

93. According to Burr, *Spoiler* was the third of three movies shot back to back, the others being *Convict 762* and *Absolution*. Bailey, Keith. "*Spoiler*: Review," http://www.badmovieplanet.com/unknownmovies/reviews/rev107.html (downloaded September 18, 2003).

94. "I want the credit A JEFF BURR FILM to mean something. My personal theory is that credit is deserved if you have total creative control on the movie ... from script development to final cut. I have had that on three movies, and they are the ones with that credit for me. Another thought is that ... would the movie exist without you? These are my guidelines, and I made [it] clear in my contracts that they CAN'T say it's a JEFF BURR MOVIE unless I have those stipulations." Weinberg, Scott. "SXSW Pre-Production: Straight Into Darkness Director Jeff Burr," http://www.efilmcritic.com/feature.php?feature=1048 (downloaded January 2, 2005).

Conclusions

1. Cronenberg is keen to point out that such an attitude and approach is far from negative but characteristic of the industry in that "you can make a good movie from anything." Indeed, *A History of Violence* was a critical success and nominated for the Academy's Best Adapted Screenplay award. Michael Rowe. "A History of Violence Lesson," *Fangoria*, 247, October 2005, p. 75–79, 98.

2. Simon Bacal. "The House of Sean S. Cunningham," *Starburst*, vol. 14, no 3, November 1991, p. 16–18 (p18).

3. McCabe, 1999, 164

4. Marc Burman. "A Real Horror Show," *The Independent*, August 21, 1992, p. 14.

5. From *Jurassic Park, Indiana Jones, Star Wars* and *The Godfather* through to the *Back to the Future* and *Lethal Weapon* series, mainstream

directors have equally exploited successful first films.

6. Cronenberg has however remade *The Fly* and in many ways provided subsequent directors with a superior example in his attitude, approach and final outcome.

7. Italian for yellow, these early works of detective fiction with Gothic overtones clearly evoked the work of Sir Arthur Conan Doyle and Edgar Allan Poe. First appearing in literary form in 1929, its cinematic counterpart arguably did not appear until 1963 with Mario Bava's *The Girl Who Knew Too Much*. For a brief introduction to the Giallo see Gary Needham, "Playing with Genre: An Introduction to the Italian Giallo," http://www.kinoeye.org/02/11/needham11.php (Downloaded: 15/03/05).

8. Most recently, Universal saw fit to release Don Mancini's *Seed of Chucky* under their newly created Rogue Pictures banner rather than bring the Universal logo into disrepute or single-handedly face any negative critical backlash to the film.

9. Lussier then went on to direct a pair of back-to-back sequels for the studio in 2003.

10. McDonagh, 1995, p. 89.

11. Michael Beeler. "Clive Barker's Hellraiser IV: Bloodline," *Cinefantastique*, vol. 27, no. 2, November 1995, p. 14–15, (p15).

12. For the opinion of such industry commentators on such a trend see Stuart Jeffries. "Desperation Part 3," *The Guardian: Section 2*, June 23, 1994, p. 11.

13. However, those franchises with a significantly higher budget, profile and potential mainstream appeal were able to afford and attract more established filmmakers from inside and outside the genre with similar promises and incentives as those previously offered to first film directors.

14. In response to such budgetary decreases and differing methods of film distribution, studios and production companies have often cited the unwritten, and recently unsubstantiated law of diminishing returns with regard to any sequel's economic success as the reasoning behind their reluctance to risk increased funds for what was expected to be a reduced return.

15. See Wood. "The American Nightmare: Horror in the 70s." in Jancovich, 2002, p. 25–32.

16. The most recent incarnation of such an approach is evident in Anderson's *Alien Vs Predator* which did not resurrect Schwarznegger's Commando or Weaver's Ripley.

17. According to Craven's publicity pitch, "it's more of a fantasy, an impressionistic thriller." Robb, 1998, p. 69.

18. Barker and Cunningham in particular envisioning an alternative narrative thread which did not feature the iconic rise of either Pinhead or Jason with respect to the *Hellraiser* and *Friday the 13th* series.

19. Steve Biodrowski. "Wes Craven: Alive and Shocking," *Cinefantastique*, vol 22, no 2, October 1991, p. 11.

20. Ibid.

21. Kirby Dick's most recent documentary *This Film is Not Yet Rated* is a belated yet vital beginning of an investigation into the inner workings and alleged double standards of the MPAA. Indeed, it is a worthy cinematic successor to Jonathan Rosenbaum's 2002 text *Movie Wars: How Hollywood and the Media Limit What Movies We Can See*.

22. Just as the *Jaws*, *Friday the 13th* and *Amityville* franchises resurrected the 3-D format and promised finality, others employed such fictional ratings as a V for violence.

23. According to the franchise's website, last year's Blood Drive encouraging audiences to donate blood, and this year 'give 'till it hurts,' collected over 10,000 liters and potentially saved over 30,000 lives. www.saw2.com (Downloaded 12/04/06).

24. Most recently, New Line actively responded to fan sites by increasing the sex, violence and bad language quotient of *Snakes on a Plane*; a B movie with an A list actor destined for a cult following.

25. Tom Shone. "Sharp Act to Follow," *The Sunday Times*, June 28, 1992, p. 10.

26. The format offers director's creative freedom on a relatively low budget/tight schedule and its success has spread into a second season as well as competition from the Stephen King-based *Nightmares and Dreamscapes* anthology series.

27. Kim Newman, "The Pleasures of Horror," *Sight and Sound / The Guardian*, London Film Festival Supplement, p. 16–18 (p16).

28. Boll's despair-inducing filmography includes such adaptations as *House of the Dead*, *Alone in the Dark*, *Bloodrayne* and *In the Name of the King: A Dungeon Siege Tale*.

29. Recent examples of this approach include *The Skeleton Key* and *The Return* starring Kate Hudson and Sarah Michelle Gellar respectively.

30. Lions Gate's role in this 70's revival, and the Hollywood horror franchise, is epitomized by such sequels as *The Devil's Rejects* and *Saw II*.

Bibliography

Andrews, Nigel. *Horror Films.* London: Admiral, 1985.
_____. *Jaws.* London: Bloomsbury, 1999.
Arroyo, Jose (ed.). *Action/Spectacle Cinema: A Sight and Sound Reader.* London: BFI Publishing, 2000.
Barker, Clive. *The Hellbound Heart.* New York: Harper, 1986 and 1991.
Baxter, John. *Steven Spielberg: The Unauthorised Biography.* London: HarperCollins, 1996.
Beard, William. *The Artist as Monster: The Cinema of David Cronenberg.* London: University of Toronto Press, 2001.
Benchley, Peter. *Jaws.* London: Pan Books, 1975.
Benshoff, Harry M. *Monsters in the Closet: Homosexuality and the Horror Film.* Manchester: Manchester University Press, 1997.
Berenstein, R. J. *Attack of the Leading Ladies: Gender and Spectatorship in Classic Horror Cinema.* Columbia: Columbia University Press, 1996.
Bergan, Robert. *Anthony Perkins: A Haunted Life.* London: Little, Brown, 1995.
Biskind, Peter. *Easy Riders, Raging Bulls.* New York: Simon and Schuster, 1998.
_____. *Down and Dirty Pictures: Miramax, Sundance and the Rise of the Independent Film.* London: Bloomsbury, 2004.
Blandford, Steve, Barry Keith Grant and Jim Huillier. *The Film Studies Dictionary.* London: Arnold, 2001.
Blatty, William Peter. *The Exorcist.* New York: Harper and Row, 1971.
_____. *Legion.* Glasgow: Fontana Collins, 1984.
_____. *Before the Exorcist: William Peter Blatty's Own Story of Taking His Novel to Film.* Eye, Suffolk: Screen Press, 1998.
Bliss, Michael. *Brian De Palma.* London: Scarecrow Press, 1983.
_____. *What Goes Around Comes Around: The Films of Jonathan Demme,* Southern Illinois University Press, 1996.
Bloch, Robert. *Psycho.* London: Corgi, 1985.
_____. *Psycho 2.* London: Corgi, 1982.
_____. *Psycho House.* New York: T. Dougherty Associates, 1990.
Bradley, Doug. *Sacred Monsters: Behind the Mask of the Horror Actor.* London: Titan, 1996.
Branston, Gill. *Cinema and Cultural Modernity.* Buckingham and Philadelphia: Open University Press, 2000.
Britton, A. (ed.). *American Nightmares: Essays on the Horror Film.* Toronto: Festival of Festivals, 1979.
Brode, Douglas. *The Films of Steven Spielberg.* New York: Carol, 1995.
Brosnan, John. *Scream.* London: Boxtree, 2000.
Budra, Paul, and Betty R. Schallenberg. *Part Two: Reflections on the Sequel.* Toronto, London: Toronto University Press, 1998.
Bussing, Sabine. *Aliens in the Home: The Child in Horror Fiction.* New York: Greenwood Press, 1987.
Butler, Ivan. *The Cinema of Roman Polanski.* London: A. Zwemmer, 1970.
_____. *Horror in the Cinema.* London: Barnes, 1979.
Carroll, Noel. *The Philosophy of Horror.* New York: Routeledge, 1990.

Caruso, Giacomo. *George A. Romero*. Venezia: Comune di Venezia, 1992.

Clarens, Carlos. *Horror Movies: An Illustrated Survey*. London: Secker and Walburg, 1968.

Clark, Randall. *At a Cinema or Drive-in Near You: The History, Culture and Politics of the American Exploitation Film*. London and New York: Garland, 1995.

Clover, Carol J. *Men, Women and Chainsaws: Gender in the Modern Horror Film*. London: British Film Institute, 1992.

Collins, Michael R. *The Films of Stephen King*. Mercer Island, Washington: Starmont Press, 1986.

Cook, Pam, and Mieke Bernink (eds.). *The Cinema Book (Second Edition)*. London: British Film Institute, 1999.

Cooper, Jeffrey. *The Nightmare on Elm Street Companion*. New York: St. Martin's Press, 1987.

_____. *The Nightmare on Elm Street, Parts 1, 2, 3: The Continuing Story*. London: Futura, 1987.

Coubro, Gerry. *Hammer and Horror: Bad Taste and Popular British Cinema*. Sheffield: Pavic, 1991.

Crane, Jonathan Lake. *Terror and Everyday Life: Singular Moments in the History of the Horror Film*. Thousand Oaks: Sage, 1994.

Creed, Barbara. *The Monstrous-Feminine: Film, Feminism and Psychoanalysis*. London: Routeledge, 1993.

Cumbow, Robert C. *Order in the Universe: The Films of John Carpenter, (Second Edition)*. Lanham, MD, and London: Scarecrow Press, 2000.

Curtis, James. *James Whale: A New World of Gods and Monsters*. Boston and London: Faber and Faber, 1998.

Derry, Charles. *Dark Dreams: A Psychological History of the Horror Film*. New York and London: Barnes and Yoseloff, 1977.

Dettmann, B., and M. Bedford. *The Horror Factory: The Horror Films of Universal 1931–1955*. New York: Gordon Press, 1976.

Dick, Bernard F. *Anatomy of Film*. New York: St. Martin's Press, 1990.

Dika, Vera. *Games of Terror: Halloween, Friday the 13th and Films of the Stalker Cycle*. New Jersey and London: Associated University Press, 1990.

Druxman, Michael B. *One Good Film Deserves Another*. London and New York: Barnes and Yoseloff, 1977.

Dyson, Jeremey. *Bright Darkness: The Lost Art of the Supernatural Horror Film*. London and Washington: Cassell, 1997.

Everson, William K. *More Classics of the Horror Film*. Secaucus, NJ: Citadel Press, 1986.

Fischer, Dennis. *Horror Film Directors 1931–1990*. Jefferson, NC: McFarland, 1991.

Fleischer, Richard. *Just Tell Me When to Cry*. New York: Carroll and Graf, 1993.

Forrest, Jennifer, and Leonard R. Koos (eds.). *Dead Ringers: The Remake in Theory and Practice*. Albany, NY: State University of New York Press, 2002.

Foster, Alan Dean. *Alien 3*. London: Warner, 1992.

Frank, Alan. *Horror Films*. London: Hamlyn, 1977.

_____. *The Films of Roger Corman: Shooting My Way Out of Trouble*. London: Batsford, 1998.

Freeland, Cynthia A. *The Naked and the Undead: Evil and the Appeal of Horror*. Boulder, Colorado, and Oxford: Westview Press, 2000.

Freer, Ian. *The Complete Spielberg*. London: Virgin, 2001.

French, Carl. *Screen Violence*. London: Bloomsbury, 1996.

Gagne, Paul. *The Zombies That Ate Pittsburgh: The Films of George Romero*. New York: Dodd and Mead, 1987.

Gelder, Ken (ed.). *The Horror Reader*. London: Routeledge, 2000.

Goldberg, Lee, Randy L'Officier, and Jean-Marc L'Officier. *The Dreamweavers: Interviews with the Fantasy Filmmakers of the 1980s*. Jefferson, NC: McFarland, 1995.

Golden, Christopher (ed.). *Horror Writers on Horror Film*. New York: Berkeley Books, 1992.

Goldman, William. *Which Lie Did I tell? Or More Adventures in the Screen Trade*. New York: Pantheon, 2000.

Gottlieb, Carl. *The Jaws Log*. New York: Dell, 1975.

Grant, Barry Keith (ed). *The Dread of Difference: Gender and Horror*. Austin, Texas: University of Texas Press, 1996.

_____ (ed). *Planks of Reason: Essays on the Horror Film*. Metuchen, New Jersey: Scarecrow Press, 1984.

Grant, Michael (ed). *The Modern Fantastic: The Films of David Cronenberg*. Trowbridge, Wilts: Flicks Books, 2000.

Gray, Beverley. *Roger Corman: An Unauthorized Biography of the Godfather of Indie Filmmaking*. Los Angeles: Renaissance Books, 2000.

Halbertsam, Judith. *Skin Shows: Gothic Horror and the Technology of Monsters*. Durham,

NC, and London: Duke University Press, 1996.
Hanke, Ken. *A Critical Guide to Horror Film Series*. New York and London: Garland, 1991.
_____. *Tim Burton: An Unauthorised Biography of the Filmmaker*. Los Angeles: Renaissance, 1999.
Hardy, Phil. *Horror Films*. London: Aurum Press, 1986.
Harris, Thomas. *Red Dragon*. London: Corgi, 1991.
_____. *The Silence of the Lambs*. London: Mandarin, 1991.
_____. *Hannibal*. London: Heinemann, 1999.
Hayes, R.M. *3-D Movies: A History and Filmography of Stereoscopic Cinema*. London: St. James Press, 1989.
Hayward, Susan. *Cinema Studies: The Key Concepts (Second Edition)*. London: Routeledge, 2000.
Heard, Christopher. *Dreaming Aloud: The Life and Films of James Cameron*. Toronto: Doubleday Canada, 1997.
Hicken, Mandy E. *Sequels*. London: Association of Assistant Librarians, 1982.
Holsten, Kim R., and Tom Winchester. *Science-Fiction, Fantasy and Horror Film Sequels, Series and Remakes*. Jefferson, NC: McFarland, 1997.
Horsely, Jake (ed.). *The Blood Poets: A Cinema of Savagery 1958–1999, Vol. 2: Millenial Blues*. London: Scarecrow, 1999.
Horton, Andrew, and Stuart Y. McDougal (eds.). *Play It Again, Sam: Retakes on Remakes*. London: University of California Press, 1998.
Howard, Joseph. *Damien: Omen II*. London: Futura, 1990.
Humphries, Reynold. *The American Horror Film: An Introduction*. Edinburgh: Edinburgh University Press, 2002.
Hutchings, Peter. *Hammer and Beyond: The British Horror Film*. Manchester: Manchester University Press, 1993.
Iaccino, James F. *Psychological Interpretations on Cinematic Terror*. Westport, CT, and London: Praeger, 1994.
Jancovich, Mark. *Horror*. London: Batsford, 1992.
_____ (ed,). *Horror: The Film Reader*. London: Routeledge, 2001.
Jaworzyn, Stefan. *The Texas Chainsaw Massacre Companion*. London: Titan, 2003.
_____ (ed.). *Shock Express 2*. London: Titan, 1994.
Jones, Stephen. *Clive Barker's A-Z of Horror*. London: BBC Books, 1997.
_____. *Creepshows: The Illustrated Stephen King Movie Guide*. London: Titan, 2001.
Kagan, Jeremy (ed). *Directors Close-up: Interviews with Directors Nominated for Outstanding Directorial Achievement in a Feature Film by the Directors Guild of America*. Boston and Oxford: Focal Press, 2000.
Kahn, James. *Poltergeist*. London and New York: Granada, 1982.
Katz, Ephraim. *The Macmillan International Film Encyclopedia (Revised by Fred Klein and Ronald Dean Nolan – 3rd Edition)*. London and Basingstoke: Macmillan, 1998.
Kaufman, Lloyd, and James Gunn. *All I Need to Know About Filmmaking I Learned from the Toxic Avenger*. New York: Berkley Boulevard Books, 1998.
Kermode, Mark. *The Exorcist*. London: British Film Institute, 1998.
King, Geoff. *New Hollywood Cinema: An Introduction*. London: I.B. Tauris, 2002.
Leigh, Janet, and Chris Nickens. *Psycho: Behind the Scenes of the Classic Chiller*. New York: Harmony Books, 1995.
Levin, Ira. *Rosemary's Baby*. London: Pan Books, 1968.
_____. *Son of Rosemary*. London and New York: Dutton, 1997.
Limbacher, James L. *Haven't I Seen You Somewhere Before: Remakes, Sequels and Series in Motion Pictures Videos and Television 1896–1990*. Pierian Press, 1979.
Lloyd, Ann. *The Films of Stephen King*. London: Brown Books, 1993.
Loynd, Ray. *The Jaws 2 Log*. New York: Dell, 1978.
McBride, Joseph. *Steven Spielberg*. London: Faber and Faber, 1997.
McCabe, Bob. *The Exorcist: Out of the Shadows*. London: Omnibus, 1999.
McCarty, John. *Splatter Movies: Breaking the Last Taboo off the Screen*. Bromley, Kent: Columbus Books, 1984.
_____. *The Official Splatter Movie Guide*. New York: St. Martin's Press, 1989.
_____. *The Modern Horror Film: 50 Contemporary Classics*. London: Carol, 1990.
_____. *The Fearmakers: The Screens' Directorial Masters of Suspense and Terror*. London: Virgin, 1995.
_____. *The Sleaze Merchants*. New York: St. Martin's Press, 1995.
_____. *Psychos: Eighty Years of Movies, Maniacs and Monstrous Deeds*. New York: St. Martin's Press, 1996.
McDonagh, Maitland. *Filmmaking on the

Fringe: The Good, the Bad, and the Deviant Directors. New York: Carol, 1995.

McDonald, Paul. *The Star System: Hollywood and the Production of Popular Identities.* London: Wallflower, 2000.

Mendix, Xavier (ed.). *Shocking Cinema of the Seventies.* Hereford: Noir, 2002.

Mettler, E., T. Forbes, and A. Ormsby. *Horror.* London: British Film Institute, 1998.

Milberg, Doris. *Repeat Performances: A Guide to Hollywood Movie Remakes.* New York: Broadway Press, 1990.

Morrison, James. *Passport to Hollywood: Hollywood Films, European Directors.* New York: State University of New York Press, 1998.

Muir, John. *Wes Craven: The Art of Horror.* Jefferson, NC, and London: McFarland, 1998.

_____. *The Films of John Carpenter.* Jefferson, NC, and London: McFarland, 2000.

Murdock, Andrew, and Rachel Aberley. *The Making of Alien Resurrection.* London: Titan, 1997.

Naremore, James (ed.). *Film Adaptation.* London: The Athlone Press, 2000.

Nelmes, Jill (ed.). *An Introduction to Film Studies.* London: Routeledge, 1996.

Newman, Howard. *The Exorcist: The Strange Story Behind the Film.* New York: Pinnacle Books, 1974.

Newman, Kim. *Nightmare Movies: A Cultural History of the Horror Film 1968–88.* London: Bloomsbury, 1988.

_____. *The BFI Companion to Horror.* London: Cassell and BFI, 1996.

Nowlan, Robert A., and Gwendolyn W. Nowlan. *Cinema Sequels and Remakes, 1903–1987.* London: McFarland, 1989.

O'Brien, Daniel. *The Hannibal Files.* London: Reynolds and Hearn, 2001.

Pallenberg, Barbara. *The Making of Exorcist II: The Heretic.* New York: Warner, 1977.

Paul, W. *Laughing Screaming: Modern Hollywood Horror and Comedy.* Columbia: Columbia University Press, 1994.

Pinedo, I.C. *Recreational Terror: Women and the Pleasures of Horror Film Viewing.* New York: State University of New York Press, 1997.

Prawer, S. S. *Caligari's Children.* Oxford: Oxford University Press, 1980.

Pye, Michael, and Linda Myles. *The Movie Brats: How the Film Generation Took Over Hollywood.* London: Faber and Faber, 1979.

Quackenbush, Robert. *Movie Monsters and Their Masters: The Birth of the Horror Film.* Chicago: Albert, Whitman, 1980.

Quarles, Mike. *Down and Dirty: Hollywood's Exploitation Filmmakers and Their Motives.* Jefferson, NC: McFarland, 1993.

Rasmussen, Randy Loren. *Children of the Night: The Six Archetypal Characters of Classic Horror Films.* Jefferson, NC: McFarland, 1998.

Ray, Fred Olen: *The New Poverty Row: Independent Filmmakers as Distributors.* Jefferson, NC: McFarland, 1991.

Rebello, Stephen. *Alfred Hitchcock and the Making of Psycho.* New York: Dembner Books, 1990.

Rigby, Jonathan. *English Gothic: A Century of Horror Cinema.* London: Reynolds and Hearn, 2000.

Robb, Brian J. *Screams and Nightmares: The Films of Wes Craven.* London: Titan, 1998.

Rodley, Chris. *Cronenberg on Cronenberg.* London: Faber and Faber, 1993.

Romero, George, and Susan Sparrow. *Dawn of the Dead.* London: Sphere, 1979.

Russo, John. *Return of the Living Dead (Original).* Middlesex, England: Hamlyn, 1979.

_____. *Return of the Living Dead (Film Edition).* London: Arrow Books, 1985.

_____. *The Complete Night of the Living Dead Film Book.* New York: Harmony Books, 1985.

Salisbury, Mark (ed.). *Burton on Burton.* Boston and London: Faber and Faber, 2000.

Sammon, Paul M. *Ridley Scott: The Making of His Movies.* London: Orion, 1999.

_____ (ed.). *Alien: The Complete Illustrated Screenplay.* London: Orion, 2000.

_____ (ed.). *Aliens: The Complete Illustrated Screenplay.* London: Orion, 2001.

Sanello, Frank. *Spielberg: The Man, the Movies, the Mythology.* Dallas: Taylor, 1996.

Schoell, William, and James Spencer. *Stay Out of the Shower: 25 Years of Shocking Films Beginning with Psycho.* New York: Dembner Books, 1985.

_____. *The Nightmare Never Ends: The Official History of Freddy Krueger and the Nightmare on Elm Street Films.* New York: Carol, 1992.

Shapiro. Marc. *James Cameron: An Unauthorized Biography.* Los Angeles, CA: Renaissance Books, 2000.

Sherman, Fraser A. *Cyborgs, Santa Claus and Satan: Science-Fiction, Fantasy and Horror Films Made for Television.* Jefferson, NC, and London: McFarland, 2000.

Silver, A., and J. Ursini (eds.). *Horror Film Reader.* New York: Limelight Editions, 2000.

Simpson, Philip L. *Psychopaths: Tracking the Serial Killer Through Contemporary Fiction and Film*. Illinois: Southern Illinois University Press, 2000.
Singer, Mark. *A Cut Above: 50 Film Directors Talk About Their Craft*. Los Angeles, California: Lone Eagle, 1998.
Skal, D.J. *The Monster Show: A Cultural History of Horror*. New York: Norton, 1993.
Soister, John. *Of Gods and Monsters: A Critical Guide to Universal Studio's Science-Fiction, Horror and Mystery Films*. Jefferson, NC, and London: McFarland, 1999.
Soren, David. *The Rise and Fall of the Horror Film*. Baltimore, MD: Midnight Marquee Press, 1997.
Staiger, Janet. *The Studio System*. New Brunswick, NJ: Rutgers University Press, 1995.
Stell, John. *Psychos, Sickos and Sequels: Horror Films of the 1980s*. Baltimore, MD: Midnight Marquee Press, 1998.
Sternfield, Jonathan. *The Look of Horror: Scary Moments from Scary Movies*. New York: Moore and Moore, 1990.
Stokes, Melvyn, and Richard Maltby (eds.). *Identifying Hollywood's Audiences: Cultural Identity and the Movies*. London: British Film Institute, 1999.
Svehla, Gary J., and Susan Svehla. *Bitches, Bimbos and Virgins: Women in the Horror Film*. Baltimore, MD: Midnight Marquee Press, 1996.
Szulkin, David. *Wes Craven's Last House on the Left: The Making of a Cult Classic*. Surrey: Fab Press, 2000.
Taylor, Philip M. *Steven Spielberg: The Man, His movies, and their Meaning (3rd Expanded Edition)*. London: BT Batsford, 1999.
Thompson, David. *The Alien Quartet*. London: Bloomsbury, 1998.
Timpone, Anthony. *Fangoria's Best Horror Films*. New York: Crescent, 1994.
Tudor, Andrew. *Monsters and Mad Scientists: A Cultural History of the Horror Movie*. London: Blackwell, 1989.
Twitchell, James B. *Dreadful Pleasures: An Anatomy of Modern Horror*. New York and Oxford: Oxford University Press, 1985.
Underwood, Tim. *Stephen King Goes to Hollywood*. New York: New American Library, 1987.
Underwood, Tim, Chuck Miller, and Jeff Conner. *Nightmare Movies: A Critical History of the Horror Film*. New York: New American Library, 1987.
Vincendau, Ginette (ed.). *Film/Literature/Heritage: A Sight and Sound Reader*. London: BFI Publishing, 2001.
Von Gunden, Kenneth. *Postmodern Auteurs: Coppola, Lucas, De Palma, Spielberg and Scorsese*. Jefferson, NC, and London: McFarland, 1991.
Waller, G. A (ed.). *American Horrors: Essays on the Modern American Horror Film*. Illinois: Illinois University Press, 1987.
Warren, Bill. *Set Visits: Interviews with 32 Horror and Science Fiction Filmmakers*. Jefferson, NC, and London: McFarland, 1997.
_____. *The Evil Dead Companion*. London: Titan, 2000.
Weaver, James, and Ron Tanborini. *Horror Films: Current Research on Audience Preferences and Reactions*. Mahwah, NJ: Lawrence Erlbaum, 1995.
Weaver, Tom. *Attack of the Monster Movie Makers: Interviews with 20 Genre Giants*. Jefferson, NC: McFarland, 1994.
Wells, Paul. *The Horror Genre: From Beelzebub to Blair Witch*. London: Wallflower, 2000.
Westfahl, G., and G. Slusser. *Nursery Realms: Children in the World of Science-Fiction, Fantasy and Horror*. Georgia: University of Georgia Press, 1999.
Wexman, Virginia Wright. *Roman Polanski*. Boston: Twayne Publishers, 1985.
Williams, Tony. *Hearths of Darkness: The Family in the American Horror Film*. New Jersey: Associated University Press, 1996.
_____. *Larry Cohen: The Radical Allegories of an Independent Filmmaker*. Jefferson, NC: McFarland, 1997.
_____. *The Cinema of George A. Romero*. Columbia: Columbia University Press, 2003.
Winecoff, Charles. *Split Image: The Life of Anthony Perkins*. New York: Dutton, 1996.
Wolf, Leonard. *Horror: A Connoisseur's Guide to Literature and Film*. New York and Oxford: Facts on File, 1989.
Wood, Robin. *Hollywood from Vietnam to Reagan*. New York and Surrey: Columbia University Press, 1986.

Index

Abbott and Costello 14, 132
Abernathy, Lewis 70
Absolution 244
The Abyss 95, 118, 151
Academy Awards 79, 82, 90, 92, 130, 134, 161, 227, 232–234, 237
Ackerman, Forrest J 78
Adaptation, literary 12–17, 19, 33, 49, 62–63, 74, 83, 90, 92–95, 114, 117, 125, 151–152, 159–161, 175, 220, 222, 229–230, 234, 237, 240
Affleck, Ben 71
Aja, Alexandre 71, 163
Akkad, Malek 144, 153, 163
Akkad, Moustapha 62
Alfred Hitchcock Presents 222
Alice 232
Alien 81–2, 108, 111, 126, 141, 145–146, 149, 225, 230
Alien 3 105, 107, 110–111, 114, 118–121, 126–128, 130, 158, 170, 239–240
Alien Nation 141
Alien Resurrection 108, 110–111, 114, 116, 127, 238
Alien vs. Predator 48, 223, 245
Aliens 95, 114, 126, 141–147, 149, 151, 233, 242–243
Alive Films 63, 230
Allen, David 83, 232
Alone in the Dark (1982) 59, 136, 241
Alone in the Dark (2005) 245
Alternative endings 17, 30, 42, 45, 53, 56, 66, 90–91, 96, 98–100, 102, 120, 125, 149, 169–170, 177, 227–228, 232, 239, 242–244
Alves, Joe 100, 232
Amazing Stories 79, 136, 152
Amelie 130
American Dream 147
American Film Market 32

American International Pictures 14–15, 30, 133, 135
American Psycho 8
American Psycho 2 112, 117, 222
An American Werewolf in London 82, 225
The Amityville Horror (1979) 234, 246
The Amityville Horror (2005) 21, 242
Amityville II: The Possession 1, 19, 116, 229
Amityville 3-D 236, 245
Amityville 4: The Evil Escapes 232, 235
Anderson, Paul W. S. 246
Andrews, Virginia 63
Anson, Jay 234
April Fool's Day 62
Arachnophobia 166
Argento, Dario 2, 160
Army of Darkness 36, 39, 44–6, 227
Arnold, Jack 14, 44, 225
Arquette, Patricia 61
Artisan 105–106, 109–113, 115, 118–119, 121, 123, 129, 231, 240, 242
Assonitis, Ovido G. 137, 242
Atkins, Peter 42, 84, 139, 234
Avco-Embassy 30, 58, 224
Avery, Roger 47, 227
Audiences, influence and role of 24, 40, 43, 45–46, 48, 59, 73, 86, 120, 126–127, 131, 148, 151, 168, 170, 174, 176, 220, 240, 246
Auteur criticism 6, 21–23, 56–58, 134, 158–160, 223

Back to the Future 246
Back to the Future Part II 231
Back to the Future Part III 45
Bad Taste 141, 237
Baker, Graham 107
Baker, Rick 82, 233
Baker, Roy Ward 133, 136
Baldwin, Michael A. 226

253

Index

Ballard, J.G. 160
Band, Charles 18, 82, 152, 154–156, 162, 230
Barker, Clive 2, 13, 42, 72, 84, 93, 95, 105, 114, 139, 162–163, 170, 175–176, 230, 241–242, 245
Basic Instinct 2 33
Basket Case 30, 32, 159
Basket Case 2 38, 42, 225
Basket Case 3: The Progeny 46–7, 227
Bates Motel 222
Batman Forever 226
Batman Returns 37, 225
Battle Beyond the Stars 134, 241
Bava, Mario 14, 52, 245
Bay, Michael 21
The Beast 95
The Beast from 20,000 Fathoms 79
The Beast Within 236
The Beastmaster 33–4, 225
Beebe, Dick 112
Beetlejuice 61
Benchley, Peter 15, 95
Bender, Jack 107, 115
Benson, Kevin 229
Bergman, Ingmar 51
Berlinger, Joe 24, 105–6, 109–121, 123–128, 130–131, 168, 237, 240
Bernardi, Barry 154, 244
Bernhard, Harvey 107, 111, 121, 140, 142–143, 163, 242
Beutel, Jonathan 141
Beyond Re-Animator 77
The Birds 17, 232
The Birds II: Land's End 142, 153, 222
Black Christmas 224
Blacula 68
Blade 95
Blade II 108, 116, 176
Blade Runner 235
Blade: The Series 222
Blade: Trinity 93, 162, 232, 236
Blair, Linda 101, 110, 240
The Blair Bitch Project 240
The Blair Witch Project 29, 30, 105–06, 173, 224, 228, 236–237
Blatty, William Peter 24, 78, 84, 89–96, 98–101, 162, 226, 234
The Blob (1958) 78
Bloch, Robert 19, 73, 89, 94, 222, 235, 238
Blood Feast 15, 79
Blood Feast 2: All U Can Eat 36
Bloodrayne 245
The Blue Iguana 93
Blue Rider Pictures 133, 240
Blythe, David 231
Body Bags 64
Body Horror 160
Bogdanovich, Peter 134
Bohem, Leslie 238
Bokencamp, Jon 238
Boll, Uwe 176, 245
Boogeyman 232
Book of Shadows: Blair Witch 2 24, 105–06, 109–121, 123–128, 168, 239, 240
Boorman, John 17, 92–4, 102, 105, 108, 110, 124–125, 127, 130–131, 168, 237–238, 240
Bota, Rick 231
Bottin, Rob 82, 141
The Boy with X-Ray Eyes 154
Boyle, Danny 69
Brainscan 64, 230
Brandner, Gary 16, 129
Brando, Marlon 233
Brandywine Productions 145
The Breed 231
Bride of Chucky 95, 108, 111, 239
The Bride of Frankenstein 5, 13, 34
Bride of Re-Animator 77
The Bride with White Hair 237
Broadstreet, Jeff 233
Brooks, Mel 82, 92, 234
Brother's Keeper 109
Browning, Tod 132, 241
Bubba Ho-Tep 49, 175
Bubba Nosferatu 175
Buechler, John Carl 83, 85, 87–8, 232, 234, 243
Bug 107
The Burning 241
Burr, Jeff 25, 132–134, 136–154, 168, 240, 243–244
Burr, William 136–137
Burroughs, William S. 160
Burrows, Saffron 224
Burton, Tim 37, 226, 234
Buyer's remorse 37–38, 102–103, 117–118

Cabal 230
Cable, rise of 20
Cahiers du Cinéma 22
Cameron, James 82, 114, 126–127, 133–139, 141–147, 149, 151, 154, 156, 158, 168, 226, 241–243
Campbell, Bruce 35, 39, 49, 224
Candyman 17, 243
Candyman 2: Farewell to the Flesh 121, 130, 236
Cannes Film Festival 32
Cannibal Holocaust 106
Cannibalism of genres and films 17–19, 29, 51, 63, 66, 72–73, 105, 115–116, 120, 145–146, 149, 154, 165, 176, 238, 243
Cannon 38, 150, 229
Cape Fear 241
Carnival of Souls (1998) 71
Carnosaur 18
Carpenter, John 28, 32, 51–2, 55, 58, 62–5, 67, 70, 76, 82, 95, 119, 140, 148, 153, 162, 175, 176, 224, 228–231, 235
Carrie (1976 film) 17, 56–7, 233
Carrie (novel) 222
Casablanca 90

Index

Cast control 40, 68, 71, 89, 96–98, 110, 136–138, 144, 165–166, 176, 225, 237–238
Castle, William 14–15, 30, 79, 151, 173, 233, 238, 244
Castle of Frankenstein 79
Cat People 237
Cellar Dweller 233
Chaney, Lon 78, 232
The Changeling 237
Chappelle, Joe 87
Chase, Chevy 68
Chaskin, David 59
Cherry Falls 231
Chicago 130
Chicago Sun-Times 32
Children of the Corn 20, 241
Children of the Corn II 241
Children of the Corn IV 140, 238, 241
Children of the Corn: Revelation 243
Children of the Living Dead 86, 234
Children Shouldn't Play with Dead Things 19, 233
Child's Play 2, 95, 222, 235
Child's Play 2 83, 93, 222, 225–226, 232
Child's Play 3 107, 115, 121, 226, 236
Christine 229
C.H.U.D. 166
Cinéfantastique 5
Citizen Kane 79
The City of Lost Children 236
Clark, Bob 19, 224
Clash of the Titans 1, 79
Classification and Ratings Administration (CARA) 41, 171
Cleopatra 232
Close Encounters of the Third Kind 235
Clover, Carol J. 7–9, 29, 84
Coen, Joel and Ethan 33
Cohen, Larry 20, 34, 43–4, 95, 109, 112, 116, 159, 225
Columbia Pictures 30, 86
Comic book adaptations 53, 235
Compass International 224
The Complete Night of the Living Dead Filmbook 94
Conan Doyle, Sir Arthur 220, 245
Conan the Barbarian 33
Condon, Bill 121, 130, 236
Conflict, source of 29–30
Continental Films 83, 224
Convict 762 244
Coppola, Francis Ford 23, 38, 72, 114, 134, 158, 241
Corman, Roger 14–15, 18, 68, 133–137, 156, 162, 176, 240
Corolco 95
Coscarelli, Don 10, 24, 27–51, 53, 55, 62, 152, 156, 160–161, 170, 175–176, 225
Coto, Manny 230
Craven, Jonathan 231
Craven, Wes 2, 17, 20, 24, 29, 48, 51–75, 93, 127, 159, 160, 162, 165–166, 171, 175–176, 219, 227–228, 231–233, 245
Crawford, Joan 238
The Crazies 225
Creative control: increased 36–37, 63, 65–66, 73, 84, 89, 108, 112, 130, 155, 169; reduced 36, 55–58, 68, 84–85, 98–100, 164, 169
The Creature 95
Creature Features 14
Creature from the Black Lagoon 14, 78, 225
The Creature Walks Among Us 44
Creepshow 1, 136, 224
Creepshow 2 83
Crichton, Michael 18
Crimes of Passion 93
Crimewave 33
Critics, role of 30, 32, 53, 66, 72–3, 79, 124–126, 128, 168, 173, 224
Critters 2 136
Cronenberg, David 5, 20, 33, 82, 136, 157, 159, 231, 233, 239, 245
Crown International 238
Cruise, Tom 222
Cunningham, Sean S. 5, 29, 51–2, 55–7, 63–5, 70, 76, 141, 146, 157, 162–163, 170, 175, 224, 227–228, 230, 236, 245
Curse of Frankenstein 14
Cursed 74, 232
Curtis, Jamie Lee 69, 100, 110, 140, 144, 153, 167, 229, 230

Daly, John 242
Damiani, Damiano 19, 229
Damien: Omen II 120, 140, 231, 236, 242
Damon, Matt 71
Dante, Joe 1, 8, 15, 17, 33, 37–8, 74, 76, 137, 225, 231, 241
Darabont, Frank 60
The Dark Half (film) 83
The Dark Half (novel) 66, 230
Darkness 232
Davenport, Harry Bromley 28, 223
David, Pierre 231
Davis, Wade 62
Dawn of the Dead (1978) 29, 34, 36, 40, 80–81, 94, 144
Dawn of the Dead (2004) 223, 227, 236
Day of the Dead (1985) 2, 45, 159, 227
Day of the Dead (2007) 89
Dead of Night 232
Deadly Blessing 53
Deadly Friend 60, 74, 229
DeCoteau, David 83
Deep Blue Sea 242
DEG (De Laurentiis Entertainment Group) 19, 42, 226
De Haven, Carter 98
De Laurentiis, Dino 33–5, 44, 58, 93, 108, 237, 241
Delicatessen 236

256 Index

Deliverance 17
Del Toro, Guillermo 108, 116, 176
De Luca, Mike 150, 244
Dementia 13 241
Demme, Jonathan 119, 125, 134, 174
Demolition Man 154
Demons 5, Exorcists 0: A Fable 101
The Dentist 152
Deodato, Ruggero 29
De Palma, Brian 17, 57
Deranged 233
Derrickson, Scott 112, 115, 127, 129–130
The Descent 177
Desperation 152
The Devil's Den 156
The Devil's Rejects 245
DeVito, Danny 37
Les Diaboliques 14
Diary of the Dead 159
Dick, Kirby 245
Die Hard 2 118
Dimension Films 20, 21, 68, 71, 74, 117, 133–134, 139, 145, 162, 164, 223, 230–232, 241
The Dinosaur and the Missing Link: A Prehistoric Tragedy 78
Direct to Video/DVD 20, 44, 117, 142, 151, 153, 164, 222, 242
Director's commentary 6, 129, 151, 177
Director's cut 95, 102–103, 129, 151, 235, 240
Directors' Guild of America (DGA) 54, 58, 73, 87, 107, 150, 228, 237
The Dirty Dozen 116
Disney 152, 228, 244
Distribution, changes in 18, 30, 52, 73, 224
Divided We Fall 134
Dr. Giggles 64, 230
Documentary: filmmaking 6, 109, 130–131, 155, 240; style 66, 116
Dog Soldiers 74, 225, 232
Dog Soldiers: Fresh Meat 232
Dominion: Prequel to the Exorcist 102–103, 112, 117, 127, 129, 140, 151, 238
Donner, Richard 38, 79, 158
Donovan, Jeffrey 113, 240
Don't Look Down 71
The Dorm That Dripped Blood 231
Douguay, Christian 240
Dourif, Brad 98–9, 235
Dracula (1931) 11, 13
Dracula Has Risen from the Grave 133
Dracula: Prince of Darkness 44
Dracula 2000 20, 162, 231
Dream Demon 229
Dreamscape 60, 228–229
Dreamworks SKG 74–5
Dreyfuss, Richard 222
Drive-in 15, 18, 79
Duel 15
Dungeonmaster 233
DVD, introduction and impact of 20–1

Eaten Alive 33
Ebert, Roger 32, 224
EC Comics 136, 147, 224
Eddie Presley 151, 155
Edmond 175
Education of a Felon 131
Edwards, Blake 89
Ellison, Harlan 242
Elvira: Mistress of the Dark v
Embassy Home Entertainment 34, 222
Empire Pictures 19, 83, 108, 152
The Empire Strikes Back 231
Englund, Robert 64–5, 67, 110, 123, 144, 229, 237
The Erotic Witch Project 240
Escape from New York 47, 229
Escape from the Planet of the Apes 140
E.T. : The Extraterrestrial 32
Evans, Robert 233
The Evil Dead 29–30, 32, 55, 173, 223–224, 228
Evil Dead II 34–5, 38, 42–4, 46, 226, 238
The Evil of Frankenstein 44, 133
Excalibur 130
The Exorcism of Emily Rose 130
The Exorcist 2, 8, 15, 17, 24, 38, 78–9, 89–93, 100, 102, 108, 116, 148, 173, 234, 236–238
The Exorcist II: The Heretic 11, 92–4, 101, 105, 107–108, 110, 112, 124, 127, 240
Exorcist III: Legion 44, 94, 96, 98–101, 103, 170, 172, 226, 235
Exorcist: The Beginning 103, 108, 129, 140, 145, 148–149, 151, 237, 243–244

Famous Monsters of Filmland 79, 82
Fangoria 2, 5, 80–2, 104, 166, 233, 243
Fantastic Factory 77
Fantasy Film Festival 136
Farmer, Todd 146
Fatal Attraction 136
Feast 71
Fields, Verna 107
Figg, Christopher 42
Filmcorp 134
The Final Conflict: The Omen III 107, 120
Final Destination 49
Final Girl 43, 55, 73, 84, 114, 144–145, 147–148
Financing: first films 29–30, 52, 55, 68, 83, 89, 105, 224; sequels 34, 36, 38–39, 46–47, 73, 129, 227, 234, 245
Fincher, David 105, 111, 118–120, 124, 127–128, 130–131, 158, 238–240
Fisher, Carrie 74
Fisher, Terence 44, 226
First film footage 43, 54, 115, 121, 148
The Flintstones 240
Flowers in the Attic 63
The Fly (1958) 78
The Fly (1986) 20, 82, 246
The Fly II 82, 87, 136, 232

Flynn, John 230
The Fog 229
Foree, Ken 144
Fortress 154
Foster, Jodie 125, 237
Fountain Society 74
Franchise: acquisition 20, 105–106, 222, 225; definition of 9–10, 220; family 70–71, 76–78, 161–163, 168, 173, 174, 232, 237; fidelity 90, 93–94, 103–105, 116, 117, 126–127, 148, 162, 165, 167, 176–177, 222; guardians 110–111, 163, 171–172; history 9–12
Francis, Freddie 133, 240
Frankenhooker 38
Frankenstein (1910) 16
Frankenstein (1931) 13, 224, 229
Frankenstein Meets the Wolf Man 223
Franklin, Richard 59, 73, 108, 115–117, 129, 225, 236–238
Freaks 224, 241
Freda, Riccardo 14
Freddy vs. Jason 48, 65, 74, 141, 144, 147, 151, 223, 233, 242–244
Freddy's Dead: The Final Nightmare 65, 123
Freddy's Nightmares: A Nightmare on Elm Street: The Series 63, 123, 222, 229–230, 237
Freeman, Morgan J. 112, 117, 222
Freiser, Eric 111
The French Connection 90
The French Connection II 18
Friday the 13th 49, 52, 56, 58–9, 70, 72–3, 81, 119, 140, 163, 170–172, 224, 227, 236, 241, 243, 246
Friday the 13th: A New Beginning 111, 127, 129, 236
Friday the 13th Part 2 58, 62, 76
Friday the 13th Part VII: The New Blood 83, 87–8, 232–234, 243
Friday the 13th Part VIII: Jason Takes Manhattan 230, 240
Friday the 13th: The Final Chapter 121, 239
Friday the 13th: The Series 222, 230
Friday the 13th 3D 245
Friedkin, William 8, 15 27, 38, 90–1, 94, 102, 107, 112, 127, 148, 173, 234–235
Fright 224
Fright Night 147
Fright Night Part II 147, 152
From Beyond 32, 144
From Dusk Till Dawn 20, 156, 234
From Dusk Till Dawn 2: Texas Blood Money 112, 164
Fulci, Lucio 19
Full Moon Entertainment 20, 83, 152–155, 223

Garris, Mick 133, 136, 142, 144–145, 148–149, 152, 175, 243–244
The Gate 225
Gayton, Joe 231
Gellar, Sarah Michelle 232, 245

George, Screaming Mad 232
Gergevicij, Viorel 155
German Expressionism 13
Get Carter 240
Ghost House Pictures 48, 175
Ghost of Frankenstein 132
Ghost Town 152, 155, 244
Giallo 160, 246
Gibson, Brian 115, 127
Giler, David 111
Ginger Snaps 74
Ginger Snaps: The Beginning 232
Ginger Snaps: Unleashed 232
The Girl Who Knew Too Much 245
Glory 240
God Told Me Too 225
The Godfather 233, 246
The Godfather: Part II 18, 38, 72, 114
Gods and Monsters 130
Goldman, William 17, 222
Goosebumps 154
Gordon, Stuart 30, 32–3, 49, 77, 152, 154, 160, 175, 224, 230
Goreteurs 77, 79–80, 83–89, 103
Gorezone 81, 233
Gorillas in the Mist 233
Gornick, Michael 83
Gottlieb, Carl 100
Governor, Richard 244
Goyer, David S. 78, 93, 162, 232, 236
Grand Guignol 80, 125
Gray Matter 131, 240
Gray Matter Productions 109
Great White 95
Green, Hilton 111
Gremlins 41, 231
Gremlins 2: The New Batch 37
Greystoke 233
The Grinch 240
Grossman, Adam 70–1, 107, 111
The Grudge 232
The Grudge 2 3
The Guardian 234
Guest, Val 44

Halcyon International Pictures 77
Halloween (1978) 1, 20, 32, 52, 55, 58, 62, 69, 73, 163, 224, 228–229, 231, 235, 241
Halloween (2007) 21
Halloween H20 140, 144, 147, 149, 230, 242, 244
Halloween Resurrection 130, 153
Halloween: The Curse of Michael Myers 87, 229
Halloween II 33, 58, 76, 107, 119, 130, 225, 229, 244
Halloween III: Season of the Witch 58, 76, 78, 100, 167, 172, 225, 235–236, 244
Halloween 4: The Return of Michael Myers 119, 130, 239
Halloween 5: The Revenge of Michael Myers 111, 129, 142, 236–237

258   Index

Hammer Films 8, 14, 44, 77, 133, 224, 226, 240
Hanbers, John 233
Hancock, John 236
The Hand That Rocks the Cradle 231
Hannah, Mark 155
Hannibal 108, 115–116, 121, 125, 131, 237, 239
Hansen, Gunnar 144
Hanson, Curtis 231
Harlin, Renny 103, 107–108, 117, 123, 129, 133, 140, 145, 148, 244
Harmon, Robert 71
Harris, Thomas 125, 237
Harron, Mary 8
Harry, Lee 115
Harry Potter 154, 220, 233
Harryhausen, Ray 45, 78–9
The Haunting 69
Haute Tension 71, 163
Haxan 29, 106
Hedden, Rob 240
The Hellbound Heart 93
Hellbound: Hellraiser II 24, 42, 86, 128, 147, 153
Hellboy 176
Hellraiser 20, 42, 95, 163, 170, 243, 246
Hellraiser: Deader 117
Hellraiser: Hellworld 117
Hellraiser: Inferno 112, 115, 127, 130
Hellraiser III: Hell on Earth 86, 115, 137, 139, 144, 147, 241–242
Hellraiser IV: Bloodline 83–4, 86–7, 229, 232, 234
Hemdale 141, 222, 236, 242
Henenlotter, Frank 27, 32, 38, 42–3, 159, 224–225
Henkel, Kim 224, 232, 235
Henrikson, Lance 144, 231
Henry: Portrait of a Serial Killer 2, 141
Hermann, Bernard 234
Hickox, Anthony 133, 136–137, 139–140, 144, 147, 153, 224, 241–243
The Hidden 116
Higgins, Claire 42
Hill, Debra 229
Hill, Walter 111
The Hills Have Eyes (1977) 51, 53, 231
The Hills Have Eyes (2006) 71, 163, 242
The Hills Have Eyes Part II 54
The Hills Have Eyes 2 75
Hiltzig, Robert 29
A History of Violence 246
Hitchcock, Alfred 8, 14, 16, 32, 41, 46, 59, 96, 114, 121, 129, 172, 222, 224–225, 237, 243
The Hitcher (2007) 21
Hitzig, Rupert 100
Hocus Pocus 152
Hodder, Kane 88
Hodges, Mike 140, 236, 242
Holland, Cecil 78
Holland, Tom 235
The Hollywood Reporter 52
Hooper, Tobe 1, 27–28, 33, 38, 42–43, 53, 55, 58, 147, 224, 226, 228–231, 237
Hopkins, Anthony 125
Hopkins, Stephen 105, 111, 114, 121, 123, 239
Home Box Office (HBO) 106
Horror-Comedy 8, 44, 46, 68–9, 74, 100–101, 106, 116, 124, 136–137, 147, 149, 152, 166, 229, 239–240
Horror genre: attraction of 28; definition 7–9
The Horror Show (aka *House III*) 63–4, 87, 230–232
Hostel 177
Hough, John 108, 237
House 29, 70, 163
House II: The Second Story 232
House of Dracula 132
House of Frankenstein 132
House of Re-Animator 77, 230
House of the Dead 245
House of Wax (1953) 44
House of Wax (2005) 226
House on Haunted Hill (1959) 14
House on Haunted Hill (1999) 112
The House on Sorority Row 231
Howard, Ron 134
The Howling 1, 8, 16–18, 74, 82, 222
The Howling II 128–129, 222
Howling III: The Marsupials 129, 240
Howling IV: The Original Nightmare 108
Howling V: The Rebirth 236
Hudson, Kate 245
Hughes, Miko 67
Humanoids from the Deep 241
Hurd, Gale Ann 141–143, 145, 242
Huston, Will 153, 155

I Know What You Did Last Summer 231
I Saw What You Did 224
If There Were Demons Then Perhaps There Were Angels : William Peter Blatty's Own Story of the Exorcist 92
I'll Tell Them I Remember You 92
In the Name of a King 245
Incidents On and Off a Mountain Road 49
Independent Film Channel 106
Indiana Jones and the Last Crusade 226, 246
Indiana Jones and the Temple of Doom 41
Interview with the Vampire 15, 18, 223
Into the Woods 223
Invaders from Mars 38
Invasion of the Body Snatchers (1956) 78
Invitation to Hell 53
Irving, Amy 57
Isaac, James 87, 141, 146, 150, 151, 231–232, 244
The Island of Dr. Moreau 240
Island of Lost Souls 132
Island of the Alive: It's Alive III 20, 44
IT 152

It Lives Again 34, 43–4
ITC 137
It's Alive 159

Jackson, Peter 141, 237
Jancovich, Mark 7, 9, 22
Jason and the Argonauts 79
Jason Goes to Hell: The Final Friday 116
Jason X 141, 145–146, 149–150, 229, 231, 243–244
Jaws 8, 15, 17, 40, 95, 137, 158, 222, 246
Jaws 2 11, 19, 38, 115, 120, 127, 137, 165, 225, 236, 238
Jaws 3-D 33, 78, 100, 225, 232, 235, 237, 241, 245
Jaws: The Revenge 108
Jeunet, Jean-Pierre 108, 110–111, 114, 116, 130, 236, 238
The Jim World's Greatest 28
Johnny Mysto: Boy Wizard 154
Jordan, Neil 15
Ju-on: The Grudge 237
Jurassic Park 17, 18, 40, 222, 246
Jurassic Park III 226

Kael, Pauline 32
Karloff, Boris 42
Kaufman, Lloyd 15
Keen, Bob 242
Kenny & Company 28
Kenton, Erle C. 132
Kermode, Mark 11, 52, 80, 103, 111, 228, 234
Kerschner, Irvin 134, 240
Killer Films 109
King, Stephen 11, 13, 17, 32–33, 66, 83, 93, 102, 152, 176, 222, 224, 229–230, 235, 240, 245
King Kong (1933) 78
King Kong (1976) 82
King Kong (2005) 223
Kinsey 130
Kneale, Nigel 225
Kotzwinkle, William 62
Krueger, Freddy 1, 19, 56, 59–63, 228–229, 233, 243
Kubrick, Stanley 89
Kuehn, Andrew J. 236
Kuhn, Robert 224
Kuppin, Larry 241, 242
Kurtzman, Robert 70, 82

Lafia, John 93, 232, 235
Lake Placid 244
Lambert, Mary 36, 40
Land of the Dead 8, 159, 172, 227, 234
Land of the Lost 151
Landau, Jon 239
Landis, John 142, 25
Landsburg, Alan 100, 235
Lane, Stephen 129, 222
Langenkamp, Heather 67

Lansdale, Joe R. 49
The Last House on the Left 51–3, 69, 106, 224, 227, 236
Lawrence, Ashley 24, 128
Leatherface: The Texas Chainsaw Massacre III 25, 133, 140–150, 152, 168, 226, 237, 243–244
The Legend of Hell House 237
Legion 94, 101
Legros, James 225
Leprechaun 20
Leprechaun 2 140
Leprechaun 3 147, 153, 240
Leprechaun in Space 153, 229
Lethal Weapon 246
Levin, Ira 95
Lewis, H.G. 15, 36, 52, 79–80, 232
Lewton, Val 176
Lifeforce 38
Lions Gate 164, 177, 222, 242, 244–245
Little, Dwight H. 119, 129–130
LL Cool J 242
Locke, Peter 52–3, 231
Logan, Bob 101
Look What's Happened to Rosemary's Baby 95, 222, 232, 236
Lord of the Rings 220
Los Angeles Times 55
Lovecraft, H.P. 13, 32, 49, 152
Lucas, George 18, 82, 158, 226, 243
Lussier, Patrick 71, 162, 231, 245
Lustig, Bill 36

Macabre 14
MacCambridge, Mercedes 243
MacLaine, Shirley 234
Macy, William H. 230
Maddalena, Marianne 231
Maddock, Brent 96
Made for TV horror 53, 63–4, 83, 95, 102, 106, 115, 123, 142, 152, 222, 229–230, 232–233, 235, 237, 242, 244
Madonna 70
Magar, Guy 243
Mamet, David 125
Mancini, Don 78, 95, 162, 232, 235–236, 245
Mancuso, Frank, Jr. 121, 171
Mandel, Robert 236
Manhunter 17, 117
Maniac Cop 36
Maniac Cop 2 36
Maniac Cop 3 46
Mann, Michael 17, 117
Manson, Marilyn 121
Marcello, Vince 71
Marcus, Adam 70, 116
Marshall, Neil 177, 225
Marshall, Paula 144
Martin 81, 225
Mastandrea, Nicholas 71, 231
Masters of Horror 49, 175, 244
Matheson, Richard 225

260 Index

Maximum Overdrive 93, 235
McCarty, John 2, 8, 27, 79–80, 96
McDonagh, Maitland 12, 23, 59, 77
McKellen, Sir Ian 221
McLean, Greg 177
McNaughton, John 141
Medak, Peter 108, 119, 121, 129–130, 237, 240
Meet the Feebles 2, 237
Memoirs of an Invisible Man 68
Metallica: Some Kind of Monster 130–131, 175
Metro-Goldwyn-Mayer (MGM) 33, 63, 111, 222
Midnight Pictures 175
Mihailoff, R.A. 144
Mil Mascaras vs. the Aztec Mummy 156
Miles, Vera 238
Miller, Jason 98–9
Miller, Victor 52, 56
Mimic 20, 108
Mimic: Sentinel 107
Mindripper 70, 231
Miner, Steve 55, 70, 89, 133, 140, 144, 147, 151, 227, 243–244
Miramax 20, 68, 74, 87, 134, 137, 139, 144, 234, 241–242
Mismarketing and publicity 6, 7, 30, 42, 45, 52, 54, 59, 70–1, 75, 95, 100, 106, 119, 123, 131, 133, 137, 140, 149, 166, 167, 172, 224, 229–230, 241–242, 245
Mission Impossible 2 240
Mr. Sardonicus 151, 244
Monash, Paul 89, 234
Monkey Shines 159
Monster from the Ocean Floor 133
Monster movies 14, 78, 151, 244
Moore, Julianne 125, 237
Mora, Philippe 108, 128–129, 236, 240
Morgan Creek 68, 96, 98, 101–103, 108, 226
Morpheus Mike 78
Motion Picture Association of America (MPAA) 15, 31, 37, 39, 41–42, 46, 52, 69, 72, 79–80, 86–8, 121, 139, 149–150, 158, 169, 171–172, 226–227, 231, 234, 239, 242, 244–245
Motion Picture Corporation of America 153
Movie Wars: How Hollywood and the Media Limit What Movies We Can See 246
Multiple scripts 62–3, 73, 107, 111–112, 123
The Mummy (1999) 223
Murphy, Eddie 68
Music of the Heart 70
Myrick, Daniel 29, 106, 109, 115, 127, 237, 240

Nakata, Hideo 237
Necronomicon 152
Negative Pick-ups 34, 52
Nelson, Ray 230
New Horizons 20, 135
New Line Cinema 19, 36, 48–49, 55–6, 59–60, 62, 64–6, 70, 72, 74 95, 108, 111, 121, 123–124, 134, 136, 140–142, 144–147, 150, 175, 223–224, 229–230, 233, 236, 238, 243–245
New World Pictures 10, 33, 42, 95, 134, 141, 241
Newman, Kim 176
Nichols, Mike 74
Nicolaou, Ted 28, 223
Night of the Demons 2 121, 140, 241
Night of the Living Dead (1968) 10–11, 15, 19, 24, 29–30, 34, 36, 79, 94, 102, 173, 228, 236, 238
Night of the Living Dead (1990) 82-7, 89, 167, 234
Night of the Scarecrow 154, 244
Nightbreed 230
Nightmare Café 64
A Nightmare on Elm Street 11, 29, 36, 50, 54–7, 59, 65, 72, 163, 166, 228
A Nightmare on Elm Street Part 2: Freddy's Revenge 11, 29, 33, 56, 59–60, 65, 124, 127, 242
A Nightmare on Elm Street 3: Dream Warriors 2, 60–1, 65, 229
A Nightmare on Elm Street 4: The Dream Master 2, 62, 108, 111, 114, 123
A Nightmare on Elm Street 5: The Dream Child 63, 105, 111, 115–116, 121, 123–124, 142, 236, 238–240
Nightmares and Dreamscapes 244–245
The Ninth Configuration 92–5
Nispel, Marcus 114, 232, 236–237
Norton, Andre 33, 225

O'Bannon, Dan 94
O'Brien, Willis H. 78–9, 89
The Offspring (aka *From a Whisper to a Scream*) 136, 154–155, 240
Oldfield, Mike 234
The Omen 17, 38, 79–80, 140, 163, 173, 238
Omen IV: The Awakening 142
O'Quinn, Terry 137–138
Orca: Killer Whale 17
Orca II 33
Orion 242
Ormsby, Alan 232
The Osbournes 131
O'Steen, Sam 232, 236
Othenin-Girard, Dominique 111, 142, 237
Oullette, Jean-Paul 42, 225
Our Town 116
The Outer Limits 242

Palace Pictures 229
Paradise Lost 109
Paradise Lost 2: Revelations 109
Paramount 52, 58, 62, 65, 68, 83, 88, 108, 121, 127, 171, 228–230, 232–233, 236, 240
Parigi, Robert 238
Pearl, Daniel 237

The People Under the Stairs 63–4
Perkins, Anthony 33, 96–7, 110, 144, 149, 225, 227, 232, 235, 237
Pet Sematary 17, 36
Pet Sematary 2 36, 40
Petty, J.T. 107
Pfeiffer, Michelle 37
Phantasm 10, 24, 27–30, 33, 49, 55, 170, 175, 224, 228
Phantasm II 31, 34–44, 226
Phantasm III 45–7, 227
Phantasm IV 45, 47, 227
Phantasm 2012 A.D. 47
Phantom of the Opera (1989) 130
Phantom Town 155
Picture Striking Company 19
Pierce, Jack P. 78, 86, 89, 232
Pierson, Jon 106
Pink Flamingos 55
Piranha 33, 137, 240
Piranha II: The Spawning 137–139, 141, 146, 154, 242
Pitt, Brad 226
Planet of the Apes 233
Platinum Dunes 21
The Player 101
Pleasence, Donald 136, 237
Polanski, Roman 15, 233, 236
Poltergeist 1, 33, 58, 228, 231
Poltergeist II: The Other Side 115, 127
Poltergeist III 115, 236
Poltergeist: The Legacy 222
Prawer, S.S. 23, 51
Prequel 19, 47, 102–103, 109, 112, 114–115, 159, 243
Price, Vincent 136, 241
Prince of Darkness 230
Prison 108
The Private Files of J. Edgar Hoover 225
Producer, role of 12, 57–8, 76–8, 86, 89–90, 98, 107, 111, 121, 138, 142–143, 163, 228, 236–237
The Producers 92
Project Greenlight 71
Prom Night 69
The Prophecy 20, 228
Prophecy 2 112, 140, 241
Psycho (1960) 8, 11; effect on genre and exhibition 14, 32–33, 89, 93, 96, 111, 114, 172–173, 224, 243
Psycho (1998) 108, 114, 222, 238,
Psycho II (film) 19, 59, 73, 116–117, 225, 237, 239
Psycho II (novel) 19, 94, 222
Psycho III 78, 96–7, 129, 225, 232, 235
Psycho IV: The Beginning 33, 142, 144–145, 148–149, 243
Psycho House 94
Pulp Fiction 227
Pulse 74, 232
Pulse Pounders 155

Pumpkinhead (aka *Vengeance: The Demon*) 82, 153
Pumpkinhead 2: Blood Wings 133, 153–154, 236, 244
Puppetmaster 20
Puppetmaster II 83, 232
Puppetmaster III: Toulon's Revenge 152
Puppetmaster 4 133, 152
Puppetmaster 5 133, 152

Quatermass and the Pit 44, 133
Quatermass II 14

Rabid 160
The Rage: Carrie II 236
Raimi, Sam 27–29, 32–4, 36, 38–40, 42–5, 48, 55, 136, 159, 175, 223–224, 226
Rambo: First Blood Part II 141, 145
Rambo III 231
Randel, Tony 24, 128, 153, 236, 241
Ratner, Brett 117, 236
Razzies 240
Reade, Walter 224
Re-Animator 30, 32–3, 57–8, 77
Red Dragon 114, 117, 149, 236
Red Eye 75, 175
Reeve, Christopher 60
Release date pressure 62, 71, 82, 87, 106, 119, 121, 150, 226, 236
Remakes 11, 20–21, 44, 69, 74, 82, 84–6, 103, 114, 117, 159, 161, 165, 175, 176, 222–223, 236–237, 240, 246
Renaissance Pictures 29
Renoir, Jean 175
Replaced directors 107, 140–143, 146, 168–169, 231, 236
Repossessed 101, 103
Republic Pictures 154
Reshoots, increase violence 58, 98–100, 113, 119, 139, 170, 229
Resident Evil 159, 227
The Return 245
Return of the Jedi 46
Return of the Living Dead (film) 103, 140, 166
Return of the Living Dead (novel) 94
Return of the Living Dead Part II 110
Return of the Living Dead Part 3 147, 150–151, 166, 241
A Return to Salem's Lot 20, 112, 116
Revenge of the Creature 225
Rice, Anne 13, 15, 222
The Ring 232, 237
The Ring Two 232, 237
Ringu 237
Risher, Sara 66
Road Games 236
Robinson, James G. 98–9
Robocop 230
Rocky 18
Rodriguez, Robert 69, 156
Rogue Pictures 245

Romeo and Juliet 231
Romero, George R. 8, 10, 15, 19, 27–28, 34, 36, 41–2, 77, 79–86, 89, 136, 159, 162, 172–173, 176, 224–225, 227, 233–234
Rosebud Releasing 35
Rosemary's Baby 15, 17, 95, 116, 123, 233
Rosenbaum, Jonathan 245
Rosenberg, Stuart 234
Rosenthal, Rick 58, 107, 119, 130, 150, 153, 229
Roth, Eli 177
Roth, Joe 118–119, 239
Rowland, Kelly 242
Rowling, J.K. 220
Ruben, Joseph 136, 228
Russell, Chuck 60–1, 228–229
Russell, Ken 93, 96
Russo, John 86, 94, 102, 236
Rydell, Mark 90

Salem's Lot 1, 44
Sanchez, Eduardo 29, 106, 109, 115, 127, 237, 240
Sargent, Joseph 108, 237
The Savage Bees 235
Savini, Tom 24, 77, 80–7, 89, 103, 141, 167–168, 233–234
Saw 173
Saw II 242, 245
Saw III 3
Scanners II: The New Order 240
Scanners III: The Takeover 240
Scary Movie 74
Schifrin, Lalo 234
Schoedsack, Ernest B. 219
Schow, David J. 147, 243
Schrader, Paul 102–103, 108, 112, 114, 117, 129, 140, 237–238
Schumacher, Joel 176
Schwarznegger, Arnold 245
Science-fiction 78, 141, 146, 153, 244
Sci-fi Channel 240
The Scooby-Doo Project 240
Scorsese, Martin 23, 134, 241
Scott, Darin 136
Scott, George C. 99
Scott, Ridley 65, 108, 115–116, 125–126, 131, 141, 149, 230, 235, 239
Scream 2, 5, 20, 68–71, 165–166, 219, 230–231
Scream 2 17, 68, 70–72, 231
Scream 3 68, 72–4, 232
Scream, Blacula, Scream 68
Scream Queen 69
Scrimm, Angus 31, 49
Season of the Witch 225
Seed of Chucky 95, 162, 232, 235–236, 245
Sequel, definition of 10
The Serpent and the Rainbow 62
Se7en 130
The 7 Faces of Death 233
The Seventh Voyage of Sinbad 79

Shapiro-Glickenhaus Entertainment (SGE) 46, 225, 227
Shaun of the Dead 227
Shaw, Larry 71
Shaye, Robert 48, 55–6, 58–9, 62, 64–5, 111, 134, 147, 163, 224, 241
Sheinberg, Sid 142
Shelley, Mary 1, 13
Sherlock Holmes 220
Sherman, Gary 115, 236
Shimzu, Takashi 237
The Shining (1980) 116, 243
The Shining (1997) 102
Shivers (film) 160
Shivers (publication) 5
Shock epilogues 17, 30, 43, 45, 47, 56–7, 63, 71, 120, 149, 169, 222, 239
Shocker 2, 63–4
Sholder, Jack 59, 119, 125, 127, 136, 239, 241–242
Showtime 49, 64, 106, 175, 222
The Silence of the Lambs 7, 119, 174, 239
Silent Night, Deadly Night Part 2 110, 115
Silver Bullet 33
Silver Bullet (production company) 155
Simpson, Michael 239–240
Sinofsky, Bruce 109, 130
Siskel, Gene 224
Skarsgard, Stellan 140
The Skeleton Key 245
Skinwalkers 244
Skipp, John 238
Slasher films 8, 19, 46, 69, 72, 74, 108, 118, 123, 138, 151, 153, 172, 229
Sleepaway Camp 29
Sleepaway Camp 2: Unhappy Campers 239–240
Sleepaway Camp 3 239–240
Sleepwalkers 152
Sleepy Hollow 234
Sluzier, George 237
Smith, Charles Martin 230, 233
Smith, Dick 79–80, 82, 89, 233
Smithee, Alan 54, 87, 150, 154
Snakes on a Plane 245
Snider, Stacey 95
Snyder, Zack 236
Society 2, 232
Soft for Digging 107
Sometimes They Come Back ... Again 107, 111
Son of Frankenstein 13, 44
Son of Kong 219
Son of Rosemary 95
Sonzero, Jim 232
Sorority House Massacre 231
Space Camp 142
Species II 108, 111, 119, 121, 240
Spector, John 238
Spence, Greg 112, 140, 238, 240
Spider-Man 235
Spiegel, Scott 112, 164
Spielberg, Steven 8, 15, 17, 18, 23, 27, 32–33,

38, 41, 70, 82, 107, 136–137, 155, 158, 176, 222, 226, 228, 231, 235
Splatter 2, 8, 44, 79–80, 82, 86, 94, 96, 233
Splatter University 231
Spoiler 154, 244
Spookies 1
Stakeout on Dope Street 241
Stallone, Sylvester 18
The Stand 47, 152
Star Wars 18, 134, 243
Starr, Bruce 110
Starship Troopers 2: Heroes of the Federation 232
Stefano, Joseph 93, 144, 243
Steinmann, Danny 111, 127, 236
The Stepfather 136–137
Stepfather 2 133, 136–137, 140, 142, 152
Stepfather III 121, 137–138, 243
Stern, Sandor 232
Stevens, Neal 238
Straight Into Darkness 155, 175
The Straight Story 240
Strait-Jacket 73, 116, 238
Stranger in Our House (aka *Summer of Fear*) 53
Streep, Meryl 70
Storm King Productions 153, 231
Student films 107, 109, 134, 147, 229, 240
Studio interference: during postproduction 16, 33, 40, 41, 54–56, 58, 74, 85–88, 113, 117–120, 137–141, 154, 169–170, 240; during production 16, 33, 40, 55–56, 74, 85–86, 88, 96–98, 100, 123–124, 145–146, 168–169, 239
Subspecies 28, 152, 223
Sundance Film Festival 32, 105, 237
Sundown: The Vampire in Retreat 136
Superman 1
Superman III 45
Superman IV: The Quest for Peace 60–1, 229
Survival Quest 33–4
Swamp Thing 53
Szwarc, Jeannot 107, 127, 165, 238

Tabloid press controversy 61, 69, 72, 92, 116, 170–173
Tacacs, Tibor 225
Talalay, Rachel 123, 240
Tales from the Crypt 233
Tales from the Darkside 83
Tallman, Patricia 85
Tapert, Robert 224
Tarantino, Quentin 156, 227
Taste the Blood of Dracula 133
Taylor, Don 140
Teaching Mrs. Tingle 72, 231
Ted Bundy 234
Tentacles 137
The Terminator 141–142, 158, 229, 242
Terminator 2: Judgment Day 95, 120
Terminator 3: Rise of the Machines 226
Terror Train 69
Test screenings 42, 56, 59, 66, 69–70, 98–9, 119, 121, 124, 149, 169–170, 174, 243–244

The Texas Chainsaw Massacre (1974) 29, 34, 53, 55, 224, 228, 237
The Texas Chainsaw Massacre (2003) 21, 114, 236, 237, 242
The Texas Chainsaw Massacre 2 38, 43–4, 144, 147, 150, 228
The Texas Chainsaw Massacre: The Beginning 3, 21
Texas Chainsaw Massacre: The Next Generation 232, 235
Thalberg, Irving 157
They 71, 232
They Live 230
They Shoot Horses Don't They? 231
The Thing 58, 82
The Thing from Another World 78
This Film Is Not Yet Rated 245
3-D technology 65, 100, 232–233, 245
Thriller 103
Tiger, Kenneth 31
The Tingler 14
Tippett, Phil 232
Title changes 56, 101, 225, 227–228, 230–231, 239
Titticut Follies 109
Tolkien, J.R.R. 220
Tonal shift: darker 37, 66, 103, 114, 121, 125, 146; lighter 45–47, 59, 62, 65, 73–74, 114, 132
Total Recall 154
The Toyer 107, 229
Trancers 152
Trans Atlantic Pictures 240
Transformers 220
Trap Door 107
Tremors (film) 7, 244
Tremors (TV series) 222
Tremors 3: Back to Perfection 96
Trenchard-Smith, Brian 108, 121, 140, 146–147
Trick or Treat 64, 230, 233
Trimark 20, 133, 140, 164–165, 240
Troll 233
Troma 15
Tuttle, William 233
Twentieth Century Fox 20, 96, 100–102, 108, 110, 118–120, 124, 129, 133, 142–144, 151, 223
28 Days Later 227
The 25th Hour v
The Twilight Zone 64
Twinkle Twinkle Killer Kane 93
2000 Maniacs 15

Underworld 156
United Artists 52, 222, 226
United Film Distribution 41, 227
Universal Studios 8, 15, 17, 21, 28, 32–3, 36, 38, 40, 42, 45, 58, 63, 65, 68, 78, 94–6, 98, 100, 107–108, 115, 121, 132, 136–137, 142, 172, 222–226, 230, 235–238, 241, 245
The Unnamable 225
The Unnamable Returns 42
Urban Legend 231

Vachon, Christine 109
Valenti, Jack 46
Valentine 231
Vampire in Brooklyn 68
Vampires v
Vampires: Los Muertos 152
Van Helsing 223
Van Sant, Gus 108, 114, 121, 126, 130, 237–238
Variety 30, 52, 140, 233
Vault of Horror 136
Verhoeven, Paul 65, 230
Vestron 19, 136
Village Voice 32
The Virgin Spring 51
Von Sydow, Max 110, 233
Vortex 224

Wagner, Bruce 60, 229
Walas, Chris 82, 84–5, 101, 232
Wallace, Tommy Lee 76, 100–101, 133, 147, 167, 229, 236
Waller, Anthony 69
Ward, Vincent 107
Warlock 34, 140, 227, 243
Warlock: Armageddon 144, 241, 243
Warlock III 111
Warner Bros. 17, 34, 37, 44, 52, 60–1, 65, 74, 86, 89–93, 102, 108, 112, 115, 124, 140, 240, 242
Waters, John 55, 79
Waxwork 136, 153
Waxwork II: Lost in Time 136, 241
Weaver, Sigourney 85, 110, 118, 120, 143–146, 237, 239, 245
Weinstein, Harvey and Bob 20, 68, 74, 134, 137–139, 232, 241–243
Weintraub, Jerry 94
Weintrob, Jed 244
Wells, H.G. 241
The Werewolf Reborn 154
Wes Craven's New Nightmare 2, 48, 66–8, 116
Westlake, Donald 136
Whale, James 5, 13, 34, 44, 132, 219
Whedon, Joss 110
When a Stranger Calls 69

Wiederhorn, Ken 110
Wilcox, Lisa 123
Wild Street Pictures 77
Wilde, Barbie 24
Wilder, Thornton 116
Wiley, Ethan 70, 232
William Peter Blatty on the Exorcist: From Novel to Film 92
Williams, Caroline 138, 144
Williams, Chuck 155
Williamson, Kevin 68, 71–2, 74
Williamson, Nicol 99
Winston, Stan 82, 153, 233
Wishmaster 20, 70, 82, 231
Wishmaster 2 242
Witchboard 225
Witchboard 2: The Devil's Doorway 225
Wolf 74
Wolf Creek 177
Wood, Ed 176
Wood, Robin 7, 16, 165
Writers Guild of America (WGA) 60, 92, 238
Wynorski, Jim 136

X-Men 235
X-Men: The Last Stand 221
X rating / Unrated/NC-17 31, 35, 41–2, 45–6, 69, 79–80, 86, 150, 171, 226–227, 231, 236–237
Xtro 28, 223

Yagher, Kevin 83–4, 86–7, 232–234
Yu, Ronny 108, 111, 133, 147, 149, 151, 237, 239, 243–244
Yuzna, Brian 57–8, 77, 133, 140, 147, 150–151, 166

Zaillian, Steven 125
Zardoz 108
Zemeckis, Robert 158
ZigZag 93
Zito, Joseph 121, 129, 236
Zombi II (aka *Zombie Flesh Eaters*) 19
Zombie, Rob 21
Zombie Prom 71